Spanish Law and Legal System

AUSTRALIA
Law Book Co.
Sydney

CANADA and USA
Carswell
Toronto

HONG KONG
Sweet & Maxwell Asia

NEW ZEALAND
Brookers
Wellington

SINGAPORE and MALAYSIA
Sweet & Maxwell Asia
Singapore and Kuala Lumpur

Spanish Law and Legal System

2nd Edition

By

ELENA MERINO-BLANCO, Lda. en Derecho

Senior Lecturer in Law, University of the West of England, Bristol

LONDON • SWEET & MAXWELL • 2006

First edition 1996
Second edition 2006

Published in 2006 by
Sweet & Maxwell Limited of
100 Avenue Road
London NW3 3PF
www.sweetandmaxwell.co.uk

Typeset by Servis Filmsetting Ltd, Manchester
Printed and bound in Great Britain by
Ashford Colour Press, Gosport, Hants.

No natural forests were destroyed to make this product; only
farmed timber was used and replanted.

ISBN-10   0-421-90230-2
ISBN-13   978-0-421-90230-5

A CIP record for this book is available from the British Library

To Alex and Pablo with all my love

Preface

Almost ten years have passed since the first edition of this work, then titled *The Spanish Legal System*, was published. In this decade Spain has consolidated itself as a key participant in European politics and is now an experienced democracy with sophisticated and well functioning institutions. A stable political and economic period has enabled the successive socialist, conservative and, again, socialist governments, to concentrate on legal reform and the provision of legal services. The current reform and modernisation of the administration of justice follows a new criminal code, a new law of civil procedure, several reforms to criminal procedure, a review of the legal professions and the introduction of several laws that adapt existing institutions to the technological progress and economic global needs which have developed.

Politically, a profound review of the territorial organisation of the state and the distribution of powers between the central state and the autonomous communities is currently under way with new *Estatutos de Autonomía* being discussed and approved by both the Autonomous Parliaments and the National Parliament in Madrid. A process of regionalisation and further independence is taking place, led by the now well established institutional framework of the autonomous communities.

Socially, Spain is now clearly a secular state in which religion is still seen as important by a large proportion of the population but where it is understood as something that belongs to and should remain within the private and personal sphere of the individual instead of influencing and dominating certain legal and civil institutions. This social evolution, which began over 20 years ago, has been reflected in the most recent changes on family law undertaken by the government of Mr Rodriguez Zapatero, the new laws of no-fault divorce and the modification of the civil code in respect of marriage. Spain has joined the few countries that have opened the institution of marriage to same-sex unions. Personal freedom and equality are seen as paramount by the state. Marriage, according to social trends common to our western European environment, has lost much of the traditional religious influence of the Catholic Church and is now purely a civil institution open to all individuals irrespective of gender or sexual orientation. Religion is also about to lose the small place it maintained in the curriculum of some state schools should the reforms in education proposed by the current government succeed.

In the preface to the first edition of this work, I referred to the absence of an accessible, easy to use introductory text on the main topics of Spanish law. The situation has not changed during the years that have passed between the first and second editions. In contrast with the literature available on the French and German Legal Systems, Spanish Law has only been marginally presented to the English reader despite the growing links between the two countries. Only specific texts on business law or buying property in Spain—the later not always written by lawyers and generally not aimed at the law reader—are available. I hope that this book will fill that gap and provide a concise, accessible and comprehensive introduction within its remit to both the Spanish legal system and some areas of Spanish substantive law. It is, of course, impossible to provide a satisfactory overview of all and every area of Spanish substantive law and I have not attempted to do so. I have selected some areas of public and private law and I have chosen topics that will usually be covered in Spanish introductory courses on the matter. The reader can then, hopefully, follow up the references provided in the footnotes and Bibliography if they wish to pursue the matter further. All the sources used for writing this book have been Spanish and therefore further or advanced study of specific areas of Spanish law would require a command of the language. However, I have tried to refer when appropriate to the websites of organisations, state departments and professional bodies that have, on occasions, information in English and can therefore be consulted easily by anybody who is not fluent in Spanish.

This second edition has gone beyond updating the topics covered in the first. The book is now divided in two main parts: the first, on the Spanish Legal System, covers the history, sources of law, legal professions and court structure; the second part covers different areas of what I will call substantive law. In the second part, I have followed the Spanish division between *derecho público* and *derecho privado* and included topics such as civil and criminal procedure in the part on *derecho público* even though for the English lawyer procedure would clearly not be a part of "Public law". This is an example of the very different meanings that legal terms and denominations have and the confusion that can arise from misuse of terminology. Throughout the book I have kept the original Spanish terminology to describe specific institutions that do not have an exact translation and attempted to explain in the text or by a footnote the meaning of the Spanish term.

The book has also an updated Glossary that should help the reader with the task of wading through these foreign italicised words that sometimes seem to inundate the text!

This book should be a self-contained manual that will hopefully be of assistance to students, academics, lawyers or individuals with an interest or connection with Spain and its legal system. Although it attempts to provide accurate, comprehensive introductory information, it should not be relied upon as the only source for providing legal advice and those seeking detailed, specific information should follow up the Bibliography.

I have attempted to state the law as of April 30, 2005, although it has been possible to include the important laws of July 2005 on the changes to the divorce law and the law allowing same-sex marriage. Any mistakes are entirely my own.

Elena Merino-Blanco
Bristol, October 2005

Contents

Table of Cases

Table of Legislation

III. *Ley*

Table of European, International and Foreign Legislation

Table of Abbreviations

AP	*Administración Pública* (Public Administration)	CP	*Código Penal* (Criminal Code)
Ap.	*Apartado* (Sub-section)	DA	*Duspisición Adicional* (Additional Disposition)
APE	*Administración Periferica del Estado* (Peripheral Administration of the State)	DGRN	*Dirección General de los Registros y el Notariados* (General Directorate of Registries and Notaries)
Art.	*Artículo* (Section (of an Act))		
ATC	*Auto del Tribunal Constitucional* (Type of decision of the Constitutional Court)	DNI	*Documento Nacional de Identidad* (National Identity Card)
BC	Brussels Convention on Jurisdiction and Enforcement of Judgments in Civil and Commercial Matters 1968	DTC	*Dictámen del Tribunal Constitucional* (Opinion of the Constitutional Court)
		EA	*Estatuto de Autonomía* (Main Law of the Autonomous Communities)
BOE	*Boletín Oficial del Estado* (Official Journal of the State		
BR	Brussels Regulation on Jurisdiction and Enforcement of Judgments in Civil and Commercial Matters(EC Council Regulation 44/2001)	EC	European Communities
		EFTA	European Free Trade Area
		EGA	*Estatuto General de la Abogacía* (General Regulations of Lawyers)
		EGPTE	*Estatuto General de Procuradores de los Tribunales* (General Regulation of Procuradores)
Cap.	*Capítulo* (Chapter)		
CC	*Código* Civil (Civil Code)		
CCom	*Código de Comercio* (Commercial Code)		
CE	*Constitución Española* (Spanish Constitution)	EOMF	*Estatuto Orgánico del Ministerio Fiscal* (General Regulation of the Public Prosecution Office)
CGAE	*Consejo General de la Abogacía Española* (General Council of Lawyers)	FCC	French Civil Code
		HL	*Ley Hipotecaria*
CGPJ	*Consejo General del Poder Juducial* (General Council of the Judiciary)	IAJD	*Impuesto de Actos Jurídicos Documentados* (Tax on the use of legal documents)

INSALUD	*Instituto Nacional de la Salud* (National Institute of Health)
INSS	*Instituto Nacional de la Seguridad Social* (National Institute of Social Security)
ISD	*Impuesto sobre sucesiones y donaciones* (Tax on inheritance and other gratuitous transfers)
ITP	*Impuesto de Transmisiones Patrimoniales* (Tax on patrimonial transfers)
IVA	*Impuesto sobre el Valor Añadido* (Value Added Tax)
J.	*Juzgado* (Court)
L.	*Ley* (Act of Parliament, law)
LA	*Ley de Arbitraje* (Arbitration Act)
LAU	*Ley de Arrendamientos Urbanos* (Landlord and Tenant Act)
LCCH	*Ley Cambiaria y del Cheque* (Bills of Exchange and Cheque Act)
LDPJ	*Ley de Demarcación y Planta Judicial* (Law on the distribution of courts and cases)
LEC	*Ley de Enjuiciamiento Civil* (Civil Procedure Act)
LECrim	*Ley de Enjuiciamiento Criminal* (Criminal Procedure Act)
LGP	*Ley Orgánica General Penitenciaria* (Prison Regulation Act)
LH	*Ley Hipotecaria* (Land Registry Act)
LJCA	*Ley de la Jurisdicción Contencioso Administrativa* (Administrative Procedure Act)
LO	*Ley Orgánica* (Type of Act of Parliament requiring special majorities for its approval)
LOACE	*Ley de Organización de la Administración Central del Estado* (Law of the Organisation of the Central Administration of the State)
LODE	*Ley Orgánica del Derecho a la Educación* (Law on the Right to Education)
LODP	*Ley Orgánica del Defensor del Pueblo* (Ombudsman Act)
LOFAGE	*Ley de Organización y Funcionamiento de la Administración General del Estado* (General Organisation of the Administration of the State Act)
LOPJ	*Ley Orgánica del Poder Judicial* (Judiciary Act)
LOREG	*Ley Orgánica del Regimen Electoral General* (General Elections Act)
LORIP	*Ley Orgánica Reguladora de la Iniciativa Popular* (Law regulating citizens' legislative initiative)
LOTC	*Ley Orgánica del Tribunal Constitucional* (Constitutional Court Act)
LOU	*Ley Orgánica de Universidades* (Universities Act)
LPH	*Ley de sobre Propiedad Horizontal* (Community of Owners in Horizontal Property Act)
LPL	*Ley de Procedimiento Laboral* (Labour Procedure Act)
LRJAE	*Ley de Regimen Jurídico de la Administración del Estado* (Legal Regulation of the Administration Act)
LRJ-PAC	*Ley de Regimen Jurídico de las Administraciones Publicas y del Procedimiento Administrativo Comun* (Legal Regulation of teh Public Administration and the Common Administrative Procedure Act)

LSC	*Ley de Seguridad Ciudadana* (Citizens' Security and Safety Act)	Secc.	*Sección* (Section)
MAP	*Ministerio de las Administraciones Publicas* (Public Administration Office)	STC	*Sentencia del Tribunal Constitucional* (Decision of the Constitutional Court)
OMEC		STJCE	*Sentencia del Tribunal de Justicia de la Comunidad* (Decision of the European Court of Justice)
PCE-PSUC	*Partido Comunista de España, Partido Socialista Unificado de Cataluña* (Communist Party–Socialist Party of Cataluña)	STS	*Sentencia del Tribunal Supremo* (Decision of the Supreme Court)
PP	*Partido Popular* (Popular Party)	TC	*Tribunal Constitucional* (Constitutional Court)
PSOE	*Partido Socialista Obrero Español* (Socialist Party)	TCEE	*Tratado de las Comunidades Europeas* (Treaty of the European Community)
R	*Reglamento* (Regulation)		
RC	*Reglamento del Congreso* (Law regulating the Congress)	Tit.	*Título* (Title)
RD	*Real Decreto* (Royal decree)	TJCE	*Tribunal de Justicia de las Comunidades Europeas* (European Court of Justice)
RDL	*Real Decreto-ley* (Law made by the Government)	TS	*Tribunal Supremo* (Supreme Court)
RGP	*Reglamento General Penitenciario* (Regulation on the General Prisons Law)	TSJ	*Tribunal Superior de Justicia* (Superior Court of Justice)
RLGP	*Reglamento de la Ley General Penitenciaria* (General Prisons Law)	TVE	*Television Española* (Spanish Television)
RRC	*Reglamento del Registro Civil* (Regulation on the Civil Registry)	UCD	*Unión de Centro Democrático* (Democratic Union Party)
RS	*Reglamento del Senado* (Law regulating the Senate)	Vol.	*Volumen* (Volume)

Chapter One
Introduction to the Spanish legal system

1. LEGAL HISTORY

HISTORICAL INTRODUCTION

Early influences

Very little is known about the peoples who inhabited the Iberian peninsula before the first Roman invasion. The first inhabitants are thought to have been Celts and Iberians and there is little evidence of their customary laws.[1] The most socially and culturally developed among the Iberian tribes were the inhabitants of the South-East due to their commercial contacts with Greeks and Phoenicians. These Iberian tribes had some written laws[2] which were customary and personal laws, meaning, only applicable to the family or local group. When contact with other groups became necessary the tribes established different agreements called *pactos de hospitalidad o clientela* (hospitality agreements) which regulated the relationships between people belonging to different groups.[3]

Iberia was incorporated with Rome after two centuries of fighting[4] and for the first time all the inhabitants of the peninsula became

---

[1] The problem with the sources of this period is the general absence of written sources; only some stones—*teseras*—hand-written in what is thought to be "Iberian" have been found. However, these cannot be translated because this language is still unknown. Francisco Tomás y Valiente, *Manual de Historia del Derecho Español* (1992) p.75. For an overview of "primitive laws" in Spain see, E. Gacto Fernández y otros, *El Derecho Histórico de los Pueblos de España* (7th edn, 1992), pp.46–55.

[2] According to the Roman historian *Estrabon* (III, 1, 6), the inhabitants of Tartessos—today's Seville—had laws in verse. See Pérez-Prendes, *"El mito de Tartessos"* (1974) 134 *Revista de Occidente*, pp.183–204.

[3] These agreements were evidenced in bronze tablets; some of these have been found by archaeologists, for example, the Bronze of Astorga. See F. Tomás y Valiente, *op. cit.*, pp.78–9.

[4] From the battle of Cissa against Carthago 218BC to 19BC, *"Hispania pacata"* under Emperor Augustus.

subject to the same political power. However, the presence of Rome and its influence was unequal in the different territories of what became Hispania. Some tribes demonstrated great resistance and offered little chance of long-term influence to their colonisers, retaining their traditions and ways of living; while other groups—mainly the Mediterranean population and the tribes of the valley of the river Guadalquivir—soon adopted the Roman culture and way of life.[5]

The main change introduced by the Romans was the urbanisation of society. Roman administrative and political life was organised around the *urbs*. However, and as a consequence of the principle of personality of the laws common to the ancient world, Roman law only applied to Roman citizens. All the other citizens of the Empire were subject to their personal laws.

The first romanisation of Hispania started with the administrative regulations dictated by Rome for the organisation and the government of the conquered territories. Hispania was organised into provinces according to a *lex provinciae* which gave legal status to the different urban and municipal entities, respecting the local laws in all matters not regulated by the *lex*. Only those who acquired Roman citizenship were subject to Roman law—the *ius civile*. The other inhabitants of the Empire were the *peregrini*, free men within the borders of the Empire whose relationships were governed by the *ius peregrinum*; the *latini*, who were an intermediate category enjoying some of the benefits of Roman citizens[6] and, therefore, were subject to Roman law in some aspects of their life[7]; and the slaves, who lacked any legal capacity. The relationships between people belonging to these different groups were articulated according to the *ius gentium*, a special system of law originating from the *ius civile* and the general rules of the other systems.

In AD212 Emperor Caracalla gave Roman citizenship to all inhabitants of the Empire except slaves. This measure did not, however, totally eliminate local pre-Roman laws, which were still applied in some areas and which undoubtedly influenced the way of understanding and applying the rules of Roman law.[8] It is not possible, therefore, to say that the same Roman law was applied throughout the territories of Hispania since local customs adapted the law to the circumstances and needs of each area.[9] Also, classical Roman law was never applied in

---

[5] This was, quite possibly, due to the fact that these peoples were accustomed to contacts with foreigners by trading with Phoenicia and Carthage.
[6] They enjoyed the *ius commercii* but not the *ius connubii, ius honorum* or the *ius sufragii*. See, F. Tomás y Valiente, *op. cit.*, p.86.
[7] The term used to designate the mixture of their own law and the *ius civile* applicable to the *latinii* was *ius latii*.
[8] F. Tomás y Valiente, *op. cit.*, p.87.
[9] See E. Gacto Fernández, *op. cit.*, pp.68–71.

Spain since this was conceived around the procedure of the *cognitio per formulas*, which was only applied in Italy, while provinces applied the *cognitio extra ordinem*. Some Roman legislation of this period was given to Hispania exclusively, such as the *lex ursonesis, lex salpesana* and the *lex malacvitana* or the "Bronzes of *Vispasa*".[10]

It was the Roman law of the postclassical period and what has been called "vulgar" Roman law,[11] which had more influence in the provinces of the Empire. The Roman Emperors tried to address the crises of the Empire in the third century by becoming more and more absolutist. The laws of the Emperor become progressively the only source of law and the great works of classical jurist-consults—Paulus, Gaius, Ulpianus and Papinianus—started to become a source of reference, since the quality of the works of the post-classical jurists was in clear decline.

While the Western Empire collapsed due to social and economic changes towards ruralisation and the feudal society of the Middle Ages, the eastern part of the Empire achieved its full splendour. Contact with the Hellenic culture, highly developed in disciplines such as logic and ethics, created a law of higher quality and sophistication than the law of the Western Empire. This culminated with the *Corpus Iuris Civilis* of Justinian AD528–533. The *Corpus Iuris Civilis* had four parts and 12 books: the *Digest* or *Pandectas*, which was a collection of the works of the great jurisprudence of the classical period; the *Institutiones*, based on the *Instituta* of Gaius written for the teaching of the law; the *Codex*, which was a code of imperial legislation from Adrian to Justinian; and the *Novella*, which contained different enactments made after the publication of the *Codex*. The importance and influence of this work was enormous since it survived the Dark Ages and was rescued by medieval Italian scholars, influencing the whole of occidental legal culture.

At the time of the fall of the Roman Empire in AD746, Hispania had already suffered the invasion of different barbarian tribes, mainly the Suevoi, Vandals and Alans. In order to fight these invasions the Roman Emperors asked for the help of another barbarian tribe, the Visigoths, who had already settled in other parts of the Empire[12] and were highly influenced by Roman culture. Their presence was not very numerous until AD507 when Alarico II was defeated in Gaul by the Francs and this began a large scale immigration towards the South.

---

[10] For more detail see, *ibid.*, pp.73–97.
[11] There is no consensus among writers about the term "vulgar Roman law". See F. Tomás y Valiente, *op. cit.*, p.94.
[12] Mainly in Gaul (France).

However, the number of Visigoths in Spain was never more than 5 per cent of the population.[13] The Visigoths were mainly peasants, with a few aristocratic families. It is doubtful whether they mixed with the Hispanic population[14] although they probably mixed with the Roman aristocracy. Their presence in Spain was very dispersed and they mainly occupied the north of the central plateau, establishing their capital in Toledo. They encountered great resistance in the North where some tribes, like the Basques, were never properly romanised or subjected to the Visigothic power.

The *leges* and *iura* of the Roman post-classical period remained in force in Gaul and Hispania long after the fall of the Empire. Most of the barbarian tribes only had customary laws, of which there is no surviving evidence. Whilst the Visigoth kings produced legislation, this co-existed with Roman law since it was primarily concerned with the distribution of land between Romans and Visigoths. The main legal works of the Visigoths were the *Código de Eurico*[15] and the *Breviario de Alarico* or *Lex Romana Visigothorum*.[16] The *Lex Romana Visigothorum* was not a compilation of Visigoth law but of Roman law. It was composed of *leges*, *iura*[17] and an *interpretatio* or interpretation of each text. Its influence was enormous and it was applied—in Hispania, and particularly in Gaul—for centuries. However, it was Recesvinto, who in AD654, produced the main work of Visigoth law, the *Liber Iudiciourum*. The *Liber* was divided into 12 books and included all the laws passed by the different Visigoth kings. It was revised on two occasions and new legislation was added to it. It was widely applied and its influence persisted well after the Moslem invasion of Spain. These three main "codes" were applied in the whole territory dominated by the Visigoths[18], although local customs were respected in those matters not covered by the Visigoth codes.

In AD711 the defeat in Guadalete meant the fall of the Visigoth monarchy and the beginning of the Moslem presence in Spain which was to remain for eight centuries. Although this factor differentiates

---

[13] F. Tomás y Valiente *op. cit.*, p.98.

[14] Due partly to the cannon laws at the time which forbade mixed marriages. This rule was later incorporated in the *Breviario*. See below.

[15] Probably passed in AD476 after the fall of the Empire. It has been described as a monument of "vulgar Roman law" although it incorporates some germanic customs, F. Tomás y Valiente, *op. cit.*, p.102.

[16] AD506.

[17] Mainly imperial constitutions and different versions of the *Instituta* of Gaius, the *Sententiae* of Paulus and the *Responsa* of Papinianus.

[18] There are important discrepancies about the "personality" of "territoriality" of Visigoth legislation. See F. Tomás y Valiente *op. cit.*, pp.107–8 for a brief explanation of the main positions and a detailed bibliography.

Spanish history from other European countries[19] the changes were not as drastic as some historians have suggested. In fact, Visigoth society was in a clear and irreparable crisis before the Moslems arrived in Spain. On the other hand, most of the Visigoth aristocracy stayed and entered into different agreements with the invaders by which the Visigoths kept most of their land and power. Also, most of the Hispano-Roman population received the "invaders" with little resistance[20] and regarded them as a possibly better alternative than the Visigoth monarchy, which anyway was really as foreign as the Moslems.

The Hispano-Roman population that stayed in the peninsula— the vast majority—was allowed to keep its religion, customs, law and property by recognising the Moslem authority and paying a tax; however, some of this population converted to Islam and became subject to Muslim law. The *Liber Iudiciourum* was still applied, although with unavoidable modifications due to the absence of an unitary power to enforce it. Also some of the parts of the *Liber*— those about political organisation, criminal law and procedure— were not tolerated by the government of Al-Andalus. The co-existence of different religions meant that different systems of law were applied to each group—Jews, Moslems and Christians— under the Moslem tolerance.[21]

The beginning of the Visigoth and Christian resistance against the Moslems—*la reconquista*[22]—meant in legal terms, the beginning of the fragmentation and diversification of the law. Different Christian kings needed the help of feudal lords who imposed their own rules within their territory and established a difference between the law applied in cities and the law of rural areas.

From the 8th until the 13th century the law became increasingly local, and after the 11th century was expressed by the different *fueros municipales*. The Christian kings of the period were weak and did not create much legislation; instead, they adopted and preserved the old law—the *Liber*. The kings did not start to create law until the sixth or seventh century, and when this happened it was in order to

---

[19] Spain was never a part of the Holy Roman Empire and the Moslem invasion and subsequent *reconquista* meant it had a different history from that of other European countries.

[20] Which explains the fact that within eight years the Moslems were in control of practically the whole of the territory, while it took two centuries for the Romans to conquer Spain.

[21] A good account of the law of the period is provided by E. Gacto Fernández, *op. cit.*, pp.144–8.

[22] For an account of this period in English, see O. Robinson, *European Legal History* (2nd edn, 1994) pp.117–19.

resolve all those situations for which the old *Liber* did not have an answer. In the new Christian kingdoms municipal law was mainly concerned with criminal, administrative or procedural law. In those areas in which the Visigoths never had effective control, i.e. the north of Spain, primitive laws were still applicable and when these people moved south, towards Castile,[23] they took their law with them—a law which was never romanised—refusing to acknowledge the *Liber* and resolving their disputes by nominating local judges.

The wars against Moslem domination lasted eight centuries, during which the different Christian kingdoms moved south as they recaptured new territories. One of the main problems of the time was the lack of population in some areas, especially on the borders of Moslem territories. In order to encourage Christian settlements in these areas the Christian kings granted a special law for each of these settlements with different privileges. These laws were known as *cartas pueblas* or *fueros*. They contained a few rules about administrative organisation and the rights over the use of the land.

In the 10th century, the King of León and the independent Count of Catalonia started to legislate, that is, to produce laws of general application for the whole of the territory under their control. The most important of these Christian laws were the *Usatges de Barcelona*, which, without derogating the *Liber*, replaced it in those areas in which it had become obsolete; the *Fuero de Aragón* and, at a later date, the *Fuero de Castilla*. In Castile a royal policy of unification of local laws was implemented by Fernando III and Alfonso X. Fernando III translated the *Liber* into Castilian calling it *Fuero Juzgo*. He chose this text as the law to be applied to all the re-conquered territories. The increasing power of the monarchy was also evident in the law of the time; Alfonso X imposed a *Fuero Real* in different areas of Castile, where it encountered severe opposition because it increased the powers of the crown and eliminated customary laws and rights.

The formation of the "ius commune"

The most important work in the history of Roman law was the *Corpus Iuris Civilis* of Justinian. However, published in AD533 after the fall of the Western Roman Empire, it was not generally known or applied in Western Europe, with the exception of the territories kept under the control of Byzantium. Although Roman legal tradition was constant in Spain through the application—albeit irregular—of the *Liber*, this was not accompanied by the study of Roman law.

---

[23] At the time dependent on the Christian kingdom of León.

In Northern Italy the tradition of studying the sources of Roman law survived during the Dark Ages and experienced a renaissance in the 7th century. One of the factors influencing the re-birth of the study of Roman law was the fact that European society at the time gravitated around two concepts: the Empire and Christianity. Charlemagne rebuilt an empire in place of the fallen Roman Empire, the "Holy Roman Empire", where all Christian people lived under the powers of the Emperor and the Pope. This Empire needed an unitary law which applied to all people; in contrast to the diversification of customs of the Germanic tribes, the law of the last great Empire seemed to provide the logical answer.

In the 6th century new manuscripts of the *Corpus* were found in Italy, and in Bologna, Innerius, a teacher of the School of Arts gave autonomy to the study of law by creating a new method: the *Gloss*.[24] The studious of Bologna worked with the original texts of the *Corpus Iuris Civilis* introducing comments and annotating the original texts at the margin with the aim of discovering and explaining the true sense of the different books of the *Codex*. The Glossators did not, however limit their work to an analysis and exegesis of Justinian's work but also cultivated other methods like the *Summa* or the *Quaestiones disputae*. The *Summa* was a systematic study of one of the books of the *Corpus*, or of a law or title of the *Digest*. The *Quaestiones disputae* consisted of the discussion of a legal problem taking into account all the different approaches from several writers, analysing these and reaching a solution which was better adjusted to justice. The important names of this school are Azzo and Accusio. The later drafted the *Glossa Ordinaria*, a collection of all previous glosses, which acquired a wide circulation being itself studied by the Post-Glossators.

Parallel to the study of the *ius civile* was the study of canon law. The increasing power of the Church meant the Popes of the seventh and eighth centuries produced an enormous amount of *Decretals* which were the object of a study similar to the study of the *ius civile*.[25]

In the 8th century, the centre for the study of law moved from Italy to France where a new method, the Commentary, started to be practised in the University of Orleans. This school tried to adapt the law to the problems of real life, abandoning to a certain extent the study of the original texts of the *Corpus* and concentrating on creating an integrated system of municipal law and Roman law. The main difference between Commentators and Glossators was that while the

---

[24] See O. Robinson, *op. cit.*, pp.42–58.
[25] The main collections are the *Decretals Gregorii IX* complied by Raimundo de Peñafort in 1234, and the *Clementinas* elaborated in 1298.

Glossators' main purpose was to find the literal sense of the different texts of the *Corpus*, the Commentators went further afield in their study, trying to discover the sense or "ratio" behind each disposition. In doing this they established the relationship of each text with the others, interpreting the rules of the *Corpus* in order to solve the practical legal problems of the time. The Commentators also produced *Consilia*, which was advice to the judges[26] and the parties in practical problems and which constituted a useful instrument for the introduction of Roman law into legal life.

The *ius commune* was a law made by lawyers—the scholars— integrated not only by Roman and canon law but also by the works of the scholars, known as "doctrinal writings".

Reception of the "ius commune" in the Spanish territories and integration of the different systems of law

Whilst it is possible to talk in general terms about the reception of the *ius commune* in countries like France by establishing a difference between the *pays de droit écrit* and the *pays de droit coutumier*[27] it is not possible to make general remarks about the situation in Spain. Although in those territories such as Catalonia, where the *Liber* had a general application, the reception of the *ius commune* was easier and more complete, each of the different kingdoms and territories adopted a different approach to the integration of the *ius commune* with the laws of the king and with their traditional laws. These differences need to be understood because they are the basis of the different civil legal systems that today still exist in Spain—*los derechos forales*.[28]

Catalonia was the Spanish territory in which the *ius commune* penetrated to the greatest extent, due to the extensive Roman and Visigoth influence, its geographical proximity to the South of France, and the continuous commercial relations with the Italian republics. After Catalonia, the new kingdoms of Valencia and Mallorca, which did not have an autonomous, developed system of customary law, were also eager to implement the *ius commune*. The small kingdom of Navarra was the territory where the *ius commune* had a later and lesser influence, followed by the Basque provinces. These were hardly romanised at all, having local and differentiated customs which were firmly entrenched in the population.

---

[26] Who at the time were not legal experts.
[27] F. Tomás y Valiente, *op. cit.*, p.201; C. Dadomo & S. Farran, *The French Legal System* (1993) p.5.
[28] "Foral laws" or regional customary laws.

In Castile and Aragón the penetration of the *ius commune* was quite complex. The local population strictly adhered to their local laws and opposed the imposition of royal legislation of Roman law. The kings oscillated in their positions as to the implementation of the *ius commune*. On one hand, the *ius commune* supported the idea of a king with power to legislate and as such was favoured by medieval kings; on the other, the *ius commune* was a highly developed system of great technical quality, which made the legislation of the king superfluous since, in theory, every problem could be resolved according to the *ius commune*. The solution to this dilemma consisted in declaring the primacy of royal legislation, recognising some traditional customary laws and the supplementary application of the *ius commune* in those areas where the above proved insufficient. However, the prestige of Roman and canon law, and the fact that the study of law at universities consisted of the study of the *ius commune*, meant that lawyers applied Roman law to resolve the cases. It was necessary for the kings to make several decisions forbidding this practice and specifying that only in the absence of royal or local rules could the parties or the judge resort to the application of Roman law. The integration of the laws in each of the different kingdoms will be considered since, as already explained, these differences in political organisation and legal institutions are the basis of the Spanish system today.

During the *Reconquista*, Spain was composed of different Christian kingdoms, to which the newly recaptured territories were incorporated with different degrees of autonomy. Some of these kingdoms were ruled by the same "Crown". This procedure culminated in 1492 when, after the conquest of Granada by Isabel and Fernando, Spain was unified under two Crowns: Castile and Aragón.[29] The "King of Spain" was officially king of all and every kingdom, "Prince of Catalonia" and "Lord of Vizcaya", but his power was unequal in the different territories because each of these kept its political personality and legal institutions and allowed the king different degrees of intervention.[30]

(1) Navarra

The small kingdom of Navarra had a uniform system of traditional local laws integrated mainly by unwritten customs and *fueros municipales*. This uniformity of local laws culminated in a general law for the whole kingdom called the *Fuero General de Navarra*. This law was respected by the different kings, who agreed to maintain the traditional law and subsequently passed little legislation. The penetration

---

[29] Which in turn are integrated by different kingdoms.
[30] See F. Tomás y Valiente, *op. cit.*, pp.282–97.

of the *ius commune* was late and minimal since there were no universities in the territory and it was only in the late 15th century that judges and lawyers started to look at the *ius commune* for answers which could not be provided by the traditional law.

(2) Aragón

In Aragón traditional laws were of a high technical quality. The original Parliament—*las Cortes*—passed laws of general application known as *Fueros*, of which the most important was the *Fuero de Aragón* of 1274. However the *Fuero* was only applicable in the absence of a special local law, which always had preference. The *ius commune* was hardly applied although the *Fuero de Aragón* of 1274 had a provision of hierarchy of sources by which, in the absence of local law and of a provision in the general *Fuero*, it was possible to judge according to canon and Roman law.

(3) Catalonia

The main characteristics of the legal system of Catalonia in the Middle Ages were the great quality of their late local laws, the powerful penetration of the *ius commune*, and the development of early legislation.[31]

The main cities of Catalonia made written compilations of their local laws—*Costums*. These *Costums* were integrated by three different elements: local customs, some of them immemorial; privileges given by the king to the locality; and decisions of the local courts.[32] Separately from the different local laws, Catalonia started developing an independent law of the Principate, the main example of which was the *Usatges*, a compilation of feudal laws. Economic changes towards a mercantile society in the 8th and 14th centuries increased the powers of cities and demands for a new legislation. This legislation was given by the king and the *Cort General*.[33] The power of the king was always limited by the *Corts*.[34]

The reception of the *ius commune* was general and extensive in Catalonia. The *Costums* established a system of hierarchy of sources by which if there were neither local customs, nor other provision by

---

[31] F. Tomás y Valiente, *op. cit.*, p.214.
[32] Among these *Costums* the most famous were: the *Costums de Tortosa* (1181) the *Consuetudines de Horta* (1296), the *Consuetudines ilerdenses* (1228), the *Recognoverunt proceres* (1284) and the *Consuetuts de la Ciudat de Barcelona* (date unknown).
[33] A parliament consisting of nobles, churchmen and the representatives of the cities.
[34] See. F. Tomás y Valiente *op. cit.*, pp.216–20.

the *Usatges*, the *Dret Comú* (*ius commune*) should be applied. Lawyers however, constantly applied the *ius commune* in the resolution of disputes to such an extent that in 1251, King Jaime I, considering that the application of Roman law was overtaking the application of specific Catalan laws, passed a restrictive order by which the pleading of Roman laws in judicial proceedings was forbidden except in cases in which there was not a local law applicable to the resolution of the dispute.

(4) Mallorca

Mallorca was a new kingdom incorporated under the Crown of Aragón but populated mainly by Catalans who imported their legal culture into the island. Mallorca did not seem to have a body of local laws and its specific law was constituted by royal legislation. The *ius commune*, either as directly applicable supplementary law or introduced by Catalan law, was widely applied. However, in 1439, in order to emphasise the autonomy of Mallorca in respect of Catalonia, a royal disposition forbade the application of the *Usatges* and declared that the supplementary law in Mallorca was the *ius commune*.

(5) Valencia

The new kingdom of Valencia, which was also incorporated under the Crown of Aragón but had autonomous political personality, was also greatly influenced by the *ius commune*. When King Jaime I decided to give a new law to Valencia this law was the *ius commune*. For four centuries, from 1229 to their expulsion in 1609, a large part of the population was integrated by the Moors who were allowed to keep some of their customs by royal decree. The local law was mainly absorbed by the *Furs* of 1240, by which different prerogatives were granted to the city of Valencia and later extended to different territories of the kingdom. Most of the rules of the *Furs* are directly taken from the *Codex* and the *Digests* of Justinian but were also influenced by canon and Catalan law.

(6) Castile

The largest and most powerful Crown of Castile, consisting of Castile and León, followed a different policy from Aragón in the respect of the autonomy of the different kingdoms. In effect Castile soon imposed its law and its political institutions on most of its territories and its kings legislated extensively. After Alfonso XI promulgated the *Ordenamiento de Alcalá* in 1348, only one law was applicable in Castile, Galicia, Asturias, León, Andalucia, Extremadura and Murcia and later to the newly acquired territories of Canarias and Granada. Only the Basque provinces kept their own law and legal institutions.

In Castile it is possible to talk about a royal legislative policy. The three early main works are the *Fuero Real*, the *Especulo* and most importantly, the main legal work of Spanish history *Las Siete Partidas*. The *Fuero Real* of 1255 was originally passed by Alfonso X for Aguilar de Campo and Sahagun. The aim of the *Fuero Real* was to supply uniform rules for the resolution of legal disputes. The *Fuero* was progressively extended to different territories, often with little or no resistance from the population, since some of these territories already had their customary laws and more importantly, regarded the *Fuero Real* as an interference with local autonomy mainly because of the provision that judges were to be designated by the king instead of chosen by the local people. This *Fuero Real* was legally influenced by the *Liber* and canon law. However, the major legal work of the time was the *Código de las Siete Partidas*. Divided into seven books it covered questions of canon law, political power, procedure, matrimonial law, contracts, succession and criminal law. It was translated into Portuguese and in the 19th and 20th centuries into English, and applied in the territories under Spanish domination in America. At the beginning it was a doctrinal text but its increasing prestige made it generally applied law until the 19th century. The influence of Roman-canon law in the *Partidas* is clear and decisive in the Spanish legal tradition.

(7) Basque country

The most distinctive feature of the territories and the peoples inhabiting what today is known as the Basque country is their language: the "*Euskera*".[35] *Euskera* is one of the rare examples of "island languages" which survived both the Indo-European and Roman influences. The Basques also avoided, to a large extent, the influences of the different cultures which invaded the Spanish peninsula through history. Confined to the remote and mountainous areas around the Pyrenees and the North of Spain, brave, and reluctant to encounter any external influence, they had little contact with the Romans, the Visigoths or the Moslems. When they descended to Castile at the time of the "reconquest" their customary laws did not seem to be homogeneous or very developed. As with their language, which had many dialects, so their customs seemed confined to small groups and communities.

---

[35] F. Tomás y Valiente, *op. cit.*, p.250.

F. Tomás y Valiente[36] points out some common characteristics of the laws of the three territories[37] during the medieval period. There is a coexistence of non-written customary law in rural areas with privileges and laws given by the King of Castile to the inhabitants of the cities (*villas*). Also, in the 14th century, in order to eliminate the violence which was an obstacle to any trade and even movement in the different territories, the inhabitants of the cities created associations called *Hermandades* or *Juntas* with capacity to dictate rules (*Ordenanzas*) for the judgment and punishment of crime. Although the Basque provinces were incorporated under the Crown of Castile the *Cortes* of Castile did not have power to legislate for Alava, Vizcaya and Guipúzcoa. In order to resist the attempt to extend to them the Castilian sources (*Fuero Real* and *Partidas*) in the 14th and 15th centuries, customary Basque laws were compiled in writing. These compilations of customs[38] and the general rules emanated from the different *Juntas*, constituted the main body of law in the provinces of Vizcaya, Alava and Guipúzcoa.

Absolutism

The powers of the King gradually increased during the 16th and 17th centuries and so did the volume of legislation. This created two main problems. The first problem was of a practical nature and this was the confusion among judges and lawyers as to which rules were still applicable and which not, since most of the new legislation did not repeal the former. The solution to this problem came by way of "compiling", that was, organising the different existing laws according to a chronological or systematic criteria in order to make it easier for the user to find the applicable provision. Most of the compilations of the time were started at instances of the king, although there were some important private collections. In general the compiler only transcribed the existing laws, organising these according to the chosen criteria but without altering the letter or substance of the provisions. However, in Castile, where the amount of legislation surpassed that in other territories, some authors attempted the difficult technique of "recasting the texts" by which all the different provisions refering to the same point were reformulated in a new one—which did not always respect the original aim and spirit of the rule. Among the most important collections of the time were the *Ordenamiento de Montalvo* of 1484 and the *Nueva Recopilación* of 1567.

---

[36] See *ibid.*, p.252.

[37] Vizcaya, Alava and Guipozcoa.

[38] *Fuero de Ayala* (1373) in Vizcaya, *Fuero Viejo de las Encarnaciones* (1394) and *Fuero Viejo de Vizcaya* (1452).

The second problem was of very different nature and related to the relationship between this increasing legislation and the different systems of law existing in Spain at the time. After the unification of Spain in 1492 following the defeat of Boabdil in Granada by Isabel I of Castile and Fernando V, Spain was ruled by a unitary Crown with different kingdoms, each of which had its own political and legal constitution which was threatened by the laws imposed by the King of Castile. The King progressively became more absolute, legislating by ways of *pragmáticas* (laws given by the King without consultation with the *Cortes* or Parliamentary assemblies) and legislating with effect in all the different territories. Felipe IV started an expansionist policy consisting of extending the political institutions of Castile to all other territories. These institutions were less democratic than those found in other territories because they granted greater powers to the King to the detriment of the local authorities. Some of the laws made by the King during this period were contrary to the laws generally approved by the different *Cortes* and assemblies and contrary to the traditional laws recognised in those territories. The solution to this conflict was found in the different legal formulas expressed by the local political organisations—*Cortes*—which, while acknowledging the power of the King to legislate, implemented the formula *obedézcase pero no se cumpla* which consisted in delaying the application of the royal legislation until the King, once he had been informed of the conflict with the local laws, resolved this in one way or another.

This formula was established by the *Cortes de Burgos* in 1379 but resistance to royal legislation and the defence of local laws was important in other kingdoms. In Navarra, where the legal system was clearly less romanised and "royalist" than in any other kingdom, a system of prior control by the *Consejo Real de Navarra* was established, by which all dispositions of the king needed to be approved by the *Consejo* before they could be applied in Navarra. This was known as the *pase foral* and was also generally practised in Guipúzcoa, Vizcaya and Alava until the 19th century. Catalonia and Aragón also protected their respective systems of law by similar formulas. In Catalonia a *constitución* passed by Fernando V in 1487, through the formula *poc valdria*, allowed the non-application of any laws contrary to the laws of the Principate. In Aragón control was effected by the *Justicia Mayor*.[39]

However, it was the Spanish War of Succession after the death of Carlos II and the triumph of Felipe V, that provided the excuse to abolish most of the local laws and effectively unify civil law in Spain.

---

[39] The *Justicia Mayor* is a typical institution of Aragón; he was a judge between the King and the kingdom. See, for an explanation of his role, F. Tomás y Valiente, *op. cit.*, p.296.

Catalonia, Aragón, Valencia and Mallorca supported the cause of Arch-Duke Carlos against the grandson of Louis XIV[40] and, when the Bourbon King won the throne, were severely punished, having their autonomy and laws curtailed.[41]

The Age of Enlightenment

The factor which was to be of greater influence on legal thought in the 18th century and which would constitute the theoretical basis for the new order of the next centuries, was the philosophical movement, which originated in the 16th and 17th centuries, based on the enlightenment of reason for the discovery of laws governing the physical world of nature. If reason could explain the functioning of nature and the laws to which this was subject, reason should also be able to explain the laws governing human nature and so draw the principles according to which men should be governed.

The School of Natural law, of which the main representatives were Grotius, Hobbes, Puffendorf and Wolff, proclaimed that philosophy would provide the general principles of Natural Law and that the legislator should create a systematic body of law based on these principles and according to which the different nations would be ruled. These principles, together with the theory of individual natural rights of Locke, Montesquieu's political theories expounded in *De L'Esprit des Lois*, and the Rousseaunian ideas of the "social contract", provided the ideological background of the Age of Enlightenment which quickly spread throughout Europe.

The legal principles of absolute monarchies by which the king could legislate according to his wishes—creating laws to which he was not subject himself—the division of society into different groups enjoying diverse privileges and the arbitrary system of justice administered by those chosen by the King, were duly criticised by Montesquieu, Kant, Mirabeau and Rousseau as contrary to reason and the natural order. Three new principles emerged from this new conception of the world: the principle of legality,[42] according to which both the universe and

---

[40] Catalonia and Aragón, followed by Mallorca and Valencia, distrusted the centralism of the Bourbons which they believed to be incompatible with the autonomy enjoyed by those regions and supported the cause of the Austro-German candidate after Felipe V was already proclaimed King of Spain.

[41] Particularly Aragón. The main consequence was that most public institutions were abolished in those territories and consequently their particular public law. Only the institutions of Navarra and the Basque provinces survived together with the Castilian ones, now extended to most territories.

[42] Recognised by the 1791 French Constitution, Tit.III, c.II, s.I, Art.3, first sentence: "There is no authority superior to the law".

human nature are subject to laws; the principle of rationality, by which those laws governing humanity are derived from the natural laws by the use of reason; and the principle of nationality, which recognises the differences existing between different nations and according to which positive law, following the principles of natural law, must be adapted to the circumstances of each nation. The philosophical and political ideas of the period were reflected by two major trends in legal history: the creation of a state of law governed by a supreme rule— the Constitution—and the codification of law.

Bourgeois revolution and liberal state

The society of the *Ancien Régime* was characterised by the differences between men who did not enjoy equal rights. Power rested upon ownership of the land which was controlled by the nobles and the Church. The King was the only person who could create law, a law which protected the interests of the dominant classes. Economic changes towards capitalism needed a new legal framework and the elimination of the old law. The new society born of the *Ancien Régime* proclaimed the equality of all men—although this was more a formal declaration used by the bourgeoisie for its own benefit rather than a real achievement—the free circulation of wealth and the liberalisation of the ownership of land. In legal terms the main difference was that the absolute monarchy was replaced by a liberal state governed by a supreme law—the Constitution.

2. CONSTITUTIONAL HISTORY

The Constitution, according to the principles and ideas of the revolutionaries and the philosophers of the Age of Enlightment, was the supreme law by which free men could decide how they wanted to organise themselves as a state.[43] The constitutional text, therefore, defined the political structure of the State and established the individual rights and freedoms of the citizens. In this respect the written constitutions of Europe of the 18th and 19th centuries served the dual purpose of being a Bill of rights and a statement of the political principles of organisation of the State.

In Spain the principles of the bourgeois revolution penetrated quite late compared to other European countries, particularly

---

[43] According to the ideas of Kant "the State is a society of free men over which nobody has power". F. Tomás y Valiente, *op. cit.*, p.422.

France, since the sociological conditions were quite different.[44] Also, the fact that France was at the time Spain's enemy, created a situation of resistance to some of the ideas exported from the neighbouring country. According to F. Tomás y Valiente[45] the revolutionary period in Spain can be divided into three phases.

The first phase extended from 1808 to 1833. Napoleon, according to his imperial plans, invaded Spain in 1808 and proclaimed José Bonaparte, his brother, King of Spain. On May 2, 1808, the War of Independence started, first as a movement to fight the invader, but later it developed into a war against the very foundations of the old regime. In a situation where there was a power vacuum—Fernando VII was absent and José Bonaparte was not recognised as the legitimate king by most of the population—the Spanish revolutionaries formed themselves into *Juntas*. All the provinces not occupied by the enemy elected their representatives in 1810 and the first *Cortes* (Parliament) met in Cádiz in order to draft a Constitution. The first Spanish Constitution was approved in Cádiz in 1812. It was strongly influenced by revolutionary ideas on the recognition of individual rights and the division of powers, establishing a Constitutional Monarchy. The Constitution of Cádiz of 1812 was a radical text which transformed society and recognised the principle of national sovereignty (Art.3, Constitution of 1812), the division of powers—with a uni-cameral Parliament which "with the King" makes the laws which are executed by the King and the courts of justice. Other important principles of this first constitutional text were the principles of unity of codes and unity of jurisdiction. However, King Fernando VII, after coming back from exile, abolished the Constitution in 1820 and the country returned to being subject to an absolute monarchy. In 1820 a liberal *coup d'état*, the *Pronunciamiento de Riego*, re-established the 1812 Constitution, which was again abolished by the King in 1823. The re-establishment of the absolutism from 1823 to 1833 meant the frustration of the revolutionary achievements.

The second period of the process took place from 1836 to 1856. During this time a Constitutional State was definitively established, the regime of land ownership modified[46] and the Church deprived of much of its power. The nobility remained a socially powerful group but was now closer to the ideas of the bourgeoisie. The Constitutions of the period (1837 and 1845) were moderate. The Constitution of

---

[44] Spain did not have such a powerful urban bourgeosie nor were the peasants so determined to break with the old regime.

[45] See F. Tomás y Valiente, *op. cit.*, p.404.

[46] On the transformation of the ownership of land or *desamortización* see, *ibid.*, pp.406–14.

1837 combined some of the ideas of the 1812 Constitution but made important concessions to the moderate sector, especially in the organisation of the powers of the State. The Parliament was now bicameral, with a Senate elected partly directly and partly by the King, and a Congress which was wholly elected. The powers of the Crown were, in general, reinforced. However, this flexible Constitution was modified in 1845 in order to change the principle of national sovereignty (sovereignty became shared between the nation and the King) and to reinforce, even more, the powers of the Crown.

The third and last stage of the revolutionary period was the most democratic. It started with the revolution of 1868 and ended with the return of a Bourbon King, Alfonso XII, in 1874. In 1868 Generals Prim, Serrano and Topete, led a revolution which ended with the expulsion of Queen Isabel II and the establishment of a new monarchy under Amadeo I of Saboya.[47] The European political climate, the loss of the colonies in America and the dissatisfaction of the working classes, together with the errors of the monarchy, created the foundations for the later republican revolution. Some consensus was reached between the bourgeoisie and the popular classes and, for the first time, universal suffrage was recognised, culminating in the 1869 Constitution which clearly recognised a wide variety of individual rights, including freedom of association, freedom of expression and religion and basic human rights. The 1869 Constitution recognised national sovereignty and included the division of powers with a clear pre-eminence of Parliament over the Executive. Important laws were passed in this period: the Criminal Code of 1870; the Organic Law of the Judiciary of 1870; and the Code of Criminal Procedure of 1872. Subsequently, the bourgeoisie became a conservative class, once it had achieved most of its demands and a new order favourable to its interests had been established.

However, the renunciation of the throne by Amadeo of Saboya, because of the impossibility of ruling a country while there were continuous political struggles between opposing parties, opened the door to the establishment of the First Spanish Republic in 1873. The 1869 Constitution remained applicable, despite the fact that it endorsed the monarchy as the form of government, while the republicans waited for a new constitution to be drafted. In 1873 a project for a republican-federal constitution was presented by a commission presided over by

---

[47] It was thought that a King belonging to a different royal family would be more suitable for the new conception of the State as a constitutional monarchy. At the time a large sector of the population, especially the regions which opposed Felipe V during the Spanish War of Succession, were against the Bourbon royal family which was identified with the absolutism of the *Ancien Régime*.

Emilio Castelar. The project retained the rights and freedoms of the 1869 Constitution and introduced Krausist ideas on a multiple conception of sovereignty recognised at different levels: individual, local, regional and federal. Indeed, the main novelty lay in the conception of Spain as a federal state, according to which several states, reflecting the historic territories, could each have their own constitution together with the generic constitution for the central State. The President of the Republic acquired some of the traditional powers of the King, becoming an arbitrator between the different territories. However, the general climate of political instability and anarchy made the implementation of the Constitution impossible and in 1874 the *coup* of General Pavía ended the republican government and the son of Isabel II, Alfonso XII, returned as King of Spain.

The monarchic return of 1874 and the moderate Constitution of 1876 meant returning to the option of a constitutional monarchy which had been unsuccessfully tried during the previous century. Even if the 1876 Constitution kept some of the rights recognised in the 1869 text, the Government enjoyed wide powers to suppress these. The State became Catholic again and the King shared sovereignty with the nation and, therefore, the power to legislate with parliament. This Constitution remained applicable for more than twenty years and important legislation of the period included the Criminal Procedure Code of 1882 and the Civil Code of 1889.

In 1917 General Primo de Rivera seized power and a dictatorship was imposed until 1931. The last government of the dictatorship in 1931 decided to call for municipal elections in order to test the political climate of the country[48] and on April 12, 1931, the socialist and republican parties obtained an overwhelming majority. King Alfonso XIII understood that the country clearly opted for a Republic and he left the country on April 14, 1931.[49] On the same day the Second Republic was peacefully proclaimed. The provisional government of the Second Republic called elections for constituent *Cortes*, after modifying the electoral laws in order to have the first truly democratic elections. Women were allowed to vote for the first time and the old electoral register was modified in order to prevent the manipulation of the electorate. This democratically elected Parliament approved the 1931 Constitution, the application of which was interrupted by the victory of General Franco in the Civil War, but had a considerable influence on the current 1978 Constitution. The Constitution of 1931 had an advanced social content. Although it recognised private ownership this was limited on the grounds of the "national interest"

---

[48] Note that the Monarchy agreed with the dictatorship.
[49] Although he did not renounce his rights to the throne.

and contained provisions according to which ownership could be nationalised, especially in respect of those services which affected the common interest. Article 1 declared Spain to be "a Republic of workers organised in a system of freedom and justice. All the powers come from the citizens". As to the territorial organisation of the State, Art.1 declared that "the Republic is an 'integral' State, recognising the autonomy of municipalities and regions". This republican constitution did not establish a federal state but lay the foundations of today's State of Autonomies because it recognised the right of the different territories to form themselves into autonomous regions and approve an *Estatuto de autonomía*.[50] Catalonia approved its *Estatuto* by a law of September 15, 1932, the Basque country by a law of October 6, 1936, and Galicia on June 28, 1936, although this last was never ratified in *Cortes*. Valencia, Aragón and Andalucia did not see their projects of *Estatuto* approved due to the outbreak of the Civil War in 1936 and the later dictatorship of General Franco following his victory.

From 1939 to 1975 Spain was under the right-wing dictatorship of General Franco who imposed an autocratic system around his person and abolished the republican Constitution and with it most of the rights and freedoms acquired during the revolutionary period. Catholic, unitary (no rights of autonomy were recognised in any of the historical regions) and highly centralised, Spain was ostracised by the international community until 1975 when, after Franco's death, the Monarchy in the person of King Juan Carlos I, was re-established.[51]

3. CODIFICATION

Codification of civil law

Although the idea of the having all the laws in a single body was not a novelty[52] the ideas of the philosophers of the Natural Law School, that the law was an organised system of rules derived from nature, was articulated by the creation of codes. A code would consist of a body of legislation which contained all the general principles on

---

[50] See below, Ch.2 pp.47–51 and Ch.7, pp.206–8.
[51] About this period and the political transition to democracy, see, among others: Paul Preston, *The Triumph of Democracy in Spain* (1986).
[52] Indeed the best example is the *Corpus Iuris Civilis* (AD527–60) and before it the *Codex Gregorianus* (AD291), *Codex Hermogenianus* (AD295) and the *Codex Theodosianus* (AD439).

which subsequent legislation would be based. The existence of a single source whereby the rights recognised by the Constitution— especially ownership and individual freedom—could be established in an universal way provided the bourgeoisie with legal certainty. A code could also be presented as the instrument with which to achieve a break with the past and consolidate the new order recognised in the constitutional text.

Prussia, Austria[53] and France were the first European countries to have codes. However, it was the French *Code Civile* of 1804 which was the greatest of them all because of its technical perfection and the fact that it was elaborated in a country which already had a bourgeoise revolution. The influence of the French Civil Code has been enormous. It was implemented and copied in several countries and inspired the codification of civil law in others, among them, Spain.

The first Spanish Civil Code was not approved until 1889, nearly a century after the French Civil Code. Although greatly influenced by the *Code Civile* in its principles, structure and systematisation, the codification of civil law in Spain presented peculiar characteristics due to the resistance of customary local laws to abolition and unification. The late publication of the Civil Code meant that during most of 19th century Spanish civil law was founded on the surviving customary local laws of the different communities[54] and the law of sources as old as the Code of the *Siete Partidas* and the *Ordenamiento de Alcalá*. In fact, it was the existence of different systems of civil law which slowed down the process of codification, together with a reaction against the centralisation of power in the 19th century. Although the Constitution of 1812 introduced the idea of drafting a civil code, several unsuccessful projects[55] were proposed until in 1885, Francisco Silvela, then Minister of Justice, presented a draft Civil Code containing important concessions for the application of *foral* and local law which would remain applicable, and establishing that the civil law contained in the Code would be supplementary in those territories which had their own customary *foral* law. According to the project of 1885 the different *foral* laws would be compiled in appendices and added to the Civil Code. The project presented by Francisco Silvela was in fact a *Ley de Bases*[56] which was to be developed by the *Comisión de Codificación*.

---

[53] On the Prussian and Austrian codification see O. Robinson, *op. cit.*, p.250; F. Tomás y Valiente, *op. cit.*, p.477.

[54] The ones which were not abolished by Felipe V. See above.

[55] For an explanation of these different projects and the problems they encountered see F. Tomás y Valiente, *op. cit.*, pp.546–50.

[56] A law establishing guidelines which were subsequently developed by a commission and later approved in Parliament.

In 1889 the Civil Code was approved and came into force on May 1, 1889. The Civil Code has a Preliminary Title on the sources, application, interpretation and efficacy of the Law. It is divided into four books: persons, property, acquisition and transfer of property and obligations. It is influenced by Castilian traditional law, particularly the Code of *Siete Partidas*, in subjects such as marriage and matrimonial property, and Roman law—as found in the *Ordenamiento de Alcalá*—in the area of contract. Principles of *foral* law are reflected in succession rules, although here the different *foral* regimes are respected. Foreign influences come mainly from the Code Napoleon and from different Ibero-American Codes, which themselves incorporated principles and ideas of the French Code. Politically the Code is a product of the liberal conception of the 19th century which is reflected in the protection of individual freedom, especially in contract law, and the protection of private ownership which is understood as an absolute right.

As far as the appendices of *foral* law originally planned are concerned, only Aragón presented its appendix in 1925. This was of poor quality and was severely critised and quickly subject to a project of reform. In 1946 a national meeting in Zaragoza rejected the idea of these appendices and agreed that different compilations should be drafted in order to elaborate a General Code of Civil law containing Common Civil law and the different aspects of *foral* law. Compilations with *foral* law were approved between 1959 and 1973, these included the laws of Catalonia, Aragón, Navarra, Baleares, Galicia, Alava and Vizcaya.[57]

Codification of criminal law

The Codification of other areas of law, envisaged since the 1812 Constitution, followed an easier path. Criminal Law, influenced by Roman law and canon law was one of the areas of law most severely criticised by the philosophers of the Age of Enlightment.[58]

Although the 1812 Constitution declared the principle of unity of Codes for the whole of the national territory, due to the political circumstances of the time[59] it was necessary to wait until the liberal triennial (1820–23) for the publication of the first Criminal Code in

---

[57] See Castán Tobeñas, *Derecho Civil Español, Común y Foral* (1982) pp.294–352 for an exposition of the different systems of *foral* law.
[58] Montesquieu, in his famous book *De L'esprit des lois* (1748) advocated a new and rational criminal law and criminal procedure since criminal law during the *Ancien Régime* took a line of extreme cruelty, especially on punishments.
[59] See above.

Spain, the *Código Penal* of 1822. This was only applied from January 1, 1823, to April 1823 when it was derogated by Fernando VII. The second Criminal Code was approved in 1848; shorter, and with a more modern approach, this was modified in 1850 by the absolutist government. The third Code was a product of the 1868 Revolution and was approved in 1870. Although originally intended only to be temporary—it was known as the "Summer Code"—paradoxically it had the longest application period. Derogated during the dictatorship of Primo de Rivera by the Criminal Code of 1928, it was re-established in 1932 during the Second Republic and modified again in 1932. The "New State" of General Franco introduced several modifications to the Criminal Code of 1870 which was formally still applicable. These culminated in 1944 with a Criminal Code in line with the principles and ideas of the *Régimen*. This Code, despite the political circumstances under which it was drafted, remained applicable, with some important modifications, after the 1978 Constitution.

Since the change of political orientation under a new democratic system, the most important reforms to the 1870 Code[60] have been effected by the *LO* 8/83, of June 25, "Partial and Urgent Reform of the Criminal Code", and the *LO* 3/89 of June 21 updating the Criminal Code, by which some of the principles contained in the Constitution were introduced into the Criminal legislation. However, the situation of Criminal law in Spain has been severely criticised from a number of different perspectives and several projects for a new Criminal Code have been unsuccessfully presented. Among these it is worth mentioning the project for Criminal Code of 1980 and the draft outline of 1983. The new Criminal Code was finally approved in 1995.[61] This introduced, as main reforms, a substantial modification of the system of punishment (according to Art.25 *CE*[62]), new types of crimes in order to reflect the changes observed in society, namely in the areas of socio-economic[63] and environmental crimes, the protection of fundamental rights such as the right to honour, with the introduction of a new and rather vague category described as "crimes against moral integrity".[64] It also proposes the modification of crimes against sexual freedom in order to depart from the traditional protection of women and to

---

[60] As subsequently modified.

[61] The new Criminal Code was approved by Congress on November 8, 1995 with the abstention vote of the Conservative group, LO 10/1995, of November 23, *Código Penal*.

[62] Art.25 *CE*: "*Las penas privativas de libertad y las medidas de seguridad estaran orientadas hacia la reeducacion y reinsercion social y no pordran consistir en trabajos forzados . . . en todo caso tendra derecho a unn trabajo remunerado . . . acceso a la cultura y al desarrollo integral de su personalidad*".

[63] Crimes relating to trade marks, intellectual property, and consumers.

[64] See Art.169 of the Project.

extend this protection to all citizens who are victims of sexual attacks without differentiating on the grounds of gender.[65] Several complementary pieces of legislation have been passed since then. Of particular importance is the regulation of the criminal responsibility of minors.[66]

Codification of commercial law

Commercial law was first codified in 1829. Since the late 18th century there had been demand for a general Code of maritime law and a general Code for commercial proceedings in order to overcome the diversification of laws produced by the different *Consulados*.[67] The *Código de Comercio* of 1829 had an excellent technical quality although it left some areas, such as the stock market, to be regulated by special legislation. However, the expansion of capitalism and the radical economic liberalism of the late 19th century soon meant that the provisions of the 1825 Commercial Code were inadequate and a new Code was drafted and approved in 1885. Very similar in its structure to the 1825 Code, the 1885 text is still applicable although a variety of laws have been passed in order to reflect changes in the commercial world. Among these the most important have been the *Ley de Sociedades Anónimas* in 1954 modified in 1989,[68] *Ley Cambiaria y del Cheque* (1985), *Ley del Mercado de Valores* (1988), *Ley General de Cooperativas* (1987), *Ley General para la Defensa de los Consumidores y Usuarios* (1984).

4. SPAIN TODAY: A SOCIAL AND DEMOCRATIC CONSTITUTIONAL STATE

On December 6, 1978, a Constitution was approved by national referendum and sanctioned by the King on December 27. It was drafted by a constitutional commission composed of representatives of the main political forces winning the 1977 elections.[69] The main aspects to be determined by the Constitution were: the definition of the form of

---

[65] See F.J. Álvarez García, *Código Penal y responsabilidad del menoz* (2005).

[66] LO 5/2000, of January 12 *de responsabilidad penal del menor*.

[67] See F. Tomás y Valiente, *op. cit.*, "Mercantile law from the XII to the XVIII Centuries" pp.346–68 and "Codification of Commercial Law" pp.507–19.

[68] By the *RDL*, 1564/1989 of December 22; see also *Ley* 19/1989 of July 25, adapting Spanish legislation on companies to EEC law.

[69] The constitutional commission was integrated by three deputies from UCD, one from PSOE, one from PCE-PSUC, one from AP and one from the Catalan minority.

government, the relationship between Church and State, the territorial structure of the State, and the powers of the Head of State and the Executive in respect of Parliament.[70] Together with these, the definition of the fundamental rights and freedoms and the establishment of a system of guarantees for the protection of these, was also in the minds of the draftsmen of the Constitution and the political forces at the time. As to the form of government—monarchy or republic—the dilemma was solved in favour of the monarchy since all political forces agreed that the price to pay for a peaceful transition to democracy was the acceptance of the monarchy as a form of government.[71] The Constitution in Art.1(3) declares that the form of government is a parliamentary monarchy.[72] Sovereignty rests upon the nation which elects its representatives to a bi-cameral Parliament.[73]

As to the relationship between Church and State, there was a considerable debate between the political parties of the left who supported a declaration of total separation of Church and State, such as the one contained in the 1931 Constitution, and the more conservative UCD (centre) and AP (right) who fought in order to preserve at least some of the powers of the Church. Article 16 represents a compromise between these two positions by declaring that, "The State has no religion . . . The public powers will, however, co-operate with the Catholic Church and other religious faiths".[74] Perhaps the major problems of the relationship between State and Church arose in connection with an area traditionally dominated by the Church—education.[75] The Catholic Church was reluctant to lose its ideological and economic monopoly on private education and the "representative political parties", the UCD and the AP ensured by the drafting of Art.27 CE, the preservation of this power.[76]

The territorial organisation of the State was one of the most difficult problems to solve, partly because even within the different political groups the position as to whether to opt for a federal or unitary state was not clearly defined. The Constitution chose, in Title

---

[70] According to M.A. Aparicio, in *Introducción al Sistema Político y Constitucional Español* (1991) p.42.

[71] See J. Solé Tura, *Los Comunistas y la Constitución* (1978) pp.69–70.

[72] See below, Ch.3, for an explanation of the role of the Crown in the Spanish System.

[73] For the role of Parliament see below, Ch.3, p.25.

[74] Art.16 CE "*Ninguna confesión tendrá caracter estatal. Los poderes públicos tendrán en cuenta las creencias religiosas de la sociedad española y mantendrán las consiguientes relaciones de cooperación con la Iglesia católica y demás confesiones.*"

[75] M.A. Aparicio, *op. cit.*, p.44.

[76] Art.27 recognises the right of creation of educational centres to individuals and groups and thereby to the Catholic Church. However the development of Art.27 has been controversial.

VIII, an unitary but decentralised State by which the different historical territories were recognised as having to achieve different degrees of autonomy according to the procedure set forth in Title VIII. Today, similarly to the Italian regional State, Spain is composed of 17 autonomous communities each of which has an autonomous Parliament and Executive[77] with powers shared with the central or national Parliament and the Executive.

As far as the definition and protection of fundamental rights and freedoms are concerned the 1978 Constitution is a progressive text along the lines of the Italian Constitution. Although it is not possible here to include a detailed study of the fundamental rights and freedoms recognised by the Constitution and the systems for their protection, a few of the most important aspects will be indicated.

The first consideration refers to the role that the fundamental rights and freedoms play in the whole legal system. To this effect Art.10(1) CE states that the laws should be interpreted according to the system of fundamental rights recognised by the Constitution. These rights and freedoms are thereby placed in a position of principles informing the interpretation and application of the rules of the whole legal system.

The second consideration relates to the guarantees established for the effective implementation and protection of fundamental rights. These guarantees are not limited to jurisdictional procedures, as indicated below, but encompass a wider system which integrates the principle of subjection of all citizens and public powers to the Law (Art.9(1) CE), with the declaration of the principle of legality of Art.53(1), according to which the regulation of the exercise of fundamental rights and freedoms is reserved to formal *leyes*, and, for some of these, to *leyes orgánicas* (Art.81)[78]; the introduction of specific institutions such as the *defensor del pueblo* (Art.54)[79]; the regulation of the right of petition (Art.29 CE) and the description of the functions of Parliament in this area.

The third point to consider is that the "Fundamental rights and duties" of Title I of the Constitution are divided into three types of rights depending on the protection available to them. The first group of rights and freedoms is integrated by Art.14—principle of equality—and Arts 15–29 CE—which include the fundamental rights and freedoms of s.1, c.2, Title I. The second group is integrated by Arts 30–38; and the third by the rights recognised in c.3, Title I, "Principles

---

[77] References are made throughout the text to the powers of the autonomous communities. See, especially, Ch.2, pp.47–51.

[78] See Ch.2, pp.31–3.

[79] See Ch.3, p.74.

informing the social and economic policy". The difference between these "types" or categories of rights, established in Art.53 CE, lies in the different form of protection against any violation of these "rights".[80] Article 53(2) makes provision for a special summary procedure for the protection of the rights recognised in Art.14 and s.1, c.2, Title I, Arts 15–29.[81] Also, these rights can be pleaded in the Constitutional Court by the procedure of *recurso de amparo*.[82] The rights recognised in c.1, should be pleaded according to ordinary proceedings and are excluded from the possibility of being protected directly by the Constitutional Court according to the procedure of *recurso de amparo*. As for the protection of the principles informing social and economic policy, Art.53(3) establishes that although these shall inform legislation and judicial practice they can only be pleaded in court according to the laws by which they have been developed.[83]

5. THE SPANISH CONCEPTION OF LAW

The word *derecho* is associated with the idea of justice and rectitude, as opposed to what is unjust, illegal or irrational.[84] When used in common language *derecho* has different meanings. First, *Derecho* (capital) means all the rules according to which society is organised. In this sense, *Derecho* is equivalent to the English word "Law". Secondly, the word *derecho* (non-capital) is used as an equivalent to the English word "right". Thirdly and last, *Derecho* is also used to designate legal science, that is, the study of the rules of law.

The first meaning of the word *Derecho*, is objective and designates the rules according to which society organises itself; but only certain type of rules can be included in the concept of legal rules. There are other rules which clearly influence and govern human behaviour but cannot be included in the term *Derecho;* these are moral, religious or

---

[80] Note that there are different classifications of fundamental rights. For example Luis López Guerra in *Introducción al Derecho Constitucional* (1994) pp.104–11, makes the distinction between "rights of freedom", "rights of participation" or political rights, "social rights" or second generation rights and, "solidarity rights" or third generation rights.

[81] *Procedimiento preferente y sumario* as developed by *Ley* 62/1978 *de protección jurisdiccional de los derechos fundamentales de la persona* of December 26. Today repealed by the *Ley* 29/1998 of July 13. See below, Ch.7, pp.208–209.

[82] See below, Ch.7, pp.202–204.

[83] For a greater detail on the exposition of the system of fundamental rights and freedoms, see M.A. Aparicio, *op. cit.*, pp.100–109 and the bibliography therein cited.

[84] Castán Tobeñas, *op. cit.*, pp.58–60.

social rules. The difference between a rule of law and other rules is that rules of law have two distinct characters: they are bi-lateral and imperative. Law is always concerned with the conduct or behaviour of a person in relationship with others; in this sense, the rule of law is bi-lateral because it creates at the same time a duty for one party and a power or right for the other.[85] Law is also imperative in the sense that every rule of law contains a mandate imposing certain behaviour on all those subject to the rule and encompasses a sanction in case of disobedience.[86]

The second meaning of the word *derecho* (right) or *derecho* in a subjective sense makes reference to the power that the legal system confers on individuals to act in a specific way and at the same time to expect a certain behaviour from others. In this sense the owner has the right of enjoyment of his property and the power to exclude others from that enjoyment, or the creditor has the right to be paid and the power to demand payment from the debtor.

The word *derecho*, comes from the latin word *directum* which is the past form of the verb *dirigere* which, according to Castán Tobeñas,[87] means "that which is according to rule" or "that which leads to an end". *Derecho* is thus, associated with the idea of "rectitude and direction".[88] It is interesting to note, however, that the Romans used the word *ius* to designate what today is known in Spanish as *Derecho* (Law). The displacement of the word *ius* for *directum* has different explanations[89] but several words connected with the Law derive from this Latin word: *justicia, justo, juez, jurídico, jurista*, etc.

6.   THE DIVISION BETWEEN PUBLIC AND PRIVATE LAW

The classical division between public and private law comes from the great Roman jurists. Ulpianus, in a definition included in the *Institutiones*, defined public law—*ius publicum*—as the law which regulates the political aspects of the State while private law—the *ius privatum*—comprises the rules which regulate the relationships of citizens

---

[85] Moral or social rules only impose duties and do not create rights or powers.
[86] This sanction can be more or less perfect depending on the case. For example in Public International law, it is difficult sometimes to impose sanctions on sovereign states.
[87] *Op. cit.*, p.58.
[88] In other languages this idea is also found in the terms used for *derecho: dret* in Catalan, *droit* in French, *diritto* in Italian, *recht* in German and "right" in English. See the very interesting etymological study by Castán Tobeñas, *op. cit.*, p.58.
[89] See, again Castán Tobeñas, *op. cit.*, p.59 and the bibliography therein provided.

among themselves. Many criteria have been discussed by scholars concerning the classification of public and private law: the type of interest—general or private, protected and/or the character, imperative or dispositive—however, all of these have been criticised and today the predominant criteria establishes the differences between private and public law on the basis of the subjects involved in the legal relationship. In this sense, public law is the part of the law which regulates relationships in which the State is involved whenever they act as such, or as the Roman jurists used to put it, whenever they exercise "*imperium*"; and private law includes all those rules which organise the relationship of private citizens between themselves.

This distinction between private and public law, which does not exist in Common Law countries, has been basic to Civil Law countries. However, the development of new branches of law and the increasing intervention of the State in many areas traditionally governed by private law has given rise to a growing scepticism as to the utility of such differentiation or even its existence to day. Some authors write about three areas of law; public, private and mixed, which of course, diminishes the importance of the original division.

The traditional branches of public law are: Constitutional law (*derecho constitucional*), criminal law (*derecho penal*), administrative law (*derecho administrativo*), procedural law (*derecho procesal*), tax law (*derecho financiero y tributario*) and public international law (*derecho internacional público*).

Private Law in turn includes civil law (*derecho civil*), commercial law (*derecho mercantil*), private international law (*internacional privado*) and originally labour law (*derecho del trabajo*), although the latter is heavily regulated by the State and can be included in the third or mixed category. I have followed the Spanish division in this book.

Chapter Two
Sources of law

1. INTRODUCTION

The expression "sources of law" can be interpreted in different ways. It can be understood as the origin of the rules of law. In this sense Parliament would be a "source of law", because the *leyes* are enacted by the Chambers of Parliament; in the same sense the Executive would be another "source of law" because it produces regulations. However, this is not the meaning that the expression "sources of law" commonly has in legal theory. When we speak about the sources of law of a given legal system what we are referring to are all those rules which constitute "the Law". From a functional perspective the sources of law are everything which provides rules for the judge when having to decide a case.[1]

Traditionally, the regulation of the sources of law was to be found in the Spanish Civil Code. The old Art.6 contained a mandate to the judge, in the absence of any rule of written law—*ley*[2]—to apply the local custom and the general principles of the law. By a law of March 17, 1973, a Preliminary Title was introduced in the 1889 Civil Code and in Art.1 the sources of the Spanish legal system were established as being: *la ley, la costumbre y los principios generales del derecho*.[3] In this preliminary title there are also rules concerning the application of the law, the interpretation of legal rules, the role of "equity"[4] and the personal, territorial and life-time effect of the laws. This group of rules has been referred to as "material constitutional law"[5] because they provide and establish the basic framework of the operation of the system. The sources of the law as defined in the Civil Code have been described as "traditional sources of law" in contrast to the

---

[1] Ignacio del Otto, *Derecho Constitucional, Sistema de Fuentes* (1991), p.72.

[2] *Ley* is a formal Act of Parliament but can also be translated as "Law" or "legislation". When referred to as a source of law, *ley* means any rule of law emanating from the State.

[3] *Ley*, in the sense explained above, custom and the general principles of the law.

[4] "Equity" or *equidad* is understood as the equivalent of justice. See below.

[5] Ignacio del Otto, *op. cit.*, p.85; against, Díez Picazo, *Sistema de Derecho Civil* (1992), Vol.I.

sources described in the 1978 Constitution. The Civil Code itself is a subsidiary source for all the other areas of the law as *derecho común ó general*, but it needs to be remembered that, for each branch of the law, the sources can be re-defined and to some extent varied. A good example of this is criminal law, where, by virtue of the "principle of legality" only written law promulgated by the State is a recognised source of law. Other examples are administrative law, tax law and labour law where the traditional sources of Art.1 of the Civil Code are limited or extended.

The sources of law in Spain can be divided into three categories: primary sources of law, which provide judges with the law directly applicable to the case; complementary sources, the power and scope of which derives from a primary source; and explanatory sources, which give guidance to the person applying the law as regards the meaning of the primary sources. What is considered to be a source of law in any given legal system is closely connected with and dependent on the legal history of the system.[6]

2.   PRIMARY SOURCES OF LAW

LA LEY (LEGISLATION)

The word *ley*, when used as synonym for legislation, has a broad meaning encompassing all written law emanating from the State: the Constitution, ordinary legislation, rules of law emanating from the government by virtue of legislative delegation or special powers derived from the Constitution[7]—*decretos-leyes*, *decretos legislativos*, and decisions of the Constitutional Court. In this respect *ley* is any rule of written law which has a certain position in the hierarchy of sources— *fuerza de ley*—and not only the rules emanating from Parliament's[8] broad category of *ley*, but rules from very different sources can be found and even the Constitution itself would be included.

However, when the Civil Code mentions *la ley* in Art.1, it is not only referring to the rules created by the State's legislative power according to different procedures and in respect of different matters, but also to

---

[6] See Ch.1 for a brief summary of the history of the Spanish legal system.
[7] See below.
[8] There is a distinction between *ley* in a formal sense, i.e. Acts of Parliament and *ley* in a material sense, i.e. general measures by another authority with the same value and position in the hierarchy of sources. For a comparison with the French legal system, see Dadomo & Farran, *op. cit.*, p.60 *et seq.*

the rules created by the Government[9] and the Public Administration in the exercise of their executive power. *Ley*, thus, is any written rule of law created by the state. All these different types of rules and the relationship between them will be examined in this chapter.

TYPES OF LEY

Leyes orgánicas[10]

When the 1978 Constitution was approved, it was difficult to achieve agreement on some fundamental matters. The political consensus, reached by the different political forces during the period of "political transition"[11] as regards the organisation of the State and the minimum levels of civil rights and liberties, could not cover all the basic aspects which make up a State. Some matters therefore had to be left to the legislator but at the same time these aspects were so fundamental that it was thought to be inappropriate to leave them to the arbitrary will of the majority political party in power. This explains why the use of *leyes orgánicas* became a necessary device.

Leyes orgánicas are a special type of statute required by the Constitution for the regulation of certain matters, subject to special requirements for the procedure of elaboration, approval, modification and derogation. Article 81 of the Constitution states that

> "*leyes orgánicas* regulate fundamental rights and civil liberties, approve of the *Estatutos de Autonomía*[12] the general electoral regime and any other matter provided for by the Constitution".

Leyes orgánicas are different from ordinary legislation in two ways: first, as to the subject matter of the regulation, they relate to specific matters (Art.81 CE); and secondly, because there are different formal requirements for their approval due to the fundamental character of the areas to which they relate.[13]

As to their position in the hierarchy of sources of law, *leyes orgánicas* are subject to the Constitution, otherwise they would be declared unconstitutional by the Constitutional Court.[14] As regards other types of *ley*, in particular ordinary legislation, *leyes orgánicas* are at the same

---

[9] *Reglamentos, decretos, ordenes.* See below.
[10] *Leyes orgánicas* could be translated by "organic laws", but this is not widely accepted terminology and therefore the original Spanish word will be used.
[11] See Ch.1, pp.22–27.
[12] See below.
[13] *Leyes orgánicas* need to be approved by an absolute majority of the Congress (Art.81 *CE*), while ordinary legislation only requires a simple majority for its approval.
[14] See below, Ch.3, pp.199–202 *et seq.*

level because they are only a different type of *ley*. Whether a matter should or should not be regulated by a *ley orgánica* depends on whether that matter is specified in Art.81 CE or another constitutional provision. If it is, then the ordinary legislator cannot regulate that matter and any ordinary *ley* purporting to do so would be unconstitutional because it would contravene Art.81 CE. If the matter is not specifically designated as requiring a *ley orgánica*, the ordinary legislator can regulate it, and the *ley ordinaria* is then subject only to the Constitution. The relationship between *leyes orgánicas* and ordinary *leyes* is, therefore, a question of subject-matter, not hierarchy. The problem arises when a *ley orgánica*, while regulating matters specified in the Constitution as requiring such legislation, goes beyond these and regulates other matters not specifically so reserved. In this case the question is, can an ordinary *ley* modify or abrogate this legislation? Article 28(2) of the LOTC[15] clearly states that the Constitutional Court can declare any *ley*, which modifies or derogates a *ley orgánica*, unconstitutional. At first, this seems to indicate that ordinary legislation cannot modify or abrogate any regulations contained in a *ley orgánica*. However, the Constitutional Court, in a decision of 1981,[16] had declared that if a *ley orgánica* regulates any other matter beyond the areas delimited in the Constitution it would only have the value of an ordinary *ley*, and as such it could be modified or abrogated, as regards these matters, by later ordinary legislation.

The matters reserved for a *ley orgánica* are listed in Art.81(1) CE. Some clarifications are necessary at this point. First, as to the "development of fundamental rights and civil liberties", the stipulation that a *ley orgánica* must be used in this area must be interpreted[17] as referring only to c.II, s.1, of Title I, Arts 15–29 CE, because this section is the only one which is entitled "Of fundamental rights and public freedoms". Any other interpretation of Art.81 CE would create the situation in which ordinary legislation would become almost redundant because Title I of the Constitution includes the principles of economic and social policy which are present in almost every regulation. Also, "development" means "development of the recognition of the right in the Constitution",[18] not every regulation on the exercise of the right, because that is a matter for an ordinary *ley* under Art.53(1) CE.[19]

---

[15] *Ley Orgánica del Tribunal Constitucional* LO 2/1979 of October 3.
[16] STC 51/81 of February 13.
[17] STC 70/1983 of August 5.
[18] STC 6/1981 of March 16.
[19] "*Los derechos y libertades reconocidos en el Capítulo segundo del presente Título vinculan a todos los poderes públicos. Solo por ley, que en todo caso deberá respetar su contenido esencial, podrá regularse el contenido de tales derechos y libertades . . .*"

Secondly, as to the regulation of the "general electoral regime" by a *ley orgánica*, the Constitutional Court understands[20] this to cover not only general elections but also local elections. This regulation by a *ley orgánica* extends to all "basic and primary aspects of the electoral regime and not only the right to vote".[21]

The approval of the *Estatutos de Autonomía* by a *ley orgánica*, will be discussed later in the context of Autonomic Laws.[22] The last matter specifically requiring a *ley orgánica* under Art.81 *CE* is an open category "any other matter as determined by the Constitution". The matters determined by the Constitution include; the regulation of the institution of the State; *Defensor del Pueblo*[23] (Art.54 *CE*), *Consejo de Estado* (Art.107 *CE*), *Tribunal Constitucional*[24] (Art.165 CE), and other important matters such as the popular legislative initiative[25] (Art.87(3) *CE*).

International treaties

(a) Incorporation into the legal system: Types of treaties

International treaties are automatically incorporated into the Spanish legal system once they have been duly signed and ratified.[26] Spain adopts a monist system of incorporation of international rules into domestic law. This means that no further action by the legislative or any other body of the State is necessary to confer binding force on an international agreement.[27] The Constitution draws a distinction between different types of treaties; in all of the them, the conditions for their validity are ex ante as to whether they have been properly entered into; if they have, they are automatically incorporated into the legal system and bind all citizens and public powers.

Three types of international treaties are identified in the Spanish Constitution:

(1) Article 93 treaties, which confer some of the powers of the State on an international organisation. For these treaties a *ley orgánica*[28] authorising the signing of the treaty is necessary.

---

[20] STC 38/1983 of May 16.
[21] STS 38/1983 of May 16.
[22] See below.
[23] LO 3/1981 of April 6, *del Defensor del Pueblo*. See below, Ch.8, pp.220–1.
[24] The Constitutional Court, *LOTC* 2/1979 of October 12.
[25] LO 3/1984 of January 26, *reguladora de la iniciativa popular*.
[26] "Any international treaty signed and ratified according to the rules of international law and this Constitution will be part of the legal system" (Art.96(1) CE).
[27] Dualist systems such as in England require an Act of Parliament to enact a treaty.
[28] This is one of the matters specifically provided for in the Constitution requiring a *ley orgánica*.

Probably the most famous and typical example of this type of treaty is the Treaty of the Accession of Spain to the European Communities, the ratification of which was authorised by a *ley orgánica*.[29]

Once the approval to ratify the treaty is given by a *ley orgánica*, the treaty will automatically be incorporated into domestic law on its publication[30] in the official journal.[31] As the international treaty has given authority to the international organisation, the legislation produced by the orgnisation—derivative or secondary law of the European Communities—will be automatically obligatory in Spain with no need for any further action by the internal powers. The Supreme Court has confirmed the "direct efficacy and supremacy of European Community Law due to the partial assignment of sovereignty to the Community Institutions".[32] Along the same lines, the Spanish Constitutional Court has expressed that "the binding force of Community Law comes from the Accession Treaty according to article 93 of the Spanish Constitution" (STC 61/1991, *caso APESCO*, F.J.4).[33]

(2) The second type of treaty is that requiring prior authorisation by Parliament through an agreement of both Chambers at the request of the Executive. These treaties, *rationae materiae*, are of a political or military character and affect the territorial integrity of the State, the rights and freedoms guaranteed in Title I of the Constitution, or create financial obligations on the State. For example, the participation of Spain in NATO required previous authorisation by Parliament. According to Art.94 (1)(a), (b), (c), (d), (e) CE, the authorisation of Parliament is necessary prior to the ratification of any treaty if this involves a modification or abrogation of any law or the need for any legislative measure for its implementation.

---

[29] LO 10/1985 of August 2, authorising the ratification of the Treaty of Accession to the European Communities, Lisbon and Madrid, June 12, 1985. The LO 411986 of November 26 authorises the ratification of the Single European Act; the LO 10/1992 of December 26 the ratification of the Treaty of the European Union; the LO 09/1998 of December 16 the Treaty of Amsterdam; and the LO 3/2001 of November 6 the Treaty of Nice.

[30] Art.96 of the Spanish Constitution.

[31] *Boletín Oficial del Estado* (BOE).

[32] STS of April 28, 1987, *Depositos Francos* (*Sala* 3, 1987); in the same sense STS of April 17, 1989, *ITE Canario* (*Sala* 3, 1989) Cdo. 2.

[33] For the most recent analysis of the relationship and applicability of European Community Law in Spain, see Pablo Perez Tremps, *Constitución Española y Comunidad Europea* (1994) pp.133, 134.

(3) Any other treaty not included in (1) or (2). The Executive can sign and ratify these treaties and there is a requirement only to inform Parliament following such ratification (Art.94(2) CE).

(b) The position of treaties in the hierarchy of sources of law

The position of international treaties is clear in respect of their sub-ordination to the Constitution.[34] There is a procedure whereby enquiries may be made to the Constitutional Court as to whether a treaty conflicts with the Constitution. The Government and/or Parliament can require the Constitutional Court to make a ruling as to whether the treaty is or is not against the Constitution.[35] If the treaty is contrary to the Constitution the latter will need to be modified before the signing of the treaty (Art.95(1) CE).[36] There is also a *post facto* control by the Constitutional Court according to Art.27(2) LOTC.[37] Since the treaty has a hierarchical position equivalent to the *ley*, the Constitutional Court can declare that all or some of the provisions of the treaty are "unconstitutional" and so inapplicable.[38]

A problem arises in respect of the relationship between treaties and ordinary laws. Treaties (without distinction) are treated in the same way as ordinary legislation as regards their constitutional control. However, other differences arise between treaties and ordinary legislation. The active force of the legislation, its capacity to abrogate or modify other rules of law, including other legislation, is not applicable to international treaties. Only when a treaty has been signed with the previous approval of the legislative power can a treaty abrogate or modify other legislation because the previous approval of Parliament means an extension or delegation of legislative power. On the other hand, the force of ordinary legislation is restricted when applied to a treaty (Art.96(1)) because the provisions of a treaty can only be modified, abrogated, or suspended in accordance with the procedure established in the treaty itself. If a provision of a treaty and a rule of domestic law are in conflict, the provision of the treaty prevails.

This particular situation regarding treaties has led to doctrinal controversy concerning the superior position of international legislation over domestic legislation. However, rather than looking at this question in terms of hierarchy, the special status of the treaty can be

---

[34] Art.95 of the Spanish Constitution *a sensu contrario*.
[35] Arts 95(2) CE and 78 LOTC. See below, Ch.7, pp.199–200.
[36] For instance Art.13(2) of the Constitution was modified on August 27, 1992, in order to allow the signing of the Single European Act.
[37] See below, Ch.7, p.202.
[38] In this case the Executive will have to take measures in order to modify its international obligations.

explained by the principle *of pacta sunt servanda* and thus the impossibility of unilateral modification of the terms or obligations assumed under a treaty.

(c) European Union law

The accession of Spain in 1986 to the then European Community and the subsequent ratification of the Single European Act and the Treaty of the European Union meant a cession of State powers in favour of an international organisation. The application and position of the original treaties in the Spanish legal system did not create major problems. The treaties are rules of International law and if properly signed they are directly applicable as a part of the national system once they have been published in the Official Journal.[39] A different problem is the applicability of the "derivative law" of the European Communities. By derivative law is meant the rules produced by the Institutions of the Community. Here, again, the Spanish legal system adopts a monist approach. In the same way as the treaties are rules of International Law directly applicable in domestic situations without the need for any further action by the internal legislative power, so is derivative law, since it is a consequence of the obligations imposed by the treaty. There is no provision other than Art.93 CE in Spanish law on which to base the application of the derivative law of the Communities. The Supreme Court has expressed and reinforced this view:

> "European Community Law has direct effect and supremacy over national law by virtue of the partial cession of sovercignty brought about by the accession to the European Community".[40]

The question of the direct effect of Community legislation has never been controversial in Spanish law, due perhaps to Spain's late joining of the Community and the numerous decisions of the European Court of Justice concerning the direct effect and supremacy of Community law. The Spanish Supreme Court has totally accepted the position of the European Court of Justice on the direct effect of regulations[41] and directives.[42]

---

[39] The problem of applicability is more difficult for States with a dualist position such as England.

[40] STS of April 28, 1987, *Depositos Francos*; also, STS of April 17, 1987, *ITE Canario*. For a general discussion on the topic, see Pablo Pérez Tremps, *op. cit.*, pp.127–49.

[41] STS of April 17, 1987, *ITE Canario*.

[42] STS of December 21, 1988, *Contrabando de Tabacos* (*Sala* 2, 1988). For more references, see Pablo Perez Tremps, *op. cit.*, p.137.

Another area concerning the relationship between Community legislation and internal rules is the question of the resolution of conflicts between rules of both systems. After the famous decision of the European Court of Justice *Costa/ENEL* (1964),[43] the principle of precedence of Community law over national law is one of the pillars on which the system rests. The Spanish Constitutional Court has held that any conflict between Community legislation and domestic legislation has to be resolved by the ordinary jurisdiction according to the principle of the supremacy of Community law.[44]

Leyes ordinarias

Since the French Revolution the word *ley* has been used to designate all the rules dictated by the organ of popular representation according to a certain procedure. *Ley* is the rule of law approved by Parliament according to the procedure established in Title III, c.2 of the 1978 Constitution[45] and the rules of law approved by the legislative organs of the Autonomous Communities.

Almost any matter can be regulated by ordinary legislation,[46] and some of these matters are specifically reserved for the *ley.*[47] However, due to the lengthy procedure for approval of ordinary legislation in Parliament and to the complexity of some of the matters that need to be regulated in modern societies, the number of formal *leyes* is relatively small compared with other types of legislation, namely *decretos-leyes* and *decretos legislativos*[48] which hierarchically are in the same position as ordinary legislation but are made by the Executive.

Decretos leyes

In cases of urgency and extreme need, the Executive has the power to introduce rules which have the force of *ley*. This power of the Executive is recognised by the Constitution (Art.86(1)) and it is

---

[43] STJCE *Costa/ENEL*, of July 15, 1964.
[44] STC 28/1991 of February 14, *Elecciones al Parlamento Europeo*. For a further discussion on the subject see. A. Sánchez Legido, *Las relaciones entre el Derecho Comunitario y el Derecho interno en la Jurisprudencia del Tribunal Constitucional* pp.184–5. Pablo Pérez Tremps, *op. cit.*, pp.146–8.
[45] See below, Ch.7, p.184.
[46] With the exception of the matters reserved to *leyes organicas* by Art.81(1) CE. See above.
[47] *Reserva de ley formal* for example the regulation of the rights and freedoms of c.2 of the Constitution can only be done by a *ley* according to Art.53(1) CE.
[48] See below.

commonplace in comparative constitutional law.[49] The limits imposed by the Constitution on this power—which indeed modifies the original division between the legislative, executive and judicial powers[50]—are both formal and substantive. The substantive limitation is that the *decreto-ley* may not affect the organisation of the basic institutions of the State, the civil rights and liberties contained in Title I of the Constitution, the organisation and powers of the Autonomous Communities or the general electoral regime. The formal limit is the need to submit the *decreto-ley* to Congress for approval and ratification within a period of thirty days. The validity of this type of legislation is therefore conditional on the ratification or rejection by Congress (Art.86(2) CE). If it is approved, Congress can "convert" the *decreto-ley* to an ordinary *ley* by an expedited procedure (Art.86(3) CE).

The existence of this power of the Government to legislate gives rise to important and difficult questions about the controls to which this type of rule is subject. The main question is the relationship between a *decreto-ley* and the subsequent *ley* of Parliament when the *decreto-ley* has been converted,[51] and whether the new *ley* and the original *decreto-ley* are two different rules which can be subjected to the control of the Constitutional Court separately, or whether the new *ley* has retroactive effects and the *decreto-ley* is a "project of *ley* with anticipated effects".[52] The Constitutional Court, in a rather unclear decision in 1983,[53] held that it is possible to question the validity of an original *decreto-ley* as to whether the requirements of "urgent and extraordinary need" were present, but when the content of the *decreto-ley* has been incorporated into a formal *ley*, what should be examined is the constitutionality of the new *ley* which thereby has "some retrospective effects". This solution seems to give the new *ley* retrospective effect which is contrary to Art.9(3) CE and also, according to some writers deprives the restrictions set out in Art.86(1) of any meaning.[54]

---

[49] Art.16 of the French Constitution, Art.81 of the German Constitution, and Art.77 Italian Constitution recognise the same power of their respective Executives. In all three the power of the government is restricted to cases of extreme urgency and/or need.

[50] As established during the French Revolution.

[51] See Ignacio del Otto, *op. cit.*, pp.206–209 for a detailed consideration and analysis of the topic.

[52] In the words of Ignacio del Otto, *op. cit.*, p.208.

[53] STC 11/1983, *caso RUMASA*. By *decreto-ley* of February 23, 1983, the Executive expropriated the *Grupo RUMASA* which belonged to J.M. Ruiz-Mateos. This *decreto-ley* was confirmed shortly afterwards by Congress according to Art.86(2) CE. On June 29, 1983, a *ley* substituted the original *decreto-ley* because it was argued that an expropriation affected fundamental rights and could not be made by this type of legislation according to Art.86(1) CE.

[54] However, the solution of the Constitutional Court is followed by the majority of writers, and warmly supported by Ignacio del Otto, *op. cit.*, pp.208–209.

Decretos legislativos

While the Executive, in the case of *decretos-leyes*, using the power given by the Constitution in Art.86, decides that the regulation of some matters requires swift action, there are other cases in which Parliament decides that some legislation would be better drafted by the Executive because of the nature of the matter. In these cases Parliament delegates its legislative power to the Executive. The legislation passed by the Executive following delegation by Parliament is called *decreto legislativo*.

Legislative delegation is a practice common in all European States. Article 82(l) of the Spanish Constitution establishes the power of Parliament to delegate to the Government the right to pass rules which have the force of *ley*. These rules are different from those mentioned previously—*decreto-ley*—for whereas with *decretos-leyes* the Government is exercising one of its own powers, here Parliament has conferred this power on the Executive which must observe the limits set out by Parliament.

Any delegation of power must be exercised within strict limitations. It can only be made for a specific matter, it must be expressly allowed by a *ley*[55] of Parliament, and for a finite period of time. It cannot apply to matters reserved for a *ley orgánica*[56] or the general budget of the State. The delegation can be articulated in two ways. In the first instance—*textos articulados*—Parliament dictates a *ley de bases*[57] fixing the principles, criteria, object, limits and scope of the delegation and the text which will be created. The second instance is the authorisation for consolidating legislation which already exists but is scattered. Here the limits are easier to establish as the Executive has to reorganise pre-existing legislation but cannot introduce or create new rules.

Control of this method of legislating can be exercised by the courts in the ordinary way once the text has come into existence. Also the enabling or delegating *ley* can establish additional controls. In the case of *decretos-legislativos* there is no control by Parliament after the promulgation of the text as is the case with *decretos-leyes*.[58] Problems arise when the Government acts *ultra vires*, that is, when it goes further than authorised by the enabling law. The doctrine has different opinions as to what happens with rules passed outside the scope of the power given by the delegation. As it is a rule having the force of law, a judge who

---

[55] A formal *ley*, approved according to the procedure of Arts 87–91 CE. See above, and for more detail Ch.7, pp.184–7.
[56] See above: matters reserved for a *ley orgánica*.
[57] Basic legislation.
[58] See above.

has to apply it has two options: not to apply that part of it which is tainted by *ultra vires*,[59] or to require the Constitutional Court to give a ruling on the constitutionality of the whole text.[60]

Reglamentos, decretos, and other administrative dispositions

The term *reglamento*[61] refers to any general legal rule dictated by the Public Administration or, more generally, by the Executive. The formalities required by these rules and the different organs from which they emanate give rise to different types of *reglamentos* which are hierarchically organised. At the top of the scale *of reglamentos* are the *decretos* of the Council of Ministers; below these, the *ordenes* of the Ministers or of the Delegated Commissions; underneath, *instrucciones* and *circulares* from inferior authorities and members of the administration. The procedure and requirements for drafting these dispositions are established by the Administrative Procedure Act 1954, Arts 129–37. *Reglamentos* are rules of law due to their generality and are different from other administrative acts which are only individual acts. These rules dictated by the Administration are always subject to the *ley* and the judge has no power to apply any reglamentary disposition which is contrary to a *ley*. A *reglamento* can also be challenged in the Administrative Court and declared null and void.

Traditionally *reglamentos* have been classified in two groups. Independent *reglamentos* or *praeter legem*, which regulate matters without legislative coverage; and executory *reglamentos*, or *reglamentos secundum legem*, which develop an existing *ley*.[62] In this case it is necessary to request the opinion of the *Consejo de Estado*.[63] A different classification is that which distinguishes between *reglamentos jurídicos* and *reglamentos administrativos*. *Reglamentos jurídicos* are

---

[59] Because, according to E. García de Enterría, *Curso de Derecho Administrativo* (1993) p.250 *et seq.*, the rules contained in the *decreto legislativo* tainted by *ultra vires* do not have the nature or the value of *ley*; they have the same value as any of the dispositions dictated by the Executive in the exercise of its regulatory power; and these regulations of the Executive need not be applied by the ordinary judge when they are contrary to a *ley* or to the Constitution. Compare, however, the view of Ignacio del Otto, *op. cit.*, pp.190–4.

[60] The Constitutional Court has affirmed its competence in this matter SSTC 29/82; 51/82; 47/84 and *Auto* 69/83 of January 17.

[61] Which can be translated by "regulation", and should not be confused with the *reglamentos* of the Chambers of Parliament which are the rules that the Chambers pass in order to organise their own functioning and which have the same value as a *ley*.

[62] A good example of this second type are the *Reglamento del Registro Civil* or the *Reglamento Hipotecario* which develop the *Ley del Registro Civil* and the *Ley Hipotecaria* respectively.

[63] Art.22(3) LO 3/1980 of April 22, *del Consejo de Estado*.

those which create or modify the rights and duties of citizens, for example the Road Traffic Code; these *reglamentos* affect citizens independently of any special relationship with the Public Administration. *Reglamentos administrativos* are those dictated by the administration for the organisation of its activities and only affect the citizen who is in a special relationship with the administration, for example, because he is a inmate in prison, or using a public hospital.[64]

The power to pass *reglamentos* is vested in the Executive by Art.97 of the Constitution,[65] but other constitutional organs of the State also enjoy "regulatory" power; these are the *Consejo General del Poder Judical*[66] and the Constitutional Court which can regulate their own organisation, personnel and services.[67] The territorial entities which have recognised autonomy by the Constitution—municipalities, provinces and Autonomous Communities[68]—also enjoy regulatory power.

La costumbre (customary laws)

According to Art.1 of the Preliminary Title of the Civil Code, *la costumbre* (Custom) is a primary source of law, the second source after the *ley*. However, this is subject to some qualifications. Custom will only be applied by a judge if there is no applicable *ley*, it cannot be contrary to morals or public order and needs to be proved.

Historically the first definition of customary laws was given in *Las Partidas*:[69] "Custom is non-written law, applied by men for a long time". This definition provides a starting point for the examination of customary laws. The first characteristic is that customs are "non-written law"; while legislation is normally written[70] customs are usually not. However, there is nothing to prevent customary laws from being compiled or reduced to writing;[71] probably the best example is provided by international trade rules such as the rules governing documentary credits transactions which have been reduced to writing[72] but

---

[64] Ignacio del Otto, *op. cit.*, p.218 and E. García de Enterría, *op. cit.*, p.257 *et seq.*

[65] *"El Gobierno . . . ejerce la función ejecutiva y la potestad reglamentaria de acuerdo con la Constitución y las leyes".*

[66] See below, Ch.3, pp.61–62.

[67] Arts 2(2) LOTC and 110 LOPJ.

[68] Art.137 CE.

[69] See Ch.1, p.12.

[70] It has to be written: Art.2 Civil Code.

[71] For example "foral laws" of customary origin had been compiled as was the *droit coutumier* in France during the sixteenth and seventeenth centuries.

[72] *Uniform Customs and Practice for Documentary Credits, Publication 500.* International Chamber of Commerce, Paris 1993.

which do not have a value other than that of mercantile usage. The fact of whether a rule is written or not, is not enough to characterise customary laws as being different from legislation. The second characteristic of customs is the origin of these rules. Customary laws, it is said, do not originate from the State but from society. This second characteristic, however, necessitates the continuous practice of the custom by the social group which has created these rules.

In order to be rules of law, customs must satisfy some requirements. The first is the existence of a practice—a "usage". This practice does not need to be for any special length of time but a single use clearly does not create a custom. The second traditional requirement for customs to be considered as sources of law is the existence of an *opinio iuris*. This means the existence of a general conviction about the obligatory character of the customary rule. Together with the requirements of "continuous and regular practice" and *opinio iuris*, the Civil Code establishes that customs cannot be contrary to morals or to public order, although if the custom is a source of law it is difficult to think how it can be immoral unless the legislator when drafting the Civil Code was thinking of uses or practices which were not customs properly so called. In order to accord with public order, since customs only apply in the absence of legislation, the public order must be established by the general principles of the law.[73]

As a source of law custom has some special features. It is an independent source since it is created and developed totally independently from any other source;[74] it is a subsidiary source because it will only apply if there is no written provision of State origin (a relevant *ley*); and it is a secondary source in the sense that it needs to be pleaded and proved to the satisfaction of the court.[75]

Depending on the relationship between customary laws and written legislation there are different types of customs: customs which are contrary to legislation—*contra legem*; customs which interpret a legal or customary rule according to the law—*consuetudo secundum legem*; and customs which regulate situations for which there is no written legislation—*extra legem* or *praeter legem*. Customs *contra legem* are excluded by Art.1 of the Civil Code because customs are only operative in the absence of legislation, never against it. As to the second type or customs *secundum legem*, their value lies in the interpretation of the application of the rules of law, but judges are not bound by this

---

[73] Note that after the 1978 Constitution the majority of the Doctrine indicate that the references to "public order" are references made to the Constitutional public order.
[74] It is due to this characteristic that custom is included among the primary sources.
[75] Since the principle *iura novit curia* does not extend to customary laws.

interpretation.[76] The third type of customs—*praeter legem*—are generally recognised by Art.1 of the Civil Code and are, thus, a source of law.

LOS PRINCIPIOS GENERALES DEL DERECHO (GENERAL PRINCIPLES OF LAW)

Much controversy surrounds the third source of law in the Spanish Civil Code—the general principles of the law. The existence of some form of "superior" principles was recognised in ancient Greece[77] and inherited by Rome where the idea of a *ratio iuris*[78] underlying the rules of law was commonly accepted. When Codification started in France the issue was much discussed. However, the French Civil Code did not contain any mention of these "natural laws" probably due to the idea that the Code was a product of reason. It was the Austrian Civil Code of 1811, the first of the modern Codes, which first contained a reference to these principles.[79] The concept of "natural legal principles" or "general principles of the law" gained popularity in modern legal theory[80] and today general principles of the law are recognised as a source of international law.[81] General principles of the law are the basic rules reflecting the convictions of a community in respect of its organisation. These general principles permeate the whole legal system. Modern constitutions make formal declarations of the values considered fundamental by the community; Art.1 of the 1978 Constitution says that the values underlying the Spanish legal system are freedom, justice, equality and political diversity. In Spanish law these general principles have a twofold function: first, they are a source of law, though a subsidiary source; secondly, they inform the other sources. A good example is provided by the principle of "equality", which is one of the fundamental values recognised by Art.1 CE and further developed in Art.14, which prohibits any

---

[76] Art.3, when setting the rules for the application and interpretation of the rules of law does not mention "usual or customary" interpretation as one of the criteria to be taken into account.

[77] Where references were made to *agrafos nomos*, or non-written law derived from nature, or moral and religious convictions.

[78] *Ratio iuris* or *natura rerum* was the law constituted or derived from the nature of things.

[79] Art.7 of the Austrian Civil Code of 1811 stated "If it is not possible to decide a question according to written law . . . it will be decided according to natural legal principles".

[80] Especially among the followers of the School of Natural Law.

[81] Art.38 of the Statute of the International Court of Justice, recognised as the most authoritative statement on the sources of international law, provides that: the Court . . . shall apply, . . . (c) "the general principles of law recognised by civilised nations".

form of discrimination. This principle informs all areas of the law, for instance civil or criminal procedure have to respect it by granting to all parties to the proceedings equal opportunities;[82] other examples of legislation incorporating this principle are the rules organising access to the civil service or employment law.

3. COMPLEMENTARY SOURCES

LA JURISPRUDENCIA[83] (CASE LAW)

Strict separation between the creation and the application of rules of law originated in the French Revolution and rests on the idea that the application of a rule of law is only an operation consisting of giving practical effect to an abstract concept which has already foreseen and provided for the consequences of any concrete case.[84]

This concept has been strongly criticised since the 19th century because in every case in which the law is applied there is a choice. The text of the rule of law is not always clear, and even if it is, the generality of its terms necessarily encompasses a certain degree of choice, with the result that the application of the law by any judge always requires the exercise of some freedom and reflects the creative aspect of the law.

In the Spanish conception of the "State of Law" or "Democratic State"[85] the principles of legal certainty, equality and unity of the law require restrictions to be imposed on the freedom of the judge. In Anglo-Saxon countries the restriction of the freedom of the judge in the exercise of this jurisdictional function is achieved by giving binding force to the criteria with which the court has decided previous cases in the past. This rule, known as *stare decisis*, originated not as an answer to the problems of applying existing rules of written law but as a substitute for it. Anglo-Saxon law is to a large extent a system of case law. Even if there is a statute (written law of Parliament) this is applied within a safe-guard provided by the previous applications of the same provision by the courts. The principle

---

[82] See below, Ch.5.

[83] Although the term *jurisprudencia* in Spanish law can be used to describe "the science of law" as in the English term "jurisprudence", it also means case law, or more exactly, the case law of the Supreme Court. The term is used here with this second meaning.

[84] According to the famous quote from Montesquieu in *De L'Esprit des Lois*: "The judge is the mouth pronouncing the words of the law".

[85] *Estado de Derecho* or *Estado Democrático de Derecho* (Art.1 CE).

of *stare decisis* operates horizontally and vertically in order to ensure uniformity of justice organised from the top of the Court structure; at the same time the possibility of abandoning the precedent, with greater or lesser freedom depending on the court, ensures the evolution of the law.

In Continental Europe limitation of the judge's freedom in the application of the law was achieved by creating a special organ, *ad hoc*, a *Tribunal de Casación*, the function of which is to elaborate a doctrine about how the rule of law must be interpreted. The origin of the system is the *réferé legislatif* introduced in France in 1790, by which, if the judge has doubts about the interpretation of a rule of law he must ask Parliament to give an interpretation. Later, a *Tribunal de Casación*—a political organ dependent on Parliament—was created for this. The *réferé legislatif* was later eliminated and the *Tribunal de Casación* became a "real" court, independent of the legislative power and with jurisdiction to rule on all mistakes on the application of the law by the judges.[86] The system has some similarities with the Anglo-Saxon system, the main difference being that only the decisions of the Supreme Court have binding force.[87]

In Spain, the 1812 Constitution, created a Supreme Court— *Tribunal Supremo*—which in principle only had jurisdiction to rule on decisions of the inferior courts which were allegedly against the law. This was done through a *recurso de nulidad*, a special type of appeal in which the Supreme Court had to determine whether the decision was null because it was found to contravene the law. In 1855 the *Ley de Enjuiciamiento Civil*[88] expanded the functions of the Supreme Court and the new appeal—*casación*—allowed the Supreme Court to decide not only if decisions were against the law, but also, whether judicial decisions of the lower courts were against the established legal doctrine[89] of the Supreme Court.[90] Today Art.1692(5) of the Civil

---

[86] In Ignacio del Otto, *op. cit.*, p.293.

[87] In Spanish law the *jurisprudencia* includes only the decisions of the Supreme Court, not the decisions of other courts, STS of June 30, 1866, and STS of February 10, 1886, among others. Castán Tobeñas, *op. cit.*, p.515.

[88] Civil Procedure Act.

[89] The term "legal doctrine" or *doctrina legal* is synonymous with *jurisprudencia*. What the Supreme Court controlled, therefore, was the respect of its own *jurisprudencia*, which brings the Spanish model closer to the Anglo-Saxon.

[90] According to Federico de Castro, *Derecho Civil de España, Parte general* T.1 (1st edn, 1942), p.418, the introduction of the ground "infringement of legal doctrine" was necessary in order to adapt the *recurso de casación*, which was imported from France to the Spanish legal tradition which acknowledged a *recurso de injusticia notoria* which was possible not only when the judge gave judgment against a written *ley* but also when the judgment was against the "straight application and interpretation of the law".

Procedure Act[91] acknowledges the possibility of an appeal in *casación* in cases in which there is an infringement of the *jurisprudencia*.[92]

The introduction of "infringement of the *jurisprudencia*" as a new ground of *casación*, has added a new dimension to the traditional debate about the nature of the decisions of the Supreme Court. It seems that if a citizen can appeal because the *jurisprudencia* has not been respected, it is because it is a source of law, and as such, it must be applied by the judge in the resolution of a case. Some authors[93] maintain that

> "the theoretical difference between continental legal systems and the Anglo-Saxon system is not so important in practical terms, because the *ley* and other officially accepted sources of law have a limited scope which is insufficient to resolve all the individual cases."

Puig Brutau affirms that,

> "Spanish Civil law is, to a certain extent, a system of law created by the judges, because judicial decisions have a highly persuasive value, independently of their formal recognition as a source of law".[94]

However, the wording of the Civil Code is clear[95] on what the sources of law are: *la ley, la costumbre y las principios generales del derecho.* The *jurisprudencia* "will complement" the legal system and is the tool by which the uniform application of the above sources of law is guaranteed.[96] The *jurisprudencia*, therefore, is a complementary source and the duty of the judiciary, therefore, is to ensure that the Supreme Court creates *jurisprudencia* and the lower courts respect it.[97]

---

[91] Introduced by the *Ley* 34/1984 of August 6 which modified the old Art.1692 of LEC.

[92] See below, Ch.6, p.125.

[93] Especially Puig Brutau, *La Jurisprudencia como fuente del Derecho* (*Interpretación creadora y arbitrio judicial*) (1951) p.7.

[94] Compare the view of F. de Castro, *op. cit.*, (2nd ed. 1949), p.508.

[95] Art.1(1) CC, "The sources of law are *la ley, la costumbre y los principios generales del derecho*".

[96] Art.1(6) CC "*La jurisprudencia complementará el ordenamiento jurídico con la doctrina que, de modo reiterado, establezca el Tribunal Supremo, al interpretar y aplicar la ley, la costumbre y los principios generales del derecho*".

[97] This is the majority view supported by Castán Tobeñas, *op. cit.*, pp.520–3; F. de Castro, *op. cit.*, p.508, Alabadalejo, *Instituciones de Derecho Civil* (1985), pp.127–47; Lacruz Berdejo, *Elementos de Derecho Civil, I* (1980), pp.61 *et seq.*

THE DECISIONS OF THE CONSTITUTIONAL COURT

The Constitutional Court is an organ of the State. The function of this Court is to interpret the Constitution and assess the conformity of the sources of law with the Constitution.[98] The decisions of the Constitutional Court are referred to as *jurisprudencia constitucional*, but their value is very different from the *jurisprudencia* of the Supreme Court because what the Constitutional Court controls is the compliance of legislation with the Constitution. When the Constitutional Court declares a statute to be unconstitutional and so null and void, this interpretation is superior to the interpretation of the legislator. This rule places the Constitutional Court's decisions on the same level as the Constitution itself in the hierarchy of sources. The decisions of the Constitutional Court have to be applied by the ordinary courts according to Art.5(1) LOPJ.[99]

4. EXPLANATORY SOURCES

LA DOCTRINA (LEGAL WRITINGS)

The third category of sources of law are those from which no directly applicable rule of law can be derived, but whose value lies in the clarification and interpretation they provide for the application of the primary sources. Among these are doctrinal and legal writings.

Legal writings were of great influence in Roman law,[1] and in historic Spanish law.[2] However, the Civil Code does not mention legal writings among the sources of law, not even with a complementary character and the Supreme Court has denied this character.[3] The value of legal writings in the system of sources is that they provide a clarification of the other primary sources of law.

---

[98] Art.1 LOTC: "The Constitutional Court is the supreme interpreter of the Constitution".

[99] Art.5(1) LOPJ: "The courts shall interpret and apply the law according to constitutional principles and the interpretation of these principles by the Constitutional Court in any type of process".

[1] See Alvaro D'Ors, "*De la prudentia iuris a la jurisprudencia del Tribunal Supremo*" in "*Información Jurídica*" (1947).

[2] In Catalonia, legal writings were a source of law accepted by the Supreme Court if uniform and widely accepted. Castán Tobeñas, *op. cit.*, pp.528–9.

[3] STS of December 10, 1894, STS of March 26, 1906, STS of June 10, 1916, among others.

5. AUTONOMY AND THE SYSTEM OF SOURCES: THE RELATIONSHIP BETWEEN STATE LAW AND THE LAW OF THE AUTONOMOUS COMMUNITIES

Autonomy is the power of individuals or groups to give themselves regulations within the framework of another, wider and superior, legal system. Spain, according to the territorial model set up by the 1978 Constitution, is a *State of Autonomies*; that is, a unitary State in which territorial entities—the Autonomous Communities—exercise the powers attributed to them by the Constitution. Amongst these powers is the power to legislate on certain matters. This produces the effect that in the Spanish legal system there are two levels or types of legislation: the rules of law of the State, which have effect in the whole country, and the rules created by the Autonomous Communities—in matters within their competence—which have effect only in the territory of the Community.

Without going into political theory and explaining the differences between a federal state and a state of autonomies a general remark seems appropriate at this stage. In a federal state the member states of the federation give themselves a Constitution within the framework of the Federal Constitution. However the main institutional rule of the Autonomous Communities—the *Estatuto de Autonomía*—is produced by the Central State. This has consequences for the status and character of the laws produced by the Autonomous Communities, because if several independent states get together in a federation their different legal systems, which were complete and provided regulation for every matter, will have to renounce those rules concerning matters which are now within the competence of the federation. In the Spanish situation, however, the departure point is a State's legal system which is complete in the sense that there are no limitations on the matters which can be regulated, and within this legal system the Autonomous Communities's sub-legal systems consist of those matters under authority of each of the autonomies. The result is that the rules of the State system on matters which are within the jurisdiction of the Autonomous Communities are not abrogated, but remain applicable, although of a supplementary character. One could say that the Spanish legal system is made of a sub-system which is complete and general, and several partial and territorial sub-systems which have a priority of application on the matters within their scope.

The *Estatuto de Autonomía* is the "basic institutional rule" of each Autonomous Community[4]; it is the *Estatuto* which creates the

---

[4] Art.147(1) CE "*Los Estatutos de Autonomía serán la norma institucional básica de cada Comunidad Autónoma . . .*".

Autonomous Community, defines its territory, and gives powers to the community. The Constitution only establishes the framework which makes possible autonomy, but it is up to the *Estatuto* to give a meaning and substance to the constitutional possibility. The *Estatutos de Autonomía* are approved by the procedure of the *leyes orgánicas*.[5] They are, therefore, laws of Parliament which, like any other, are sanctioned by the King. However, there are important differences between an *Estatuto de Autonomía* and other laws of Parliament. Before the *Estatuto* can be approved by Parliament there is a whole procedure, called *proceso de iniciativa autonómica*, by which the different provinces express their will to become an Autonomous Community that needs to be followed. The Constitution establishes two procedures of access to autonomy: the so called "quick way" or *vía rápida* (Art.151 CE), and the "normal way" or *vía normal* (Arts 143, 144 and 146 CE). The *vía rápida* allows a greater initial autonomy.[6] In order to be able to obtain autonomy, the municipalities of the territories involved must vote and choose to become autonomous and integrated into a Community. Parliament can only intervene to grant autonomy to a single province without historic tradition (Art.144 CE),[7] or when it is necessary in order not to leave a single province which has not integrated into an Autonomous Community.[8] The drafting of the *Estatuto* is done by the representatives of the province,[9] the *diputados* and *senadores*[10] elected by the province which is to become an Autonomous Community. The draft is sent to Parliament where it needs to be approved by the procedure of a *ley orgánica*. The *Estatuto de Autonomía* will, once approved, specify the powers of the Autonomous Community according to the maximum limits fixed by the Constitution depending on which type of procedure was followed.[11] The *Estatuto de Autonomía* is, therefore, a rule approved by Parliament, with special characteristics, and subject to the Constitution.

All the Autonomous Communities have legislative power by virtue of their respective *Estatuto de Autonomía*. The legislation produced by the Autonomous Communities' legislative power[12] can be in

---

[5] Although with some important differences which justify a separate study.
[6] Arts 148 and 149 CE.
[7] This was the case of Madrid, today the Autonomous Community of Madrid.
[8] This was the case of Segovia.
[9] Members of the *Diputación* of each province.
[10] Members of Parliament, of the *Congreso* and *Senado* respectively.
[11] See Ignacio de Otto, *op. cit.*, pp.259–63 for a detailed account of these procedures and in general of the whole topic.
[12] The Autonomous Communities have an "Autonomic Parliament" elected by the residents of the Community. The best study on the autonomous communities is, S.Muñoz Machado, *Derecho Público de las Comunidades Autónomas* (1982 and 1984) Also E. García de Enterría, *op. cit.*, p.279 *et seq.*

the form of *ley*[13] promulgated and published by the President of the Autonomous Community.[14] These dispositions are published in the Official Journal of the Autonomous Communities[15] and in the State or general Official Journal (BOE). The only difference between the *ley* of the State and a *ley* of an Autonomous Community is that if the Government challenges the constitutionality of legislation of an Autonomous Community, application of this legislation is suspended until the matter is resolved by the Constitutional Court.[16] The Autonomous Communities can also delegate legislative power to their Executive and so legislate in the form of *decretos legislativos*. Urgent legislation by *decreto-ley* is not possible as this possibility has not been established in any *Estatuto de Autonomía*. However, all the *Estatutos de Autonomía* mention the power to pass *reglamentos* (by the Executive of the Autonomous Community).

The idea of "autonomy" is based on a principle of equality between the rules of the State and the rules of the Autonomous Communities. The system works on the basis of the distribution of matters. Any rule of the system as a whole, including the State sub-system and autonomous sub-systems, is only valid if it has been made under the relevant and necessary authority. This would seem logical and straightforward enough, and it is. The problem, however, arises because the distribution of matters is not neat and clear cut. For each matter there can be a distribution of functions between the State and the Autonomous Community. A matter can be attributed to the Autonomous Community or the State "exclusively", in which case, whoever exercises the power over that matter can legislate and develop it with complementary rules. For example the Constitution says that the State has exclusive competence in respect of defence.[17] In such a case it is clear that no Autonomous Community can dictate any rules on the matter. On the other hand, the Autonomous Communities have the exclusive right to fix municipal limits in their territory and the State has no competence at all in such matter. However the distribution of authority between the State and the Autonomous Communities is often made according to issues concerning the same matter. For instance, the State will have legislative competence or power to regulate the matter and the Autonomous Community will have executive power over it; or the State will have competence over basic legislation and the Autonomous Community

---

[13] Each *Estatuto de Autonomía* will determine the legislative initiative.
[14] In the King's name.
[15] *Boletin Oficial de La Comunidad Autónoma.*
[16] Art.340 LOTC and Art.161(2) CE.
[17] Art.149(1) (5) CE.

will have competence to develop further complementary legislation. This type of competence is called "shares competence" or "shared jurisdiction". The final way in which the division of legislative power can occur is in the case of "concurrent jurisdiction". In this case both the State and the Autonomous Community have the same, identical jurisdiction, to legislate over a certain matter.[18] In this case, when the Central State—or the federation, if it happens in a federal state—exercises its power to legislate over the matter, the legislation of the State will prevail over that of the Autonomous Community. This principle is established in Art.149(3) of the 1978 Constitution.[19] Distribution of authority in the Spanish legal systems is either exclusive—to the State or to the Autonomous Community—or shared between these entities in different ways. To date the Constitutional Court has never had to use the rule in Art.149(3) and has resolved every conflict between the State and the Autonomous Communities by applying the rules relating to the distribution of powers.

The last principle which it is necessary to mention in the context of the relationship between the law of the State and the law of the Autonomous Communities is that the law of the Central State is supplementary to the law of the Autonomous Communities (Art.149(2) *CE*). This principle complies with the initial aim of the system by recognising Autonomous Communities with a different degree of autonomy.

6.   INTERPRETATION, APPLICATION AND EFFICACY OF THE LAWS

INTERPRETATION OF THE LAW

The application of the law by the judge for the resolution of a case brought before him is a complex intellectual activity by which the judge, even if he is deprived of the "power to create law", needs to analyse the facts of the case and apply to those facts a rule of law as indicated by the provisions on sources of law and their hierarchy. Before the judge can apply any of the sources of law he needs to be sure of the meaning of that particular rule of law. Sometimes this

---

[18] This type of distribution is frequent in federal states see Art.72.1 *Ley Fundamental de Bonn*.
[19] The conflict is only of academic interest because the distribution of competences by the different *Estatutos de Autonomía* has not left any matter subject to concurrent powers of the State and an autonomous community.

meaning will appear clear from the words of the text of the statute, but in other cases the meaning may not be clear at first, or it may not be clear whether that rule should be applied to the actual facts of the case. In this case the judge will have to proceed to interpret the rule of law according to the provisions of the Civil Code, which, in Art.3, establishes the criteria for the interpretation of the different laws.

Interpretation is the search for the true meaning of the law. Every rule of law needs to be interpreted in order to be applied, not only legislation but also customs and general principles. It is, however, the interpretation of legislation[20] which is at issue most often due to its primacy in the hierarchy of sources.[21] Article 3 of the Civil Code indicates four ways of arriving at the meaning of the rule: literal, logical, historical and systematic. These different methods do not produce different types of interpretation; there is not a "literal interpretation" as opposed to, or different from an "historical interpretation". What Art.3 of the Civil Code does is to establish an order to follow in order to arrive at the meaning of the rule of law.

In the first stage, when the judge is considering the application of a rule of law, he will look at the words used by the legislator, or in which the custom is expressed, and try to find the meaning of those words according to the usual sense of the word or, if it is a technical word, according to the technical meaning. In some cases, this will be enough. However, the task of interpretation never ends at this point because it is necessary to find the "spirit of the rule".[22] The "spirit of the rule", the *ratio legis*, is found by applying a logical or rational criteria in order to arrive at why that rule exists and at its true meaning. Closely connected with the logical interpretation is the systematic approach, by which the rule which is being interpreted is placed in relation with other rules governing the same legal institution in order to discover the principles informing that institution. The last of the interpretative guides given by the Code is the "historical element". This means that if, after the preceeding criteria have been applied, the meaning of the rule is still not clear, an investigation of the antecedents of the rule—since most rules of law are the product of a long evolution—may throw some light as to the purpose and sense to be given to the rule.[23] However, the value of the historical element is

---

[20] In the wide sense explained above, including regulations and any other rule given by the State.

[21] Here the focus of study is on the interpretation of legislation.

[22] Art.3(1) CC *in fine*: "*Las normas se interpretarán según el sentido propio de sus palabras . . . atendiendo fundamentalmente al espíritu y finalidad de aquellas*". Also, STS of June 27, 1941.

[23] These antecedents can be more or less remote, for instance in the case of legislation the preparatory works or "exposition of motives" can be consulted. An investigation

only relative, because Art.3(1) CC *in fine* adds that the rules need to be interpreted according to the social reality of the time in which they have to be applied. It can well be the case that certain rules, for instance a particular statute, was passed a long time ago and it now needs to be interpreted according to the current social circumstances in a way which may be quite different from the original intention of the legislator or from previous interpretations given to the same statute in the past.[24]

Although the judge will be the person who most often is faced with the task of interpreting rules of law in order to apply these to the resolution of cases he is by no means the only possible interpreter. Traditionally there has been a distinction between different types of interpretation depending on the person performing it. It is common[25] to distinguish between "public" and "private" interpretation. Public interpretation is the interpretation made by any authority or agency of the State or Public Administration, for instance judges when applying the law—*interpretación usual* (usual interpretation)—or Parliament which can dictate a new law to clarify previous legislation—*interpretación auténtica* (authentic interpretation). Private interpretation is that done by individuals and it is also known as doctrinal interpretation. Its value depends on the prestige of the author and it is only indicative.

According to its effect, interpretation can be extensive or restrictive, depending on whether it extends or restricts the application of the rule of law to situations or cases that seem to be included or not included in the words.

THE ROLE OF "EQUITY"

The Civil Code, in Art.3, mentions *la equidad* ("equity")[26] as an element to be considered when applying the law. *Equidad*,[27] according to Castán Tobeñas,[28] has two connected meanings. First, it means the adaptation of the rule of law to the circumstances of the actual

---

into historical or Roman law can help to understand some of today's legal institutions, or a comparative study of foreign codes, especially the French Civil Code due to its influence on the Spanish Codification.

[24] See in this sense, Rafael Ruiz Manteca, *Introducción al Derecho y Derecho Constitucional* (1994), p.56.

[25] See R. Riz Manteca, *op. cit.*, p.59; Castán Tobeñas, *op. cit.*, p.489.

[26] "Equity" because it is not to be confused with what is understood as equity in English law. *Equidad*, in Spanish law, means justice.

[27] In order to avoid confusion the Spanish word will be used.

[28] *op. cit.*, p.506.

case[29] and, secondly, it means the mitigation of the consequences of the rule of law in a particular case.[30] Equity is therefore a method of the application of the law. This method is, however, restricted as to its application by the courts. The Civil Code, in Art.3, forbids the judge to base the resolution of a case exclusively in equity except when he is expressly so allowed.[31] In this sense, "equity" is not a source of law. The role of "equity" is much more restricted in Spanish law, and in general in all Civil law systems, than in English law.

Where "equity" has a role to play is in the application of the general principles of the law since it enables these to be adapted to the circumstances of the case.

EFFICACY OF THE LAWS: TERRITORIAL APPLICATION AND TIME-SPAN

The rules of law are limited in their application both in space and time. Usually, the laws given by a State are applicable only in the territory of that State[32]—including jurisdictional waters and air-space—since International Law recognises a State's sovereignty and the power to exclude the application of foreign laws in the national territory. There are two principles which govern the "spatial" application of the law: the principle of territoriality and the principle of personality. The principle of territoriality means that the law is only applicable in the territory of the State in which it was dictated and it applies to all people in the territory whether foreigners or nationals. Examples of territorial laws are criminal laws or laws relating to public security. The principle of personality, on the other hand, links the application of the law to people; certain laws are given for certain people and are applied to them wherever they are. The principle of personality of the law was common in primitive laws[33] and it was applied in the time of the Roman Empire. Roman citizens were subject to the *ius civile*, other inhabitants of the Empire to their own personal laws, and the relationships between people belonging to different groups was regulated by the *ius gentium*. Today's legal systems have a combination of both principles for the application of the law. Spanish law, adheres to the principle of territoriality of criminal and public order laws and recognises the principle of personality of the laws in aspects such as legal capacity or status of natural persons.

---

[29] According to Greek concept of *epiqueya*.
[30] According to the Christian idea of *humanitas*, *benignitas* or *pietas*. See Castán Tobeñas, *op. cit.*, p.506.
[31] See Arts 3(2) CC and 1154 CC.
[32] There are exceptions to this rule, but the study of this belongs to Private International Law.
[33] See above, Ch.1.

The question is particularly important in the Spanish legal system because, as has been previously explained, different systems of civil law co-exist. In private law, Spanish Civil law, as contained in the Civil Code, co-exists with different systems of *foral* law applicable in the historic territories. This phenomena is known as "inter-regional law" and the rules for the application of one or other systems of law are found in the Preliminary Title of the Civil Code.[34] Their application is governed by the principle of personality articulated according to the concept of *vecindad civil* (civil domicile). Article 4 CC determines the domicile of a person for this purpose and the consequence of being subject to the rules of the Civil Code or *foral* law for the areas in which these are different from the former.

The second question relating to the application of the rules of law makes reference to their life-span. Laws do not exist forever but change and are replaced by new rules. The laws start to have effect at the time when a law comes into force and ends when the law is repealed. Legislation comes into force from the time established by the legislation itself. A certain *ley* can state that it shall be applicable on the day following its publication in the BOE, or in three months or a year. If nothing is said the Civil Code in Art.2(l) establishes that legislation will be applicable after a period of 20 days following its publication in the BOE. This period of 20 days is known as *vacatio legs* and the purpose of it is to give time to those who are subject to the law to become acquainted with its provisions before the law is applicable.

Legislation ceases to be applicable for different reasons. The first one is when a particular *ley* is expressly repealed by later legislation (*derogación expresa*); or, when the contents of later legislation are incompatible with the contents of previous legislation[35] (*derogación implicita*). Only legislation can repeal legislation. The different rules should have at least the same position in the hierarchy of sources; for instance a *formal ley* cannot be repealed by an administrative regulation but only by another *ley*. In other cases a law can cease being applicable because it was dictated for a specific period only, or if the purpose of the law was to regulate a specific situation which has now disappeared. In these two cases some writers refer to *leyes temporales* (temporary legislation).

Closely connected with the questions of life-span of the laws is the problem of the "retrospective" or "non-retrospective" effect of the law; in other words, whether a new law has effect on situations created

---

[34] Arts 13–17 CC.
[35] For instance many laws approved during the dictatorship of General Franco were repealed in this way.

or existing before the new law was dictated. Article 2(3) of the Civil Code enunciates the general principle of non-retrospective effect of the law "unless something different is provided". The vague formula of Art.2(3) reflects the reality of this problem of whether to apply a new law and its consequences to old situations or not. In principle, legislation is passed for the regulation of future situations but there are two considerations to take into account when choosing between the retrospective or non-retrospective effect of legislation: legal certainty and the changing social reality.

In effect, legal certainty would be hindered if individuals could not foresee the consequences attached to the legal relationships they enter into because at any time a new rule can be approved and this new rule can determine totally different consequences. The principle of legal certainty seems better guaranteed by establishing a system of non-retrospectivity of the law and this is indeed the principle applicable in areas such a criminal law or administrative law as stated in the Constitution.[36]

On the other hand, the need to adapt the law to the changing circumstances of social life can in some instances justify the retrospectivity of some legislation. This retrospectivity can have different degrees of applicability. The first degree is when the new law is applied only to those effects of a pre-existing legal relationship which actually occur after the entry into force of the new law. The second is when the new law is applied to effects of the pre-existing relationship which started before the new law was approved but which still have not finished. The third degree is when the new law is applicable to all the effects of the relationship annulling previous effects, and reshaping this legal relationship into a new one. This last case is extremely rare because of the serious consequences it has for legal certainty. It is generally associated with policy decisions such as those which happened after the Civil War when the *Ley de Matrimonio Civil*, approved during the Second Republic, and the *Ley de Divorcio* were declared null and void with retrospective effects and many people found themselves not "married" to their "spouses".

In order to smooth the transition for the applicability of a new law and avoid or minimise problems of retrospective or non-retrospective effect—since most legal relationships have a continuous duration—the laws establish particular rules known as "transitory law" or *disposiciones transitorias*, by which it is stated to which part of the relationship or to which effects each law, the old or the new, should be applied.

---

[36] Art.9(3) CE: "*Le Constitución garantiza . . . la irretroactividad de las disposiciones sancionadoras no favorables o restrictivas de derechos individuales. . . .*"

Chapter Three
Courts and court structure

1. THE JUDICIAL POWER: COURTS AND COURT STRUCTURE

The role of the judiciary in the different legal systems today is better understood by looking back in history. Modern anthropology has established that in primitive societies judges developed before the institution of the legislator.[1] Legal systems were created by the accumulation, and latter organisation and rationalisation, of case law. This was the situation in Roman law and accounts for the meaning of the term *iurisdictio*—the saying of the law. The judge, therefore, in the early stages of the creation of legal systems, appears to have had a major role in the production of rules of law. It was in the development of modern systems that the position of the "administration of justice"[2] changed and became centralised. In England this started in the twelfth century when itinerant judges gave judgement in the different courts in the name of the King, thereby starting the unification of legal customs and rules which became what is known as *common law*. In France the evolution started when the *Parlement* of Paris extended its jurisdiction to other territories,[3] and ended in the recognition of the supremacy of the King's justice as being more general and uniform than the "justice" of the different feudal lords. Later, the French Revolution, in order to avoid the concentration of powers in a sole organ and to guarantee the supremacy of Parliament as the expression of popular sovereignty, established the strict separation of powers and this idea has permeated contemporary legal thinking for a long time.

However, in the period between the two world wars the initial suspicion of the revolutionaries towards the judge was replaced, to a certain extent, by a suspicion towards the legislator and correspondingly, with a hope that the judge would correct any errors made by Parliament. It was during that period that the Constitutional Courts

---

[1] A. Torres del Moral, *op. cit.*, p.251 referring to Max Weber's theory.
[2] Understood here as the role of the judges in administering justice in a concrete case.
[3] See C. Dadomo & S. Farran, *op. cit.*, 46.

were created, with the function of controlling the validity of laws passed by Parliament, taking as a touchstone the Constitution itself.

Today, the tendency is to acknowledge that there is always a creative role involved in the application of the law which, combined with the power given to judges to control the legality of administrative action, and the constitutionality of the legal rules of the system, make some legal writers doubt the politically neutral role assigned to the judge.[4]

Having said that, constitutional states are organised according to the idea of the "material division of functions" and "formal division of powers".[5] The judicial power is exercised by the organs of the State, which according to the Constitution and other laws, have the function of resolving conflicts arising in the application and interpretation of the law.[6] These organs are judges—*jueces*—and magistrates—*magistrados*.[7] Judges are independent, irremovable, responsible and subject only to the Law (Art.117(1) CE).[8] Only judges exercise the judicial power and although they rely on a variety of personnel in their service for the administration of justice (for example, judicial secretaries, officials, agents, forensic doctors[9]), these do not have judicial power and constitute what is called the "administration of the administration of justice"[10] in the sense of all the personal and material means at the service of the judge for the exercise of his judicial power. The difference between the "judicial power" and the "administration of justice" is important because it reveals the dual nature of the task of imparting justice. On one hand, it is a power of the State—the judicial power—on the other, it is a function, a public service. In this second sense the Executive is responsible for the functioning of this service in the same way as it is responsible for the defence of the State.

As one of the powers of the State in charge of the "jurisdictional function", the judicial power is unitary. The principle of "unity of

---

[4] See A. Torres de Moral *op. cit.*, p.254.
[5] According to the terminology used by J. Garcia Morillo in L. López Guerra y otros, edn, *op. cit.*, p.223.
[6] Art.117 CE "*la justicia se administra . . . por jueces y magistrados, integrantes del poder judicial*".
[7] The term "magistrate" is used although it is not equivalent to the English "magistrate". In Spanish Law *magistrados* are a higher category of professional judges. The word "Judge" is used here to designate both *Jueces* and *Magistrados* unless a distinction is necessary.
[8] "*. . . independientes, inamovibles, responsables y sometidos únicamente al imperio de la ley*".
[9] See Ch.4, "The legal professions", pp.91–2.
[10] J. Garcia Morillo, in Luis López Guerra y otros ed., *op. cit.*, p.255.

jurisdiction" is important because there is only one judicial power in Spain. The division of the State into Autonomous Communities does not affect the unity of jurisdiction; Autonomous Communities have executive and legislative power but not judicial power. The courts situated in the territory of the Autonomous Communities are courts of the State.[11] All the courts are included in the judicial power (Art.3(1) LOPJ). This unity of judicial power also excludes the existence of special courts (Arts 26 and 117(6) CE) and any possibility of the Public Administration imposing punishment involving the deprivation of freedom. The only and relative exception to the unity of jurisdiction is the existence of a military jurisdiction (Art.117(5) CE). This jurisdiction is limited to matters qualified as "military crimes" under the Military Criminal Code and to the special cases of state of siege, alarm or exception—*estado de sitio, alarma ó excepción* (LOPJ and Art.9(2)). In any case, military jurisdiction is part of the judicial power.[12]

The judicial power is also "general" because the jurisdiction "extends to all the people, all the matters and all the territory" (Art.4 LOPJ).[13] The only exception to this principle is the person of the King (Art.56(3) CE) who enjoys special and total immunity; otherwise the judicial power has jurisdiction over any case involving any person, throughout the national territory. This obviously includes the Public Administration the activities of which are subject to the Law (Art.103). This is different from the French legal system where, due mainly to historical reasons,[14] the administrative courts are separate from the ordinary courts. The only area of administrative activity which is not controlled by the judiciary is the evaluation of "opportunity of administrative action" because this evaluation is left to the Parliament.

Article 117(3) of the Constitution also states that the exercise of the jurisdictional function is *exclusive*, belonging only to judges, who must "judge and execute the judgements". The judge stands in a position of independence, in the sense that he is not subject to orders, directions or instructions by any other of the powers of the State, not even by other judges, and it is from this neutral position that he resolves conflicts between individuals or between individuals and the State.

---

[11] See below, *Tribunales Superiores de Justicia.*
[12] Indeed there is a "Military Chamber" in the Supreme Court. See below.
[13] "*la jurisdicción se extiende a todas las personas, todas las materias y todo el territorio español*".
[14] See Dadomo & Farran, *op. cit.*, p.45.

ORGANISATION AND GOVERNMENT OF THE JUDICIARY: EL CONSEJO GENERAL DEL PODER JUDICIAL

While the constitutional theory of the last century emphatically endorsed the independence of the Judiciary and the separation of powers, for a long time judicial power was governed by the Executive through the Ministry of Justice. If the judge is to be neutral, subject only to the law, and independent of any other power in reaching his decisions, it is necessary to ensure that the personal position or professional future of judges is not left in the hands of the Executive. Otherwise, it would be easy to punish those members of the judiciary who, in applying the law, did not favour the political group in power. Conversely those judges seeking promotion would only need to ensure that their line of decision-making was sympathetic to the current government.

It was the French Constitution of the IVth Republic which first created a *Conseil de la Magistrature*,[15] an independent organ of government of the Judiciary. This has survived until today although it has lost some of its original functions. The Italian Constitution also established a similar organ, which inspired the legislator when creating the Spanish *Consejo General del Poder Judicial*. Portugal and Greece also have this type of organ, while in the United Kingdom and the United States the Executive retains authority over the organisation of the Judiciary.

The Spanish Constitution of 1978, in trying to guarantee the neutrality and independence of judges, created a special organ of government of the Judiciary called *Consejo General del Poder Judicial* (General Council of the Judiciary)[16] and supported this organ with a number of guarantees (Art.122(2) CE). This organ is composed of 21 members, 12 of whom must be chosen from judges and eight from lawyers of recognised standing. The *ley orgánica* developing this constitutional provision—*Ley Orgánica 6/85 del Poder Judicial* (LOPJ)[17]—establishes that the members of the CGPJ should be chosen by both Chambers of Parliament, in equal numbers, by majority of three-fifths. Once the members have been chosen they elect the President of the Supreme Court who will also be the President of the *Consejo*. Their mandate lasts five years and, with the exception of the President, they cannot be re-elected. The

---

[15] A. Torres del Moral *op. cit.*, p.284.
[16] The Spanish terminology will be retained and it will be referred to as the *Consejo* in this chapter or the CGPJ. Visit *www.poderjudicial.es*.
[17] As amended, especially by the LO 19/2003 of December 23 of modification of the LO 6/1985 of July 1 *del Poder Judicial* and the LO 1/2001 of June 28.

Consejo General del Poder Juducial is a constitutional organ of the State like Congress, Senate or the Government and as such is endorsed with guarantees that enable it to perform its constitutional duty of preserving the independence of judges and magistrates. The CGPJ can as any other constitutional organ bring a *conflicto de competencias* to the Constitutional Court against other constitutional organs.

The main functions of the CGPJ are connected with the organisation of the Judiciary in the context of the nomination of judges, their promotion, sanctions and suspension from the exercise of their functions. In this sense the Constitutional Court has described the CGPJ as the "administration of the Administration of justice".[18] The *Consejo* does not have total discretion concerning these nominations and promotions, since most of these are carefully regulated by statute. The only discretion relates to the nomination of the presidents of the *Tribunales Superiores de Justicia* and the judges of the *Tribunal Supremo*. Even these must comply with previously stipulated conditions. The *Consejo* also inspects the *Juzgados y Tribunales*,[19] (Arts 107(4), 348–77 LOPJ). It sends an annual report to Parliament about the situation, functioning and problems—if any—of the courts, and it has the capacity to submit reports about any proposed legislation affecting the Judiciary. Other functions are the capacity to nominate two of the members of the Constitutional Court[20] and it is consulted on the nomination of the *Fiscal General del Estado* (the Attorney-General).[21]

The CGPJ has been criticised for being a highly political organ due to the procedure for selecting its members. This was changed from the original LOPJ of 1980, where 12 of its members were chosen by judges, to the election of its 20 members by Parliament[22] in the 1985 version.

CLASSIFICATION OF COURTS

The structure of the judicial power is organised according to three different and concurrent criteria: subject matter of the dispute, territory and hierarchy of courts. According to the subject matter of the dispute the jurisdiction is divided into four categories—*ordenes*

---

[18]   STC 108/1986, of July 26.
[19]   Courts. *Juzgado* is used to indicate a unipersonal court, while *Tribunal* is used for collegiate organs.
[20]   See below p.97.
[21]   The CGPJ has an excellent website which can be consulted for statistics. See above, *www.poderjudicial.es.*
[22]   And therefore, by the different political groups.

jurisdiccionales (Art.9(2) LOPJ): civil—for claims based on or related to civil or commercial issues; criminal—claims based on violations of the criminal code; social—claims based on or related to employment or social security; and administrative, for claims based on acts performed by the public jurisdiction. There is also a Military Chamber in the Supreme Court, *Juzgados de menores* and *Juzgados de Vigilancia penitenciaria.*

The national territory is divided for jurisdictional purposes into different areas (Art.30 LOPJ): municipalities (*municipios*), judicial districts (*partidos judiciales*), provinces (*provincias*), Autonomous Communities (*Comunidades Autonomas*), and the whole of the national territory, over which two courts have jurisdiction, the *Tribunal Supremo* (Supreme Court) (Art.123(1) CE and Art.52 LOPJ) and the *Audienca Nacional* (National Court) (Art.62 LOPJ). Most of these divisions coincide with the administrative division of the territory; the only exception is *partidos judiciales* which are based on a special jurisdictional concept and so need to be delimited by a special law (*Ley* 38/88, *de demarcación y planta judicial*, modified by the *Ley* 3/92).

Each territorial unit has a specific type of court. Municipalities have *Juzgados de paz*[23] (Art.99(1) LOPJ), *partidos judiciales*, or one or several *Juzgados de Primera Instancia e Instrucción*[24] (Art.84 LOPJ). Provinces have an *Audiencia provincial*[25] (Art.80 LOPJ), *Juzgados de lo penal, lo social, de Vigilancia penitenciaria, de menores*, *Juzgados contencioso administrativos*[26] (Arts 89 (bis), 90, 92 and 97 LOPJ) and *Juzgados de lo Mercantil* (Arts 86 bis LOPJ), since September 1, 2004. Each Autonomous Community has a *Tribunal Superior de Justicia* (Arts 152(1) CE and 71 LOPJ); and there is a *Tribunal Supremo* and an *Audiencia Nacional* with jurisdiction over the whole territory.

Usually each court has its seat in the capital of the territorial unit to which it belongs, with the exception of the *Tribunales Superiores de Justicia*[27] which sometimes, according to the *Estatuto de Autonomia* of the community, have their seats somewhere different from the capital of the autonomous territory.[28] However, it is possible to establish Chambers, (*Salas*), of the *Tribunales Superiores de Justicia* in other localities depending on the volume of affairs and

---

[23] Justice of the Peace.
[24] First Instance Courts.
[25] Provincial Court.
[26] Administrative matters courts.
[27] Superior Courts of Justice.
[28] Notwithstanding the fact that the *Tribunales Superiores del Justicia* are organs of the State in the Autonomous Community and that the Autonomous Communities do not have an independent judicial power.

taking into consideration geographical circumstances. Also the *Audiencia Provincial* can open sections in places other than the capital of the province.

Hierarchically although each judge is independent and his decisions are not bound by any other court but only by the Law,[29] the organisation of the courts provides a system of appeals against the decisions of lower courts to higher courts and to the Supreme Court.

The Supreme Court

The *Tribunal Supremo* is the Supreme Court of the jurisdictional order (Art.123 CE and Art.53 LOPJ). It has jurisdiction throughout the national territory and it is based in Madrid. It is divided into five Chambers: civil, criminal, administrative, social and military.

Composition

The Supreme Court is composed of a President[30] of the Supreme Court, a further five Persidents—one for each Chamber—the judges designated by law, a secretary, a Vice-President and other non-judicial personnel. The public prosecution is represented by the Attorney-General, and several other public prosecutors.

Jurisdiction

The Supreme Court has jurisdiction in civil, criminal, administrative, social and military matters. There are, consequently, five different Chambers which are in charge of the cases in each area.

Civil Chamber
The Civil chamber has jurisdiction over the *recursos de casación y revisión* and the *recurso en interest de le ley*[31], cases concerning the civil liability of the President of the Government, the Presidents the Congress, the Senate, the Supreme Court, the Constitutional Court, *Diputados* and *Senadores*, Members of the *Consejo General del Poder Judicial*, Judges of the Constitutional and Supreme Courts, Presidents and Judges of the *Audiencia Nacional* or of the *Tribunales Superiores de*

---

[29] Although it is necessary to qualify this statement in respect of the effect of decisions of the Supreme Court. See Ch.2, "*La Jurisprudencia*" and *Recurso de casación.*
[30] The President of the Supreme Court is also the President of the *Consejo General del Poder Judicial.* See above, p.79.
[31] See Ch.5, pp.125–127.

Justicia, the Attorney General, high government officers, and petitions for the enforcement of foreign judgments.[32]

Criminal Chamber

This has jurisdiction in all cases of *recursos de casación* and *revisión* against decisions of the *Audiencia Provincial* and *Audiencia Nacional* and criminal actions against any of the person mentioned above for whom the Civil Chamber has special jurisdiction in civil matters.

Administrative Chamber

The Administrative Chamber of the Supreme Court has sole jurisdiction in all cases of *recursos* against the decisions of the Council of Ministers, or against decisions of the *Consejo General del Poder Judicial*, or against decisions of the organs of Government of the Chambers of Parliament and other high organs of the State. It also has jurisdiction on *recursos de casación* against decisions of the *Audiencia Nacional* and decisions of the *Tribunales Superiores de Justicia* relating to acts of the Autonomous Communities, and *recursos* against the resolutions of the *Tribunal de Cuentas*.

Social Chamber

The Social Chamber has jurisdiction over the *recursos de casación* and *revisión* and any other extraordinary *recurso* as established by the *Ley de Procedimiento laboral* of April 27, 1990.

Military Chamber[33]

Recursos de casación and *revisión* against the resolutions of the *Tribunal Militar Central* and of the *Tribunals Militares Territoriales* are heard by this Chamber as are proceedings against high members of the military which are not disciplinary sanctions. Also heard are *recursos* in jurisdictional conflicts and petitions in error regarding the liability of the State established by the military jurisdictions.

There are also other organs in the Supreme Court such as the Chamber of Conflicts.

Audiencia nacional

This is a collegiate Court based in Madrid with jurisdiction in administrative, criminal and labour matters for the whole of the national territory. It currently has four chambers: *de apelación*,[34] *de*

---

[32] For statistics about the volume of cases in the last few years visit *www.podejudicial.org/CGPJ.*
[33] Created by LO 4/1987.
[34] Appeal chamber created by the LO 19/2003 of modification of the LOPJ, Art.64.

la penal (criminal), *de lo contencioso* (administrative) and *de lo social* (labour).

Criminal matters

In criminal matters this court has jurisdiction in cases involving: crimes against the Crown, the high organs of the nation, or the government in the form of counterfeit and monetary crimes, drug trafficking, food and drugs crimes, crimes committed outside the national territory but which the Spanish courts are responsible according to international treaties, terrorism, extradition of prisoners and *recursos* against decisions of the *Juzgados Centrales de Instrucción*.

The new appeal chamber of the *Audiencia Nacional* will hear appeals against decisions of the *Sala de Penal*, relieving the overload of the second chamber of the Supreme Court.

Administrative matters

In administrative matters it has jurisdiction over *recursos* against acts and decisions of Ministers and Secretaries of State.

Labour matters

In labour matters it has jurisdiction over any dispute concerning collective bargaining agreements of national application.[35]

Tribunales superiores de justicia

These courts were created by the LOPJ of 1985[36] and have jurisdiction in civil, criminal, administrative and social matters in the territory of the Autonomous Community where they have their seat. They came into operation on May 22, 1989, and replaced the *Audiencias Territoriales* which had existed previously.

Jurisdiction

Civil matters

These courts have jurisdiction to hear: *recursos de casación* of decisions of courts within the territory of the Autonomous Community when the *recurso* is based on an infraction of rules of civil, *foral* or special law of the Community and when the *Estatuto de Autonomía* of

---

[35] From May 22, 1989, when the *Tribunal Central de Trabajo* was abolished.
[36] Their jurisdiction has been subsequently modified in 2003 by the LO 19/2003 of modification of the LOPJ.

the Community has delegated this jurisdiction to the TSJ.[37] They may also hear *recursos de revisión* based on rules of civil, *foral* or special law of that Community (Art.73(b) LOPJ), actions for civil liability of the President or of Members of Government and Parliament of the Community—if the *Estatuto de Autonomía* does not confer jurisdiction on the Supreme Court—and civil liability of judges of the *Audiencia Provincial* having a seat in the Autonomous Community (Art.73 LOPJ).

Criminal matters

The *Tribunal Superior de Justicia* has jurisdiction over all the actions provided for in the *Estatuto de Autonomía*,[38] and over both the *instrucción*[39] and judgment of actions against judges and *fiscales* in the exercise of their function, except when this is the responsibility of the Supreme Court.

Administrative matters

These courts have jurisdiction at first instance in the case of the *recurso contencioso-administrativo* against acts and dispositions of the organs of the administration of the State, where jurisdiction is not given to any other court. They also have jurisdiction to deal with *recursos contenciosos* against administrative rulings of the *Consejo de Gobierno* of the Autonomous Community where they have their seat, its President or *Consejeros*;[40] *recursos* against the organs of government of the Autonomous Parliament, and *recurso contencioso-electoral* against the decisions of the electoral administration concerning nominations of Presidents of local corporations.

As second instance courts they have jurisdiction to hear all the *recursos* against decisions of courts situated in the Autonomous Community in administrative matters.

Social matters

Since 1989 the TSJ has replaced the *Tribunal Central de Trabajo*. At first instance, this court has jurisdiction to hear any dispute between employees and employers which falls outside the jurisdiction of a

---

[37] *Estatuto de Autonomia del Pais Vasco* (Art.14 LO 7/79), *Cataluña* (Art.19 LO 4/78), *Galicia* (Art.22 LO 1/81), *Murcia* (Art.35 LO 4/82), *Valencia* (Art.40 LO 5/82), *Aragón* (Art.29 LO 6/82) *Navarra* (Art.61 LO 13/82), *Extremadura* (Art.45 LO 1/83), *Islas Baleares* (Art.49 LO 2/83), all the other *Estatutos* expressly exclude this function.
[38] As an example, Cataluña gives jurisdiction to these courts to hear criminal actions against members of the Autonomous Parliament (Arts 26 and 31 LO 4/79).
[39] See below, Ch.6.
[40] Equivalent to Ministers but at a regional level.

Juzgado de lo Social. At second instance they hear any *recursos* against decisions of the *Juzgados de lo social* based in the Autonomous Community and conflicts of competence between these courts. Article 7 of the LPL of April 27, 1990, also gives jurisdiction over the formation and recognition of trade unions and business associations, modification of their *estatutos*, protection of the right to belong to a trade union, collective conflicts and appeals against collective bargaining agreements with effects restricted to the territory of the Autonomous Community.

Audiencias provinciales

These are collegiate courts with jurisdiction in civil and criminal matters in the territory of a province.[41]

Jurisdiction

Civil matters
In civil matters these courts have jurisdiction to hear *recursos* against resolutions of the *Juzgados de Primera Instancia* of the province (Art.82 LOPJ). They also have jurisdiction over conflicts of jurisdiction between courts situated in the province and in proceedings for the removal of judges from particular cases.[42]

Criminal matters
In criminal matters the *Audiencias* are mixed courts because they have jurisdiction to decide in the first instance on criminal proceedings concerning serious crimes—*delitos graves*—together with a significant appellate capacity.

According to Art.82 LOPJ, as modified by the LO 7/88 of December 28, the *Audiencia Provincial* has jurisdiction in criminal actions not conferred on other courts, on *recursos* against criminal resolutions dictated by the *Juzgados de Instruccion y de lo Penal* in the province, *recursos* against resolutions of the *Juzgados de Vigilancia Penitenciaria* in matters relating to the enforcement of punishments in criminal cases, *recursos* against decisions made by the *Juzgados de Instrucción* in first instance proceedings for minor crimes, and *recursos* against decisions of the *Juzgados de menores.*

---

[41] In Spain there are 52 provinces.
[42] *Recusación de magistrados.*

Juzgados de primera instancia e instrucción

These courts are composed of a single judge with jurisdiction in civil and criminal matters in a territory of a *partido judicial*. Their name, in theory, explains their jurisdiction; first instance in civil cases and *instrucción* in criminal cases. However, in practice, the jurisdiction of these courts extends beyond these matters because in civil matters they have jurisdiction to hear certain appeals and also for the enforcement of judgments; in criminal matters they actually decide some cases.[43] They have no jurisdiction in social or administrative matters.

Since 1974 some of these courts have separated criminal and civil matters, creating *Juzgados de Primera Instancia* for civil matters and *Juzgados de Instrucción* for criminal matters. Moreover, in some places, such as Madrid, the *Juzgados de Primera Instancia* have specialised, creating *Juzgados de Familia* for family law disputes and special *Juzgados* for cases involving mentally handicapped people. All these courts are *Juzgados de Primera Instancia* in spite of their specialised nature.

Jurisdiction

Civil matters

In civil matters they hear and decide any case in which the amount of the claim is more than €60[44] and any other special proceedings.[45] They also hear all proceedings concerning matters regulated by special legislation, including matrimonial causes, civil proceedings for violations of fundamental rights, protection of the right to honour, privacy and personal image, bankruptcy, succession matters and, at second instance, appeals against decisions of the *Juzgados de Paz*.

Criminal matters

According to Art.87 LOPJ, as modified by LO 7/88 the *Juzgados de Primera Instancia e Instrucción* carry out the stage of "instruction" of those cases in which the decision corresponds to the *Audiencia Provincial* and the *Juzgados de lo penal*.[46] They also have jurisdiction for the adjudication of minor offences, proceedings of *habeas corpus* according to the LO 6/84, appeals against resolutions of the *Juzgados*

---

[43] See Ch.6, for an explanation of the different stages of the proceedings.
[44] Approximately £40.
[45] Such as *interdictos, juicios de retracto, juicio ejecutivo, alimentos provisionales.*
[46] It is important to emphasise the distinction between instruction and judgment in criminal proceedings. These are carried out by different courts in order to guarantee the rights of the citizen. See below, Ch.6.

de paz within the territorial limit of their jurisdiction and jurisdiction to authorise searches of private dwellings.

Juzgados de lo penal

These unipersonal courts were introduced by the LO 7/88 as a consequence of the decision of the Constitutional Court[47] declaring unconstitutional the fact that the same court "instructing" or investigating a criminal case was the court giving the judgment.

These courts have jurisdiction in criminal matters within the territory of a province. According to Art.14 LECrim, they have jurisdiction to judge crimes punishable with imprisonment of less than six years, with pecuniary sanctions or with any sanction not exceeding six years, and confiscation of a driving licence—whatever the period—and any minor offences committed in connection with crimes punished as mentioned above. In all these cases these courts apply the new *Procedimiento Abreviado*.[48] There are 143 *Juzgados de lo Penal* in Spain and they came into operation on September 15, 1989.

Juzgados centrales de instrucción

These courts were created by the *RD-Ley* of January 4, 1977, and they are *Juzgados de Instrucción* but with jurisdiction in the whole of the national territory. Their seat is in Madrid (Arts 1 and 6 LO 7/88) and their composition is exactly the same as that of any other *Juzgado de Instrucción*. They carry out the "instruction stage" of cases which will be decided by the *Juzgado Central de lo Penal* or the *Audiencia Nacional*.

Juzgado central de lo penal

Created by the LO 7/88 the *Juzgado Central de lo Penal*, with its seat in Madrid and jurisdiction in the national territory, is the competent court for those matters which would be heard by the *Audienca Nacional* but are of less importance, that is, crimes for which the punishment is less than seven years imprisonment, pecuniary sanctions of any amount or withdrawal of a driving licence. The "instruction" for these cases is the same as to the *Juzgados Centrales de Instrucción*.

---

[47] STC of July 12, 1988.
[48] See below, Ch.6.

Juzgados de lo contencioso-administrativo

These courts have not yet been created. The idea of the LOPJ was to create one such court in each provincial capital to decide at first or only instance all administrative appeals. Until they are created the *Tribunal Superior de Justicia* of the relevant Community hears all cases concerning administrative matters.

Juzgados de lo social

These courts replace the old *Magistraturas de Trabajo* which were courts dependent on the *Ministerio de Trabajo y Seguridad Social*. Today the *Juzgados de lo Social* are proper jurisdictional organs with jurisdiction in any matters related to employment contracts or social security obligations arising in the province for which they have jurisdiction.

Juzgados de lo mercantil

The *Juzgados de lo mercantil* are courts specialised on commercial matters. The first of these courts was created on September 1, 2004, and for the time being not many cases have been brought up to these courts.[49]

These courts were introduced by the LO 8/2003 *para la reforma concursal* but the jurisdiction of these courts extends to other commercial matters,[50] such as:

- intellectual property law claims. These claims are usually dealt with by the *procedimiento monitorio*[51];
- contracts of transport;
- free competition and trade;
- maritime law.

The aim of having specialised courts with specialised judges has been promoted in the last modification of the LOPJ.

Juzgados de vigilancia penitenciaria

These courts belong to the criminal order and are located in the capital of the province although it is possible to establish them in

---

[49] See comments by the Ilustre Colegio de Procuradores de Las Palmas, *www.icplpa.org/modules/news/*.
[50] Art.86 *bis LOPJ* as amended by the LO 8/2003.
[51] See Ch.5, "Civil Proceedings", p.120.

other localities. Their function is the enforcement of criminal decisions imposing loss of freedom and other security measures; they also safeguard the rights of prisoners.

Juzgados de menores

These juvenile courts are in charge of criminal offences committed by minors and the supervision of any educational or other measures imposed upon them.

Juzgados de paz

These are the only courts where the judge is a non-professional judge. Article 99 LOPJ declares that all the municipalities which do not have a *Juzgados de Primera Instancia e Instrucción* shall have a *Juzgados de Paz* with a *Juez de Paz* who performs his function gratuitously and who does not need to have any professional qualification. This "judge" is nominated by the Chamber of Government of the *Tribunal Superior de Justicia* from among the persons proposed by the respective *Ayuntamiento*.[52] They have jurisdiction over minor civil and criminal cases.

2.   EL MINISTERIO FISCAL (THE PUBLIC PROSECUTION SERVICE)

Although the public prosecution service is not a part of the judicial power[53]—because the judicial function belongs exclusively to judges and magistrates—its function and activities are so closely connected with the judicial power that it is regulated under this title in the Constitution. The main function of the public prosecution is to "promote the cause of justice in defence of legality, of the rights of the citizens and of the public interest".[54]

The public prosecution is regulated by its own *Estatuto Orgánico*[55] by which it is given "organic autonomy in the Judicial power". It has

---

[52] The *Ayuntamiento* (town hall) chooses a person from candidates who voluntarily nominate themselves.

[53] See J. Garcia Morillo, *op. cit.*, p.247.

[54] Art.124(1) *CE "La función del Ministerio fiscal es promover la acción de la justicia en defensa de la legalidad, de los derechos de los ciudadanos y del interes público tutelado por la ley"*.

[55] *Ley* 12/2000 of December 28, of modification of the *Estatuto Orgánico del Ministerio Fiscal* (EOMF); developed by the RD 545/83.

its own resources and personnel and is organised according to the principle of "unity of action". All the members of the prosecution service are subject to hierarchical organisation with the Attorney-General at the top (Arts 22, 25 and 27 EOMF). The Attorney-General (*Fiscal General del Estado*) is appointed by the Government (Art.124 CE) because the public prosecution is a key function in the criminal policy of the Executive. Together with these principles of unity of action and hierarchy, the public prosecution is subject to the principles of neutrality and legality.[56]

The usual activity of the prosecution is to bring charges in criminal proceedings. However, in comparison with other countries, the public prosecution does not have the exclusive right of prosecution because this can also be started by the victim or by a third party by the mechanism of "a popular action" of Art.125 CE.[57] The public prosecution also participates in other proceedings, such as proceedings before the Constitutional Court[58] where it has a separate office—*Fiscalía ante el Tribunal Constitucional*.

---

[56] As with any other organ, including the Public Administration, it is subject to the Law (Art.103 CE).

[57] See below, Ch.6, p.168 *et seq.*

[58] See below.

Chapter Four
The legal professions

1. Introduction: legal education in Spain

It is necessary to have obtained the title of *licenciado en derecho*[1] in order to practice any legal trade in Spain.[2] This is obtained after completing the approved course of studies in a Law faculty. The study of law has recently been changed after nearly half a century[3] and today the old programme of studies of 1953 co-exists with the new programme, which is being gradually implemented in the different faculties. According to the old programme, everybody aiming to obtain the title of *licenciado en derecho* had to follow a compulsory programme consisting of the study and corresponding examinations of 25 compulsory law subjects, covering virtually all the branches of law. Today, the new programme is designed to offer some compulsory subjects for all universities (*materias troncales*), some compulsory subjects for each university, and some optional subjects. Each subject, according to the new plan, carries a certain number of credits and in order to obtain the title of *licenciado* the number of credits will vary from 350 to 400 depending on the University. The major innovations of the new programme were introduced in order to attain some kind of homogeneity with legal education in Europe and include the introduction of a compulsory subject called "Institutional Community Law"[4] and

---

[1] Equivalent, to a certain extent, to Bachelor in Law but with certain differences because the course of studies is longer and more comprehensive than the English equivalent and at the end of it law graduates are qualified to practice as lawyers by registering in a *Colegio de Abogados*. This, however, is due to change in the future, see below, discussion of the project to reform access to the professional careers of *abogados* and *procuradores*.

[2] Alegría Borrás, *Legal Education and Training in Tomorrow's Europe* (paper presented at a conference on Legal Education in Europe, Metz, October 1994).

[3] *Real Decreto* 1497/1987 of November 27, about "General principles common to study programmes for obtaining of official degrees in Universities" and 1424/1990 of October 26, "Principles concerning the study of programmes tending towards the obtaining of the title of *licenciado en derecho*".

[4] In the old plan of studies there was no subject called "European Community law" although the study of the institutions of European law was included in different topics —public law II, public international law and administrative law—mainly with references to substantive law where appropriate in the other subjects.

a *Practicum*, which is intended to offer some integrated practice of law—although the content of this varies from institution to institution. The assessment of students falls within the discretion of each university according to the controversial new *Ley Orgánica* 2/2001 of December 21 *de universidades* (LOU)[5]. There is no compulsory final exam; usually there is one final exam for each subject to be held in June of the academic year, with the possibility of resitting the examination up to a maximum of five times per module. Exams are oral or written depending on each department and usually each student goes through a combination of both written unseen papers and orals in the course of his degree.

Many students commence law studies in Spain but usually only a percentage complete them. The study of law in Spain is not regarded as the main step to becoming a practicing lawyer,[6] but rather as a means of gaining a solid legal foundation in order to engage in a diverse range of legal professions or in industry or business. The term "legal profession" has, therefore, a much wider meaning than in England because not only does it refer to barristers or solicitors but to all those professionals who, holding a law degree, have any kind of involvement with legal matters. It includes: judges, *fiscales*, civil servants in different departments of the public administration, *abogados*, corporate lawyers, *procuradores*, judicial secretaries, notaries and public registrars.

It is important to note that it is not possible to practice any legal profession without the title of *licenciado en derecho* which can only be obtained by following the course of studies described above. There is no provision or possibility for graduates from other disciplines undertaking any type of "conversion course"—such as, for instance, the "Postgraduate Diploma in Law" in England—in order to qualify to start any legal profession.[7]

After obtaining the title of *licenciado en derecho* the new graduate has different possibilities if he wishes to pursue a legal career. He can register with a *Colegio de Abogados* and become a practicing lawyer.[8]

---

[5] The LOU was approved by the government of the *Partido Popular* and had numerous criticisms during the period of comments. It was challenged by all opposition parties mostly on points regulating the self-government of universities. The LOU introduced some much needed measures to reduce the endogamyc composition of some universities and the system of employing academic personnel on temporary contracts. For an overview of the main debate see *www.el-mundo.es/especiales/2001/10/sociedad/educacion*.

[6] Indeed only a small percentage of law graduates became *abogados en ejercicio* despite the automatic qualification they obtain.

[7] Compare with the survey on the education of solicitors in England in "Solicitors in private practice" *New Law Journal* (1992) pp.833–4.

[8] See below.

He can prepare for some of the public competitive exams (*oposiciones*) in order to become a judge, a public prosecutor, a notary, a registrar or a civil servant. He can work for business or industry or engage in postgraduate studies.

Postgraduate studies in law[9] are divided into two main types; those relating to obtaining a doctorate in law and those which lead to other diplomas. Doctoral studies are regulated by the Government and are delivered by the different departments of law faculties. Their aim is to provide specialisation of knowledge and training in research techniques. Studies are divided into a series of taught lectures and seminars and the presentation of a thesis on a legal topic under the approval and supervision of a university department or a scientific body, e.g. the *Consejo Superior de Investigaciones Científicas*.[10] Each department has discretion to accept students for postgraduate courses. It is usually the director of the department who makes the selection, taking into account the marks obtained during the university degree and/or any other relevant experience. When a student is accepted by a department, he is appointed a director of studies who must hold a doctorate and be a member of that department. Once the student has obtained a "certificate of competence" issued by the department and submitted a thesis which is evaluated by a five-member jury, he will be awarded the title of Doctor in Law. The title of doctor is required in order to become a university lecturer in the category of *Profesor Titular de Universidad* and further to progress towards the category of *Catedrático de Universidad*.[11]

2. ABOGADOS[12]

It was the increase in the number of laws and the application of these rules to increasingly complicated cases that historically led to the creation of professional courts and the need to have professionals, familiar with the complications and technicalities of the law, to stand for the rights of the parties demanding justice.[13] This was how the *abogados* (*patroni, defensores, causidici o vozeros* in historic law) and *procuradores*, originated.

---

[9] Arts 37 and 38 LO 6/2001 of December 21.
[10] High Council of Scientific Research.
[11] See Arts 48–55 LO 6/2001. Today it is only possible for those without doctorates to teach in universities as *profesores asociados*.
[12] The term *abogados* or lawyers will be used throughout since this does not translate as either solicitors or barristers but indicates a combination of both.
[13] J. Almagro Nosete, *Instituciones de Derecho Procesal*, Tomo I (1993), p.132.

The complete defence of the parties in Spanish law involves two professionals an *abogado* and a *procurador*. First, the profession of *abogado* will be considered and then, the role of the *procurador*.

The profession of *abogado* is a liberal and independent profession dedicated to the advice, conciliation and defence of public and private interests through the application of legal science and technique. *Abogados* give a service to society in the public interest.[14] They give this exclusivity: only *abogados* can carry out the legal defence of the parties.[15]

The denomination of *abogado* applies to a *licenciado en derecho* belonging to a *Colegio de Abogados* as a practising member, who has a professional address and professionally exercises the right of defence and direction of the parties in all types of litigation, or gives legal advice outside any proceedings.[16] *Abogados* are organised into public law corporations called *Colegios de Abogados*,[17] and it is a necessary requirement to be incorporated to one of these *Colegios* in order to practice as an *abogado*. It is possible to be a member of a *Colegio de Abogados* as a non-practising lawyer if all the requirements for incorporation are met.[18] Only practising lawyers can be called *abogados*.

Those who have practised law for at least 20 years but are currently not doing so can called themselves *abogado "sin ejercicio"*[19] as a different category to the *abogado no ejerciente* for non-practising lawyers who have either never practised before or who have done so for a period of less than 20 years. The differentiation between those two lies on the greater degree of accomplishment with legal practice that somebody who has 20 years in the profession is presumed to have and it will have relevance if the person who used this denomination or the denomination of *abogado no ejerciente* gives advisory services as a consultant or *"asesor"*.

There are in excess of 100,000 *abogados* registered in 84 *Colegios de Abogados*.[20] Of these 100,000 approximately 80 per cent are practising members and the rest are registered as non-practising members.

The following requirements must be complied with in order to become a member of a *Colegio de Abogados*. It is necessary to have Spanish nationality or nationality of any country of the European

---

[14] Art.1 of the *Estatuto General de la Abogacía* (EGA), approved by the *Real Decreto* 658/2001 of June 22.

[15] Assisted by *procuradores* as prescribed by law. See below.

[16] Art.436 LOPJ and Art.6 of the EGA.

[17] Regulated in the EGA Arts 2, 3 and 4.

[18] Art.9(4) EGA.

[19] Art.9(3) EGA (RD 658/2001).

[20] One of each provincial capital and the rest in mayor cities. See *www.cgae.es*.

Community,[21] to have reached majority, to hold the title of *licenciado en derecho*, not to have any criminal record preventing the exercise of the profession, to pay the registration fee,[22] to join the *Mutualidad General de Previsión de la Abogacía*, and to obtain a licence of economic activities.

The new *Estatuto General de La Abogacía* (EGA) of 2001 has changed the old and very criticised system whereby *abogados* could only practice in the territorial area of the *colegio* where they were registered, except in the case of appeals if the appellate court was situated in a different territorial demarcacion. Today this has changed and there is a system of *Colegiacion Unica* that habilitates the *abogado* to practice in the whole of the Spanish territory or the territory of any of the members of the European Union subject to the requirements outlined below.[23] The only requirement that an *abogado* must fulfil if he wishes to practise in the territory of a *colegio* different to that of registration is to communicate this to the *colegio* of the territory where he intends to practice. This is done by notifying the *colegio* of origin or by notifying any of the entities mentioned in Art.17 EGA.

Advocacy is a liberal profession in the sense that the *abogado* gives a service without any subjection to the person to whom the service is given. It is also an intellectual profession because it encompasses the application of legal science, and it is independent because the *abogado* is only subject to the moral, deontological and technical demands of his profession.[24]

They are some circumstances in which the exercise of advocacy is forbidden. These are: any physical or mental disability which, by its nature or circumstance makes it impossible to carry out the defence of private interests; suspension or disability due to a judicial decision or disciplinary sanctions imposed by the *Colegio de Abogados*. The exercise of advocacy is also incompatible with the posts of President of the Government, Minister, Secretary of State, Subsecretary,

---

[21] The extension to nationals of other states which are members of the European Community was brought into effect by the RD 147/1991 of February 15, in order to adapt Spanish legislation to Art.52. of the European Community Treaty, by which nationality cannot be a reason for restricting access to the legal professions. In any case this requirement can be dispensed with if all the others are complied with for nationals of non-EEC states. See Art.13(1), EGA, RD 658/2001.

[22] The amount varies from one *Colegio* to another but it is around €800 to €1400 for the first registration. To this it is necessary to add the monthly fees that vary depending on whether the registration is as a practising or not practising lawyer and on the years that the *abogado* has been registered. Visit the webpage of the CGAE *www.cgae.es* for links to all the *Colegios de Abogados* in Spain. It is possible to check the fees for each of them on line.

[23] See Art.17 EGA, RD 658/2001.

[24] Almagro Nosete, *op. cit.*, p.132.

Director General and high positions of the public administration, *procurador*, judge, public prosecutor and judicial secretaries, Secretary of the *Consejo General de Poder Judicial*, and any other public post which expressly forbids. It is also impossible to act as *abogado* in a case where the judge is a member of the family of the *abogado* within the second degree of consanguinity. Civil servants can practice advocacy although they cannot act in cases in which the Ministry or Department where they are posted is involved. (See Arts 21–26 EGA.)

Lawyers can now advertise their services according to Art.25 of the new *Estatuto de la Abogacía* provided that the publicity is "true, loyal, and does not incite to unnecessary litigation", does not reveal details of clients and does not use the logo of a *Colegio de Abogados*. This is a change from the old *Estatuto* which forbade publicity.

There are no compulsory training periods to be completed in order to become an *abogado* in Spain, although in practice most graduates will either join a course of legal practice in schools sponsored by the *Colegios de Abogados* or join a law firm in the unofficial category of *pasante*.[25] This situation has been an issue for a long time and finally the *Anteprojecto de ley sobre el acceso a las profesiones de abogado y procurador de los tribunales* has reached the *Consejo de Ministros*.[26] It is hoped that this legislation will finally be approved during the current mandate of the Socialist Party. It has got the support of the *Consejo General de La Abogacía*[27] but it has been heavily opposed by law students and universities.[28] The supporters of the proposed new law base their arguments on the lack of preparation for the practice of law that students acquire in universities. The current system, they argue, allows unprepared graduates to call themselves *abogados* by the right of automatic incorporation to a *colegio* with the problems of inadequate advice that they potentially can give to clients. The system proposed will require that all law graduates that wish to

---

[25] Which roughly means "trainee" but due to the lack of regulation amounts in many cases to abuses by the law firms both as to the length of time for which one is considered to be a "trainee" and to the remuneration during this period, which varies from nothing to £400 a month. In this respect it would be preferable to establish some regulation of the *pasantía* and make it a compulsory but limited stage.

[26] The final version that the author had access to is the definitive version approved by the Consejo de Ministros on July 22, 2005. It can be accessed at *www.mje.es*.

[27] See declaration from Carnicer Diaz, president of the CGAE on May 14, 2002, and June 28, 2002, about the need for such legislation, *www.cgae.es/prensa/articulos/prensa_020628_1.htm*. The subject was raised in the *Congreso de la Abogacía Espanola de Leon* (1970), *Palma* (1989), *Coruña* (1995); *Sevilla* (1999) and *Salamanca* (2003) also by *Procuradores* in the National Congress of 2000 and the VII *Congreso International del Comité de Postulantes de Mallorca* (2004).

[28] *www.elmundo.es/universidad/2003/10/20/actualidad/1*.

incorporate into a *colegio* either as *abogados* or *procuradores*, since the regulation will cover both professions, will have to pass an exam about the practice of law and a second exercise about knowledge of the Code of Professional Conduct of Lawyers. It is not intended to re-examine knowledge already tested in universities. In order to pass these exams the candidates will attend either an *Escuela de Práctica Jurídica* of a *colegio* or one of the accredited courses imparted by Universities that will be approved by the Ministry of Education. They will also have to spend a period of time under the supervision of a practising *abogado* or *procurador*. There are no requirements for the continuous training for *abogados*, although in practice the different *colegios* organise courses and seminars in various legal areas of current interest.[29]

The main duties of *abogados* are connected with their function of legal defence. *Abogados* collaborate with the administration of justice by defending the legal interests they represent. They have duties towards their clients, their colleagues and the courts. Their remunerations are not subject to any fixed fee and they enjoy the benefit of a special proceeding for the payment of their fees regulated by Art.35 of the LEC 2000.[30] The *Colegios de Abogados* publish indicative guidelines about legal fees, but each *abogado* is free to fix these. However, it is forbidden to fix the fees as a percentage of the amount obtained in the proceedings—*pacto de quota litis* or contingent fees.[31] This prohibition also extends to the so-called *pacto palmario*, by which the *abogado* obtains a fee superior to the one originally fixed if he wins the case. The respective *Colegio de Abogados* will sanction any of these practices.

All practising lawyers belonging to a *Colegio de Abogados* have a duty to give free legal advice to those entitled to legal aid.[32] This is called *turno de oficio*. Also, in criminal cases outside the scope of legal aid, all the *abogados* have the duty to defend any person who so requests. If the services are given to somebody entitled to legal aid, the State will compensate the *abogado* for his services; if the person to whom services are given is not entitled to legal aid the duty solicitor has the right to demand payment on his normal terms from the

---

[29] See B.M. Cremades, "La formación continua del abogado" *La Ley*, October 12, 1993.
[30] The *abogado* and also the *procurador* can, if their client refuses to pay, present a note with their fees to the court which will order enforcement of the debt.
[31] The prohibition originated in Roman and canon law and was introduced by the Historic law in Spain: *Fuero Real; Las Partidas* and *Novísima Recopilación*; it was later forgotten by the LO of 1870 but reintroduced by the *Estatuto de la Abogacia* of 1946 and today is contained in Art.44 EGA (2001).
[32] Art.57 of the EGA. See also Ch.5, "Legal Aid", p.135

beginning of the case. For those criminal cases with a potential punishment of six or more years of prison there is a special *turno de oficio* with *abogados* that have at least five years of professional experience.[33]

Article 10 of the LEC[34] prescribes the compulsory intervention of *abogado* in all types of proceedings except in acts of conciliation, oral proceedings, acts of voluntary jurisdiction or the adoption of urgent measures. In all other cases the signature of an *abogado* is a requisite to the acceptance of the claim by the court. In criminal proceedings the assistance of an *abogado* is compulsory.

Spanish law firms—*bufetes*—are usually specialised. They are much smaller than English law firms although there is a tendency in big cities to establish larger practices. There is no differentiation between associates and partners, although in practice, there is a hierarchy between different *abogados* of the same firm, especially in larger ones, based on experience and professional standing. The *Estatuto de la Abogacía* of 2001 makes provision for what are called *despachos colectivos*.[35] It eliminates the maximum number of 20 members that was fixed by the old *Estatuto* and it also allows the creation of multiprofessional practices in which *abogados* associate with compatible professionals, for example tax advisors, architects or town planning experts in order to offer a more complete service to the public. In the case of multi-professional practices each professional will be subject to the rules of their own profession and their compulsory insurances and liabilities. This is a much welcomed addition which allows a more dynamic and modern approach to the provision of legal services. In big cities like Madrid and Barcelona or Valencia, and also in tourist destinations where the number of foreigners accessing legal services is greater, these multi-professional practices are growing and becoming successful. In most of Spain law firms still retain a somewhat traditional character.

FOREIGN LAWYERS

Foreign lawyers wanting to practice in Spain need to have their professional qualification recognised and be admitted to one of the different *Colegios de Abogados* (or *de Procuradores*, as the case may be).

The recognition of foreign professional titles and qualifications follows a different procedure according to the country where the foreign lawyer qualified.

---

[33] Art.45, EGA.
[34] Art.31, EGA.
[35] Collective offices.

Lawyers from the EU or the EEE

There are different ways in which a lawyer from the EU or the EEE can practise in Spain. He can practise as a professional under the principle of free movement of services (Directive 77/249/CEE and RD 607/1986/1988). It is possible to obtain a card indicating the title of *"Abogado Europeo"*—European Lawyers according to the Directive. He can also practise once the original title has been recognised and the foreign lawyer has passed an exam on Spanish law and professional deontology.[36] It is possible to dispense with the exam in exceptional circumstances if the foreign lawyer whose title has been recognised can prove that his experience in Spain and knowledge of Spanish law are well established. The application for recognition of the foreign qualification must be sent to the *Ministerio de Justicia* enclosing a copy of the passport or other document stating the nationality of the applicant, a copy of the professional title, an academic certification stating subjects taken, length of time over which the title was obtained and the approximate number of contact hours for each subject. The *Ministerio de Justicia* will decide within a period of four months whether to recognise the title or not as valid for practising in Spain. At the end of the four months it will notify the applicant as to whether he has been successful in his application or not and if he has been successful as to whether he is required to take an exam on Spanish law before he can proceed to register in a *Colegio de Abogados*.

The examination for foreign lawyers include matters such as constitutional and administrative law; fundamental rights and freedoms; civil law, obligations, property, family and succession; company law and commercial law; criminal law; labour law and professional deontology. The aim of the examination is clear: law is a nationally bound subject and excellent knowledge of foreign law does not prove minimum knowledge of national law. These exams take place at least once a year and it is possible to obtain copies of the specific subjects from any of the offices of the *Ministerio de Justicia*.[37] The exam itself consists of a practical case on one or several of the subjects listed above that must be resolved by the applicant and read aloud to the *Comision de Evaluación*. The candidate can take as many legal texts and reference books as he wishes to resolve the case. He has six hours to do so. After this the examination panel will ask different questions related to the practical case, the Spanish court system and the rules of

---

[36] This is done according to the European Directive 89/48/CEE and the Spanish RD 1665/1991 and OM 30-4-1-1996, which lie down the specific conditions for the recognition of degrees.

[37] See *www.justicia.es*.

professional conduct. The Panel will then decide whether the candidate has passed the exam or not.[38] The *Comisión de Evaluación* is an administrative body and as such must act according to the rules set up in the *Ley* 30/1992 of November 26 *de Régimen Jurídico de las Administraciones Públicas y del Procedimiento Administrativo Común*. Decisions of the panel can be challenged by filing a *"recurso de alzada"* that will be resolved by the Director General of Relations with the Administration of Justice.

Practice is also possible by opening a permanent office according to the Directive 98/5/CE and the RD 936/2001. In this case the foreign lawyer must also pass an exam on Spanish law and professional conduct.

In all cases the foreign lawyer has a choice as to whether he wishes to practice keeping his original qualification in which case he will have to act alongside a Spanish lawyer in order to stand in court or assist those in custody or whether he wishes to fully integrate on the Spanish Bar. If the later, the foreign lawyer needs to prove a continuous and effective practice in Spain during a minimum of three years.

Lawyers who do not come from the EU or EEE

These lawyers do not benefit from the principles of free movement of persons and services or freedom of establishment of the European Union.

The foreign lawyer must request the recognition of his academic title and professional qualification and a *"dispensa legal de nacionalidad"* or legal dispensation of nationality.[39]

In order to have the foreign title recognised (*homologado*) in Spain, it is necessary to fill in an application form to the *Ministerio de Educación Cultura y Deporte* enclosing an authentic copy of a document proving the identity and nationality of the applicant[40]; original certification of the academic title and receipt of payment of the required fee. It is optional to include any extra information such as programmes of the different subjects studied during the degree.

---

[38] The Comision will publish a list of successful candidates within three days from days. More information can be obtained contacting the Oficina General de Informacion (Del Ministerio de Justicia): C/ San Bernardo 45, Madrid 28045; or the *Consejo General de La Abogacía Espanola*, *www.cgae.es* or the *Consejo General de Colegios de Procuradores*, *www.cgpe.es*.

[39] See RD 86/1987 of January 16 for the recognition of foreign University Degrees; Orden ECD/272/2002 of February 11 and OMEC of July 21, 1995, establishing the general criteria for setting exams for candidates who wish to have their title recognised.

[40] An authentic copy is a copy that has been certified as true according to the original by an administrative authority or by a notary.

Foreign documents must be official and must have the *Apostilla de la Haya*[41] and be translated into Spanish by an official translator.[42]

A special panel called *Consejo de Coordinación Universitaria* will decide whether the degree can be recognised (*homologado*) if the studies are clearly equivalent, as may be the case with many science degrees, engineering or computing science; or whether it can even be recognised that the applicant needs to sit and pass an exam in order to prove knowledge of those areas that have not been studied in the foreign university, which would be the case with law degrees; or, whether there is no possibility of recognition at all because the programme of studies was so fundamentally different that there would be no parity with the same Spanish graduates. This would mean a potential further exam which the candidate would have to pass and will cover all the compulsory subjects of the degree chosen and can be taken at any of the Spanish public universities.

In addition, to have their title recognised foreign lawyers also have to apply for an "official dispensation of nationality". This request must be addressed to the Ministry of Justice indicating the *Colegio de Abogados* (or *Procuradores*) that they wish to join because in order to belong to a *Colegio de Abogados* it is necessary to be a Spanish national.

3.   PROCURADORES

Procuradores are lawyers who represent[43] the parties in court and other official departments through a power of attorney given by the person requiring their services. They also collaborate with the *abogado* through the reception and communication of documents received from the court. Their profession is defined as a liberal and independent profession and is regulated by the *Estatuto General de Procuradores de los Tribunales*, approved by RD 1281/2002 December 5. *Procuradores* are organised in *Colegios de Procuradores*, which are public law entities governed by the *Consejo General de Ilustres Colegios de Procuradores de los Tribunales de España*.[44] In order to register in one of these *Colegios* it is necessary to have Spanish nationality, to have reached the age of majority, to hold the

---

[41] *Apostilla de la Haya* or general certification for foreign document Convention XII of the Hague Conference on Private International Law of 1961.

[42] In Spain translators are registered and belong to an official organisation or *Colegio de Traductores Jurados*.

[43] As distinct from *abogados* who advise and defend their clients. Although see Art.3(4) RD 1281/2002 and below.

[44] See *www.cgpe.es* for information on regulation and a list of all *colegios*.

title of *licenciado en derecho* and to have obtained the title of *procurador*, which is given by the Ministry of Justice once applicants have fulfilled the other requirements.[45] They also have to pay the required fee and join the *Mutualidad de Previsión de los Procuradores de los Tribunales de España*; deposit a bond and swear an oath to the Court where they are intending to practice.

The intervention of a *procurador* is compulsory in civil proceedings with the exception of those proceedings mentioned in Art.10 *LEC*.[46] In criminal proceedings their intervention is always compulsory.

In order to act as a *procurador* it is necessary to have a power of attorney—*poder suficiente*—given by the client, which enables the *procurador* to act as the legal representative of the client. Historically, the client approached the *procurador*, gave him a power of attorney and advanced some money for starting the proceedings, leaving to the *procurador* the choice of the *abogado*. Today the practice is different because clients approach their *abogados* first and usually these appoint a *procurador*.

Procuradores can only practice within the territorial demarcation of their *colegio de procuradores* (Art.13 EGPTE). *Procuradores* are subject to similar incompatibilities as *abogados* and they have civil, criminal and disciplinary responsibilities in the exercise of their profession. Since the distinction between *abogados* and *procuradores* does not exist in all EU countries, the EU regulations for freedom of establishment and rendering of services apply to both these professionals.[47]

If the project of a law to regulate entry to the careers of *abogados* and *procuradores* succeeds in parliament, those wishing to join this career will have to take the same practical exam and period of placement with a *procurador* established by the anteprojecto.[48]

4.   REPRESENTATION AND DEFENCE OF THE STATE: ABOGADOS DEL ESTADO

The representation and defence of the State, its constitutional organs and the Administration, corresponds to the *Cuerpo de Abogados del Estado-Dirección del Servicio judicio del Estado*.[49] In

---

[45] Art.8 RD 1281/2002.
[46] They coincide with cases in which the intervention of an *abogado* is not compulsory.
[47] See above, "Foreign lawyers".
[48] See above—*Anteprojecto de ley sobre el ingreso a las profesiones de abogado y procurador de 22 julio 2005.*
[49] Regulated by the *ley* 52/1997 of November 27.

some cases it is possible to give the legal defence of the State, or organs mentioned above, to a private practitioner specially designated for this task (Art.447(1) LO 6/1985 of July 1).

This body of lawyers is dependent on the Ministry of Justice and it is composed of legal professionals who hold a law degree and join this body by passing a competitive examination consisting of both theoretical and practical exercises on legal matters. These lawyers represent the State and the Administration in all legal proceedings and also advise the Autonomous Communities.[50]

The *Abogados del Estado* represent the State in front of *Tribunal Constitucional* when legislation approved is challenged in the constitutional court,[51] the *Tribunal de Cuentas*[52] and the *Tribunal Supremo*.[53]

5.   JUECES Y MAGISTRADOS

Access to a judicial career is based on a distinction between three types of judges.[54] *Magistrados del Tribunal Supremo*,[55] *Magistrados*[56] and *Jueces*[57] (Art.299 LOPJ). All members of the judiciary are covered by these categories including civil registrars. With the exception of the *Jueces de Paz*, who are appointed by the *Consejo General del Poder Judicial* following a proposal by the municipal authorities, all other judges and magistrates hold a law degree. *Jueces de Paz* have very limited functions in minor civil and criminal cases.[58]

There are two ways of becoming a judge, either by passing a competitive examination[59]—*turno normal*—set by the *Centro de Estudios Judiciales*, taking the courses and final examination also set by the

---

[50] They are regulated by the RD 997/2003 of July 25, but see also RD 1474/2000 of August.

[51] Regulated by the *Ley Orgánica 2/1979, of October 3, del Tribunal Constitucional (Artículo 82(2)); Real Decreto 1425/1980, of July 11, de Creación de la Abogacía del Estado ante el Tribunal Constitucional; Orden of April 2, 1981, de estructura orgánica de la Abogacía del Estado ante el Tribunal Constitucional.*

[52] See Art.49 of the LO 21/1982, of May 12 *del Tribunal de Cuentas.*

[53] Visit *www.justicia.es* the website of information to the citizen of the *Ministerio de Justicia*, and follow links to "organos" where the *Cuerpo de Abogados de Estado* can be found.

[54] Alegría Borrás, *op. cit.*, p.10.

[55] Judges of the Supreme Court.

[56] Judges sitting in higher courts.

[57] All other judges; used in general to designate both *Magistrados* and *jueces.*

[58] See sections on *Juicio Oral* and *Jueces de Paz* in Ch.5.

[59] For which it is necessary to hold a law degree.

Centro de Estudios Judiciales, or by selective competition amongst lawyers of recognised standing with at least six years of private practice. For each four places, three are reserved for the *turno normal* and one for an applicant selected by competitive entry. The entrance exam consists of three different examinations. Failure of one of them leads to exclusion. Two of the examinations are theoretical and one is practical. The examinations cover General Theory of the Law, Constitutional Law, Civil Law, Criminal Law, Commercial Law, Administrative Law and Civil and Criminal Procedure. Once the examination has been passed and the candidate has completed the course offered by the *Centro de Estudios Judiciales* and its assessment requirements, the *Consejo General del Poder Judicial* can award the title of Judge.[60]

There are three ways of becoming a *Magistrado*. A third of the places are filled by the judges who are highest in the hierarchy, a third by way of competitive examinations amongst judges, and a third is reserved for practising lawyers of recognised standing with at least 10 years of professional experience.

There are two ways in which to become a *Magistrado* of the Supreme Court.[61] For each five posts, four are filled by those members of the Judiciary who have held the position of magistrate for at least 10 years and have been members of the Judiciary for at least 20 years. The candidate for the fifth post is elected from among lawyers of recognised standing with at least 20 years of practice in the area of law of the chamber of the Supreme Court to which they are appointed.[62]

The continual training of judges is actively organised by the *Consejo General del Poder Judicial* with provincial and local training schemes, and is adapted to the needs of the members of the Judiciary. This training is voluntary.

Judges enjoy a special status in order to guarantee the proper performance of their duties in administering justice. They are independent, irremovable and subject only to the law (Art.117 CE). Their independence must be respected by all citizens and public powers. If a judge feels that his independence is being threatened he will inform the CGPJ who will then take the necessary measures. The independence of judges, which is necessary for the rightful application of the law, is also guaranteed by establishing two procedures by which a judge can be required or voluntarily abstain from resolving a case due to personal or professional connections with the parties involved or with the subject-matter. These are known as *abstención* and *recusación* and are regulated in Art.219 LOPJ.

---

[60] Alegría Borrás, *op. cit.*, p.10.
[61] The highest post in judicial hierarchy.
[62] These Chambers are civil, criminal, administrative or social.

Judges can be held civilly, criminally and disciplinary responsible in the exercise of their functions and are subject to a strict regime of incompatibilities in order to guarantee their independence in the application of the law. Judges can only be dismissed, transferred, suspended or forced to retire according to the terms provided by law. The independence of judges from other powers, especially from the Government, is achieved by providing the judiciary with a system of self-government: the *Consejo General del Poder Judicial*.[63] Judges in Spain are anonymous in the sense that they do not enjoy the publicity that they do in England. Decisions are not published with the name of the judge. However, a recent phenomenon has appeared in Spanish society mainly linked to the big scandals of political corruption which have shocked public opinion. This is known as the *super-jueces*[64] by which certain judges, mainly the ones of the *Audiencia Nacional* in charge of special crimes and political corruption, have become national heroes and are well known by the public due to extensive media coverage of notorious trials, in particular the ones involving Members of Parliament and Government.[65]

Together with the judges and magistrate members of the judicial career, there are also other judges known as *jueces temporales*. These temporary judges are not members of the Judiciary although they can give judgments. Temporary personnel are divided between *Magistrados Suplentes* and *Jueces de Provisión Temporal*.

The *Magistrados Suplentes* are appointed in exceptional circumstances when it is impossible to appoint a *Magistrado de Carrera*[66] (Art.200 LOPJ). They are selected from among the members of a list drafted by the CGPJ. The office of *Magistrado Suplente* is an honorary post, even if remunerated. These can only be selected from those who fulfil the requirements to enter the Judiciary, with preference being given to persons who have performed judicial or academic functions in the past.[67]

The *jueces de provisión temporal* are appointed by the *Tribunal Superior de Justicia*, giving preferences to those who are doctors in law, who have passed the competitive exams for other legal careers,[68] or who have had academic experience. They can be nominated for

---

[63] See above, Ch.3, p.79.

[64] Literally "Super-Judges".

[65] Names of judges like Baltasar Garzón, Marino Barbero, Mariñas, Ana Ferrer, are common knowledge as public opinion follows big cases of political corruption due to the extensive media coverage.

[66] This is a professional judge, a member of the Judiciary.

[67] It is common to appoint university professors specialised in the area that the *Magistrado Suplente* has to cover.

[68] For instance Civil Servants.

a year with the possibility of extension for a further year. The post is remunerated.

Today, 80 per cent of the successful candidates to the competitive exams for joining the judicial career are women. Although women make only 40 per cent of the total number of judges in Spain it is expected that in the next five years there will be more than a 50 per cent number of women judges. This is common with countries like France where women also make half of the judiciary. However, it does not appear that women are governing the judiciary or reaching the high posts of the profession, at least not yet. Of the 95 judges on the *Tribunal Supremo* only one is a woman; there is only one vocal in *el Consejo general del Poder Judicial* and the 17 *tribunales Superiores de Justicia* of the Autonomous Communities have male presidents.[69]

6. *FISCALES*

Fiscales[70], according to the Constitution are in charge of upholding the law and ensuring the application of justice by defending the rights of citizens, the public interest and the independence of the courts (Art.124 CE[71]).

The *Ministerio Fiscal* has independent means for the performance of these functions. It operates through different agencies.[72] The most important authority of the *Ministerio Fiscal* is the *Fiscal General del Estado* nominated by the King and elected by the Government following consultation with the *Consejo General del Poder Judicial*.[73]

In order to be a member of the *Carrera Fiscal*, it is necessary to hold a degree in law and to pass a competitive entry examination in common with the examination which must be passed by judges. *Jueces* and *Fiscales* have a common access to the profession. After the first exam has been passed the candidates must choose (the one with the higher

---

[69] See www.juezas.es.

[70] Public Prosecutors.

[71] Art.124 CE: "*EL Ministerio fiscal . . . tine por misión promover la accion de la justicia en defensa de la legalidad de los derechos e los ciudadanos y del interés público tutelado por la Ley, de oficio o a petición de los interesados, asi como velar por la independencia de os tribunales y procurar ante estos la satisfacción del interés social*".

[72] These agencies are: *el Fiscal General del Estado, el Consejo Fiscal, la Junta de Fiscales de Sala, la Fiscalía del Tribunal Supremo, la Fiscalía de Tribunal Constitucional, la Fiscala de la Audiencia Nacional, las Fiscalias de los Tribunales Superiores de Justicia de las Comunidades Autonomas, las Fiscalias de las Audiencias Territoriales*.

[73] See Ch.3, p.61

marks have preference of choice) whether they wish to opt for the judicial career or to the *cuerpo de fiscals*. It is after this choice that they pursue different studies and tests of aptitude. Their place in the hierarchy, honours and remuneration are similar to those of judges and they are subject to the same civil, criminal and disciplinary liability and have the same rights of independence and irremovability.

Within its main function of "upholding the law and ensuring the application of justice" the *Ministerio Fiscal* intervenes in a variety of proceedings. It is in charge of the civil and criminal actions arising as a consequence of the commission of a criminal offence, intervenes in all proceedings concerning the civil status of natural persons and in the defence of the legality in proceedings involving those subject to guardianship, ensuring respect of their rights. It also intervenes in proceedings of the Constitutional Court[74] and in any proceedings involving the infringement of fundamental rights of citizens. Recently its functions have been expanded in criminal proceedings by the LO 7/88,[75] which confers limited capacity for investigations on the public prosecution, beyond its traditional function of guaranteeing the rights of the suspect and the victim and the application of the law.[76]

Fiscales are governed by the Ley 12/2000 of December 28, *de modificación del Estatuto Orgánico del Ministerio Fiscal*. They can join the *Asociaciones de Fiscales*, a body created in 1980.[77]

7. SECRETARIOS JUDICIALES

In the second rank of importance according to their function in the administration of justice and just below judges, are the *Secretarios Judiciales*.[78] This body of law graduates is in charge of running the courts and has the task of directing the *Oficina Judicial* and organising the proceedings.

Secretarios de Justicia hold a law degree and have passed a competitive entry examination and a course organised by the *Centro de Estudios Judiciales*. They are attached to the Ministry of Justice[79] and

---

[74] *ibid.*
[75] See Ch.6
[76] See Ch.3, p.72 and Ch.6, p.140.
[77] See *www.asoc-fiscales.org*.
[78] Court Clerks. Their status, functions and duties are regulated by the LOPJ Art.472 to 483 and RD 429/88 of April 29, approving the *Reglamento Orgánico de Secretarios Judiciales*.
[79] They are, therefore, a part of the Public Administration compared to judges who are ingrated within the Judicial Power.

assist the judges in the administration of justice. They are subject to a similar regime of incompatibilities as judges, with the exception that secretaries can participate as candidates in local elections.[80]

Their functions fall mainly under the heading of assisting judges in the function of administering justice. They have custody of all documentation, depositions and any objects connected with the judicial proceedings; they keep all books and records of the judicial activities of the Court; they also practice all notifications and communications related to the proceedings. The *Secretarios Judicales* are in charge of the *Oficina Judicial* and exercise direct control over all the auxiliaries[81] of the judge. As is the case with judges, *Secretarios Judiciales* are subject to civil, criminal and disciplinary liability. The role and importance of the *Secretarios Judiciales* has been extended with the modification of the LOPJ by *Ley* 8/2003 that recognises the crucial role of these officials.

8. Auxiliary personnel in the administration of justice

Oficiales, auxilares y agentes[82]

There are other civil servants within the Ministry of Justice whose work supports that of judges, magistrates and public prosecutors in the administration of justice. These are the *oficiales, auxiliaries* and *agents*. They are in charge of the day to day running of the courts or agencies to which they are attached and their functions are administrative. They do not need to hold a law degree and they are civil servants of "Grade B" or "C" depending on whether they have primary or secondary education. Entry is by means of a competitive examination.

Policía judicial

The judicial police is not a separate body from the general police but includes all those members of the police force who are directly under the orders of the courts and the *Ministerio Fiscal* (Art.126 CE). According to the LOPJ (Arts 443 to 445) the functions of the judicial police can be summarised as providing assistance to the courts of

---

[80] From which judges are precluded.
[81] See below.
[82] Officials, auxiliaries and agents.

justice and the *Ministerio Fiscal* in the investigation of crimes and the search of criminals. This is a duty of all members of the police force but the judicial police specifically assist the courts in any situation which requires the use of force or public coercion.[83]

OTHER TECHNICAL AUXILIARIES OF THE ADMINISTRATION OF JUSTICE

These are professionals from different disciplines who assist the courts in their role of administering justice. The common feature of all of them is that they are experts in different areas of knowledge at the service of the administration of justice. Some of them are civil servants and others are independent professionals.

Forensic doctors have a wide input in criminal cases. They determine the time and causes of death and give a report in all cases involving offences against physical integrity. They are appointed by the State.

Doctors of the Civil Registry provide reports for all those cases concerning the civil status of individuals, for instance in the ascertainment of birth or death.

Translators and interpreters make official translations of foreign documents and verify private translations. They also provide an interpretation service when one of the parties to the proceedings requires this.

The Institute of Toxicology, which is part of the Ministry of Justice, provides all the required information in this area (Art.505 LOPJ).

The National Institute of Medicine and Security in the Workplace, advises the Social Courts on specific areas related to security and hygiene in the workplace.

9.   CIVIL SERVANTS

The highest category in the civil service, Grade "A", is open only to graduates including, but not exclusively, law graduates. A large proportion of the graduates holding a title of *Licenciado en Derecho* will prepare for the competitive exams in order to become civil servants, partly due to the difficulties in securing employment nowadays. This category of higher civil servants includes diplomats who must pass a competitive examination requiring a university degree and perfect knowledge of at least two foreign languages. The subject matter of this examination covers topics of law and politics,

---

[83] For more detail see Ch.6, pp.151 *et seq.*

current affairs and general knowledge. A large proportion of the members of the Diplomatic Service are, in fact, law graduates. After passing the examinations the successful candidate must take a course in the *Escuela Diplomática* and obtain a certificate of completion. After that they become members of the diplomatic corps and enjoy all the related privileges and dignities. They can take postings abroad and occupy one of the posts at the Ministry of External Affairs.

Certain bodies of the administration do require a degree in law; these are the *Cuerpo de Letrados del Tribunal Constitutional, Letrados de las Cortes* and *Abogados del Estado*.

10. NOTARIOS

Notarios[84] are legal professional whose function consists in conferring authenticity on documents by which the parties effect different legal transactions. This function is exclusive to them and the documents drafted by them enjoy a presumption of authenticity; that is, their content is presumed to be the truth unless falsity is proved in the corresponding criminal proceeding.

The profession of *notario* has a dual nature in Spain. On one hand, *notarios* have a delegated power from the State and they perform a public service—the authentication of documents. In this respect the number of notaries is *numerus clausus*, their fees are fixed and they are subject to various rules of conduct and competence which assimilates them to civil servants. On the other hand, *notarios* are liberal professionals who exercise an independent activity giving advice[85] to the parties on the drafting of private documents. However, even when providing legal advice *notarios* have a very different role from *abogados* since they are impartial and do not act on behalf of any of the parties. What a *notario* attempts to do is to explain the legal consequences of the documents that the parties want to have drafted.

Notarios are dependent on the Ministry of Justice and belong to professional bodies—*Colegios de Notarios*—presided over by the *Consejo Superior del Notariado*. The *Consejo Superior del Notariado* is at the head of all the notaries' associations and performs a function similar to that of the *Consejo General de la Abogacía*, that is, it represents the

---

[84] Visit *www.notariado.org*.
[85] *Notarios* can give legal advice in any area. However, they are precluded from exercising the representation and defence of clients in courts, which is reserved for *abogados* and *procuradores*.

interests of notaries, drafts guidelines for practice and liaises with other legal bodies. *Notarios* are independent in the exercise of their functions and are subject to civil, criminal and disciplinary liability in the same way as any other legal professionals.

The delegation of powers from the State means that the principle of freedom of establishment of Arts 52 *et seq.* of the TCEE justifies the application of the exception contained in Art.55 TCEE.

In order to be awarded a *Notaría* (the office of a *notario*) it is necessary to hold a degree in law and to pass a competitive examination, traditionally regarded as being very difficult both in terms of the actual examination and as regards the tough competition for the few places of *notario* available. Once the examination has been successfully passed the new notary will be asked to deposit a bond or security and will be granted a licence and appointed to a specific office. There are three types of *Notarías* depending on the population of the town where the *notario* has been appointed.

The functions of *notarios* are regulated by the *Ley del Notariado* of May 28, 1862, and the *Reglamento Notarial* of June 2, 1994 (modified by *RD* 1209/1984 of June 8, *RD* 1728/1991 of November 29 and RD 2537/1994 of December 29).

Since the concept of authentic documents of "public faith" is unknown to common law lawyers, this concept may be explained by the function performed by the *notario* throughout the legal system. Legal certainty, in the sense of the possibility given to citizens to foresee the consequences of their acts, is of foremost importance in civil law systems. This is achieved by a variety of means including the establishment of the sources of law, the principle of legality, the publicity of the laws, the subjection of the judge to the established sources and, as Rodriguez Pinero[86] suggests, by the existence of professionals—*notarios*—who prevent conflicts by conferring certainty on the documents that they authorise. In conferring authenticity to documents notaries must comply with several requirements.

Public documents are those authorised by a *notario*, they are presumed to represent the truth and, therefore, they can constitute *títulos ejecutivos*.[87] This is achieved by subjecting the activities of notaries to certain principles.[88] The first of these is the principle of "authorship

---

[86] In Vol. *"La fé pública"*, *Jornadas organizadas por el Ministerio de Justicia y el Consejo Superior del Notariado*, Madrid, 1994; cited by A. Gomez-Martinho Faerna, *"La situación y la organización del notariado en los paises miembros de la Union Europea" LA LEY*, n. 3775, (May 9, 1995).

[87] They are "enforceable". See Ch.5.

[88] See Jose-Maria de Prada, *"La forma de los actos jurídicos privados y la seguridad jurídica" Seminario sobre Seguridad Jurídica* (1990); cited in detail in Augusto Gomez-Martinho Faerna, *op. cit.*, p.2.

of the document". The *notario* drafts the document once the parties have declared their intentions and the parties later express their agreement with the document.[89] These documents are drafted according to the principles established in notarial regulations (*Ley del Notariado* and *Reglamento del Notariado*), that is, according to Art.147 of the *Reglamento Notarial*, by listening to each of the parties, giving legal form to the intentions of the parties and informing each of them of the consequences of what is being drafted. In doing all this the *notario* is impartial. Whilst *abogados* advise their clients and protect their interests, notaries, given their dual public and private function, act in the interest of both parties and the Law. Once a document has been drafted, the notary keeps the original which becomes a "Protocol" from which he can issue a copy to the parties if they so request. The *Protocolo Notarial* is secret—Art.274 of the *Reglamento Notarial*—and the possibility of obtaining copies is carefully regulated in order to avoid forgeries, alterations or obliterations and even loss of the document.

The intervention of a *notario* is required by law in a number of transactions: transfer of real estate, constitution of companies, donations between spouses, contracts determining or altering the economic consequences of marriage, mortgages, creation of easements and declaration of heirs (Art.1280 CC).

---

[89] Art.1216 CC, Art.1 of the *Ley del Notariado* and Art.2 of the *Reglamento del Notarial*.

THE LEGAL PROFESSIONS

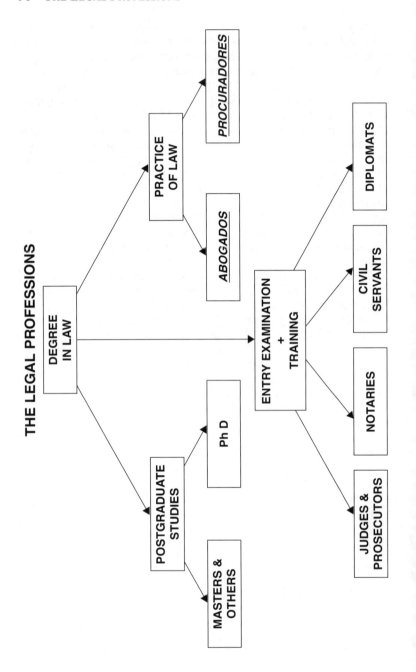

Chapter Five
Civil procedure

1. GENERAL CHARACTERISTICS

INQUISITORIAL AND ADVERSARIAL PROCEEDINGS

There are two models of civil proceedings in legal and comparative history: inquisitorial and adversarial proceedings. In the inquisitorial model the judge controls the proceedings and the parties passively await a decision of the judge. Inquisitorial proceedings are written— as a guarantee of protection for the parties from the great powers of the instructing judge—and secret. They are usually open to review by a different court. Adversarial proceedings, on the other hand, are based on the existence of a duality of parties who stand in a position of "contradiction". These parties are in control of the proceedings from beginning to end and can terminate the proceedings at any point by amicable settlement. The judge is a spectator—though a qualified one—of the activity of the parties. The choice between a procedure based mainly on one or other model depends primarily on the subject-matter of the dispute, although the history of different legal systems has an undoubted influence. In most cases, however, the actual proceedings have elements of both the inquisitorial and adversarial models.

Together with these two models there are two main principles according to which judicial proceedings can be organised: the "dispositive principle" (*principio dispositivo*) and the "principle of officiality" (*principio de oficialidad*). In all proceedings inspired by the "dispositive principle" there are two parties in a position of "contradiction"; these parties have full powers over their substantive and procedural rights. The plaintiff[1] bring proceedings against the other party, the defendant.[2] Both plaintiff and defendant have equal rights of audience and equal opportunities for the protection of their rights; they can present any evidence they think relevant and have the right to end

---

[1] In Spanish the plaintiff is called *actor* or *demandante*.
[2] *Demandado*.

the proceedings because these are only an instrument for the protection of substantive rights that can be disposed of at any time.

In proceedings inspired by the "principle of officiality" the judge is under the obligation to initiate the proceedings, ensuring compliance with all the necessary requirements and carrying the proceedings through to a conclusion. Whilst, in order to implement the "dispositive principle", it is necessary to have a procedure based on the adversarial model, it is not strictly necessary to have an inquisitorial procedure in all proceedings inspired by the "principle of officiality". This is the case in Spanish judicial proceedings, which are inspired by both the "officiality" and "dispositive principle" and which incorporate elements of the inquisitorial and adversarial models.

Spanish civil proceedings are adversarial and mainly based on the "dispositive principle" according to which the partes are in control of the proceedings, however, there are some elements derived from the "principle of officiality". These elements were introduced by the *Ley* 10/1984 whereby the judge had to ensure ex officio that he had jurisdiction[3] and that the right type of proceedings had been started.[4] The LEC of 2000 takes this further by greatly enhancing the powers of the judge.[5] This is a trend that has been observed even in common law jurisdictions[6] but the Spanish new civil procedure goes a step further by authorising the judge to suggest the practice of new evidence if he believes that certain facts have not been proved by the evidence proposed by the parties[7]; and he can decide according to different legal principles than those suggested by the parties[8] with the only limitation that he must respect the petition made by the parties.[9]

Spanish criminal proceedings, while based on the "principle of officiality", incorporate elements of both inquisitorial and adversarial proceedings. In the standard criminal procedure[10] there is an initial stage—*sumario ó fase de instrucción*—which is clearly inquisitorial, written and secret; the judge has wide powers of investigation although this judge is different from the judge giving the judgment.

---

[3] Art.74 LEC 1881 as amended.

[4] Art.694 LEC 1881 as amended.

[5] See, for a good introductory overview to the new law the *Estudio Preliminar* to the *Ley* 1/2000 of January, 7, by F. Cordon Moreno, in the *Ley de Enjuiciamiento Civil*, ed. Aranzadi, (2000) p.14.

[6] Jolowicz, *Adversarial and Inquisitorial Models of Civil procedure*, ICLQ vol.52, April 2003 pp.281–295.

[7] Arts 429(1)(II), 435(2) and 282, LEC.

[8] Art.218(1)(II) LEC 2000.

[9] For a discussion on the relationship between the principles of *iura novit curia* and the dispositive principle see Jolowicz, op. cit. p.292 where he compares the French and the English systems of civil procedure.

[10] The *Juicio por delitos graves*, see below, Ch.6, pp.159–166.

The second stage of the proceedings—*fase de plenario ó juicio oral*—is, however, oral, public and contradictory. In criminal proceedings the subject-matter of the proceedings is beyond the control of the parties. The judge can, and must, start the proceedings *ex officio* once there is enough evidence of the commission of a crime. Even in the second stage, or *juicio oral*, the parties do not have the power to terminate the proceedings[11] because the Public Prosecutor has the obligation to prosecute in all cases prescribed by law.

ORALITY AND WRITTEN PROCEEDINGS

Article 120 of the Spanish Constitution states that "the proceedings will mainly be oral".[12] This general provision is complemented by Art.229(1) LOPJ which contains a similar declaration.[13] For a long time both statements were more a declaration of intention to guide the legislator in future reforms than a fact, because the majority of Spanish proceedings were written with the exception of employment disputes. The reform of the LEC has given a greater emphasis to oral proceedings (*juicio verbal*) and, mostly to the *principio de inmediación*, connected with oral procedures in the sense that the judge is present with the parties during the practice of evidence and statements.[14] What the Constitution seems to indicate is that proceedings should be public, and publicity has historically been connected with orality. Article 24 CE recognises the right to a "public hearing" as a guarantee for the defendant without precluding that some activities may be carried out in secret, if necessary, for the security of one of the parties or society.

2.   SOURCES OF CIVIL PROCEDURE

The main source of civil procedure in Spain is the *Ley de Enjuiciamiento Civil* (LEC) of January 7, 2000.[15] The old *Ley de Enjuiciamiento Civil* of 1881 (as amended) had been criticised by some writers[16] because it was basically constructed around the long

---

[11] See below, Ch.6 p.158.
[12] Art.120 CE: "*El procedimento será predominantemente oral, sobre todo en materia criminal.*"
[13] Art.229(1) LOPJ: "*las actuaciones judiciales serán predominantemente orales, sobre todo en material criminal, sin perjuicio de la documentación*".
[14] See Art.137 LEC 2000, Arts 229(2) LOPJ and 313 of the LEC 1881.
[15] *Ley* 1/2000 of January 7.
[16] See J. Almagro Nosete, *op. cit.*, pp.34 and 35.

and mainly written "common procedure" of Spanish historical law.[17] This law had several reforms, the most important of which were the *Ley* 34/1984 of August 6, by which it was intended to start the transformation of Spanish civil proceedings towards a more modern model, adapted to the changes in circumstances and social demands, and the *Ley* 10/1992 of April 30 *de Medidas Urgentes de Reforma Procesal*, which was mainly directed at better resourcing of the administration of justice and had minor consequences for the regulation of the different civil proceedings. Today the new LEC of 2000 gives a coherent and much needed unitary and modern regulation to what had become the obsolete system of civil procedure.

Together with the LEC, the basic law on civil—and any type—of procedures, is the *Ley Orgánica del Poder Judicial,* LO 6/1985 of July 1 which has important provisions affecting the organisation of the Judiciary and principles of procedure. This has been developed by the *Ley* 38/1988 *de demarcación y planta judicial* and the RD 122/1989 of February 3.

MAIN CHARACTERISTICS AND STRUCTURE OF THE LEY 1/2000 OF CIVIL PROCEDURE

The old law of civil procedure 1881 was based on the dispositive principle, as we said in the first edition of the book, and according to this principle the judge played a passive role, almost like an arbiter to a private dispute, engaged when requested by the parties who were the true motor of the proceedings.

The new law changes the axis of the relationship between the judge and the parties. Civil proceedings under the Civil Procedure Code of 2000 are still based on the dispositive principle since they are designed to protect private, civil rights over which the parties have full powers of disposition and can, at anytime decide to withdraw their petition or settle their claim in or out of court but the judge has become an informed active judge with enhanced powers.[18]

The main principles informing the LEC 2000 can be summarised into two: the dispositive principle and the *principio de inmediacion*.

Structure of the new law

The new law of civil procedure is divided in four major parts that correspond to the common denomination of "Books". These are:

---

[17] See above, Ch.1, p.11.
[18] See above.

- Book 1: General provisions common to all civil proceedings;
- Book 2: Declarative proceedings;
- Book 3: Enforcement and provisional measures;
- Book 4: Special proceedings. These are divided into three types of proceedings each regulated in a different "Title":
  - (a) Title 1: proceedings about civil status and include: general capacity, filiation, proceedings for separation and divorce and adoption.
  - (b) Title II: "Judicial Division of Property" is divided into two Chapters. Chapter one for Division of the Estate in Inheritance proceedings and Chapter two regulates proceedings for the liquidation of the economic matrimonial regime.
  - (c) The last title, among the special proceedings is Title III regulating the new *"procedimiento monitorio"*[19] and the execution of bills of exchange, cheques and promissory notes (*juicio cambiario*).

General provisions

The first part of the law deals with those matters that are common to all civil proceedings such as capacity be to a party to the proceedings, representation, capacity to stand in court; jurisdiction and channels to challenge this; challenges to the capacity of a particular judge[20] to hear a particular case, rules for the counting of time, working days, presentation of documents, costs and other charges.

Foreigners have got the same rights of access to the Spanish courts as Spanish nationals subject to the general criteria of jurisdiction of the courts[21] by a combination of Arts 24 CE,[22] 13(1) and 27 CC.[23]

Articles 23 to 34 of the new LEC regulate the involvement of professionals on the defence and representation of the parties. It is compulsory for all but certain proceedings listed below to engage the professional services of an *abogado* and a *procurador.*[24] The only cases in which the parties can conduct the proceedings themselves without

---

[19] This new procedure will be explained in detail below.

[20] Known as *"recusación"* in Spanish Law.

[21] See above or below (include somewhere) and Arts 4, 9(1), 9(2) and 21 *et seq.* LOPJ.

[22] Art. 24 CE, *principio de tutela jurisdiccional efectiva.*

[23] See also LO 7/1985 of July 1, on rights and duties of foreigners in Spain, declared partially unconstitutional by the Constitutional Court. See STC 115/1987 of July 7 (RTC 1987, 115).

[24] For an explanation on the role of these professionals see Ch.4, *The Legal Professions*, above.

being represented by experts are: in *juicios verbales*[25]—if the claim is under €950; in the initial petition on the new *procedimiento monito-rio* (see below) and in cases requesting urgent provisional measures or challenging decisions on the right to free legal assistance.[26]

Even in the cases just mentioned, where it is possible to dispense with the services on an *abogado, procurador*, or both it is possible for those entitled to free legal assistance to request the services of these professionals. The court hearing the case will suspend the proceedings until a decision is made as to whether free legal assistance has been granted or not.[27] If free legal assistance is not granted the party who requested it has the option of proceeding without it or withdrawing from the proceedings if he is the plaintiff.

Matters excluded from the new law

Three areas of regulation are specifically excluded by the new LEC that defers its regulation to special legislation that is to be passed in the near future.

1. Recognition and enforcement of foreign judgments and other documents

The LEC in Art.523 refers to international Conventions or other documents, and to a new law that is due to be passed in the near future regulating in a coherent way this increasingly important area.[28] For the time being the old regulation of the LEC 1881 is still in force. Judgments of EU countries enjoy the semi-automatic recognition and enforcement awarded by the EC Council Regulation 44/2001.

2. Voluntary jurisdiction

It is envisaged that a new law will regulate this area coherently. In the meantime the regulation of the old LEC applies.[29]

---

[25] See below, *Juicio verbal*.

[26] See Art.23 LEC for a detailed list of those cases in which it is possible to dispense with the services of the *procurador* and Art.31 for those cases in which it is possible to proceed without an *abogado*. Note that there is some overlap in those articles but not exact correspondence.

[27] See Art.32 LEC, Art.6(3) of the *Ley de Asistencia Jurídica Gratuita* and Art.24(3) of the CE.

[28] The LEC gave a period of six months for the remission of the project on this new law to Parliament (D.F.20). Until the entry in force of the new law, foreign decisions are executed in Spain according to the old system of the LEC. See below, *Enforcement of foreign judgements*.

[29] Again, the period of 12 months suggested by the LEC has gone and no project has been approved.

3. Bankruptcy proceedings

A new substantive law on bankruptcy was due to be approved shortly after the LEC 2000 came into force and it was thought it would provide a more coherent regulation of both the substantive and procedural issues. The new law was approved by Parliament on July 22, 2003: *ley 22/2003 Concursal de 9 de Julio*.[30]

3. INTERNATIONAL JURISDICTION OF THE SPANISH COURTS

Jurisdiction is the authority which a court has to decide matters that are litigated before it or to take cognisance of matters presented in a formal way for its decision.[31] From the point of view of anybody considering starting judicial proceedings, the first question which should be asked is: does the court have jurisdiction? When considering the international jurisdiction of the Spanish courts, the question of whether or not the Spanish Courts have jurisdiction to hear a specific matter is the first step in order to determine the appropriate court in which to lodge the case.

In principle each country is free to decide which cases its courts are going to be competent to hear and to decide. This is a matter to be regulated by domestic law. However, even if each country is free to decide virtually any case litigated in its courts, it does not mean that this is the best option in terms of policy because it might by inappropriate to overload the courts with cases which have little or no connection with the country. Different countries have approached the question of international jurisdiction following different policy principles; England, for instance, has a wide scope of international jurisdiction by which the courts of England and Wales are competent to hear and decide virtually any case served on a defendant present in England:

"whoever is served with the King's writ and can be compelled consequently to submit to the decree made is a person over whom the courts have jurisdiction".[32]

Courts in other countries, for instance France, have international jurisdiction in any case involving a French national.[33] The Spanish law

---

[30] The full text of the law can be found at *http://civil.udg.es/normacivil/estatal/contract/L22-03.htm*.

[31] Mozley & Whitley's *Law Dictionary* (10th edn, 1988).

[32] *John Russell & Co Ltd v Cayzer, Irveine and Co Ltd* [1916] 2 A.C. 298 at 302, HL.

[33] Art.14 of the French Civil Code.

on international jurisdiction was substantially changed in 1986 with the establishment of a system based on the Brussels Convention[34] criteria on international jurisdiction.

To some extent it seems only good sense to limit jurisdiction to those cases in which an eventual decision can be executed in the national territory. This is why different countries impose upon themselves certain limits in the exercise of jurisdiction by their own courts. These limits are usually established in two ways, by international bilateral or multinational Conventions and by domestic rules of private international law on jurisdiction. Together with this, it is important to add the exceptions to the jurisdiction of country's courts imposed by public international law in the form of "immunity from jurisdiction" for Heads of State and diplomatic personnel. This exception is specifically made in the LOPJ Art.21(2). This immunity from jurisdiction covers foreign states—*par in parem non habet imperium*—although in public international law there is a distinction between acts of the state as a state and its commercial acts as a private person.[35] The most important treaties concerning the immunity of foreign personnel are the Vienna Convention on Diplomatic Relations 1961, the Vienna Convention on Consular Relations 1963 and the Convention on Special Missions 1969.

The most important multilateral agreements limiting the jurisdiction of the Spanish courts are the Warsaw Convention on International Air Transport 1929, the Geneva Convention on Carriage of Goods by Road 1956, the Convention Relating to the Arrest of Sea-Going Ships of 1952, and the Brussels Convention on Liability for Oil Pollution Damage of 1969. These conventions confer jurisdiction on a certain state to hear and adjudicate certain matters and so deprive all other member states which are signatories to the convention of any jurisdiction.

Spain is also party to a large number of bilateral agreements on jurisdiction, the main object of which are to facilitate the execution of decisions in the two countries which are signatories to the treaties by establishing rules on international jurisdiction.[36]

---

[34] Brussels Convention on Jurisdiction and Enforcement of Judgements in Civil and Commercial Matters 1968. Replaced for all but judgments proceeding from Denmark by the EC Council Regulation 44/2001 of December 22. See below.
[35] See amongst others M. N. Shaw, *International Law* (1991) pp.430–80 for a detailed study on immunities from jurisdiction in public international law.
[36] There are bilateral treaties with France: *Convenio de 289 de mayo de 1969*, with Colombia: *Convenio de 30 de mayo de 1908*; with Italy: *Convenio de 22 de mayo de 1973*; with Germany. *Convenio de 14 de Noviembre de 1983*; with Austria: *Convenio de 17 de febrero de 1984*; with Czechoslovakia: *Convenio de 4 de mayo de 1987*; with Israel: *Convenio de 30 de mayo de 1989*; with Mexico: *Convenio de 17 de abril de 1991*.

However, and without diminishing the importance of any of these conventions, the most important convention in terms of international jurisdiction is the Brussels Convention of September 17, 1968, on International Jurisdiction and Recognition of Decisions in Civil and Commercial Matters (hereinafter Brussels Convention or BC), and the Lugano Convention which is a parallel convention to the Brussels Convention, between EC/EFTA Countries.[37] The Brussels convention has been replaced by the EC Council Regulation 44/2001, herein after the Brussels Regulation (see Art.68 BR).

It is possible to suggest that the world is now divided into two groups of countries as to jurisdictional effects (in the international context): those countries which are party to the Brussels Regulation and/or Lugano Conventions and those which are not. In certain circumstances in civil and commercial cases (Art.1 BR),[38] the Brussels Regulation substitutes the national private international law rules on jurisdiction. These circumstances are, namely when a defendant is domiciled in a state which is a member to the Convention, in certain exclusive jurisdiction areas (Art.22 BR), and in jurisdiction agreements with some connecting factors (Art.23 BR). If these connecting factors are not present or if the country is not a party to the Conventions it is up to the law of any country to decide when and in what circumstances they are going to hear and decide a case.

The LOPJ 1985 sets out in detail, in Arts 21–5, the matters over which the Spanish courts have international jurisdiction. The general rule is that Spanish courts have jurisdiction over persons domiciled in Spain and/or where there is submission to the Spanish courts (Art.22(2) LOPJ). Submission can be express, that is, by agreement to submit any dispute to the Spanish courts, or tacit, by the parties appearing and contesting the case on its merits. Regardless of the above criteria, Spanish courts retain exclusive jurisdiction over matters involving real rights, incorporation, validity and dissolution of companies domiciled in Spanish territory, the validity of entries on public registers, the recognition and execution of foreign judgments and arbitration awards (Art.22(1) LOPJ). In these instances of exclusive jurisdiction, the nationality or domicile of the parties is totally irrelevant; also, because this competence is exclusive, no decision affecting these matters which is given by a foreign court will be enforced in Spain.

Spanish courts also retain jurisdiction over matters such as contracts made in Spain (between Spaniards, between foreigners or between Spaniards and foreigners) or when Spain is the place of performance

---

[37] See Peter North, *Private International Law* (13th edn, 1998) pp.180–1.
[38] See Case 29/76, *LTV v Eurocontrol*: [1976] E.C.R. 1541 and P. North, *op. cit.*, pp.286–8, as to the meaning of civil and commercial matters.

of the contractual obligation; in extra-contractual obligations, when the tort was committed in Spain or both author and victim have their habitual residence in Spain; in succession matters when the deceased had his last domicile in Spain or immovable property in the country (Art.22(3)).[39]

In criminal matters Spanish courts have jurisdiction over all crimes committed within Spanish territory and over specific crimes committed by Spanish citizens abroad. In administrative matters Spanish courts have jurisdiction over claims involving acts performed by the Spanish public administration. In labour matters, the labour courts protect worker's rights and so different rules apply from ordinary civil cases. Jurisdiction is decided on the basis of the place of performance of the contract of employment. If both employer and employee are Spanish and the contract is performed abroad the Spanish court retains jurisdiction.

The Spanish courts will examine their own international jurisdiction *ex officio* and abstain when they are lacking it, especially in cases in which exclusive jurisdiction is given to the courts of another country by virtue of an International Treaty,[40] but also when the criteria of Art.22 LOPJ are not present. Otherwise it is up to the defendant to challenge the international jurisdiction of the Spanish courts; if he does not, he must submit to the court (Art.22(2) LOPJ). If the defendant wants to challenge the jurisdiction of a Spanish Court, he must do so by applying for a stay of the action on the basis of lack of jurisdiction; the procedure is called *declinatoria international*,[41] and it must be done at the time of appearance and before contesting the case on its merits, otherwise the defendant implicitly submits to the jurisdiction of the court.

4.   COURTS OF FIRST INSTANCE IN CIVIL PROCEEDINGS

One it has been decided that the Spanish Courts have jurisdiction to hear and decide the case, it is necessary to determine which court will be the court with jurisdiction over that specific matter. This is

---

[39] See the long list of connecting factors of Art.22(3) LOPJ which can be compared *mutatis mutandis* with the "special jurisdiction" of Arts 5–21 of the Brussels Regulation.

[40] Art.26 Brussels Regulation and Art.19 Lugano Convention.

[41] Similar to the *declinatoria* for lack of territorial competence (see below), and accepted by the Supreme Court in its decisions of STS of July 1, 1897, confirmed by STS of February 22, 1960 and STS of May 30, 1961 as the appropriate procedure for challenging questions of international jurisdiction.

mainly done according to the subject-matter of the dispute (*jurisidic-ción por razón del objeto*) and the claim of the plaintiff.

According to the subject matter of the dispute the case will be decided by one of the four "jurisdictional orders": civil, criminal, administrative or social.[42] The judge is under an obligation to examine his own jurisdiction on the basis of the subject matter of the claim and to refuse jurisdiction if it belongs to a court of a different "order".[43] The parties cannot "give" jurisdiction to judges of a different order.[44] If the judge fails to realise his lack of jurisdiction according to the subject matter, the parties can exercise the "exception of lack of jurisdiction" (Art.39 LEC). Together with this, both parties—or the public prosecutor in cases in which his intervention is prescribed by law—can challenge the jurisdiction by means of a "conflict of jurisdiction" (Art.43 LOPJ), at any time during the proceedings. This is decided by a different judge who will, once he has heard the parties and examined the case, require the judge who is currently hearing the case to abstain if he believes that the case must be decided by different order of courts. If both judges disagree as to whether there is a lack of competence they must refer the matter to the Supreme Court, where a special "Chamber of Conflicts"[45] will determine which type of court shall decide the case (Arts 42–8 LOPJ).

The second problem of jurisdiction regards the choice of higher or lower courts within one "jurisdictional order", that is, which of the civil courts, for instance the *Juzgados de Primera Instancia e Instrucción* or the *Tribunal Superior de Justicia*, has jurisdiction to hear at first instance a particular claim. This is determined by the type of proceedings which are applicable for the resolution of the dispute. In civil matters this will normally depend on the amount of money of the claim although there are some cases in which know-ledge of a specific matter means that the dispute will be allocated to certain courts regardless of the amount of the claim. For instance, a decision concerning the enforcement of arbitration awards falls under the *Jueces de Primera Instancia*,[46] as does the enforcement of foreign decisions once they have obtained the *exequatur*[47] regardless

---

[42] See above Ch.3, p.62
[43] Art.38 LEC.
[44] Art.9(6) LOPJ: "*la jurisdicción por razón del objeto es improrrogable*".
[45] Art.42 LOPJ, *Sala de Conflictos*. This special chamber is composed of the President of the Supreme Court and two judges; one for each *orden* in conflict.
[46] Art.46 *Ley de Arbitraje, Ley* 60/2003 of December 23.
[47] *Exequatur* is the procedure by which a foreign judicial decision is equated to a Spanish decision and so can be enforced by the national courts. This procedure is regulated in Arts 951–6 LEC and the applicable jurisdiction corresponds to that of the Supreme Court.

of the amount of the arbitral award or foreign judgment (Arts 545–547 LEC).

Due to the nature of the case, the Supreme Court has jurisdiction over civil and criminal suits brought against members of Government, members of Parliament and magistrates (Art.56(2) LOPJ). The *Tribunales Superiores de Justicia* have jurisdiction over civil and criminal cases involving members of the autonomous government or parliament (Art.73(2)(a) LOPJ), and the *Audiencia Nacional* over matters of particular national interest such as crimes against the Crown, currency counterfeit and extradition proceedings.

If there is no provision that a case should be heard by a specific court because of the subject-matter, then, the determination of the type of judge who will hear the case at first instance depends on the amount of money of the claim (*la cuantía del litigio*). The relevant amount is what the plaintiff asks for in his petition. This amount will determine two different but connected issues; first, it will determine the type of proceedings (Arts 248–250 LEC): proceedings for larger claims—*juicio ordinario*,[48] or oral proceedings—*juicio verbal*.[49] Secondly, it will determine the type of judge of first instance. In principle the judges of first instance (*Jueces de Primera Instancia*) hear of all proceedings after the modification of the *jucio verbal* by Arts 437–447 LEC. The Code of Civil Procedure (LEC) establishes detailed rules for the calculation of the *cuantía* when this is unclear (Art.251 LEC).

Once the type of judge and the type of proceeding has been determined, it is necessary to choose among courts of equal rank but with jurisdiction over different parts of the national territory. This question is perceived by the legislator as a secondary problem and so freedom is given to the parties to choose a particular forum. Territorial jurisdiction has a dispositive character (it is *prorrogable* in the words of the LEC, Art.54), and thus parties might submit by agreement or by appearance to any court having "objective jurisdiction". Otherwise the Spanish Civil Procedure Act lists a series of criteria applicable to the different types of cases: for example, in suits regarding contractual obligations court of the place of performance of the obligation has jurisdiction; in suits regarding rights over personal or real property the domicile of the defendant is relevant (Arts 52 and 63 LEC). The only exceptions to the principle that the parties have freedom to choose the forum re: in landlord and tenant disputes, when the courts where the property is situated have jurisdiction (Art.121 LAU); in matrimonial proceedings, when it is the court of

---

[48] Art.249 LEC.
[49] Claims under €3,000, Art.250.2 LEC.

the spouses domicile (Disp. Adic. 3, *Ley* of July 20, 1980); in damages arising out of road traffic accidents the courts of the place where the accident happened (Disp. Adic. 1, LO 3/89 of July 29), and in cases concerning patents and trade marks the judge of first instance will be the judge of the *Tribunal Superior de Justicia* the Autonomous Community where the defendant has his domicile (Art.122(2)—Patent law—and Art.40—Trade Marks law).

The last question concerning venue relates to the court having jurisdiction to hear appeals against the decision of the competent court of any other matters relevant to the litigation.[50] This includes questions concerning which court is competent to enforce the decision. All these matters are referred to as "functional competence"—*competencia funcional* (Art.62 LEC).

5.   MAIN CIVIL PROCEEDINGS

PROCEEDINGS FOR PROVISIONAL REMEDIES

Medidas Cautelares, or provisional remedies, are those which provide provisional relief to the plaintiff until the case is fully decided in court. The type of provisional remedies proceedings available is of paramount importance when planning litigation in a foreign country. It would be of little or no help to the owner of a right, if the law acknowledged the existence of that right and was prepared to defend and protect it but, due to the unavoidable length of time that judicial proceedings take, it could not do so until the enjoyment of the right was impossible. Provisional remedies are important because they provide immediate and fast relief to the person whose right is being infringed, without prejudicing the innocence or guilt of the defendant which will be established and if necessary condemned after the plenary procedure has taken place.

For the first time there is a general and unitary regulation of provisional measures. These measures are generic although Art.727 LEC 2000 lists those most used.

All provisional measures must be requested by the plaintiff (Art.721 LEC), the court cannot order provisional measures of its own accord nor can it order measures more burdensome than those requested by the plaintiff. Parties to arbitral proceedings taking place in Spain, or to judicial proceedings taking place abroad can

---

[50]   For instance conflicts of jurisdiction, see above.

also request provisional measures from the Spanish courts (Art.722 *LEC* 2000).

General Characteristics (Art.726)

The court can adopt any measures that will ensure the effective protection of the right to judicial protection. It will always ensure that it adopts the measure that is less burdensome for the defendant provided that the interests of the plaintiff are duly protected.

Traditionally there have been three conditions that it was necessary to satisfy in order to be successful in an application for provisional measures. These conditions are still reflected in Art.728 of the *LEC* 2000: danger due to delays in the proceedings, *periculum in mora, fumus bonis iuris*, or indication of having a good right or a good arguable case on the merits, and the giving of a caution or deposit that can cover the damages caused by imposing the precautionary measure onto the defendant's property.

Specific provisional measures mentioned in Art.727 LEC are:

- attachment (*embargo preventivo*);
- intervention or judicial administration of property in litigation;
- deposit of movables;
- drafting an inventory of property;
- inscription in public registries (*anotacion preventiva de la demanda*);
- other entries in public registries;
- judicial order to stop an activity, service or other conduct;
- intervention and attachment of monies and bank accounts;
- deposit of works deemed in contravention to the laws of intellectual property;
- suspension of company agreements.

The time to request the court to issue a precautionary measure is at the beginning of the proceedings, with the main petition.[51] It is necessary to enclose all documents justifying the need for the court to adopt such measure/s and the concurrence of the requirements of Art.728.[52] The court will, as a general rule, hear the defendant before granting such measures unless the plaintiff can make a sufficient case about the importance of swift action *before* hearing the defendant. The court has five days to notify the defendant of the petition of provisional measures against him and will call a hearing with both parties within a

---

[51] Art.730 LEC 2000.
[52] Art.732 LEC 2000.

period of ten days. The court will then decide within five days whether the measure/s requested is granted. Both parties can appeal the decision of the court of granting—or not granting—the measures.[53]

Precautionary measures can be changed or modified if it is deemed necessary by the court or previously requested by the party affected by it in one or another way. They will be discharged completely once a firm decision has been delivered by the court about the dispute or if the plaintiff abandons the proceedings by *renuncia* or *desistimiento*. The defendant against whom a precautionary measure is ordered can always offer what is called a *"caución sustitutoria"*. This *caución* is deposit of a sufficient amount on the courts opinion to cover an eventual decision against him. The court will look at the circumstances of the case, including what type of measures were requested by the plaintiff and what was the purpose of those before it decides to accept the *caución sustitutoria.*[54]

DECLARATIVE PROCEEDINGS

Ordinary declarative proceedings apply to the resolution of most civil and commercial matters. One of the main achievements of the current law of civil procedure in Spain has been the simplification of declarative proceedings into two: the *"juicio ordinario"* (ordinary proceedings) and the *"juicio verbal"* (oral proceedings).[55] The choice between one or another is determined by the value of the claim or the subject matter of the action.[56]

Irrespective of the amount or value of the claim the *juicio ordinario* will be the procedural channel for all cases referring to:

- protection of the right to honour, privacy, and own image and the protection of other fundamental rights. In these cases the Ministerio Fiscal will always be a party to the proceedings;
- challenges to the validity of agreements adopted by general assemblies or collegiate bodies of companies;
- protection of free competition and trade, intellectual property rights, patents and trade marks. If the claim is only of monetary value the case will be decided by the proceeding appropriate to the amount of the claim;
- cases relating to general conditions in contracts;
- cases relating to landlord or tenant disputes in either urban or rustic land;

---

[53] See Arts 730–738 LEC 2000.
[54] Arts 746 and 747 LEC.
[55] Art.248 LEC.
[56] Arts 249–250 LEC.

- cases originating in the *Ley de Propiedad Horizontal*[57] that are not only a request for the payment of money;
- any case in which the claim is for an amount above €3,000 or where it is impossible to determine the amount of the claim.

The *juicio verbal* will be the procedure used for claims of less than €900 and those cases indicted in Art.250 LEC, which are:

- actions for the payment of the rent in landlord and tenant cases;
- actions requesting repossession of land by the owner at the end of a tenancy, or usufruct;
- actions requesting the possession of property acquired by inheritance;
- the old *interdictos*, which are orders involving the protection of possession of the person who has been disturbed,[58] orders against new constructions or orders requesting the demolition or repair of dangerous buildings or trees[59];
- maintenance orders;
- actions of rectification of incorrect information;
- actions relating to the sale on instalments of movable property;
- actions relating to contracts of leasing that have been registered in the special register of sales by instalment.[60]

Articles 251, 252 and 253 of the LEC give detailed rules for the calculation of the amount of the claim.

Phases of the juicio ordinario

The *juicio ordinario* is modelled in the *juicio de menor cuantía*[61] with important improvements.

La demanda (The claim)
All civil proceedings in Spain start by filing a claim form called *demanda*. This *demanda* can be *declarativa* (declarative) if what is sought from the court is a declaration about the existence, creation, modification or extinction of a legal relationship, or a declaration obliging the defendant to do or not to do something; or the *demanda* can be *ejecutiva* (enforceable) when the request of the plaintiff is for

---

[57] Reference to the *Ley*. See Ch.10, pp.270–272.
[58] See Ch.10, Possession and Ownership, p.261.
[59] Art.250(4), (5), (6) LEC.
[60] *Registro de ventas a plazos.*
[61] See, Merino-Blanco *The Spanish Legal System* (1st edn, Sweet & Maxwell, 1996), p.145.

the enforcement of a declarative judgment or for the seizure and sale of the defendant's assets as a way of compensation for the defendant's unperformed obligation. In this second case the plaintiff must present a *título ejecutivo*[62] together with his *demanda*.

This first document, the *demanda* or writ of complaint, must comply with several requirements both formal and substantive. These requirements are specified in Art.399 LEC. Formally, it must contain a heading consisting of a generic invocation to the judge to whom the complaint is addressed, the full names of the plaintiff and his *procurador* and the name and address—if known—of the defendant, or as much information as possible in order to identify him,[63] an exposition of the facts—*fundamentos de derecho*—and a *petitum* or claim to the courts stating what relief is sought. It is also important to enclose a statement by which it is submitted that the *procurador* has a legally sufficient power of attorney. These documents should be presented in as many copies as there are parties to the trial, they should be drafted in Spanish or in any other of the official languages (Catalan, Euskera, Gallego) and the trial can proceed in any of these languages if none of the parties object to this. If one party objects, all documentation and proceedings must be translated into Spanish. Foreign documents should be translated into Spanish, preferably by a sworn translation as if this is not done the defendant might challenge the accuracy of the translation and delay the proceedings. If some of these requirements are not complied with the defendant can file a dilatory exception for defects in the formalities.

Once the action has been filed any limitation period is interrupted and the presumption of good faith ceases to have effect (for instance in cases concerning possession in good faith). Also the subject matter of the claim becomes *lis pendens* and no other proceedings can be started in a different court involving the same parties and the same cause of action.

Service on the defendant

Once the *demanda* has been filed and the court has accepted jurisdiction, the claim form is served on the defendant. Service is effected either by personal service on the defendant's domicile,[64] by registered mail with acknowledgement of receipt or by publication of *edictos*, by public notice in the *Diario de avisos* and the Official Journal of the

---

[62] See below, enforcement of judicial decisions and *juicio ejecutivo*.
[63] A nickname or alias would be enough if the real name is unknown.
[64] Art.155 LEC.

province (Arts 156–161 LEC). Service on a defendant who is outside the jurisdiction is effected according to the procedure set forth in international treaties on the matter.

The *emplazamiento* is important because it is one of the requirements of the principle of contradiction *audiatur et altera pars* and, if it is not properly observed, can give rise to *recurso de casación*[65] and *recurso de amparo* for violation of Art.24(1) CE.[66]

La contestación a la demanda (The response)

Article 404 LEC gives the defendant 20 days from the day of receipt to answer the *demanda*. At this point the defendant can do three things: not appear, appear and contest the *demanda* or appear and challenge any of the requirements of the proceedings by way of a dilatory exception.

If the defendant does not appear before the court at the relevant time, the court will consider that the *demanda* has been answered and will carry out the proceedings in default of the defendant's presence.[67] All subsequent communication will be made by publication in Court—*notificación en estrados*, with the Court Clerk reading any communication aloud in the presence of two witnesses who will sign the record along with him. The fact that the defendant does not appear does not mean that he admits the plaintiff's claim and so does not result in an automatic judgment. In fact, the defendant can appear at any stage in the proceedings and in certain cases even have these re-opened after judgment has been given.[68]

If the defendant does appear, this does not automatically mean that he submits to the jurisdiction of the court, because he can file a dilatory exception—*excepciones dilatorias*—challenging some or all of the requirements of the process. These exceptions must be filed before the time for the answer has expired.[69] The exceptions are of paramount importance if for instance the defendant challenges the international jurisdiction of the court, because if the exception is not duly filed at the right time, the defendant will be deemed to have submitted according to Art.22 LOPJ. These exceptions can be of two types: procedural and substantive and are *numerus clausus* accorindg to the LEC. The dilatory exceptions are: lack of jurisdiction—*falta de jurisdicción o compe-*

---

[65] See below.
[66] The Constitutional Court understands that the Court may "adopt any measure necessary to guarantee the presence of the defendant" STC of June 3, 1987, extending beyond mere formalities, STC of November 3, 1987.
[67] The defendant is declared *en rebeldía*.
[68] See below, *Recursos*.
[69] Within the first six days of the 20 days given to the defendant to contest the *demanda*.

tencia (Art.533(1) LEC);[70] lack of personal or procedural capacity of the plaintiff—*falta de personalidad del demandante* (Art.533(2) LEC), or lack of representation when this is necessary; defects in the power of attorney of the plaintiff's *procurador* (Art.533(3) LEC); lack of personal or procedural capacity of the defendant—*falta de personalidad del demandado* (Art.533(4) LEC)[71]; *lis alibi pendens* (Art.533(5) LEC); lack of formalities or defects in the *demanda* (Art.533(6) LEC); non-exhaustion of administrative remedies prior to the judicial process (Art.533(7) LEC). To these it is necessary to add the agreement to submit to arbitration according to the *Ley* 60/2003 of December 23 (Art.23) and the *cautio iudicatum solvi* (Art.534 LEC), by which, when the plaintiff is a foreigner and the defendant is Spanish, the defendant can request the deposit of security from the plaintiff to cover eventual costs incurred in litigation and damages; the defendant has to prove that, in the country of origin of the plaintiff, a similar measure is applied to Spanish plaintiffs.[72]

These dilatory exceptions must be raised in the first six days of the period given to the defendant for the response and they interrupt the proceedings[73] until they are resolved. If they are not proposed within this time the defendant can include them in his answer to the *demanda*, in which case they do not suspend the proceedings (Arts 536(2) and 542(1) LEC). Once these exceptions have been formulated they are passed to the plaintiff during the next three days and resolved by incidental proceedings (Art.537 LEC). If the judge accepts one or several of these exceptions and they were raised before the response, the proceedings will be suspended until the defect has been made good. It is possible to appeal against a decision on the existence of one of these exceptions (Art.538(3) LEC). If the exceptions were raised at the same time as the response they will be resolved in the main decision and the appeal will be against this.

The defendant can, of course, appear and contest the case on its merits. The *contestación a la demanda* is the procedural expression of

---

[70] Which can be lack of international jurisdiction, lack of jurisdiction by reasons of the object (conflict between an ordinary or special jurisdiction), by reason of the subject-matter (between criminal and civil jurisdiction), lack of territorial jurisdiction (Art.79 LEC), or lack of functional jurisdiction.

[71] When he lacks the character or representation with which he has been sued.

[72] The Supreme Court has always been very restrictive in the application of the requirement and today the scope of this exception is very limited due to the existence of several bilateral and multilateral treaties on the matter. The most important of these treaties is the Hague Convention of 1905, modified by the Hague Convention of 1954 (ratified by Spain in 1961) which suppresses the requirement of *cautio iucatum solvi* for nationals of all the countries which are signatories to the Convention.

[73] This is only for the *juicio ordinario* (Art.535(1) LEC); for all the others these are included in the response.

the principle of equality of the parties[74] and the constitutional right of defence of Art.24(1) CE. The *contestación a la demanda* is symmetrical to the *demanda* itself (Arts. 399 and 405 LEC 2000)[75] and it must contain all peremptory pleas, dilatory pleas not previously raised and, if applicable, a counterclaim (*demanda de reconvención*). If the defendant in his response not only denies the facts alleged by the plaintiff or their legal effects or both, but he also raises new facts, two things can happen: one those new facts constitute a substantive exception to the plaintiff's claim, or two they are an independent claim—a counterclaim.

If they constitute a counterclaim this will be a new action which will be decided in principle in the same proceedings provided the judge originally in charge of the case is competent (this means competent by reason of the subject matter of the counterclaim as well as that of the original claim). There is no requirement for the counterclaim to have any connection with the original claim although it will usually do so.[76] The counterclaim, once it has been established, has the same effects of *lis alibi pendens* as any other *demanda* and it is not possible for the original plaintiff to start new proceedings based on the facts of the counterclaim.

The last of the possible responses of the defendant is acceptance of the facts and their consequences as expressed in the *demanda*. This is called *allanamiento* and can be done orally or in writing provided it is express. However, it cannot be done in certain types of procedures, for instance it is impossible in proceedings not governed by the dispositive principle, such as proceedings relating to the civil status of natural persons[77] when the rights are not renounceable or when the public interest or the interest of third parties is involved.[78]

Audiencia previa al juicio (Arts 414–430 LEC)

This is very similar to the public audience in the old *juicio de menor cuantía*. Three days after the answer to the claim both parties are summoned to appear in court where the judge will ask the parties if they wish to reach an agreement and end the proceedings at this stage. The parties must be assisted by an *abogado* at this appearance.[79]

---

[74] See above, "Principles of procedure".
[75] "*El demandado formulará la contestación en los términos prevenidos para la demanda*".
[76] The only limit is that the judge must have jurisdiction based on the subject matter.
[77] A resolution of divorce would, for instance, be impossible.
[78] As in criminal proceedings.
[79] Art.414 LEC.

If the parties do not agree and want to continue pursuing the proceedings the judge will hear each of them in turn. This is the time to correct minor defects, rectify errors and request the presentation of evidence.

A marked improvement in respect of the *juicio de menor cuantía* is that there is now a comprehensive regulation of the treatment and resolution of any procedural matters that has been put forward by the parties. These can be: lack of capacity or representation (Art.418 LEC); admission—or not—of accumulation of claims (Art.419 LEC); defects and lack of capacity of one of the parties in cases of plurality of parties (Art.420 LEC); *lis alibi pendens* (Art.421); allegations that the proceedings chosen are wrong according to the type of claim or the amount of the claim (Arts 422 and 423 LEC); defects in the claim (Art.424 LEC); or any other procedural defect (Art.425).

At this stage the parties must also put forward any further arguments that they may have once they have seen the reply by the defendant and also can challenge the authenticity of any documents presented by the opposing party (Arts 426 and 427). If the facts are not controversial and the dispute involves only a legal point the judge must give a decision within 20 working days. If the facts are controversial or disputed the parties must request the presentation and practice of evidence (Art.429 LEC).

Evidence

Evidence is a procedural activity to persuade the judge of the veracity of the facts alleged by the parties. Only disputed facts are subject to evidence—*thema probandi*. Facts admitted by both parties, confessed by any of them, or simply notorious, need not be proved. However it is not only facts that need to be proved because sometimes legal points need to be established by evidence; a good example of this is foreign law,[80] customs[81] and commercial usages.[82]

Evidence must be requested by the parties but the LEC leaves the door open to the judge who can decide that further evidence is necessary.[83]

---

[80] The judge has the obligation to apply the choice of law rules but the person who was to rely on foreign law needs to prove its content. See Art.12(6) CC.

[81] Customs are a source of law according to Art.1 CC but they also need to be proved.

[82] Art.281 LEC for the first time lists the object of evidence, before it was dispersed in several pieces of legislation.

[83] Art.282 LEC, compare with Art.550 LEC 1881.

Means of evidence

Chapters 5 and 6 of the second book of the LEC contain the general rules of evidence applicable to any type of proceedings. Article 299 lists the means of evidence as being: interrogation of the parties by the judge; public documents; private documents; experts' reports; judicial examination; and interrogation of witnesses. To this rather traditional list the law also adds those means for the reproduction of sound or image or electronic or other instruments that allow the recording of data. The list is not closed and the legislator leaves the door open to any other mean of evidence that can be adequate to prove facts relevant to the proceedings. All evidence must be practised in front of the judge.

The burden of proof

The party who alleges a fact or series of facts must prove them. The plaintiff, therefore, has to prove all constitutive facts or facts in which the obligation is based, for example the existence of a contract. The defendant, on the other hand has to prove any mitigating or extenuating circumstances. These can be of two types in Spanish law: *hechos impeditivos*, which make the performance of the obligation impossible, or *hechos extintivos*, which wipe out the obligation altogether.

Weighing up of evidence

Presumptions
Experience teaches that certain consequences usually follow certain acts. Presumptions are established by the legislator and they are generally based on rules of experience although sometimes reflect policy decisions (for example the presumption that an individual under a certain age is not criminally responsible). Legal presumptions can be absolute, not admitting counter-evidence—like the example just seen about minimum criminal age; or relative, called also presumptions *iuris tantum*, which admit counter evidence. A good example of the later is the presumption of good faith in Art.434 of the Civil Code.

El juicio
Once evidence has been accepted the court will fix a date for the hearing that needs to be within a month of the *audiencia previa*.[84] In this hearing (*juicio*) all personal evidence, such as interrogations,

---

[84] Due to the principle of *concentración de actuaciones* of Art.433 LEC.

questioning witnesses, all written and oral reports of experts, will be heard and any examinations from the court will take place.

After the practice of evidence the parties have an opportunity to present their conclusions about disputed facts and advance their legal arguments.

After the hearing the court will make a decision within 20 days.

EL JUICIO ORAL

This is the second type of proceeding regulated by the LEC and it follows the model of the old *juicio oral* of the LEC 1881 but with some important changes. As the name indicates it is a predominantly oral procedure for claims under €3,000 and those claims *ratione materiae* indicated in Art.250 LEC.

The *juicio oral* starts by a short written claim or *demanda sucinta* (Art.437 LEC) that must indicate clearly who the parties are, where they are domiciled and what is the actual and exact petition of the plaintiff. If the claim is for less than €900 the claim form can be filed using the pre-printed forms available in court to this effect.[85] The aim of this pre-printed form is to make access to the court for relatively minor claims easy and as informal as possible.

There are strict limits about accumulation of actions or *reconvencion*[86] in this type of proceedings (Art.438 LEC) and only those facts or rather claims that have a direct relationship with the claim originating the *juicio verbal* are admissible.

The judge will examine its own jurisdiction and within the period of five working days will accept or reject the claim. If the claim is accepted, a copy of the claim form will be sent to the defendant and both parties will be called to a hearing that will take place between 10 and 20 days from the date of notification.

At the hearing the parties will each expand on their respective arguments and any evidence will be practised. The practice of evidence follows the same rules than for the *juicio ordinario*.[87]

The judge will then conclude the hearing and dictate a decision in the period of 10 working days. Certain decisions given in a *juicio oral* do not have the effect of *cosa juzgada* because the LEC has brought some of the summary proceedings of the old LEC 1881 within the

---

[85] Most forms for these proceedings can be obtained on line from *www.mju.es/canalciudano*.

[86] *Reconvención* is the technical Spanish legal term for the counter demand that the defendant can establish.

[87] See above and also *Capítulos* V and VI of *Título* I of *Libro* II of the LEC 2000. Arts 281 *et seq.*

realm of the *juicio oral*. These are proceedings for the protection of the enjoyment of possession and other real rights[88] when the property is not registered and in which the means of evidence of the parties are limited. If the parties wish a final decision on any of those situations or rights they can choose to go to the channel of the *juicio ordinario*.

PROCEDIMIENTO MONITORIO

This new procedure has been introduced by the LEC 2000 and a special procedure for the enforcement of monetary obligations that must be certain, documented and due and under €30,000. This procedure substitutes the old *juicio ejecutivo* of the LEC 1881.

The aim of the *procedimiento monitorio* is that a quick channel for the enforcement of those well documented obligations, to which there is or should be no defence to payment, should be provided.

The party initiating the proceedings must hold one of the documents listed in Art.812 LEC 2000:

- a document signed by the debtor acknowledging the existence of a monetary debt of a liquidated amount, a bill, invoice or other document commonly used that evidences the existence of that debt;
- a document proving a debt in the contributions towards a community of owners under the new law of horizontal property.

In this new type of summary proceedings the party seeking payment does not need to be represented by an *abogado* or *procurador* (Art.814(2)) and only needs to fill in a special pre-printed form[89] and present this form together with one of the documents listed in Art.812 to the Court of First Instance of the domicile of the debtor.[90]

The debtor has 20 days to either pay or oppose the demand for payment.[91] If the debtor does not appear to pay or challenge the demand the court will direct enforcement that will take place according to the general procedure for the enforcement of judicial decisions.

If the debtor opposes the requirement of payment he must do this in writing, and, depending on the amount of money that is being discussed, the intervention of *abogado* and *procurador* signing this oppos-

---

[88] These are some of the old *interdictos* or special procedures for the protection of possession (irrespective of ownership). See Ch.10, "Property", p.261.
[89] This and other forms can be obtained at *www.justicia.es*, under the section "Canal Ciudadano".
[90] Art.813 LEC.
[91] Art.815 LEC.

ition may be necessary (Art.818). If the amount in dispute is within the limits of the *juicio verbal* the judge will resolve this immediately. If the amount is over that the judge will pass on the opposition to the plaintiff who will have to start the corresponding civil proceedings.

JUICIO CAMBIARIO

This special procedure can only take place for the enforcement of bills of exchange, cheques and promissory notes according to the provisions of the *Ley Cambiaria y del Cheque*.[92] It has substituted the old *juicio ejecutivo* that included these mercantile instruments.

The court with jurisdiction is the court of first instance of the domicile of the defendant. The plaintiff will start the proceedings by presenting a short written request together with the bill of exchange or cheque. The court will look at documents and if they are found to be in order will: request payment from the debtor in the next 10 days; proceed to freeze and/or charge enough of the debtor's assets to satisfy the amount due plus interests, court costs and other expenses in case the debtor refuses to pay.

The debtor will have to pay, and if he does so will also have to pay court costs so far,[93] or oppose the request based in one of the reasons listed in Art.67 of the LCCH.[94] If neither of these two things is done the court will, after the period of 10 days, order enforcement. If the debtor opposes the court will conduct a hearing according to the same procedure as for the *juicio verbal* (Art.443 LEC) and give a decision.

Court decisions in these proceedings have full effect of *res iuducata* (Art.827) in respect of all points that were decided, for example, existence of the debt and identity of debtor.

6. RECURSOS (APPEALS)

The system of *recursos* has been another of the areas that has been substantially modified by the new civil procedure law. There are now six different *recursos* in Spanish civil procedure: *recurso de reposición, recurso de apelación, recurso extraordinario for infracción procesal, recurso de casación, recurso en interés de la ley* and *recurso de queja*.

The main novelties in this new scheme of *recursos* lie in the disappearance of the *recurso de súplica* that is now included within the

---

[92] *Ley Cambiaria y del Cheque, Ley* 19/1985, of July 16, modified by the Disp. Final 10 of the LEC 2000.
[93] Art.822 LEC.
[94] Art.67 lists the personal defences to payment accepted by the *Ley Cambiaria*.

recurso de reposición, the creation of the new *recurso en interés de la ley* and a *recurso extraordinario por infracción procesal* that excludes challenges to the application of procedural laws from the domain of the *recursos de casación*. We will see all of these in order.

RECURSO DE REPOSICIÓN[95]

This is an ordinary appeal against decisions of the court that is decided by the same court that gave the decision under appeal. The *recurso* seeks the revocation of an interlocutory decision and its substitution by a new one.

RECURSO DE APELACIÓN (CHART OF SYSTEM OF APPEALS)

This is an ordinary appeal against any definitive decision. The court *ad quem* examines the decision of the court *ad quo* as to its substance and formalities. The new regulation includes a new system of preparation of the appeal[96] that must be lodged with the court *ad quo*—the court that gave the decision that is being challenged—in the period of five days. The court examines whether the conditions for the appeal are met and if so will give notice to the plaintiff of a period of 20 days in which to appeal. If the court thinks that the conditions are not met it will communicate this to the appellant. The only avenue then open to the appellant is to appeal this *auto*[97] by filing a *recurso de queja*.

The plaintiff will present the appeal proper to the court together with any documents deemed necessary. The court will pass all the documents and the appeal to those who can oppose the appeal or contest it on its merits. The court that gave the original decision which now subject to the appeal—the court *ad quo*—will the pass all documents, including the original decision to the court *ad quem*. This court is:

- the *Juzgado de Primera Instancia*, for appeals against decisions of the *Juzgados de Paz*;
- the *Audiencia Provincial*, for appeals against decisions of the *Juzgados de Primera Instancia*.

The court hearing the appeal will request all evidence and call a hearing if there are new documents or evidence has been proposed by the parties. A decision will be made within the 10 days from the date of the hearing.

---

[95] Arts 451 and 454 LEC.
[96] Art.457 LEC.
[97] The court's decision will be in the form of an *auto*.

CHART OF CIVIL COURTS

```
                    ┌─────────────────────┐
              ┌────►│     TRIBUNAL         │
              │     │     SUPREMO          │
              │     └─────────────────────┘
              │                ▲
              │     ┌─────────────────────┐
              │     │ TRIBUNAL SUPERIOR    │
              │     │   DE JUSTICIA        │
              │     └─────────────────────┘
              │                ▲
              │     ┌─────────────────────┐
              └─────┤     AUDIENCIA        │
                    │     PROVINCIAL       │
                    └─────────────────────┘
                               ▲
                    ┌─────────────────────┐
                    │     JUZGADO          │
                    │   DE 1a. INSTANCIA   │
                    └─────────────────────┘
                               ▲
                    ┌─────────────────────┐
                    │     JUZGADO          │
                    │     DE PAZ           │
                    └─────────────────────┘
```

Note: The arrows indicate the system of appeal to higher courts.

This decision given by a court in the second instance (appeal) can only be challenged by a *recurso de casación* or *recurso extraordinario por infracción procesal*.

RECURSO EXTRAORDINARIO POR INFRACCIÓN PROCESAL (ARTS 468–476 LEC 2000)

This is an extraordinary *recurso* against decisions on appeal of the *Audiencia Provincial*. The competent court to hear this *recurso* is the *Sala Civil* of the *Tribunal Superior de Justicia*.

This is a new *recurso* created by the LEC 2000 that extracts the breaches of procedural law from the scope of the *recurso de casación* where they were usually resolved.

The grounds for this appeal are listed in Art.469 LEC:

- breach of the rules of objective or functional jurisdiction[98];
- breach of the procedural rules on reaching a the decision by the court[99];
- breach of the procedural rules at some stage in the proceedings when this breach could have produced a situation whereby one of the parties could not defend his position[1];
- when the rights of Art.24 of the Constitution have not been respected by the civil court.[2]

The party who wants to make an appeal on one of these grounds must present a preparatory written statement to the court that gave the decision within five working days since the date when the decision was notified to him. If all the formal and substantive requirements for the appeal are met, the court will accept it and the party who started the appeal must then prepare an *escrito de interposición* in which he will indicate if he wishes any further evidence to be practised. The court will then send all relevant materials to the *Tribunal Superior de Justicia*.

The *Tribunal Superior de Justicia* will pass the case onto the *Magistrado Ponente*[3] who will decide whether or not to proceed depending on his appreciation as to whether the conditions set by Arts 468 and 469 are met. These conditions are set to avoid unnecessary appeals by requesting that if the breach could be remedied by the court which committed it, the party must request this to the court first.

If the *recurso* is admitted both parties will be called to a hearing. Any evidence will take place according to the rules for the practice of evidence in the *juicio verbal*.

The court will make a decision in the 20 days following the hearing. If the decision appreciates that there was lack of jurisdiction by reason of the subject matter, or lack of functional jurisdiction, it will discount the decision made under those circumstances and notify the parties of their right to start proceedings again in the competent

---

[98] For objective and functional jurisdiction see above.

[99] For example because the period of time that one of the parties has to present documents was not observed.

[1] One of the parties was not granted right of audience, or evidence crucial to his case was wrongly rejected.

[2] Art.24 of the Constitution: *derecho a la tutela judicial efectiva*. Note that this is also a fundamental right and allows the parties to resort to the protection of the Constitutional Court under the procedure of the *recurso de amparo* once all ordinary appeals have been exhausted. See Ch.8, pp.202–3.

[3] This is the judge in charge of writing the report and checking that all requirements are present. It is also the judge who will lead the case in the court.

court. For any of the other grounds the court will declare the decision void and return the parties to the position they were into at the time when the infraction took place.

Against the decision of the *Sala de lo Civil* of the *Tribunal Superior de Justicia* the only possible appeal is the *recurso en interes de la ley* in front of the Supreme Court.

RECURSO DE CASACIÓN

The *recurso de casación* has also been modified by the LEC 2000. First, all infractions of procedural rules are now processed through the *recurso extraordinario por infracción procesal* just seen; but second and more important there is now the possibility of appeals against the decisions of the *Audiencia Provincial* when the matter under appeal has an "*interés casacional*".[4]

The remote origins of the *recurso de casación* can be found in the *querella nulitatis* of Roman law. Closer origins can be found in French Law in the *Conseils des Parties of the Ancien Regime* and the *Tribunal de Cassation* created by the French Revolution.[5] This *recurso* is a jurisdictional appeal although in its origins had a political meaning. Today it is partly an instrument of enforcement of the law amongst the judges.[6] The *recurso de casación* is not a new hearing. It is not possible at this stage to introduce new facts or to discuss factual problems already raised. The Supreme Court will only examine the regularity in the application of the law.[7]

The *recurso de casación* is still an extraordinary appeal because it is only possible in those cases fixed by Art.477 LEC 2000. The only decisions susceptible to *casación* are decisions dictated in second instance by the *Audiencias Provinciales* in the cases of jurisdictional protection of fundamental rights, except the rights recognised by Art.24 of the Constitution[8]; or in cases when the matter is over €150,000 or when the resolution has "*casational*" interest". A decision or resolution has got this special interest if the decision goes against the doctrine of the Supreme Court on this matter, or resolves matters over which there are

---

[4]   Art.477(3) LEC 2000. We will look at what this means in detail below.

[5]   See Ramos Mendez, *op. cit.* p.759.

[6]   See Ch.2, "Sources of Law", "*Jurisprudencia*", pp.45–47 about the role of judges creating law and the control of legality in the application of the law made by the judges themselves through the system of appeals.

[7]   Art.477 stresses this by stating that, "*El recurso de casación habra de fundarse como motivo unico, en la infracción de normas aplicables para resolver las cuestiones objeto del proceso*".

[8]   Art.477(2)(1). This is because the rights recognised by Art.24 are the object of the new *recurso por infracción de ley procesal*.

contradictory decisions[9] of the *Audiencias Provinciales*; or applies rules that have only been in force for a maximum of five years and in respect of which there is not previous *"jurisprudencia"* or doctrine of the Supreme Court in respect of similar rules.

The *Tribunales Superiores de Justicia* can also resolve *recursos de casación* when the decisions present this special interest because it goes against previous doctrine of the *Tribunal Superior de Justicia* of that particular autonomous community or because there is no previous doctrine in this point. The *Tribunal Superior de Justicia* can only decide if the infraction is of *foral* or special law of the Autonomous Community and if the *Estatuto de Autonomia* for that particular community has specifically stated that its *Tribunal Superior de Justicia* will have this particular role.

Following the new procedure established by the LEC 2000 for this *recurso* the appeal has to be "prepared" in the court that gave the decision that is going to be challenged and this needs to be done within five working days following the day of notification of the decision. It is necessary to state the right that the appellant believes has been violated, the rule of law that has been misapplied or the previous court decisions of the Supreme Court that have not been followed.

Effects

The effects of *casación* are only applicable to the decision that has been the subject matter of the appeal. The court will quash or confirm totally or partially the decision. If the *casación* was based on Art.477(2)(3) the court will quash the decision challenged and decide the case on the merits. The new decision will not have any effects over legal situations already created by previous decisions, other than the decision being challenged.

RECURSO EN INTERES DE LA LEY

This is an extraordinary appeal against the decisions of the *Tribunales Superiores de Justicia* in cases of *recursos extraordinarios por infracción de ley procesal* when the different Chambers of the TSJs have different criteria.

If a decision is the object of a *recurso de amparo*[10] it is excluded from this appeal.

---

[9] The law uses the word *"jurisprudencia"*. See Ch.2, "Sources of law".
[10] This will be for cases in which Art.24 of the Constitution—*derecho a la tutela judicial efectiva*—is said to had been violated. For an explanation on the *recurso de amparo* see Ch.8, pp.202–3.

The appeal can only be brought up by the *Ministerio Fiscal*, the *Defensor del Pueblo*, or those public law entities that by reason of their role have an interest on the unity and homogeneity of the *doctrina jurisprudencial* in procedural matters. It is, therefore, not an appeal open to the parties directly.

The *recurso en interés de ley* can be started up to a year after the decision object of the challenge was given. The competent court is the Civil Chamber of the Supreme Court. The legislator has been careful in avoiding confrontation or overlap between the *Tribunal Supremo* and the *Tribunal Constitucional* and has requested that a certification is presented in order to open this *recurso* stating that the decision is not the subject matter of any *recurso de amparo* in the Constitutional Court and that the period of time for starting a *recurso de amparo* has lapsed.

The consequences of this regulation for the system of sources are important. We saw in Ch.2 that in civil law systems court decisions are not sources of law in theory, although in practice the "*doctrina*" of the Supreme Court has always been of extreme importance and contradiction with this was one of the old grounds of *casación*. The new system of appeals reinforces the view that the decisions of the higher courts have more value than just symbolic authority in the system of sources. Article 493 goes as far as saying that the decision of the court will be published in the BOE and will complement the legal system, binding all judges and courts in the civil system. With due respect there are two contradictory words within the Article: "*complementará*" (will be complementary)[11] and "*vinculará*" (will be binding).

RECURSO DE QUEJA (ARTS 494–508)

This is a *recurso* against the decisions refusing admission of the *recursos de apelación, extraordinario por infracción procesal* or *casación*.

7.   ENFORCEMENT OF JUDGMENTS AND OTHER DOCUMENTS

A judgment must be definitive in order to enforceable. A judgment is definitive when the time for lodging an appeal has lapsed or when they are just not grounds for appeal. In some cases, however, the court

---

[11] This word, we said in Ch.2, with reference to the sources of law, was chosen because it is said that the system of sources is complete and court decisions or rather the doctrine of the Supreme Court can only complement an already complete system.

will enforce decisions that are not definitive. This is called *ejecución provisional* and must meet strict criteria established by the LEC[12] to ensure that no irreversible damage is inflicted.

Despite the heading not only judgments can or are enforced by the courts: arbitral decisions (*laudos arbitrales*) and certain public documents can also be enforced according to Art.517.

ENFORCEMENT OF JUDGMENTS

The enforcement of judicial and extrajudicial decisions has received for the first time in Spanish Civil procedure a unitary regulation. The jurisdiction to enforce judicial or extrajudicial decisions is determined by Art.545 of the LEC, which distinguishes between the former and the latter in terms of competent court. For judicial decisions the court that gave the decision is the court with jurisdiction to enforce the judgement (Art.545(1)). In the case or arbitral awards, enforcement corresponds to the court of first instance of the place where the award was given (Art.545(2)). For all other documents and decisions the law makes a remission to the general forums of Arts 50 and 51 LEC: for individuals, the court of the domicile of the defendant and for companies the place of their domicile or the place of the domicile of the directors.

All proceedings for the enforcement of civil decisions—judicial or extrajudicial—are stared by a request by the party in the form of a *demanda ejecutiva* or claim for enforcement (Art.549(1) LEC) due to the *principio dispositivo*. The person who wishes to enforce a judicial decision has five years from the date when the decision became firm. After five years decisions are no longer enforceable.[13] The LEC itself clearly establishes the form of this *demanda* or claim and the documents that must be presented with it when requesting enforcement (Arts 549 and 550 LEC). The parties must be represented by *abogado* and *procurador* (Art.539).

The enforcement of civil decisions is often patrimonial and the object against which enforcement is directed is the property of the debtor (Art.1911 SCC).[14] The first step to enforcement is to establish what property exactly belongs to the debtor and what property does not. If the property or right can be registered the court will follow the indication of ownership of the registry, otherwise and in the absence of documents of title it will take into account a simple appearance of

---

[12] Art.524 *et seq.*, "*De la ejecucion provisional . . .*"
[13] This time limit is a *plazo de caducidad* and it is different from the general rule of the Civil Code that allows 15 years. See Art.515 LEC and 1915 SCC.
[14] See Cordon Moreno, op. cit., p.31.

ownership (Art.593 LEC) that can, of course, be contested by a third party if there is a reason to do so.[15]

Judgments ordering the debtor to pay a certain amount of money are the simplest to enforce. The court will charge the goods of the debtor and proceed to a judicial auction of those to raise the required money. Orders for specific performance are enforced by fixing a period for performance and awarding damages to the plaintiff if performance does not take place. Those damages are aimed at enabling the plaintiff to request a similar performance by a third party if the obligation of the debtor is not of a personal type[16] or to receive damages for the loss that the breach of the defendant's obligation has caused him.

Resolutions on matrimonial proceedings are entered into the Civil Registry and the judge will adopt whatever measures are necessary in order to guarantee compliance with the conditions agreed during the proceedings[17] (Arts 90 and 91 CC).

There is in the LEC 2000 a more exhaustive regulation of the position of the third parties in the enforcement of judgements. These third parties may be involved because of a rule imposing joint liability like in the case of heirs (Art.540 LEC) who in Spanish law fulfil the debts of the testator with their own property,[18] or in the case of the "*sociedad de gananciales*"[19] where the property that integrates the common fund must be used to fulfil the debts of any of the parties (Art.541 LEC). Article 583 LEC leaves the door open for any other party whose property has been affected by the enforcement to express their views and/or challenge the enforcement.

ENFORCEMENT OF FOREIGN JUDGMENTS

Before starting proceedings for the enforcement of a foreign judgment in any country, and therefore in Spain, there are some practical considerations which need to be taken into account. The first of these is to ensure that the defendant, against whom judgment is going to be enforced, has assets in Spain. There is little point otherwise in going through the whole procedure of enforcement. Ascertaining the

---

[15] The third party must start what is called a "*terceria de dominio*", because if it does not challenge the court's decision to direct the enforcement against his own property it may lose if it is sold in public auction.

[16] See below, Ch.9, "Obligations", p.233.

[17] These may have to do with visits to children, payment of maintenance, rights of grandparents to visit, see Ch.11, "Family Law", 301–6.

[18] Unless they accept the inheritance "*a beneficio de inventario*" see Ch.12, "Succession", p.317.

[19] See Ch.11, pp.298–9 for an explanation of this matrimonial regime and its consequences.

existence of the defendant's assets is however, a difficult matter. The plaintiff can search in the Land Registry of the place where he believes the defendant's property is situated or otherwise seek enforcement at the place of business of the defendant if this is known.

Being a foreign party to the proceedings, as will be the case if, for instance, an English plaintiff wishes to enforce an English judgment against a defendant in Spain, is also expensive and time-consuming and the overall cost implications must be weighed in relation to the value of the judgment and the possibilities of enforcement.

The main costs and difficulties are in relation to preventing the disposal of the defendant's assets before enforcement is granted,[20] obtaining of a power of attorney to conduct litigation in Spain and employing a local lawyer and *procurador* who will, almost undoubtedly, ask for advance payment of their fees and other expenses.

It might be worth considering before the beginning of an action whether it is more convenient to sue directly in Spain and then seek enforcement of the Spanish judgment or to start the action in England and seek enforcement of the later judgment at a later date. Although the enforcement of English judgments in Spain has been considerably simplified since the implementation of the Brussels Convention,[21] the experienced international lawyer will always weigh up both possibilities.

Methods of enforcement of foreign judgments in Spain[22]

Before a foreign judgment can be enforced in Spain it needs to be authorised. Once this is done enforcement will proceed in the ordinary ways common to local and foreign judgments. The regulation of the enforcement of foreign judgments can be found in Arts 951 to 958 of the LEC which differentiate between three different systems.

Conventional system

The first of these systems is the conventional system which applies when there is an international convention with the country of origin of the judgment.[23] In the past most of these treaties were bilateral and established the requirements for the execution of judgments from each

---

[20] Which can be done by an *embargo preventivo*. See above.
[21] See below.
[22] A new law for the regulation of the enforcement of foreign judgments needs to be passed quickly to the LEC 2000. Until then the burdensome system of the old LEC 1881 remains applicable.
[23] Such treaties exist with Colombia, *Convenio* of December 26, 1908; Czechoslovakia, November 21, 1927; Switzerland, November 19, 1896; France, May 28, 1969; Italy, May 22, 1973; Austria, February 17, 1984; Germany, November 14, 1983.

signatory country to the other. Today the most important conventions on enforcement of foreign judgments are the Brussels Regulation and Lugano Convention, which articulate a simplified system of enforcement which relies heavily on jurisdictional criteria concerning which country has jurisdiction in the first place to decide the case. If these criteria of international jurisdiction are respected, the enforcement of judgments in other states which are members of the convention is almost automatic.

The Brussels and Lugano Conventions apply only to civil and commercial matters and specifically exclude questions of status or legal capacity of natural persons, rights in property arising out of a matrimonial relationship, wills and succession, bankruptcy, social security and arbitration.[24]

The actual procedure for the enforcement of judgments as implemented in Spain by Instrument 2362 (BOE January 28, 1991), states that the court with jurisdiction for the enforcement of foreign judgments in Spain is the *tribunal de primera instancia* of the place where the defendant is domiciled (Art.32 Brussels Regulations and Art.10 of Instrument 2362). If the defendant is not domiciled in the member state where enforcement is sought, jurisdiction of the relevant court shall be determined by reference to the court of the place where judgment is to be enforced (for instance where the defendant has assets or real property).

The plaintiff must make an application to the court accompanied by the following documentation (Arts 46 and 47 of Instrument 2362): an authentic copy of the foreign judgment (Art.53 BR)—if judgment was given in default he must also present a copy of the documentation evidencing proof of service of the writ on the defendant—and proof that the judgment is enforceable in the country of origin and that notice of the judgment has been served; if the applicant for enforcement qualifies for legal aid in his country of origin he must present documentation to this effect and he will be automatically entitled to legal aid in Spain (Art.44 of Instrument 2362 and Art.50 BR). The plaintiff must also provide the court with an address for service and, when possible, with an address for service on the defendant. As a general requirement for any foreign party to proceedings in Spain the applicant must have executed a power of attorney in favour of a Spanish lawyer and *procurador* empowering these persons to act for him. All these documents must be translated into Spanish by a legal translator or a similar authorised person in the country of origin, if requested by the court (Art.48 of Instrument 2362).

Once these documents have been presented, the judge cannot

---

[24] See Art.1 BC. Also see Cheshire and North, *op. cit.*, pp.288–9.

examine substantive issues, nor are the parties allowed to intervene or make any representations. A decision must be given by the judge in "a short period of time" (Art.34 of Instrument 2362). Recognition, according to the Regulation, can only be refused on the grounds of Art.43 BR, when such enforcement is contrary to the rules of *ordre public*, when judgment has been given in default and service has not been properly effected on the defendant, or when the judgment conflicts with another judgment previously given by the Spanish Courts in an action between the same parties. Recognition can also be refused in cases concerning the status of natural persons, rights in property arising out of matrimonial relationships, wills or succession, in cases in which the court of the state of origin has decided a preliminary question which conflicts with a rule of the private international law of the state in which recognition is sought, unless, however, the same result would have been reached by the application of the rules of private international rules of that state.[25]

Article 28 provides defences for enforcement in two situations, both when the judgment was given without observing the jurisdictional provisions of s.3 of the Regulation (insurance matters, consumer contract or exclusive jurisdiction) because jurisdiction in these matters is to a large extent mandatory,[26] and when the case is provided for under Art.69. Article 69 refers to the situation in which a contracting state has entered into an agreement with a non-contracting state as to the non-recognition of foreign judgments given in other contracting states against defendants of that non-contracting state.[27]

The judge is under a duty to examine whether any of these defences applies in so far as this appears from the judgment or is known to the court.[28]

If enforcement of the foreign judgment is authorised, the defendant can appeal to the *Audiencia Provincial* on the following grounds: first, that the rules of Title III of the Regulation do not apply; secondly, that the judgment was not enforceable in the country in which it was given; and thirdly, that one of the defences acceptable under the Regulation apply. This must be done within the period of one month

---

[25] Even if the question of status of natural persons is outside the scope of the conventions, a judgment will not be excluded if such matters arise as an incidental issue; for instance, in cases of maintenance orders it would be necessary to determine whether the parties were married. Maintenance judgments are enforceable under the Convention but the state in whose courts the order has to be enforced will not do so if, according to its own private international law rules, the parties were never married in the first case.

[26] See P. North, *op. cit.*, pp.306–13 and p.433.

[27] It will refer to cases provided for in the conventions with non-contracting states.

[28] Cheshire and North, *op. cit.*, p.421.

from when the notification of enforcement was given. The only appeal against the decision of the *Audiencia Provincial* is the *recurso de casación* to the Supreme Court.[29]

System of reciprocity

If there is no treaty between Spain and the country of origin of the judgment, the foreign judgment will have the same effect that Spanish judgments have in that country (Art.952 LEC). The person seeking enforcement must prove this.

Suppletory regime—exequatur

If there is no treaty or a system of reciprocity has not been established by the plaintiff the foreign decision needs to be recognised[30] before enforcement is possible. This control or authorisation is known as *exequatur* and the Supreme Court has jurisdiction for this procedure. The following requirements need to be complied with (Art.954 LEC). First, the foreign judgment must have been given in a personal action; secondly, the foreign judgment must not have been given in default;[31] thirdly, the underlying obligation in the foreign proceedings must be lawful in Spain; and fourthly the foreign judgment must meet all the requirements for validity in the country where it was given, as well as being duly certified according to the requirements for foreign documents in Spain.

The procedure for *exequatur* is complex, expensive and time-consuming. The party initiating the proceedings must submit a translation of the foreign judgment and file all the necessary documents together with a *demanda* to the Supreme Court. The court will then examine the requirements. If it thinks these are met it will start the proceedings according to the procedure for *juicios ordinario*.[32] The burden of proving any alleged fact lies on the plaintiff. The defendant can appear and contest the proceedings. If the Court thinks that all the conditions of Art.954 are satisfied, the foreign judgment will be recognised and then it is possible to enforce it in Spain. Enforcement rests with the Courts of First Instance.

Since *exequatur proceedings* can take one and a half years to complete, the plaintiff would, in most cases, seek an *embargo preventivo*

---

[29] See above for the grounds of *casación*.

[30] *Homologada.*

[31] STS of April 15, 1986, relaxes this requirement by demanding proper service on the defendant. If proper service has been effected the judgment can be recognised.

[32] See above.

according to the provisions of Art.1400 LEC—similar to a Mareva injunction—with the purpose of preventing the defendant from disposing of his assets outside the jurisdiction before the judgment is enforced.

8. JUDICIAL COSTS

Litigating is expensive. It causes expense to the parties who must pay for all those involved on their side and to the State which must organise the administration of justice. It is not surprising that many disputes do not reach the courts because the cost of starting and pursuing the proceedings would be higher than the eventual compensation if the case were to be won.

The costs of litigating are varied. Some of them, including costs for legal advice, certifications and documents, occur before the actual proceedings start. Other expenses arise once the proceedings have started and because of the proceedings. These are known as judicial costs in *stricto sensu*. Although the *Ley* 25/1986 of December 24, abolished the fee payable to the court—*tasas judiciales*—these have been reintroduced on April 1, 2003, for civil and administrative litigation.[33] Individuals and small businesses are excluded from payment as well as any non-commercial organisation.[34] There is also a general exemption for cases about civil status of individuals, family or succession and in the case of administrative procedings any case that involves the protection of fundamental rights, or the challenge of general rules of the administration.

In all other cases the *tasa* is due and proof of payment is necessary in order to begin proceedings. The amount of this *tasa* varies depending on the type of procedure that is being initiated and on the value of the claim. The first amount of the tax is integrated by a fixed amount that varies depending on the length and complexity of the procedure chosen and therefore of the cost that the Administration of Justice incurs. As an example the *juicio verbal* has a fixed fee of €80, the *juicio ordinario* €150, appeals are charged at €300 and *recursos of casación* and *infracción procesal* at €600. This is a small cost compared to the real cost of these proceedings.[35]

---

[33] Arts 35 and 36 of the *Ley* 53/2002, of December 30 *de Medidas Fiscales, Adminsitrativas y del Orden Social* (BOE December 31, 2002).
[34] *Ley* 49/2002 of December 23 *de entidades sin fines lucrativos y de mecenazgo*.
[35] "Modelo 696" is the form to fill in with indication of chargeable tracts, type and fixed amount. See *www.mju.es.*

Together with this we need to take into account the fee payable to the *procurador* and the fees of the *abogado*.[36] The fees of experts employed during the litigation and expenses payable to witnesses will also add to the legal bill. As a general rule each party pays its own costs (Art.241 LEC) as they become due. This must not be confused with the *condena en costas* regulated later in Arts 394–398. The *Ley* 1/2000 follows the tradition of imposing the payments of all costs at the time of the decision to the party whose claim has been rejected. This is know as *criterio de vencimiento objetivo* and applies with certain limits such as the finding of bad faith in the winner by the court, or cases where the *Ministerio Fiscal* sees its claim rejected. There is a limit as to how much the party who has lost has to pay, particularly as to the charges of lawyers and other professionals not subject to a fixed fee. The costs can never exceed one third of the whole amount of the claim (Art.394(3)).

9.   LEGAL AID

The financial burden of judicial—or arbitral—proceedings could amount to an effective lack of access to the administration of justice if there were no provisions for those with limited economic means to have access to free or reduced cost legal services. Article 119(f) the Constitution proclaimed that "justice shall be free on those terms specified by law"[37] and several laws have been passed since then to regulate and specify the cases when access to the courts will be free. In Spain this is known as *beneficio de justicia gratuita*.

Those who can prove limited means will be exempt from any payment to the court or to witnesses, experts and others and will be entitled to the free services of an *abogado* and *procurador*. It is understood that those whose whole maximum family income is less than twice the amount of the minimum monthly wage are entitled to exemption[38]; this amount can be increased to four times the minimum wage if the applicant has got dependants, ill relatives or particularly

---

[36] That is negotiable between the *abogado* and his client, although the CGAE publishes a list of recommended charges. See the CGAE website. The fees are usually higher that those indicated the CGAE and the respective *Colegio de Abogados*.

[37] "*La justicia será gratuita cuando asi lo disponga la ley y, en todo caso, respecto a quienes acrediten insuficiencia de recursos para litigar*" ("Justice will be free when the law so regulates . . .") (Art.110 CE). This law is the *Ley* 1/1996 of January 10, *de Asistencia Jurídica Gratuita*; *Real Decreto* 996/2003, of July 25.

[38] The current minimum wage or *salario mínimo interprofesional* is of €451.20 a month or €15.04 a day.

difficult family circumstances.[39] Foreigners legally resident in Spain have the same rights and Spanish Citizens.[40]

The party who wishes to request free legal aid must fill in an application form and out together several documents[41] in the *Colegio de Abogados* where the case is taking place or the court of his domicile if the proceedings have not started yet. The *Colegio* will examine all documentation and make a decision as to whether the claim has got any legal basis or merits and the party is entitled or not to the benefit. If the party is entitled it will notify the applicant and name a provisional lawyer who will advise on the matter. It will also notify the *Colegio de procuradores* who will allocate a *procurador* within three days.

If the application is rejected the applicant can request that the *Comisión de Asistencia Jurídica Gratuita* looks at his case. The *Comisión* will decide in the period of 30 days.

---

[39] Ley 40/2003, of November 18, *de Protección de las familias numerosas.*

[40] In Criminal litigation even those foreigners not legally resident are entitled to the free assistance of an *abogado* and *procurador*; the same is true for all foreigners in proceedings involving the *Ley de Extranjería.*

[41] This application form is available from the information services of the local *Colegio de Abogados.* The provincial departments of the *Consejeria de Justicia y Administraciones Publicas*, the *Comisiones de Asistencia Juridica Gratuita* and the courts themselves.

Chapter Six
Criminal procedure

1. CRIMINAL LAW AND CRIMINAL PROCEDURE

Criminal procedure is that branch of procedure which regulates the proceedings by which the courts can punish criminal offences.[1]

There is an important connection between substantive criminal law and criminal procedure. Only the facts described and established in the Criminal Code as constituting a criminal offence[2] can initiate the commencement of criminal proceedings. Substantive criminal law, also, can be applied only by the courts which have the relevant jurisdiction.[3] The importance of the rights involved, and the seriousness of the consequences of infringing those rights, means that only the State, through its courts, decides if a criminal offence has been committed and the punishment that this deserves.

There are two main types of offences according to the Spanish Criminal Code—*delitos* and *faltas*.[4] *Delitos* are serious offences, and are subdivided into major offences or crimes—*delitos graves*, and less serious offences—*delitos menos graves*. *Faltas* are minor offences. This distinction is important because it will determine the type of procedure to be followed, in the same way as the amount of the claim determines the type of civil proceedings.

2. PRINCIPLES OF CRIMINAL PROCEDURE

The important consequences of the commission of a crime both for the victim and for the perpetrator, and the seriousness of the punishment attached to that commission, means that criminal procedure

---

[1] J.L. Gómez Colomer, *El Proceso Penal Español para no juristas*. (1993) p.43.

[2] Only the law can establish which facts constitute a criminal offence. These facts need to have been previously established by a *ley* according to the principle of legality, as must the punishment attached to the commission of an offence. Articles 1, 2 and 3 of the *Código Penal* 1995.

[3] Art.117 CE.

[4] Arts 10–13 of the *Código Penal* LO 10/1995, of November 23.

is subject to a variety of principles which guarantee the rights of both the victim and the accused. Some of these principles are established by the Constitution itself and therefore can be protected by the *recurso de amparo* before the Constitutional Court.[5]

Criminal proceedings are organised according to different principles from those governing civil proceedings. In civil proceedings the parties control the action and the judge is a qualified spectator of the activities of both parties who could, at any stage, end the proceedings by settling their dispute. In criminal proceedings the judge plays an active role while the parties do not control the commencement or end of the proceedings.[6] This is because in civil matters the parties are free to enter into legal relationships and agree a solution if a dispute arises. Criminal law, on the other hand, is a branch of public law which protects the right of freedom in all its possible manifestations. The State has the duty to protect all public and private interests which are infringed as a consequence of the commission of a criminal offence. In order to fulfil this duty, the State has the monopoly of the *ius puniendi*—the right to punish those who attack and endanger freedom. The right of the State to punish is organised according to strict principles in order to avoid the misuse of power. These principles are the principles of criminal procedure, since the only channel by which the State can punish individuals is through a process in which there are a number of guarantees.

In this respect criminal proceedings are "necessary".[7] The "principle of necessity" of criminal proceedings encompasses other subsidiary principles. The first of these is the principle of officiality. According to this principle the existence and commencement of criminal proceedings does not depend on the will of the individual.[8] Criminal proceedings are started by the court once it has knowledge of the commission of a crime. Also, even if the parties can bring any evidence they wish, the direction of the proceedings rests on the judge who can refer to and search for any evidence he considers appropriate and necessary without any intervention of the parties;[9] he is unrestricted in the evaluation of this evidence and will give judgment according to his own conscience. The judge, also, directs the proceedings until the end

---

[5] Articles 24 and 25 CE.

[6] With the exceptions mentioned below.

[7] Civil proceedings are not "necessary" because the parties can organise their civil relationships and dispose of their rights privately; the State only intervenes when one of the parties so demands.

[8] The only exceptions are the so called "private" and "semi-private" criminal offences. See below.

[9] Especially during the instruction, which is governed by the inquisitorial principle giving wide powers to the judge (Arts 299, 483, 701(vi), 708 and 729(2) LEC).

and the parties cannot agree or decide on the termination of the proceedings.[10]

In order to protect individual rights from the great powers of the judge in criminal proceedings, the exercise of these is governed by strict formalities which must be respected or will otherwise constitute a ground for *casación*. Criminal proceedings are oral (Art.120(2) CE) and public (Arts 24(2), 120(1) CE and 232 LOPJ).[11]

Although the parties in criminal proceedings do not stand in an equivalent position to the parties in civil proceedings, it is possible to say that there is a duality of positions, namely one party which accuses and the other party who is accused and who must defend. Both parties are in a position of contradiction, and the party who is being accused has the right to be heard—principle of audience—before she or he can be condemned. The principle of contradiction or audience has constitutional status. Article 24 of the CE prohibits lack of defence and ensures a procedure which has guarantees. Accordingly, both parties have the right to know all the facts and evidence presented in order to organise their defence or accusation. Also, in criminal proceedings, it is not possible to give a judgment in default. If the defendant is not present the proceedings can not take place. Finally, the principle of equality, which also informs civil proceedings, is of paramount importance in criminal proceedings where the parties have the same opportunities to establish their positions and the same rights of audience.[12]

3. SOURCES OF CRIMINAL PROCEDURE

In Ch.2 we saw that the sources of law vary from one branch of the law to another, depending on the nature of the rights involved and the purpose of the regulation. Criminal law and criminal procedure are subject to the "principle of legality", which means that the only type of rule of law which can determine which actions constitute a criminal offence is a rule with the force of *ley*.[13] There is no scope for administrative regulations or customs in this area.

The main sources of criminal procedure are the Constitution, which establishes the main principles informing the regulation of this

---

[10] Principle of *impulso procesal de oficio* (Arts 237 LOPJ and 215 LECrim).
[11] Even if there is a preliminary or first stage—*Fase de Instrucción o Sumario*—which is written and secret.
[12] Despite the major role played by the prosecution in the instruction of criminal proceedings.
[13] See Arts 1, 2 and 3 CP 1995; Art.25.1, 1.1, 9.3, 53.1 and 81.1 CE; Art.43 LO 5/2000 of January 12 *De responsabilidad penal del menor*.

type of proceedings (Arts 24, 120 CE) and the *Ley de Enjuiciamiento Criminal* (Criminal Procedure Act) of 1882 as amended.[14] The reform of the centenary law of criminal procedure was one of the points agreed by the *Pacto para la Reforma de la Justicia* between the PSOE and the PP signed on May 31, 2001.[15] The LECrim of 1885 has been complemented, modified and adapted to the new realities in multiple occasions but it will certainly benefit form a general reform similar to that of Civil Procedure which overhauls the structure, principles and types of proceedings available.

Much has changed since the first edition of this book. A new Criminal Code has demanded new ways of processing claims in criminal proceedings. We will look at the principal modifications. Only the State—the Central State—can regulate criminal proceedings (Art.149(1)(6) CE). The Autonomous Communities have no power to legislate on procedural or substantive criminal law matters.

The decisions of the Constitutional Court on matters affecting any rights of individuals which are closely connected with procedural matters, have a binding effect on judges as to the interpretation of constitutional rules (Art.40(2) LOTC) and therefore can be included within the sources of criminal law.[16]

4.   PARTIES

In criminal proceedings there is a duality of positions: accusation and accused. This is not equivalent to the plaintiff and defendant of civil procedure because the accusation in criminal proceedings is, or can be brought by a variety of persons. This is due to the fact that not only the person suffering the consequences of the crime is a victim, but the whole society may be affected. Therefore, the right to start criminal proceedings is vested in several persons.

The accusation, in Spanish criminal proceedings is drawn up in the first place by the public prosecutor—*el Ministerio Fiscal*.[17] The public prosecutor represents the public interest, not only the interests of the victim. In the exercise of these functions all the circumstances of the case will be considered and a request may be made that the proceedings stop or that changes or amendments are made to the original

---

[14] Many modifications on criminal procedure have been subsequently introduced by *ley orgánica*. See below.

[15] See *www.elpais.es/articulo/elpporesp/20030917elpepunac_7/Tes/el%20Pacto%*.

[16] *ibid.*

[17] See above, Ch.3, pp.72–73 .

charges, if it is considered that there is not enough evidence against the presumptive culprit. This office is also under an obligation to ensure that all the procedural guarantees are respected (Arts 2 and 781 LECrim; Arts 2–6 EMF).[18]

The main function of the public prosecutor is the exercise of the "public criminal action" in all criminal proceedings, except in those cases in which the intervention and consent of the victim are necessary for the initiation of the proceedings.[19] For this purpose, criminal offences can be classed as public, semi-public or private, according to who can or must start the proceedings. "Public" criminal offences—which are the majority—are those which should be prosecuted *ex officio*. This means that the public prosecution can and must initiate the prosecution once it has notice of the commission of the crime, independently of the response of the victim, who can remain passive or even "forgive" the offender. This eventual "forgiveness" does not affect the prosecution of the crime by the State through the public prosecutor.[20] "Semi-public" criminal offences are those in which it is necessary that there has been a previous report of the offence by the victim (or a close relative of the victim, or by the public prosecutor in the case of minors or persons without full legal capacity) in order to commence the prosecution. Once this report has been made the public prosecutor has the obligation to proceed with the accusation. Traditionally these offences were offences against sexual freedom, or domestic offences for which the legislator preferred to give the persons involved the choice as to whether to start proceedings or not.[21] "Private" offences are those in which in public prosecutor does not intervene at any stage.[22]

Together with the "criminal action" the public prosecutor will undertake the "civil action" (Art.108 LECrim) if the victim has not reserved the right to start the action for civil damages in civil proceedings.[23]

Not only the public prosecutor can start criminal proceedings. Any citizen can do so subject to a few restrictions. This is a major departure from other legal systems in which the prosecution belongs exclusively to the state—for instance in countries like France or Italy. There is, however, a difference depending on whether the person who starts

---

[18] See Ch.4, pp.89–90, *Estatuto Orgánico del Ministerio Fiscal.*

[19] Art.105 LECrim and Art.85 CP.

[20] Art.107 LECrim.

[21] Today this list has been extended to include rape and sexual abuses (Art.443 CP), slander and libel (Art.463 and 467 CP and Art.4 of *L*62/1978), family desertion (Art.487 CP), public scandal (Art.431 CP), damages for reckless driving when the amount of these is over the compulsory insurance limit (Art.563 CP). For a complete list see. J. Gómez Colomer, *op. cit.*, p.116.

[22] Arts 104 and 105 LECrim and Art.191 CP.

[23] Art.109 CP.

criminal proceedings is also the victim of the criminal action or not. If he is the victim he is referred to as the "private prosecutor"—*acusador particular*.[24] If he is not the victim, he is referred to as the "popular prosecutor"—*acusador popular*.[25]

The private prosecutor will be the only party in the accusation of "private crimes" in which the public prosecution does not take part. In this case he can discontinue the proceedings, withdraw the charges against the accused or forgive him, in which case there will be no punishment.

The victim of the crime can decide whether he or she wishes to request civil damages in the criminal proceedings or prefers to start separate civil proceedings. He has the right to waive the claim for civil damages. This waiver must be express and conclusive (Art.110 LECrim) and will not have any consequences on the criminal action which will proceed with the few exceptions of the "totally private crimes".

The "popular" prosecutor can be any Spanish citizen, over 18, in possession of full civil rights. It is not possible to prosecute a spouse as a "popular prosecutor", except for crimes against close relatives of the prosecuting spouse. The "popular" prosecutor needs to be represented by an *abogado* and a *procurador* and deposit a security *caución* with the court (Art.280 LECrim). Once he has done so and presented a *querella*[26] he becomes party to the proceedings with full rights and duties.

The defendant in criminal proceedings receives a variety of denominations depending on which stage of the trial he is at: suspect, arrested, presumptive culprit, accused, or simply, defendant. The minimum age for criminal liability is 16 years (Art.8(2) CP),[27] and only physical persons can be defendants in criminal proceedings.[28] Because of the severe consequences of an eventual judicial decision determining his culpability, the defendant's position is protected by the law. The guarantees or rights of the defendant have the character of fundamental rights and are established by the Constitution in Arts 17 and 24. The infringement of any of these is a ground for the *recurso de amparo*.[29] The defendant has, first, the right to an ordinary,

---

[24] Art. 270(II) LECrim, the victim can be a Spanish national or a foreigner.

[25] In this case it is necessary to be a Spanish citizen (Art.101 LECrim).

[26] This is the name of the initiating claim if brought up by individuals. See below.

[27] See Art.66 CP. Article 8(2) CP73 still in force according to the *Disposicion derogatoria* 1 of the CP.

[28] This raises important and difficult questions as to the responsibility of companies and juristic persons. The general solution is to charge the director or administrator of the company. See Art.31 CP.

[29] See *recurso de amparo* to the Constitutional Court. Ch.7, pp. 202–3.

pre-determined judge.[30] This means a total prohibition on "exceptional courts" appointed for the sole purpose of judging a particular case, and gives the defendant the guarantee that his case will be decided impartially by a professional judge who will be subject only to the law in arriving at his decision.[31] Secondly, the defendant has the right of defence and the right to be assisted by a professional lawyer (Art. 24 CE). If the defendant does not designate a lawyer of his choice to conduct the defence of his case, the court will designate one *ex officio* from among the lawyers registered at the local bar. This lawyer is called *abogado de oficio*.[32] Thirdly, the defendant has the right to be informed of the charges against him and of the state of the proceedings. Fourthly, the defendant has the right to use all evidence in his defence including the right of not making any declarations which can be prejudicial to his position.[33] Fifthly, every person has the right to the "presumption of innocence", which means that until all charges have been duly and sufficiently proved and the judge has given a verdict of culpability, the defendant is innocent. Consequently, it is the prosecution which must prove and establish the culpability of the defendant, not the defendant who must prove his innocence. Sixthly and lastly, nobody can be arrested except in the cases and circumstances determined by the law.

According to Art.109 CP, every person who is criminally liable, is also responsible for the civil damages caused by the commission of the offence. This civil liability, according to Art.110 CP and Art.100 LECrim, extends to restitution of the object of the crime, if this was against property and/or compensation for physical and moral damages.[34] The compensation for moral damages extends to the family of the victim.[35]

Criminal liability is personal, and therefore, only the author of the offence can be held responsible for it. However, civil liability arising out of the commission of a criminal offence can extend to persons other than those who committed the offence. If the author of the

---

[30] Art.24(2) CE and Arts 446, 447, 448 and 449 CP.

[31] The judge can be prosecuted if he acts unfairly. See above Arts 446 *et seq.* CP.

[32] Similar to the "duty solicitor" in England. His services will be free of charge if the defendant is entitled to free legal aid. Otherwise he can fix a charge.

[33] This right commences from the moment when the presumptive culprit is conducted to the police station where he can insist on keeping silent and insist on answering only to the judge (Art.520(2)(a) LECrim).

[34] Pain and suffering. See *Ley* 35/1995 of December 11 on help to the victims of violent crimes against sexual freedom.

[35] There is a special compensation for the victims of terrorist attacks that includes extraordinary Social Security pensions. See Arts 36, 38 and 39 of the *Ley* 41/1994 of December 30.

offence is a minor or does not enjoy full capacity, his parents or guardians are responsible for the civil damages arising from the criminal action. Also persons with a duty of care are held responsible for the civil consequences of actions of the persons under their care.[36]

The instructing judge determines who is the person with civil liability, at the instance of the civil claimant,[37] and will demand that this person provides bail to cover the eventual damages imposed. From this moment the person charged with a civil claim becomes a party to the proceedings with full rights and duties.

5. THE COURT

The court with jurisdiction to hear criminal cases is determined by taking into account the importance and severity of the punishment attached to the actual offence. This criteria also determines the type of offence—*delitos graves* (crimes), *delitos menos graves* (serious offences) and *faltas* (minor offences). Together with this, some offences are heard by specific courts taking into consideration the capacity of the person committing the offence; in this context offences perpetrated by Members of Parliament[38] are judged by the Criminal Chamber of the Supreme Court, irrespective of the classification of the offence.

Minor offences (*faltas*) are decided by the *Juzgado de Instrucción*[39] of the place where the offence was committed (Art.15(1) LECrim) with the exception of very minor cases in which a decision can be made by the *Juez de Paz*.[40] For the decision of serious offences (*delitos menos graves*)[41] either the *Juez de lo Penal* of the place where the offence was committed or the *Juez Central de lo Penal* has jurisdiction. Cases involving very serious offences and crimes (*delitos graves*) are decided by the *Audiencia Provincial* of the province where the crime was committed.[42]

---

[36] See Art.106(2) CE of 272 CP and LO 5/2000 of January 12 *de responsabilidad penal de los menores*, Art.61.

[37] This can be the private prosecutor or the public prosecutor.

[38] See Art.118 bis LECrim as introduced by the LO 7/2002 of July 5 *de Reforma parcial de la Ley Enjuiciamiento Criminal*.

[39] See above, Ch.3 under section on *Juzgados de Primera Instancia e Instrucción*.

[40] Arts 385, 590, 594, 596 and minor offences of Tit. I and II of the Criminal Code.

[41] *Delitos menos graves* are those offences which are punishable by imprisonment of less than six years, a fine of whatever amount, deprivation of a driving licence or any other punishment of less than six years.

[42] For information on which cases are decided by the *Audiencia Nacional*, *Tribunales Superiores de Justicia* or *Tribunal Supremo* see Ch.3, pp.64–9.

CHART OF CRIMINAL COURTS

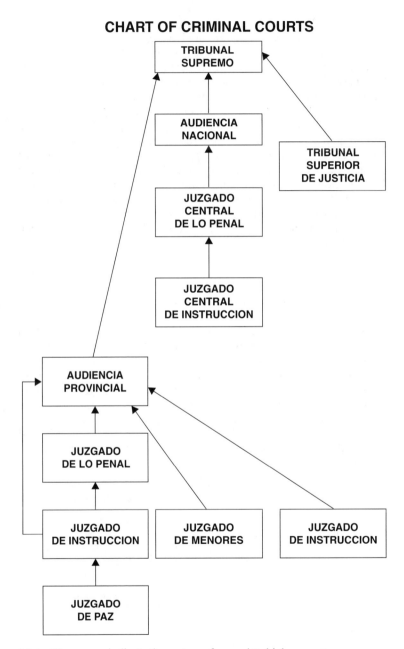

Note: The arrows indicate the system of appeal to higher courts.

In criminal proceedings, at least for serious offences and crimes, there are two clear and differentiated stages—the *instrucción*,[43] and the public hearing. These are carried out by different courts in most cases and by different judges with the exception introduced by the LO 8/2002 of October 24 for *juicios rapidos e inmediatos de faltas*.[44] The court with jurisdiction for the "instruction" of criminal cases is the *Juez de Instrucción* or the *Juez Central de Instrucción*. For cases decided by the *Tribunal Supremo* or *Tribunal Superior de Justicia*, a special judge is designated from the Criminal Chamber of these courts to carry out the *instrucción* of the case. This judge will not participate in the public hearing or in the final decision since the Constitutional Court has declared unconstitutional the decision of a criminal case by the instructing judge.[45] Appeals against criminal decisions, when these are possible,[46] are decided by the superior courts. The enforcement is always made by the judge or court which gave judgment.

6.   MAIN CRIMINAL PROCEEDINGS

There are four "ordinary" types of criminal proceedings in Spain for serious crimes (*delitos*) and two types of *juicios de faltas*. Together with these there are what are called special proceedings because of the person charged, the type of offence or both. These are the procedure against *Diputados* and *Senadores*,[47] the procedure against members of the autonomous parliaments,[48] the procedure for extradition,[49] and the procedure when minors are involved in a criminal case.[50] Since the LO 2/2000 of January 12 of criminal responsibility of minors, only those that are 18 years old or more

---

[43] Meaning the first phase of the proceeding where the judge gathers evidence. See below.

[44] See below for an explanation of this new type of proceedings.

[45] STC of July 12, 1988. This decision of the Constitutional Court has been reflected by the LO 7/88 which specifies the obligation to nominate a separate judge for the instruction of the cases decided in the *Tribunal Supremo* and the *Tribunal Superior de Justicia*.

[46] See below.

[47] Art.71 CE. See LO 7/2002 of July 5 that introduces Art.118 *bis* in the LECrim modifying this procedure. See also Arts 750–756 LECrim and Arts 10–14 of the *Reglamento del Congreso* and the *Reglamento del Senado*.

[48] Regulated in the *Estatuto de Autonomía* of each Community.

[49] *Ley* 4/1985 of March 21.

[50] See Art.19 CP and LO 5/2000 of January 12 of Criminal responsibility of minors.

can be held criminally liable. The law also establishes the special procedure to follow in cases involving minors and the role of the *Ministerio Fiscal*.[51] This regulation aims at protecting both the minor and the victim of the crime.[52] Other proceedings are special because they deal with facts and activities which are not offences typified by the Criminal Code but by other laws. Of these the most significant is the *proceso militar penal* for crimes typified by the Military Criminal Code.[53]

The application or choice among ordinary criminal proceedings is related to the seriousness of the offence and the duration and type of punishment that can become applicable.

PROCEDIMIENTO ORDINARIO

This is the procedure to follow when we are looking at a serious crime. It was originally the main procedure regulated in the LECrim and references in this chapter are to this type of procedure unless otherwise stated. This procedure is for serious crimes that have attached a punishment of prison for nine or more years.

PROCEDIMIENTO ABREVIADO

This procedure is regulated in the LECrim Arts 757 *et seq*. It applies in cases of crimes that can have a punishment of prison of less than nine years or crimes that have any other type of punishment whatever the amount or duration.

JUICIO RÁPIDO

This procedure was introduced in 2002[54] and it is regulated in Arts 795–803 LECrim with the supplementary application of the rules of the *procedimiento abreviado*. The *juicio rápido para determinados delitos* is available for those offences in which the punishment cannot exceed five years of prison, or if the punishment includes prison when all other sanctions do not exceed 10 years. The proceedings need to be started with a police report (*atestado policial*); the defendant must be identified and arrested or identified and notified to attend the

---

[51] See Arts 16–42 LO 2/2000.
[52] *See Exposición de Motivos* of the LO 2/2000.
[53] LO 4/1987 of July 15 on military jurisdiction and LO 2/1989 of April 13 on military procedure.
[54] LO 8/2002 of October 24.

Juzgados de Guardia and must have committed a flagrant crime from the list included in the *Ley* 38/2002.[55]

This procedure is a faster version of the already abbreviated *procedimiento abreviado* for those cases in which a person was caught in the act of a crime and the crime, by its nature, has a punishment no higher than five years of prison or 10 years of other punishment. In these cases it is thought the protection of the victim is better provided for by a fast mechanism for charging and convicting the person accused. The evidence available makes this possible without any risk of invading the legitimate rights to a fair trial of the person accused.

PROCEDIMIENTO DEL JURADO

On May 22, 1995, the LO 5/1995 *Ley Orgánica del Tribunal Jurado* introduced the institution of the jury to Spanish criminal procedure according to the general provision of Art.125 CE. This provided that the participation of citizens in the administration of justice was to be effected by two main mechanisms; the "popular action"[56] and the jury.

The institution of the jury in criminal proceedings has had a controversial history in Spain. Traditionally favoured by liberals and condemned by conservative governments,[57] the institution of the jury appears today to be related to the fundamental right of citizens to participate in public matters (Art.23(1) CE) and, in particular, in the administration of justice (Art.125 CE).

The LO 5/95 of May 22, is due to enter into force six months after its publication[58] and there have already been some "test-runs" for trials with a jury. The institution of the jury in criminal proceedings has had a controversial history in Spain. Traditionally favoured by liberals and condemned by conservative governments,[59] the institution of the jury appears today to be related to the fundamental right of citizens to participate in public matters (Art.23(1) CE) and, in particular, in the administration of justice (Art.125 CE).

Being a juror is at the same time, and according to the LO 5/95, a

---

[55] It includes: physical or mental violence against relatives; theft; road traffic accidents; and crimes against public health, intellectual or industrial property. See Arts 263, 368, 270, 273, 274 and 275 CP 1995.

[56] See above.

[57] There were provisions for a jury in the Constitutions of 1812, 1837, 1869 and 1931.

[58] *Disposición final quinta* LO 5/95 with the exceptions made in this disposition concerning ch.II of the law (Selection of Juries) and the *disposición transitoria tercera*, which will become enforceable two months from the date of publication. The LO 5/95 of May 22, was published on May 23, 1995.

[59] There were provisions for a jury in the Constitutions of 1812, 1837, 1869 and 1931.

right and a duty of citizens. Chapter II of the LO 5/95 specifies who can and should be a juror, how jurors are to be appointed and duties of jurors, as well as the roles which are incompatible with that of being a juror.

Trials by jury are limited to certain types of crime.[60] These are crimes against human life (Arts 138–140 CP), crimes committed by civil servants in the exercise of their duties (Arts 413–415, 419–426, 428–430, 432–434, 436–440 and 471 CP), the crime of omission of duty of help (Arts 196 and 197 CP), trespass[61] (Arts 202–204 CP) and crimes against the environment (Arts 352–354 CP—especially intentional fires or *incendios forestales*). Jurisdiction for these trials traditionally belonged to the *Audiencia Provincial* and the intervention of the jury is limited to trials in the *Audiencia Provincial* or another court with jurisdiction according to the status of the person accused.[62] There is no intervention of a jury in trials in the *Audiencia Nacional*.[63]

The *Tribunal del Jurado* is composed of nine jurors and a judge who acts as the President. The function of the jury is to give a verdict declaring whether the facts indicated by the presiding judge are proved or not. The jury also declares whether the accused is guilty or not guilty of the criminal actions accepted as forming the charge by the judge (Art.3 LO 5/95). The judge in turn issues a sentence according to the jury's verdict, imposes a punishment and decides, if it is applicable, the civil liability of the accused.

The introduction of trial by jury made necessary the modification of certain procedural rules which did not provide an adequate framework for this new development. In this respect, the *Exposición de Motivos* of the LO 5/95, makes some important remarks and explains the reforms which are to be introduced in Spanish criminal proceedings for trials by jury. Contrary to the theory that it is only necessary to modify that part of the procedure in which the jury intervenes, that is, the *juicio oral*, the legislator has opted for some changes in both stages of the Spanish system. Article 24 of the LO 5/95, effectively created a new type of criminal proceedings, the Trial by Jury, which is regulated in Arts 24–70 of the LO 5/59, while the LECrim provides subsidiary guidelines for matters not specifically provided for in the new regulations. The aim of these reforms is to adapt the most difficult techni-

---

[60] Art.1(2) LOPJ.
[61] Note than in Spain trespassing is a criminal offence.
[62] *i.e.* special jurisdiction in cases concerning Members of Parliament and members of the Government. See above.
[63] Which in any case has special jurisdiction because of the subject matter of the crime. See above, Ch.3, pp.65–6.

calities of Spanish criminal proceedings, which were initially designed for professional judges, to the needs and limitations of non-professional jurors on one hand, and on the other, to reinforce the value of evidence stated in the *juicio oral*, since most judges in fact decide on the basis of the evidence available from the *sumario* or *instrucción*. In order to achieve these two main aims, the main changes introduced are: the need for a well-founded claim for the start of oral proceedings—in which the facts that are going to be subject to evidence are clearly stated; reinforcement of the neutrality of the investigating judge by establishing that a party—different from the judge—needs to start the accusation while the judge decides whether it is convenient to proceed with the investigations or not; and, the introduction of several dispositions relating to the oral trial itself addressed to provide an adequate framework for the decision of the jury (Arts 42–65 LO 5/95).

JUICIO INMEDIATO DE FALTAS

Applicable in those cases where the judicial police is aware of facts that may amount to one of the conducts typified in Arts 617, 620 or 623 CP[64] had been committed. In these cases the judicial police prepares a report (*atestado*) that is passed onto the *Juzgado de Guardia*. The parties can be assisted by a lawyer if they so wish. The *Juez de Guardia* will celebrate the *juicio* and dictate a decision in the same procedural act. This decision can be appealed in the five days following its notification. Once the decision is firm it will be enforced in the ordinary manner.[65]

JUICIO PARA OTRAS FALTAS

These "other minor offences" are those of the Libro III of the Criminal Code and not included in Art.962 of the LECrim or any other special legislation.[66] This is a short and fast procedure for relatively minor offences in which all judicial actuations take place in the same act. It starts with a *denuncia* or *querella* and the absence of the accused is not an impediment for the proceedings to take place, providing that he was properly notified of the proceedings. The person accused is presumed to agree with the facts alledged by the accusation and there will be a conclusion condemning the person charged if the facts of the accusation are proved.

---

[64] These are minor offences against the physical integrity or property of people.

[65] Arts 969, 974 and 975 LECrim and Art.712 LEC for civil responsibility.

[66] Minor offences of falsification of money, minor offences against public property, cruelty to animals, offences caused by unattended dangerous animals (Arts 629–637 CP).

7. STAGES IN CRIMINAL PROCEEDINGS

In criminal proceedings there are several clearly differentiated stages. Some of these take place before the actual court commencement of the proceedings and their function is to establish whether or not there is enough evidence to initiate criminal proceedings against the defendant.

PRELIMINARY STAGE

Before criminal proceedings can be started it is necessary to determine various issues, the first being whether an offence has actually been committed and the circumstances in which this happened. In order to do this, several investigations need to take place. These investigations are usually carried out by the judicial police. Secondly, and once it has been established that a criminal offence has been committed, it is necessary to determine who is the person responsible for it. Further investigations are then required in order to find and identify the author (unless he presents himself to the judge or the police and confesses to the commission of the crime).[67] These investigations are also carried out by the judicial police.[68] Only after these two points have been established can the prosecution start the criminal procedure.

(i) The judicial police

The body of the judicial police[69] is an auxiliary of the judicial power,[70] the public prosecution and—since it performs a public service—to some extent of the citizens.[71] Article 126 CE states that the function of the judicial police is to assist the judge and the public prosecutor in the investigations of crimes and the identification of the person responsible for these. The judicial police is subject to the orders received by the judge and the public prosecutor (Art.283 LECrim).

The judicial police will start investigations once it has been instructed to do so and will communicate any knowledge of facts which might constitute a criminal offence to the judge. If the criminal

---

[67] This is not conclusive because in any event a procedure is necessary before anybody can be convicted of a criminal offence.

[68] See below.

[69] See De Llera Suanez-Barcena, *Derecho Procesal Penal* (Valencia, 1997), pp.67–92, for a detailed and excellent account of the functions of the judicial police.

[70] See above, Ch.4, p.91.

[71] J.L. Gómez Colomer, *op. cit.*, p.152.

offence is a *delito público*, then the judicial police has the duty to investigate all the events which took place in the territorial district under their jurisdiction. If the offence is a *delito privado*, which can only be prosecuted if the victim so desires, the judicial police will have the same obligation to investigate the facts and to identify the criminal once it has been requested to do so.[72]

The judicial police body is dependent on the Ministry of Internal Affairs (*Ministerio del Interior*) (Art.31 LO 2/1986) even if its members are subject to the orders of the judge or public prosecutor. They will perform any acts in which public coercion, entry into and search of private dwellings are necessary.

(ii) Starting criminal proceedings

The initiation of criminal proceedings requires an act—just as civil proceeding are started by the issue of claim form—which can be carried out by citizens or by the State. Citizens can start the proceedings by a *denuncia*[73] or by a *querella*.[74] The State can initiate the proceedings ex officio or by special requirement of the Executive.

La denuncia

A *denuncia* is a declaration of knowledge by a private person who has notice of the commission of a criminal offence and thereby communicates this knowledge to the court. This can be done orally or in writing. The *denuncia* is made to the judge, usually the duty judge—*Juez de guardia*[75]—the public prosecutor or the police. As a result of its general duty to investigate and report every fact which might constitute an offence, the reports of the police (*atestados policiales*)—according to Art.297 LECrim—are also a *denuncia*. The person who makes this declaration of knowledge does not necessarily become a party to the proceedings although he will at least be called as a witness.

---

[72] Their obligations are specifically regulated in the RD 769/1987 of June 19, which develops the LO 2/1986 of May 13.

[73] This term could be translated by "complaint" or "information". The original Spanish terminology will be used because there is another type of complaint, *querella*, with special characteristics.

[74] There is no direct and accurate translation of this term into English. This is a special type of complaint in those criminal offences which can only be prosecuted with the consent of the victim. See above on certain offences against sexual freedom, libel and slander.

[75] See Arts 259, 262 and 264 LECrim.

Although every citizen has a general ethical duty to report any knowledge of the commission of a criminal offence, certain persons, due to their personal circumstances or their relationship with the offender, are excepted from this duty. These persons are minors and mentally disabled people (Art.260 LECrim), the spouse, close relatives and descendants of the perpetrator (Art.261 LECrim), the lawyers of the offender (Art.263 LECrim) and Catholic priests in respect of facts, knowledge of which was acquired under confession, according to Canon Law (Art.263 LECrim). On the other hand some people have a special duty or obligation to report their knowledge of the commission of a criminal offence because of their profession, for example the police and the public prosecution service.

Once a *denuncia* has been made, the court has the obligation to start investigations. If the report was made to the police, it will be passed on to the judge who will determine whether the facts reported constitute a criminal offence. If so, the judge will pass the information to the public prosecutor and to the persons who are accused of the commission of the offence (Art.118 LECrim). If the facts reported do not constitute a criminal offence the *denuncia* will be dismissed.

The person making the *denuncia* has no further obligations, unless he wishes to become a party in a private or popular accusation, depending on the circumstances. He will also be protected if his security is endangered by the fact of reporting the criminal offence. However, if he acted maliciously when making the *denuncia* he could be criminally liable (Art.456 CP—*denuncia falsa*—and Art.457 CP—*simulación de delito*).

La querella

The second type of declaration which starts criminal proceedings is called *querella*. This is a complaint made with the intention of becoming a party to the proceedings. This complaint is made formally, in writing, to the judge with jurisdiction to hear the case.[76]

The distinction between public, semi-public and private criminal offences becomes relevant again in order to analyse who can make a *querella*. In the case of public criminal offences—*delitos perseguibles de oficio*—this report or complaint can be made by the victim,[77] any

---

[76] This is different from the case of a *denuncia* which could be presented to the duty judge, the police or the public prosecutor.

[77] Which will become the "private" accusation.

Spanish citizen,[78] or the public prosecutor. The latter, is under an obligation to do so.[79] In cases of "semi-public" offences, once the victim has presented the *denuncia*, the public prosecutor has the duty to prepare and present a *querella*. The victim can also do so if he wishes.[80] No other person is entitled to make a *querella* in this case. In "private" criminal offences only the victim can formulate a *querella*.[81]

This complaint is a formal declaration which must be signed by an *abogado* and a *procurador* and addressed to the court with jurisdiction. It must identify the person against whom it is made, give a detailed account of the facts believed to constitute a criminal offence and the relevant law, with a request to carry out whatever investigations are necessary in order to determine the actual commission of the offence by the suspect. It also has to state any precautionary measures to be taken and include a petition as to the civil liability or otherwise state the reservation of the right to start civil proceedings later. With the *querella* it is necessary to enclose the power of attorney of the *abogado* and *procurador* and any other documents relevant to the case.

If the *querella* is accepted by the court this produces important effects. The person signing it becomes a party to the proceedings, the judge will order the carrying out of the investigations requested, unless these are against the law or unnecessary (Arts 311 and 312 LECrim) and will serve it on the defendant who now becomes the accused and as such has the rights of defence stated in Art.118 LECrim and should be represented by a lawyer.

Initiation ex officio

The judge who has knowledge of the commission of a criminal offence must communicate this knowledge to the public prosecutor in order to allow him to make a *querella*. The court which has decided a case can also initiate criminal proceedings against the person who started these if there is a case of *denuncia falsa*.[82]

A special form of criminal proceedings applies in the case of defamation against foreign Heads of State or diplomatic personnel because of the political connotations. These cases can only be started when the Executive so requests.[83]

---

[78] The "popular" accusation.
[79] See Art.271 LECrim, Art.19(1) LOPJ, and Arts 3, 4 and 5 EOMF.
[80] Arts 104, 105 and 270 LECrim.
[81] Art.104 LECrim, Art.4(1) Ley 62/1978, Art.215(1) CP.
[82] False indictment, Arts 205–207 CP and 456–457 CP.
[83] Art.457 CP.

(iii) Precautionary measures

If in civil proceedings it is sometimes necessary to impose certain precautionary measures in order to ensure that the judicial decision can be enforced in the future, this is even more necessary in criminal proceedings. The investigations can take a long time and the period between the completion of these and the date of the public hearing can vary considerably. If one considers that the author of the offence could face a punishment amounting to imprisonment of up to 20 years, it is not surprising that he may try to hide, leave the country or change identity. Also, in the same way as the civil defendant might try to dispose of his assets and alienate these from his estate in order to frustrate the claims of the plaintiff, the person who is liable for civil damages arising out of a criminal offence may also try to alienate his estate or change the ownership of it in order to frustrate a monetary punishment or liability for civil damages.

Precautionary measures in criminal law try to avoid the above situations. These measures can be addressed to persons or to property. Measures imposed on persons are the *citación cautelar* (cautionary summons), *detención* (arrest), *prisión provisional* (pre-trial custody), *libertad provisional* (freedom on bail). Measures applied to property are basically two, *la fianza* (bail) and *el embargo* (attachment).

La citación cautelar

This is a summons to the person whose participation in the criminal acts appears likely from the investigations of the judge to appear and make a statement to the instructing judge or to the public prosecutor (Arts 486 to 488 LECrim). If the person summoned to appear and make a statement does not do so he will be arrested (Art.487 LECrim).

La detención[84]

Since freedom of movement is a constitutional and fundamental right (Art.17(1) CE) a person can only be arrested according to the rules established in the Constitution and the LECrim (Art.17 CE and 389 LECrim). It is also necessary to distinguish between arrest as a precautionary measure before the trial and arrest as an executory measure.

---

[84] See the useful and clear explanation of this measure in Richard Vogler, *op. cit.*, pp.28–39.

As a precautionary measure it is only possible to arrest a person who is about to commit a crime (Art. 490 LECrim), or who is caught in flagrant commission of a crime. The courts are very strict on the need to establish these circumstances and the police must justify and prove that they exist.

Preventive detention or arrest can only last for a maximum of 72 hours. After this time the person arrested must either be conducted to the judge to declare or he must be allowed to go (Art.17(2) CE). Only in cases of terrorist activities can this detention be extended to a maximum period of five days (Art.520 (bis)(1) LECrim). This detention can be carried out by the police in the circumstances mentioned above or ordered by the judge.

The person arrested has the right to be told of the reasons for his detention; his rights also include the right to remain silent (Art.520 LECrim), the right to request the assistance of a lawyer to help with the enquiries at the police station or by the judge, the right to communicate the detention to a member of the family or any other person, the right to be examined only by a doctor, the right to a translator if the person arrested does not speak or understand Spanish, and, in the case of minors or people with disabilities, the right to notify parents or guardians at once.[85] If any of these rights are denied, or the person arrested has suffered ill-treatment or been held at the police station for longer than the maximum allowed[86] he is entitled to ask of *Habeas Corpus*. *Habeas Corpus* is a fundamental right that each person has to request judicial protection against illegal detention or other violation of rights deriving from it. It is recognised in Art.17(4) CE and developed by the LO 6/1984 of May 24.

The *Ley de Seguridad Ciudadana* (LSC) of 1992 has introduced a special type of "arrest"[87] the features of which are constitutionally more than dubious. Effectively Art.20 of the LSC allows the police, while exercising their functions of protecting citizens' security,[88] to request any person to identify himself. If the person so requested fails to produce proof of identity,[89] or refuses to do so he can be taken to the police station and be "detained". In order to make the detention legal the conditions of Art.490 LECrim must be present,[90]

---

[85] In the case of a foreigner the consular authority must also be notified of the detention Art.520. LECrim.

[86] 72 hours, or five days in cases of terrorism.

[87] Called *retención*.

[88] Which of course, is not a clear concept.

[89] In Spain every citizen has an identity card, *Documento Nacional de Identidad (DNI)*, which he is obliged to carry or to produce for the Police and other authorities on request. Foreigners must produce their passports.

[90] Flagrant commission of a crime.

if not the detention is illegal and Art.20 of the LSC cannot dero-gate from Art.490 LECrim and even less Art.25(3) or 17(2) CE.[91] The police should, therefore, be cautions in the exercise of the powers given to them by the LSC and ensure that the person who is being arrested falls under one of the categories of article 490 LECrim.

La prisión provisional (pre-trial custody)

The regulation of pre-trial custody has been modified successively since the 1978 Constitution. The presumption of innocence and the right of freedom of movement of all citizens requests a tight control over the regulation of this measure. The old law of criminal proce-dure of 1885 was modified in 1985,[92] in 1980,[93] 1984[94] and 1995[95] and by the abundant decisions of the constitutional court.[96]

The State has the duty to punish crimes effectively on the one hand and the duty to guarantee personal freedom on the other,[97] and some-where in between the regulation of provisional prison has finally found a balance that incorporates the constitutional court findings and guidelines with the LO 13/2003 of October 24.[98]

The Constitutional Court had long established that in order to be constitutional the regulation of provisional prison has to be organ-ised according to the two principles that establish that pre-trial custody is on the one hand exceptional and that it is proportional. The constitution guarantees the freedom of all citizens in Art.17 and the general rule in criminal procedure in Spain is that of freedom of the accused during the proceedings. All restrictions of freedom must be regulated by law and this must be done according to a rule of

---

[91] Arts 25(3) and 17 CE—rights of freedom and security. Nobody can be deprived of freedom and provisional detention cannot last longer than strictly necessary and never more than 72 hours.

[92] *Ley* 16/1980 of April 22.

[93] LO 7/1983 of April 23.

[94] LO 10/1984 of December 26.

[95] LO 5/1995 of May 22.

[96] The most important of which are the decisions of: STC 41/1982 about the balanc-ing of the duties of the state to protect the freedom of all citizens according to Art.17 of the constitution and the duty to prosecute and punish crimes effectively; and the STC 47/2000 that declared Arts 503 and 504 of the LECrim unconstitutional.

[97] See STC 41/1982 that establishes that " . . . *la prisión provisional se situa . . . entre el deber estatal de perseguir eficazmente el delito, por un lado, y el deber estatal de asegu-rar el ámbito de la libertad del ciudadano, por otro. . . .*"

[98] LO 13/2003, of October 24, *de Reforma de la Ley de Enjuiciamiento Criminal en materia de prisión provisional.*

proportionality. Proportionality means that the means used—in this case to deprive the accused of freedom—must be proportional to the end, i.e. the effective punishment of crimes. The Constitutional Court has established[99] that only when it is strictly necessary for the continuance of the proceedings and the enforcement of the sentence or when it is necessary in order to avoid the risk of the commission of another crime is this type of prison acceptable.

The new law of 2003 has taken the constitutional court guidelines into account and established in Art.503 that pre-trial custody will only be ordered when there is a risk that the accused will disappear, than the accused will destroy or eliminate evidence relevant to the proceedings or that he will commit a new crime. In the later case it is important to remember that Spanish criminal proceedings are informed by the "presumption of innocence" and therefore the risk that the accused may commit a new crime must be real. Article 503 of the LECrim establishes a very detailed list for the evaluation of these circumstances. It is also necessary that the crime is punished with at least two years of prison.

Provisional prison can only last while the circumstances justifying it are present, for example if there is a risk that the accused may destroy evidence relative to the proceedings, this risk will disappear when all evidence has be collated and evaluated by the court. There is also an absolute limit as to how long a person can be detained without a trial and a decision,[1] and the new regulation of Art.504 lays the limits for the different scenarios with the overall aim that nobody can be in provisional custody for longer that they will be in prison if they were finally declared guilty of the commission of the crime.

The request for provisional prison can only be made by the accusation or the Ministerio Fiscal. The judge before making a decision must hear all parties and evaluate the evidence in front of him.[2] Of particular concern are those cases in which there is a secret summary, as all individuals have the right to know what are they being accused of. Article 506 establishes the minimum content that the *auto* of the judge must have while allowing him to withhold information if this is deemed necessary for the investigations, to obtain evidence and for the general conduct of the proceedings.

It is possible to appeal the decisions declaring or denying pre-trial custody according to Art.766 LECrim.

---

[99] STC 47/2000.
[1] Art.504 LECrim as amended by the *Ley* 13/2003 following allegations that the previous regulation was against Art.5(3) of the European Convention on Human Rights.
[2] Art.505 LECrim.

Libertad provisional (Freedom on bail)

Freedom on bail, is allowed to those suspects for whom an order of pre-trial custody is not justified. It consists of the imposition of certain obligations on the suspect which limit his freedom and performance of which is guaranteed by the bail given to the court (Arts 529–42 LECrim). It usually consists of obliging the suspect to appear before the court periodically[3] and to remain at the disposition of the court (Art.530 LECrim), not being allowed to leave the country or to change residence without previous notification and the consent of the court.

Other measures

Other measures imposed by the court can be directed against the property of the suspect in order to satisfy any eventual fine, the civil liability and the legal costs of the proceedings. These can be imposed at the same time as a personal measure limiting freedom, or independently. Basically there are two such measures: *embargo* (attachment)—which has the same characteristics as the attachment ordered in civil proceedings—and *fianza* (bail).[4]

The final type of measures that the judge can impose before the trial are connected with the punishment attached to certain offences. These include suspension of office for judges, public prosecutors, *secretarios judiciales*, and any other personnel auxiliary to the judge, in criminal cases brought against any of these persons in connection with the exercise of their functions;[5] and the provisional forfeiture and suspension of driving licence.[6]

LA INSTRUCCIÓN

Once criminal proceedings have been formally started, the first stage of the proceedings—*la instrucción*—begins. *La instrucción* has the object of ascertaining the facts and the perpetrator of the crime in order to formalise the request for punishment. In this respect this is a preparatory stage for the oral public hearing—*jucio oral*—during which the judge will definitively establish the innocence or culpability of the accused.

---

[3] Customarily on the 1st and 15th of each month.
[4] See Arts 589–614 *LE*Crim.
[5] See Criminal Code Arts 463–467, 529–534 and 537–542 CP for a list of these offences.
[6] Arts 379–385 CP.

The *instrucción* is conducted by a judge—*el Juez Instructor*—who must be different from the judge conducting the public hearing. The instructing judge has wide powers in order to clarify all the circumstances and facts which might or might not constitute a criminal offence. These powers can imply the restriction of some fundamental rights in order to guarantee the success of the investigations and are therefore carefully regulated by the LECrim.

The *instrucción*, also called summary—*sumario*—is clearly inquisitorial and usually secret, with a judge who controls the proceedings, orders investigations and has wide powers concerning the imposition of any urgent measures considered necessary for the clarification of the facts or the identification of the presumptive culprit.

Whilst the judge has the power to conduct any investigations he thinks appropriate, the parties—both the prosecutor and the defendant—can request the judge to undertake further investigations. These will be carried out by the judge himself or with the assistance of the judicial police or experts—for example, forensic doctors, graphologists or ballistic experts.

Investigations by the judge

The first act of investigation that the judge will undertake is a visual inspection (*inspección ocular*) by personally going to the place where the events took place.[7] He will then make a report describing what he has seen and will take any fingerprints, photographs or any other evidence available and interrogate witnesses if they are available. This is regulated in Arts 326–333 LEC.

The judge will then examine the object of the crime (*cuerpo del delito*). This can be a person or an object. If it is a person it might be necessary to identify the corpse, or to carry out an autopsy in order to determine the time and causes of death.[8] It might also be necessary to conduct other medical examinations in cases of physical injuries not amounting to death. If it is an object, the judge will describe it if this is possible, and make enquiries about its previous state. He will also try to determine the value of the object, which is important in order to determine the eventual punishment and the civil liability.

The next investigation by the judge is directed at the suspect and its purpose is the identification of the author of the offence. Once the judge has done this, he will have to determine if the presumptive author has the necessary capacity to be held criminally liable, i.e. the

---

[7] He is obliged to do so by Art.336 LECrim.
[8] This is necessary in all cases of violent death or when there is suspicion of foul play concerning the cause of death (Art.343 LECrim).

presumptive author will not be criminally liable if he is under 16, or mentally disabled. The judge can also request information about the suspect[9] from any public authorities. After this, he will take a statement from the suspect. At this point it is important to remember that the right not to incriminate oneself and the presumption of innocence are recognised by Art.24 of the Constitution.

The defendant in criminal proceedings might have already been arrested by the police. If this is so, he must be brought before the instructing judge to make a statement within 24 hours. In his statement, besides the right to remain silent and not to declare anything which may be prejudicial to his position, the suspect cannot be compelled to take an oath. He can demand the presence of his lawyer and, if he is a foreigner, of a translator. Any kind of coercion or torture is strictly forbidden and will give rise to criminal liability of the persons involved in these acts.[10] The aim of this interrogation is to confirm or determine the identity of the suspect and his participation in the commission of the criminal offence. To this effect the judge can, for example, request the suspect to write some words in order to check if he is the author of documents which were allegedly written by him. The judge will enquire about previous conduct or morals and the general life-style of the defendant but these questions may not be trick questions intended to entrap the suspect. The clerk (*secretario judicial*) will keep a record of everything which is done. The statement given by the suspect is written down and everybody who is present—suspect, judge, suspect's lawyer, court clerk and translator—will sign it. The suspect cannot be obliged to sign it unless he totally agrees that what has been written is exactly his declaration. If the suspect admits the facts, this does not amount to a confession with the same effects that a confession has in civil proceedings,[11] because it is only possible to convict somebody at the public hearing. If the suspect was previously arrested by the police and made a statement in the police station, he might not be required to do so again, but simply to ratify the previous one before a judge. The suspect has the right to make as many statements as he wishes to the judge (Art.400 LECrim).

---

[9] The circumstances of the accused can be taken into account for the punishment. For example, if he has already been convicted of the same crime previously the punishment will be increased (Arts 10(15), 61(2) and 61(6) LECrim).

[10] Spain is a party to the European Convention on the Prevention of Torture, November 26, 1987 and a signatory to the main human rights treaties like the European Convention of Human Rights of November 4, 1950. The European Chart of Fundamental Rights of December 7, 2000, is also applicable in Spain.

[11] See Ch.5.

Once the judge has taken a statement from the suspect, he will do the same with any witnesses.[12] If there are any discrepancies between the statements of the witnesses and the defendant, or between the different defendants if there are more than one, the judge will arrange a confrontation (*careo*).[13] This confrontation takes place in front of the judge and the *secretario judicial*. The latter will read to all the parties present at the confrontation, the statements already made and remind the witnesses that these have been made under oath and the consequences of false declarations. He will then ask each of the witnesses if they confirm their statements. If there are contradictions at this stage the judge will request the parties to agree in their statements. The *secretario* will keep a record of the whole procedure and this record will be given to all the parties to sign.

Some of the investigations conducted by the judge during the *instrucción* could, as indicated previously, limit the fundamental rights recognised by the Constitution or international conventions ratified by Spain.[14] Most of these investigations will, in practice, be carried out by the police who must in any case possess a warrant from the judge authorising their activities. The types of activities include entry to public or private places,[15] and the interception of personal communications which can be postal, telephonic or telegraphic and presumably nowadays, informatic. This interception of personal communications can only be made in respect of the person accused of the commission of a crime, and in no case can it affect the lawyer in charge of the case since he is under a duty of confidence to his client.[16]

Since the establishment of a democracy in Spain, these activities have been performed with sufficient guarantees, always with a judicial warrant and any proof obtained outside the judge's authorisation is considered illegal and inadmissible. However the approval of the LO *de Seguridad Ciudadana* by Parliament has created controversy among lawyers, politicians and citizens. This law allows the police to enter and search a private dwelling when the police know that a drug-related offence is being committed. While fully appreciating the importance and magnitude of the problem of drug-related crime in Spain in recent times, this regulation seems most unfortunate in that it does not require any judicial intervention before the police can enter a private residence. This will, no doubt, give rise to complaints

---

[12] Witnesses make depositions under oath (Arts 410–450 LECrim).
[13] Arts 451–455 LECrim.
[14] For instance the Rome Convention of Human Rights and Individual Freedoms of 1950 (ratified by Spain in 1979).
[15] This is contrary to Art.18 CE which guarantees the inviolability of private dwellings.
[16] See J. Tome, *op. cit.*, p.238.

that will have to be decided by the Constitutional Court, since the LSC clearly infringes constitutional and internationally recognised fundamental rights.

The final investigation which can be authorised by a judge and which can conflict with a fundamental right is a physical inspection in the form of blood, semen, saliva, urine or other body fluids' tests. Vaginal or anal inspections, X-rays, psychiatric or psychological tests, alcohol and drugs tests must only be carried out when it is strictly necessary since Art.15 of the Constitution guarantees the right to physical integrity. In order to carry out any of these investigations it is necessary to obtain a judicial warrant. They can never be ordered or carried out at the request of the public prosecutor or the police unless the person subject to them expressly consents and they will only be undertaken by an expert, i.e. a doctor. The only exception to this is in the case of alcohol tests taken by the police during routine checks in order to determine whether the offence of driving under the influence of alcohol (Art. 379 CP) is being committed. This test can be used as evidence at the trial and it is carried out by the police in accordance with the LECrim and various administrative regulations on the matter.[17] The Constitutional Court has declared that this investigation does not infringe any constitutional rights and has established special guarantees[18] in order to ensure that the rights of defence and the principle of contradiction are respected. The public prosecutor has the right to be kept informed of the progress of the procedure by the instructing judge (Art.306 LECrim) and in certain cases (Arts 785 (bis) and 789(3) LECrim) carries out some of the preparatory enquiries.[19]

Charges: el procesamiento

Charging somebody means formally accusing that person of the commission of a certain crime.[20] This is necessary in order to open the oral hearing and it is done by the instructing judge (Art.384 LECrim). In order to charge the suspect it is necessary to establish the existence of "rational evidence of the commission of a crime by a specific person".[21] This decision of the judge—*auto*—can be

---

[17] Base 4, *Ley* 18/1989, July 25; Art.12(2) of the *texto articulado* approved by RDL 339/1990 of March 2; and Arts 20–25 of the *Reglamento General de la Circulación* approved by RD 13/1992 of January 17.
[18] STS 5/1989 and STC 3/1990, of January 15. See J. Tomé, *op. cit.*, pp.226–227.
[19] The role of the public prosecutor is greater under the Abbreviated Procedure. See below.
[20] *Mozley & Whiteley's Law Dictionary op. cit.*, p.234.
[21] Art.384(I) LECrim.

appealed.[22] The charge is not necessary in the abbreviated proceedings nor in proceedings for minor offences.[23]

Once the judge considers that all the investigations are complete he will end the *sumario* (Art.622 LECrim). The prosecutor can then request that the dosier is sent to the *Audiencia Provincial*. If the judge who carried out the *instrucción* considers that the facts constitute a minor offence (*faltas*), he will send the dossier to the *Juez de lo Penal*. If he considers that it is a major offence or a crime (*delitos*), the judge will send the dossier with all the documentation to the court which has jurisdiction to decide the case—the *Audiencia Provincial* or the *Tribunal Superior de Justicia*. This decision will be communicated to the private prosecution, if there is one, even if he is only acting as civil actor, requesting him to appear at the *Audiencia Provincial* within 10 days or at the *Tribunal Superior de Justica* within the period of 15 days. A copy of all these documents will be sent to the public prosecutor (Art.623 LECrim). The *Audiencia Provincial* or the *Tribunal Superior de Justicia*, will examine the dossier sent by the judge and will confirm whether the *instrución* is complete or not. If the court thinks that further investigations need to be carried out it will send the documents back to the "instructing" judge with instructions as to any new investigations which need to be undertaken (Art.631 LECrim). If the *Audiencia* or the *Tribunal Superior de Justice* considers that the *instrución* is complete it will dictate a resolution declaring that this is so and decide whether the public hearing should take place or whether the proceeding should be stayed because of lack of evidence (Art.632 LECrim).

THE PUBLIC HEARING

Submissions by the parties

Once the case has been admitted for public hearing, the parties to the proceedings need to elaborate certain documents in order to make their petitions and positions clear and definitive in the light of the evidence provided by the *instrucción*.

In proceedings for *delitos graves*, this consists of the presentation to the court of the *escrito de calificación provisional* by the prosecutors,

---

[22] Art.384 LECrim.

[23] In proceedings for minor offences the person is charged by being notified to appear at an oral hearing (Art.962(I) LECrim). In the "abbreviated proceedings" (Art.790 LECrim) the person is charged when any precautionary measures are taken against him by an *escrito de acusación*.

in which they request the presentation of the evidence they deem necessary. The same document must be presented by the accused indicting the evidence he intends to rely on for his defence. The court will decide whether to accept the evidence proposed and indicate a date for the start of the public hearing. This will be notified to both parties. Once this is done some preparatory activities must be undertaken in order to present the proposed evidence, for example notifications to the witnesses and experts and requests for documents.

The trial

The court for the trial will be composed of three judges,[24] one of whom will be the President who will control the proceedings. Until the LO 5/95 of May 22, there was no jury in Spain although the Constitution had a provision for this in Art.125. This article has now been developed and although at the time of writing trial by jury has still not been implemented, the new regulation will be considered below.

The trial is public unless it is necessary to protect the victim or his family (Art.680 LECrim) and the Press is admitted. The defendant is present and he is represented by his *abogado* and *procurador* and a translator if he does not speak Spanish (Arts 688–40 LECrim).

The trial will start with the clerk reading aloud the background to the case and all the details of the file, including the commencement of the *sumario*, the investigations undertaken and any precautionary measures taken, for instance whether the defendant is in custody or at liberty on bail. He will also read the submissions of the parties (*calificaciones*), the evidence proposed to be presented by them and whether it has or has not been accepted by the court (Art.701 LECrim*)*.

Then, depending on whether the offence with which the defendant is charged carries a punishment involving imprisonment of more than six years or not, the judge will ask the defendant whether he accepts the facts or not, including civil damages. If the offence committed is punishable with imprisonment of more than six years the case automatically proceeds to trial and the court will not ask the defendant whether or not he pleads guilty. If the offence carries a punishment of less than six years imprisonment or other type of penalty, the president of the court will ask the defendant in clear and concise terms whether he pleads guilty or not. The defendant is under no obligation to answer at this stage, and he or his lawyer can demand that the case proceeds to trial. Even if the defendant pleads

---

[24] In cases for *delitos* heard by the *Audiencia Provincial* or *Tribunal Superior de Justicia*.

guilty, the court has to demand the consent of his lawyer. If the lawyer refuses to accept the plea of guilty the case has to proceed to trial despite what the defendant has said. Also, the court must be satisfied from the file that the defendant is guilty before sentencing. If the court is not satisfied, the case will proceed to trial, even if the defendant and his lawyer have accepted the plea of guilty (Arts 688–99 LECrim).

Evidence

At the public hearing, the witnesses will make their statements under oath.[25] First, the witnesses for the prosecution are called and then the defence witnesses. Witnesses must wait outside the court-room and are called by the president in the order proposed by the parties in their submissions. All persons called to be witnesses in criminal proceedings must attend, otherwise they face a severe penalty (Arts 410, 420 and 702 LECrim). They can also be criminally charged for false statements (Art.433 LECrim and Arts 326–8 CP). If a witness, because of illness or disability, cannot appear at the court hearing the judge will take a statement at his home and read this at the hearing. The witnesses are questioned first by the lawyer of the party who called them and then by the other party. The defendant can be called to give evidence either by the prosecution or by the defence. He is the only person who does not need to take an oath as he can not be forced to declare against himself. The president of the court can intervene at any time to clarify matters. He must also prevent, either on his own initiative or at the request of the prosecutor or the defence lawyer, questions which are captious, suggestive or impertinent (Art.708 LECrim). The witness can refer to documentary or other evidence if this has already been accepted by the court (Art.712 LECrim). If the witnesses contradict each other or the defendant's and the witnesses statements are contradictory, the judge can call a confrontation (*careo*) ensuring that no insults or threats happen during this confrontation. The defendant can remain silent, although this might be seen as indicative of guilt.

After the witnesses have made their statements any other evidence is produced. There are no fixed rules concerning the weighing up of the evidence by the court. The court is free to attach whatever weight it thinks appropriate to all statements and evidence presented, although it cannot act unreasonably. No evidence which has been obtained illegally, for instance illegal telephonic interceptions, or the

---

[25] Arts 701–722 LECrim.

opening of correspondence without a court warrant, will be accepted. Nor will evidence obtained as a result of a violation of basic human rights, for instance by torture, be accepted (Art.11 LOPJ).[26]

Definitive submissions

The original submissions of the parties (*escritos de calificaciones*) were based on the investigations and evidence available during the instruction. At this stage the parties have heard all the evidence of the oral hearing and might wish to alter their original submissions.

After the presentation of evidence the parties have two choices; either they can confirm their original submissions, in which case, they may do so orally and the court clerk will make a note which will be added to the dossier or, the parties, or one of them, can decide to alter the original submissions. This must be done in writing. At this stage, the prosecutor can charge the defendant with a different offence which may be more or less serious.

The definitive submissions or the ratified ones—*calificaciones definitivas*—form the basis for the accusation.[27] These submissions are the ones by which the court is bound in its decision, since the sentence dictated by the court must resolve all the points raised in these submissions, and only those.[28] According to the *principio acusatorio*[29] a person needs to be charged before he can be convicted. It is, therefore, not possible for the court to charge somebody with a crime of which he has not been accused by the prosecution and consequently against which he has not had the possibility of defending.

However, different problems can arise at this stage. For example, the court might believe that once all evidence has been heard a crime has taken place and that it has been committed by the defendant. The prosecution might, on the other hand, have withdrawn the charges. If the court were to condemn the defendant without accusation it would amount to an infringement of the accusatory principle. It also could amount to denial of the right of defence if the crime the court believes the defendant has committed is different from the crime with which he was originally charged, because, in this case, the defendant would not have been given the opportunity to be heard and to conduct his defence. Conversely a similar problem may arise when the court

---

[26] The persons involved in obtaining such evidence can be charged in criminal proceedings.

[27] See J. Tomé *op. cit.*, p.313.

[28] *Principio de congruencia.*

[29] Which govern criminal proceedings during the second stage, or public hearing.

believes that mitigating circumstances exist and these have not been pleaded by the accusation or the defence.

The solution to these problems can be found in Art.733 of the LECrim which provides that,

> "if on the basis of the evidence presented, the court understands that specification of charges has been made on the basis of *clear mistake*, the president of the court can ask the prosecution and/or the defence whether they believe the facts constitute the offence that has been described in the specification of charges or a different one as suggested by the court, or whether the prosecution or the defence think that any mitigating circumstances have taken place".[30]

This exceptional power of the court should be applied with moderation. There is considerable *jurisprudencia* of the Supreme Court on the application of this provision of the LECrim by the courts.[31] In general it is possible to charge the defendant with a different offence if this is of the same nature,[32] provided that a circumstance exempting or reducing liability has not been raised by the prosecution or the defence.[33] It is not possible, however for the court to suggest that a circumstance increasing liability has taken place because it would amount to a denial of the right of defence.[34]

The definitive submissions are made orally to the court. First, the president of the court permits the public prosecutor to speak, followed by the lawyer of the private or popular prosecution and then the lawyer of the civil plaintiff, if any. The last person to make definitive submissions is the defence. These submissions must state the facts which the party making the submission considers proved according to the evidence put forward during the trial, the legal clarification of those facts, i.e. which offence is charged, any

---

[30] Art.733 LECrim "*si juzgando por el resultado de las pruebas entendiera el tribunal que el hecho justiciable ha sido calificado con manifiesto error, podra el Presidente emplear la siguiente formula: Sin que sea visto prejuzgar el fallo definitivo sobre las conclusiones de la acusacion y la defensa el Tribunal desea que el Fiscal y los defensores del procesado le ilustren acerca de si el hecho justiciable constituye el delito de . . . o si existe la circunstancia eximente de responsabilidad a que se refiere el num . . . del art 8 del CP*".

[31] See J. Tomé, *op. cit.*, pp.314–316 for a detailed explanation of this point.

[32] STS of November 4, 1986, and June 16, 1988, and STC of April 18, 1981, October 10, 1986 and December 29, 1989.

[33] STS of September 30, 1988.

[34] STC of December 29, 1989; STS of November 4, 1986, June 17, 1989, and February 25, 1991.

extenuating, aggravating or mitigating circumstances and the evidence supporting these.

After all parties have submitted their conclusions and before the president declares the trial to be *listo para sentencia*,[35] he will ask the defendant if he wishes to make any final statement. After this, the President announces that the trial is closed (Arts 739 and 740) and will ask the public to leave the courtroom. All the parties will be asked to sign the record.

The court will then retire to consider its verdict.

The Sentencia

Once the trial has been closed the court has five days in which to give a verdict. However, because of the overload that Spanish courts have, this period can be longer. The court will conduct its discussions privately on the same day or the next business day. One of the judges of the court—*el Magistrado Ponente*—is in charge of summarising the case and gives his opinion on the case. After this all the judges vote. Decisions are made by a simple majority of votes and all issues must be considered separately (Arts 741–2). The court must decide on the innocence or guilt of the defendant and the issues of civil liability raised. It must he remembered that up until now the presumption of innocence applies[36] and any doubts or deadlocks must be decided in favour of the defendant—*in dubio pro reo*.

The *Sentencia* must acquit or condemn the defendant (Arts 141 and 742 LECrim). The document containing the *sentencia* has three parts. The first part is called *encabezamiento*, and states: the place and date of the decision, the court dictating it, the facts leading to the opening of the proceedings, the names, addresses and occupations of the parties, and the name of the *Magistrado Ponente* and the other judges. It also has a number as required by the LOPJ in order to keep a special record of all decisions, and an indication as to whether the public prosecution has been a party to the proceedings or not.

The second part is a summary of the facts—*antecentes de hecho*[37]—in which all the facts connected with the final verdict must be stated. It is also necessary to make a clear declaration as to the facts considered to be proved[38] and of the conclusions of the parties,

---

[35] Literally "ready or sentence".

[36] Except in serious drug related offences.

[37] The LOPJ has substituted the traditional denomination *resultandos* by the term *antecedentes de hecho*.

[38] It is not possible to declare somebody guilty of an offence which has not been proved, STS of November 14, 1981.

including whether the court has used the power included in Art.733 LECrim.[39]

The third part of the decision is called *fundamentos de derecho*, in which the court, according to Art.142 LECrim, expresses the application of the law to the facts proved. It must contain the legal and doctrinal justification as to the classification of the facts considered to be proved as a criminal offence.[40] It must also explain, in legal terms, the participation of the defendant in the commission of the offence and the existence of any aggravating, or mitigating circumstances. In a separate paragraph it must state the legal implications as to civil liability and the imposition of the *costas*.[41] All legal rules applicable to the case must be stated and properly cited.

The last part of the decision is the verdict—*el fallo*—which will declare whether the defendant is guilty or innocent and decide the *costas* and any civil liability (Art.142 LECrim).

The judgment—*sentencia*—must be written and signed by the judge or judges. It must be made public by being read aloud by the *Magistrado Ponente* in court. After this the original is filed in the record of judgments (Art.159 LECrim and Art.266 LOPJ) where all judgments have a number and are kept in chronological order. A true copy is made by the clerk who will include it in the record of the case. The judgment will be notified to the parties and their *procuradores*.[42]

8. *RECURSOS*[43]

Depending on which court dictated the judgment the parties have different possibilities of challenging the decision.

For judgments given in abbreviated proceedings,[44] it is possible to appeal the decision of the *Juez de Paz, Juez de lo Penal*, or the *Juez Central de lo Penal* (Art.795 LECrim). The *recurso de apelación* must be made within ten days from the date of judgment. In order to be

---

[39] See above, p.184.
[40] For instance the court will say: "the facts declared to be proved constitute a criminal offence, typified in art . . . of the Criminal Code with the punishment of . . ."
[41] The expenses caused by the proceedings. See below.
[42] Remember that the role of the *procurador* is to liaise between the court and his client. See Ch.4, pp.84–5.
[43] The Spanish terminology is retained because, as explained earlier, this word has a wider meaning than the term "appeal".
[44] And in *juicios de faltas,* where an appeal is possible to the *Juez de Primera Instancia*.

admissible the party appealing must have suffered prejudice as a result of the judicial decision. The appeal must be made in writing, stating all relevant submissions and include a petition to the court (Art.795(2)). This appeal must be lodged with the trial court. The grounds of appeal depend on a mistake of the facts by the trial judge, or a mistake in law or in procedure.

The judge, if he considers that there are grounds for appeal, will pass the submissions to the other party who has the right to make his own declarations, and will then refer the whole dossier to the higher court for decision. This higher court[45] will then re-try the case. It is possible to introduce new evidence in the circumstances stated in Art.795(3),[46] although the appellate court must abide by the evidence already accepted in the original trial. The procedure at this stage is mainly written and there is no need for a public hearing (Art.795(8)) although this is possible. The court will then give its judgment (Art.796 LECrim).

Further appeal is only possible either by the *recurso de casación* or the *recurso extraordinario de queja* and only on the specific grounds fixed for each of these.

The judgments of the *Audiencia Provincial* and the *Audiencia Nacional* in proceedings for serious crimes are final, the only appeal against them which is possible is the *recurso de casación* and the *recurso de queja*.

The *recurso de casación* is only available on points of law or procedure, never on the appreciation of the facts by the court. This *recurso* is not possible against the decisions of the Supreme Court (Art.847(II) *LE*Crim) or decisions of the *Juez de lo Penal* and the *Juez de Paz* in proceedings for minor offences.[47]

The grounds for *casación* depend on a mistake in law—*infracción de ley* (Art.849(1) and (2) LECrim) and the breach of formalities in the proceedings—*quebrantamiento de forma*, (Arts 850 and 851 LECrim).

Mistakes in law can be of two types: infringement of a substantive rule of law, i.e. a rule of the Criminal Code; or mistakes in the appreciation of documentary evidence. Although the Supreme Court does not analyse questions of fact, or evidence, an exception is made when the judge clearly made a mistake as to the evidence presented by documents which was not contradicted by other evidence.

---

[45] The *Audiencia Provincial* in appeals against decisions of the *Juzgados de lo Penal* and the *Audiencia Nacional* for appeals against decisions of the *Juzgado Central de lo Penal*.

[46] Evidence which could have been presented before, or the presentation of which was wrongly rejected by the trial judge.

[47] Against the latter two the *recurso de apelación* is available.

Infringement of procedure or lack of formalities can occur either during the proceedings or during the elaboration of the judgment by the court.

If the Supreme Court considers that there has been a mistake in law, it will pass its own judgment to resolve the case. In accordance with the principle of *reformatio in peius* (Art.902) this new judgment cannot impose a punishment higher than the punishment imposed in the first and now annulled judgment.[48]

If there has been lack of formalities, the case will return to the original trial court which must re-try it from the point in the proceedings where the infringement happened (Art.901 (bis)(a)) and dictate a new decision.

The last available *recurso* is the *recurso extraorinario de revisión*. This is an extraordinary procedure against definitive judgments which can only be initiated when new facts prove that the person has been punished on erroneous grounds because new facts or documents are discovered after the end of the proceedings. The court with jurisdiction to hear of this *recurso* is the Supreme Court. Locus standi for the commencement of this *recurso* lies with the prosecutor of the Supreme Court—*Fiscal del Tribunal Supremo*—(Art.957), but the person who was wrongly punished, or his relatives, can request the Minister of Justice to open investigations in order to ascertain the existence of the grounds for *revisión* (Art.955 LECrim). It these grounds exist, the Minister will request the Prosecutor of the Supreme Court to initiate the *recurso*. The grounds for the *recurso de revisión*—which are stated in Art.954 LECrim—are, first, when more than one person has been condemned and contradictory sentences have been passed for the commission of an offence which only one of them could have committed; secondly, when a person was condemned on the basis of evidence provided by documents or witnesses' statements which were later declared false in a criminal procedure; thirdly, when a person was condemned for the manslaughter of a person who is proved to be alive after the sentence; and fourthly, when, after the sentence, new facts establish the innocence of the person condemned.[49]

The procedure for the *recurso de revisión* is written; the prosecutor and the person condemned make their submissions to the court. The Supreme Court will decide whether the decision needs to be annulled and, depending on the circumstances of the case, whether a new trial

---

[48] *STC* of 84/1985 of July 8.
[49] The Constitution guarantees compensation by the State for judicial error (Art.121; also the LOPJ Arts 292–297).

is necessary. If the person condemned is later found to have been innocent, he or his next of kin will be entitled to compensation for damages by the State and to the rehabilitation of his name. Even if the person wrongly declared guilty is already dead his widow or descendants can request the procedure of *revisión* in order to rehabilitate his memory and prosecute the real author of the offence.[50]

9. Costs and legal aid

The costs incurred in criminal proceedings include the fees of the *abogado* and *procurador*[51] (Arts 241(2) and (3) LECrim), the fees payable to experts, the expenses of witnesses and any other expenses, such as public notices in official journals (Art.241(4) LECrim).

The judge in the final judgment must make a decision as to liability for costs. The principle, in criminal procedure, is that the winner does not pay any costs, but that these are borne by the person who loses. This principle is complemented by the rule of bad faith, by which any party who started the proceedings in bad faith will have to pay the costs.[52] In respect of the defendant, there are two possible situations. The first is that he is declared guilty, in which case he will have to pay all costs (Art.240 LECrim) and Arts 123 and 124 CP). The second is that he is declared innocent in which case he will not have to pay costs (Art. 240 LECrim) in respect of expenses incurred by the proceedings, but he will still have to pay his lawyers, witnesses and experts (Art.242 LECrim), unless the person bringing the private accusation acted in bad faith. The costs are calculated according to the criteria of Art.242 LECrim.

There is provision for legal aid or *beneficio de justicia gratuita*, for those persons who do not have sufficient economic means to litigate. The *beneficio* will be awarded according to the criteria of Arts 123–5 LECrim, taking into account the economic circumstances of the claimant and his family (Arts 126 and 127 LECrim). If legal aid is awarded, the beneficiary will be exempted from payment of any fees and will be represented by an *abogado* and *procurador de oficio* paid by the State (Art.440(2) LOPJ).

---

[50] Arts 960 and 961 LECrim.

[51] The latter charges an *arancel* or fixed fee.

[52] The application of this principle in criminal procedure is however, reduced because if the judge or the public prosecution do not think that the facts amount to a criminal offence or that the evidence available indicates that the defendant might have committed the offence, they will order a stay of the proceedings. The private prosecutor will then have to pay the costs incurred up to that stage.

The judge who has jurisdiction over the case will decide on the award of free legal aid. Both Spanish citizens and foreigners can enjoy this benefit.

10.   ENFORCEMENT

Judgments in criminal proceedings, unless these end in acquittal, need to be enforced by the State. Article 117 CE establishes that the execution or enforcement of judgments in all cases must be carried out by the judicial power. The different types of sentences that can be imposed will require a different machinery of enforcement. Punishments in Spain can be divided into the following groups: imprisonment, punishments restrictive of rights other than freedom, punishments restricting freedom of residence, others.

The first type of punishment, imprisonment, is the most important because of the consequences it has for the person condemned. Prison sentences are arranged in steps and degrees.[53] Their duration can vary from six months to 20 years.[54] There is no death penalty in Spain except for military crimes in times of war.[55] If the person condemned has not got a criminal record and the punishment imposed is imprisonment for less than two years, the judge can suspend the sentence (Art.80(2) CP) on condition that the person condemned does not commit any offence in the next five years.[56] This measure was introduced in order to solve two problems—overcrowding in Spanish prisons, and the constitutional mandate that punishments should be directed at the re-education and rehabilitation of the delinquent and that consequently the effects of imprisonment for less than a year could theoretically be worse than leaving him at liberty.[57]

In all cases of prison sentences there are two types of judges who intervene in the enforcement of the sentence, the judge who dictated it and the *Juez de Vigilancia Penitenciaria*.[58] This latter type of judge was created by the LO 1/1979 *General Penitenciaria* (LGP)[59] with the

---

[53] See *Código Penal* 1995, *Libro* I, *Titulo* III.
[54] Art.36 CP.
[55] Art.15 CE.
[56] See also, Art.36 CP.
[57] Note that the Criminal Code of 1995 has reduced the maximum term of punishment and has increased to two years the possibility of suspension.
[58] Prison Judge.
[59] The LO 1/79 was modified by the LO 6/2003 of June 30 in order to facilitate access to education of inmates.

specific function of supervising the enforcement of prison sentences, safeguarding respect for the fundamental rights of inmates and any other matters connected with the above, for instance: granting parole, authorising sanctions against inmates in prison, concessions of benefits to inmates, changes of regime or remission.[60]

There are three types of prisons in Spain: *establecimientos preventivos*—remand prisons—(Arts 7(a) and 81(1) LGP), *establecimientos de cumplimiento de penas*—ordinary prisons—which can be of two types, ordinary or open (Arts 7(b) and 9 LGP) and *establecimientos especiales*—special prisons—i.e. psychiatric hospitals, general hospital or "rehabilitation" centres (Arts 7(c) 11 LGP).

Each prisoner is subject to an examination by a team composed of a criminologist, a psychologist, a social worker and a teacher, in order to determine the "criminological type", and the possibilities of rehabilitation and social reintegration. They will decide to which type of prison the prisoner must be sent to and will give him a "grade" (Art.74(2) LGP and Art.242(2) RLGP). There are four grades: first grade or closed prison regime (Art.46 RGP), in which case the convicted prisoner is sent to an ordinary prison; second grade or ordinary regime (Art.44 RGP), whereby the prisoner is also sent to an ordinary prison, but the regime is more open than in the first degree; third grade or open regime (Art.45 RGP), for prisoners sent to an "open prison", where the prison regime is based on two elements, namely the trust given to the prisoner and the absence of obstacles preventing escape,[61] and fourth degree or parole (Art.58 RGP), for prisoners who have already served three-quarters of their prison sentence and who provide guarantees that they will live a "normal life".

Fines are enforced by the court, which will request payment from the convicted. One of the novelties of the 1995 Criminal Code was the introduction of the "*días multa*".[62] If the convicted refuses to pay the court will execute the fine in the same way in which civil monetary decisions are enforced,[63] or, if this is unsuccessful the court will arrest the convicted person with one day of arrest being the equivalent of two unpaid daily quotas or tariffs.[64]

---

[60] See J.L. Gómez Colomer, *op. cit.*, pp.309–311 and R. Vogler, *op. cit.*, pp.89 and 90
[61] The advantages, according to J. L. Gómez Colomer, are that this system is more in accordance with the aims of social rehabilitation, improves physical and mental health, stimulates "normal" family relationships, is less expensive, encourages and facilitates the finding of employment and solves the sexual problems of prisoners. The only inconvenience is the possibility of escape, which, according to the same author, is statistically very low. *op. cit.*, p.318.
[62] Art.50 CP.
[63] See Ch.5, pp.128–9.
[64] See Art.53 CP.

Other type of punishments can consist of the restriction of certain rights other than freedom of movement, for example, deprivation of driving licence (Art.789(2) LECrim) suspension from public office or restriction on the exercise of private professions (Arts 39–49 CP) or the imposition of community work.

Chapter Seven
Constitutional law

1. THE CROWN

Spain, according to Art.1 of the Constitution, is "a social and democratic State of Law" in which sovereignty rests on the nation and the political form of government is a parliamentary monarchy.[1] In a parliamentary monarchy the king is a separate institution from the executive, and the Government is responsible to Parliament as opposed to "pure constitutional monarchies" in which the king is the holder of the executive power and there is no provision for liability of the executive to parliament.

The 1978 Constitution drafted the main lines defining the physiognomy of the Spanish monarchy. However it is not possible to reduce the different forms of government to legal terms because within the framework of a constitution it is possible to find great varieties concerning the form of government. A clear example is provided by the United States, the history of which presents certain periods when Congress was prevalent, others, including the present, of presidential pre-eminence, and even times when it was possible to talk about a "government of the judges".[2] It is also important to note that the extent to which constitutional powers are exercised by the monarch will depend on external and political factors such as the system of political parties. In Britain, a classical example of a typical parliamentary monarchy, the intervention of the monarch in the formation of governments has been drastically reduced since the 19th century due to the rigid "Two-Party System", but this intervention would increase if this system of parties changed.[3]

---

[1] Art.1 CE "España se constituye en un Estado social y democrático de Derecho . . . La soberanía nacional reside en el pueblo español . . . La forma política del Estado español; es la Monarquía parlamentaria."
[2] Miguel Satrústegui in Luis López Guerra y otros, Derecho Constitucional (1992), Vol.II p.17.
[3] A. Hauriou, Droit Constitutionnel et Institutions Politiques (1974), pp.465–8.

FUNCTIONS OF THE KING

The King of Spain is the Head of State.[4] The King is a constitutional organ of the State and his functions are defined by the constitutional text. As a constitutional organ the King is in a position of parity with all the other constitutional organs as none of them is subordinate to the others. As Head of State, on the other hand, the King enjoys formal supremacy and higher dignities and honours.[5] He is also the symbol of the "unity and permanence" of the State. This function, which is common to Heads of State,[6] has an historical meaning since the monarchy has traditionally been a symbol of the territorial unity of a number of different kingdoms and territories in Spain.[7] The King stands in a position of neutrality, guaranteeing the regular functions of the institutions of the State.[8] He acts as a special type of arbitrator[9] and represents the State in international relations, signing international treaties and declarations of war or peace.[10] The powers of the King are at the service of State politics as directed by the Executive and authorised by the Parliament.

The King is also the head of the armed forces (Art.62(h) CE) and guarantees the Constitution and the Constitutional order by carrying out the last step of the main acts of the State: he sanctions Acts of Parliament, the celebration of treaties, the convocation of referendum. As head of the armed forces his position is distinct from the military hierarchy because the King is in a position of institutional supremacy which has both a civil and a military character. This is crucial in times when the Executive is unable to govern because the orders of the King must be followed by the armed forces, according to military discipline.[11]

All the acts of the King as the Head of State need to be endorsed by a different constitutional organ, which will be held responsible for

---

[4] Art.56(1) CE "*El Rey es el jefe del Estado . . .*".

[5] The Constitution itself starts with the Crown, before it defines the other powers of the State.

[6] See Art.5 of the French Constitution or Art.87 of the Italian Constitution.

[7] See, Ch.1 for an overview of the history of the different kingdoms that integrate what today is known as Spain and, for a more detailed analysis, Miguel Satrústregui, *op. cit.*, p.19.

[8] Art.56(1) CE "*El Rey arbitra y modera el funcionamiento regular de las instituciones*".

[9] Special, because sometimes his function is to impose the choice of the Congress for instance when he proposes a candidate for president in the absence of a majority party in Congress (Art.62(3) CE).

[10] Arts 63(2) and 62(3) CE.

[11] This aspect of the orders of the King was evident on the night of February 23, 1981, when an attempted coup was successfully aborted due to the intervention of the King.

these.[12] The responsibility of the endorser extends to the content and formalities of the act except when the person endorsing the act has not participated in the procedure of production of the act; for example, when the President of the Government countersigns or endorses the nomination of the members of the Constitutional Court proposed by Parliament, the President is only responsible for the formal requirements of the procedure.

2.   LAS CORTES GENERALES (PARLIAMENT)

Parliament is the main institution of the State. As Art.66 CE states, Parliament is the representative of the nation and its functions can safely be described as the main functions of the State: legislative (producing the main rules of the system), budgetary (authorising the expenses of the State) and of control of the Government. Parliament also authorises the international obligations of the State and proposes candidates for other constitutional organs such as the Ombudsman (*defensor del pueblo*).

In a democratic system Parliament is the forum where all the major decisions affecting society are taken and where the different political forces can express their views and give their consent or disapproval to the acts of the Government.

Freedom of Parliament is limited only by the Constitution and the principle of national sovereignty. According to this principle, sovereignty rests on the nation and not with Parliament. Parliament is only a representative of the citizens and so it must seek their specific consent before taking important decisions, for example in cases of reform of the Constitution or the *Estatutos de Automomía*.[13] On the other hand the Constitution itself limits the freedom of Parliament when it legislates, and demands respect for the "fundamental rights and freedoms" recognised in the Constitution.[14] A further control on the legislative function of Parliament is provided by the Constitutional Court which supervises the adequacy of, and respect for the Constitutional order, by the different laws approved by Parliament.[15]

This system of control of the different organs of the State by other organs is a typical of democratic societies and guarantees that there are no abuses of power by any of the organs of the State.

---

[12] Art.64(2) *CE "De los actos del Rey serán responsables las personas que los refrenden".*
[13] See more on current reforms to the *Estatutos de Autonomía* below, p.206.
[14] See above, Ch.2 p.32.
[15] *Recurso ó cuestión de inconstitucionalidad*, Arts 27 and 37 LOTC. See below, p.199.

COMPOSITION

The Spanish Parliament has two chambers: *el Congreso de los Diputados* (the Congress of Deputies) and *el Senado* (the Senate).[16] According to the Constitution the bi-cameral system is a consequence of the recognition of the right to autonomy of the regions and nationalities (Art.2 CE). The *Senado* is meant to be the chamber of territorial representation—such as is found in federal systems—while the *Congreso* is the chamber of popular representation. The members of each chamber are elected according to different electoral systems to reflect the different character and function of each chamber.

The Spanish bi-cameralism had been described[17] as "asymmetrical and uneven" because each chamber has a different function with powers which are exclusive to that chamber and in respect of which the other has no power at all,[18] which makes them asymmetrical; they are uneven, because the *Congreso* is in a position of clear superiority over the *Senado*, both in the relationship with the Executive and in the legislative proceedings whereby the *Congreso* can decide whether or not it accepts any modifications introduced by the *Senado*.

Due to the nature of Parliament as a deliberative organ with a large number of members, the Chambers are organised so as to achieve efficiency in the performance of their functions. The Chambers are organised by dividing their functions between "government agencies" and "functioning agencies". Each Chamber has a President, elected by the members of that Chamber at the beginning of a new Parliament, who co-ordinates the work of the Chamber and represents it when necessary. It also has a Board—*Mesa*—elected by the Members of Parliament, which is composed of the President of the Chamber, four Vice-Presidents in the Congress and two in the Senate, and several secretaries (Art.30(2) RC and Art.5(1) RS). The Board has administrative functions and in fact organises all the work of the Chamber. Together with these there is a *Junta de Portavoces*. This is a modern agency which reflects the reality of the political forces in Parliament. Each parliamentary group has a representative in the *Junta*. There is also a representative from the Executive, and it is chaired by the President of the Chamber.

How the Chamber actually works depends on the nature of the matter. The main decisions will be taken in a plennary session—*el Pleno*, by all the Members of the Chamber sitting to the right and left

---

[16] Art.66 CE.
[17] M. Satrústegui. *op. cit.*, p.69.
[18] The *Congreso* appoints the President (Art.99 CE) and ratifies *decretos ley* (Art.86 CE) while the *Senado* has exclusive powers relating to the autonomous communities.

of the hemicycle according to political orientation,[19] or by different commissions—*Comisiones*—(Art.75(1) CE). Since the normal functioning of Parliament nowadays would be impossible if every member had to give his point of view, because of the diversity, complexity and technicalities of modern regulations, the Chambers have a series of organs, called *Comisiones*, which study in detail the different proposed regulations and the technicalities involved therein. The draft legislation of these *Comisiones* is called *Dictamen* and this will usually be not only the basis of later discussion by the *Pleno*, but in general, very similar to the definitive text adopted. The *Comisiones* of the Chambers have full legislative power in most matters. They can definitively approve *proyectos* or *proposiciones de ley* without the need for ratification or approval by the *Pleno*, the intervention of which is only necessary in particularly important matters such as modifications to the Constitution, international matters, *leyes orgánicas* and *leyes de bases*, and the approval of the general budget (Art.75(3) CE).[20]

There are different types of *Comisiones*; usually each of them works in a delimited area which corresponds to a ministerial department of the Government, for instance, industry. These are called *Comisiones permanentes legislativas*. It is intended that these *Comisiones* reproduce the *Pleno* on a small scale and so they are composed of representatives of different parliamentary groups. They also have a president and a board. There are other types of *Comisiones* which are "special", and are created by the Chamber in order to study a specific matter, and which will be dissolved once this special project has been completed; a good example is the creation of the special commission for the investigation of party funding.

Members of Parliament of the same political ideology need to be grouped in what are called parliamentary groups. These groups represent a political ideology. If a member does not identify with any of these formations they integrate with what is called a "mixed group"— *Grupo mixto*—since it is compulsory to be integrated into a group. The minimum number of Members of Parliament for the creation of a parliamentary group is 15 members for Congress and 10 for the Senate. Members of the same party must all belong to the same group, otherwise artificial groups will be created in order to obtain greater voice and power. The function of these groups can be described as political on the one hand, because they either support or challenge the politics of the Executive; and technical on the other,

---

[19] i.e. the denomination of groups of left and right.
[20] See for the requirements of these Ch.2, pp.32 and 40.

because the different agencies of Parliament, *Juntas*, *Mesas* and *Comisiones*, will be created by the members of the different groups.[21]

STATUS OF MEMBERS OF PARLIAMENT

Historically, democratic societies grant the chambers of Parliament and its members guarantees and privileges for the better performance of their functions. These are not rights of individual members of the Parliament but real rules of law which will be applied *ex lege* by the courts if the situation for which they exist arises. These prerogatives cannot, therefore, be renounced. There are two types of prerogative; the ones enjoyed by the Chambers (*Congreso and Senado*) and the ones enjoyed by their members. In the former group the most relevant is the power that each Chamber has to regulate its own functioning (Art.72(1) CE). These regulations are known as *Reglamento*[22] and are the main source of law for the regulation of the activities of each Chamber.

The Constitution[23] specifies some of the main aspects of the functioning of Parliament, but due to the general character of the constitutional text the importance of the *Reglamentos* is crucial. A *Reglamento* is approved by the absolute majority of each Chamber, a procedure which guarantees protection of the interests of the minority groups. The *Reglamentos* are not *leyes* in the formal sense of the word because they are not made according to the legislative procedure[24]—they are not sanctioned by the King or published in the *BOE*; but they enjoy *fuerza de ley*[25] and are subject to the control of the Constitutional Court according to Art.27(2) LOTC. The Chambers also have the power to approve their own budget for the exercise of their functions (Art.72(1) CE) and they have "inviolability" which means that nobody can be held liable for the activities of the Parliament as such (Art.63 CE).

Members of Parliament also enjoy different guarantees to ensure the best performance of their duties. These can be described as the *Estatuto de los Parlamentarios*, which includes the different prerogatives, guarantees and obligations attached to the condition of being a Member of Parliament. Included in these rules are certain duties; for example the incompatibility of being a Member of Parliament with

---

[21] For more information about parliamentary groups see: Arts 23–8 RC and 28–34 RS and J.M. Morales Arroyo, *Los Grupos Parlamentarios* (1990). Reformed on September 26, 1996 and May 11, 2000.

[22] There is a *Reglamento del Congreso* (of February 10, 1982) and a *Reglamento del Senado* of May 3, 1994, modified in 1995 and 2000.

[23] Arts 73, 75(1), 76, 78, 79 and 80 CE.

[24] See below.

[25] STC 118/88, *Caso Roca*.

certain other public positions (for instance it is not possible to be a judge and a Member of Parliament) in order to guarantee the independence of the office of the member and the obligation of accepting the Constitution (Art.20(3) RC and Arts 11 and 12 RS).[26] Others are rights such as the protection, immunity and special jurisdiction of Members of Parliament. Members of Parliament are protected so that their declarations in the Chambers of Parliament do not attract negative consequences or legal sanctions. This protection covers any declaration made in Parliament, but excludes, for instance, opinions expressed by Members of Parliament outside any parliamentary activity.[27]

A different right of Members of Parliament is the right of immunity by which no criminal action can be brought against them as a consequence of their political activities. This latter right is very different from the former since it only extends to criminal actions. The immunity does not exclude criminal prosecution of a Member of Parliament but it aims to guarantee that any prosecution is not started for a political reasons. It is given effect by establishing a procedure by which, before a criminal action is started against the member of one of the Chambers, a *supplicatorio* or petition must be made to the respective Chamber, which will then decide whether there is a political motivation or retaliation in starting the proceedings. If the Chamber thinks that there are no political reasons behind the action, it might authorise the action to proceed but at this point, the third prerogative arises. This is, that any criminal action against a member of Parliament will be heard and decided by the Supreme Court (Art.71(3) CE). This is known as the "special jurisdiction" of *Diputados y Senadores*. The privilege of immunity has a clear political nature and it is not strictly a right of the individual member, because the Chamber might deny the possibility of prosecution even if the member asks for it to be permitted. This immunity of jurisdiction obviously does not cover cases in which the member of Parliament is caught in the flagrant commission of a crime.

The LO 7/2002 of July 5 modified the procedure for criminal actions against Members of Parliament on the grounds that the right of defence guaranteed to all citizens[28] was jeopardised by the so-called prerogatives and procedural privileges granted to Members of Parliament. Many of the allegations and accusations against Members of Parliament are politically motivated as we have noted. The secret of the *suplicatorio* meant that in many occasions a

---

[26] See STC 119/90, *Caso Idigoras-Aizpurúa-Alcalde.*
[27] Compare STC 51/85 *Caso Castells* and *STC* 30/86 *Caso Casa de Juntas de Guernica.*
[28] By Art.24(2) CE—*Derecho a la tutela judicial efectiva.*

Member of Parliament only knew through the press that a case had been brought against him without any possibility at that stage to provide his version of the facts or prepare his defence appropriately. The new features introduced in 2002 allow the Member of Parliament to know immediately of any *denuncia* or *querella* brought up against him. He can, at this stage, become a party to the proceedings and provide any evidence to the judge. This does respect Art.71(2) CE because at this point the Member of Parliament has not been charged with any criminal offence. If charges are brought, then the authorisation of Parliament becomes necessary. The Second Chamber of the Supreme Court was already accepting declarations of Members of Parliament duly represented by an *abogado* and *procurador*.[29]

Different in character, but related to the former, is the question of remuneration of Members of Parliament. In order to ensure that no economic factors would influence the political views of Members of Parliament and that every citizen has access to political activity it was necessary to provide Members of Parliament with an independent allowance.[30] Today the salary of Members of Parliament in Spain is fixed by the *Reglamento* of each Chamber (Art.8(1) RC and Art.23(1) RS).

THE LAW-MAKING PROCESS

It has been stated that one of the functions of Parliament is the elaboration of laws. In parliamentary monarchies the legislative power, or the capacity to make the rules of law that are to define the system, is vested in Parliament.[31] This does not mean that Parliament has the sole power to make laws because in modern societies, due to the complexity of the matters that need to be regulated, the Executive is increasingly producing rules through its own reglamentary power and by using the mechanism of "urgent legislation". However, even in those instances in which the Executive plays a leading role as to the volume of legislation, its activities of law-making are controlled by Parliament; either by a posteriori control and ratification of urgent legislation[32]; or by the principle of the hierarchy of sources, by which any *reglamento* produced by the Executive in the exercise of its legislative power must be subject to laws previously approved by

---

[29] See Art.118 *bis* LECrim., *www.porticolegal.com/pa_ley.php?ref=849*.

[30] It also establishes the definitive separation from a system of "imperative mandate" to pure representation.

[31] Even if the Executive can dictate rules of law—*reglamentos*—these are subject to the laws dictated by Parliament.

[32] See *Decretos leyes*, Ch.2, pp.38–9.

Parliament (*leyes*) on the matter. Otherwise the laws made by the Executive (*reglamentos*), will be illegal and thus not applicable.[33]

Before describing the procedure of law-making, it is necessary to indicate who are the subjects, or entities, vested with what is called "legislative initiative". In other words, who can initiate or ask Parliament to produce a rule of law having the force of *ley*. Historically this power was linked to the question of who had sovereignty: the king, the government, parliament or the nation. Today the Spanish legal system, while recognising that sovereignty rests on the nation,[34] acknowledges a diversity of subjects with the power of "legislative initiative".

Article 87 of the Constitution vests the full ordinary legislative initiative in the Government, the Congress and the Senate. It also vests this power in the governments and assemblies of the Autonomous Communities (Art.87(2)),[35] and, with some limitations (Art.87(3))[36] in the nation. All these five subjects have the power to initiate the law making process, but with important differences.

Since the Executive is in charge of national politics most of the proposals for legislation will actually come from it. The Constitution accordingly vests full power to start the law-making procedure in the Government. The Executive will draft a "project of law"—*projecto de ley*—which needs to be approved by the Council of Ministers and then referred to Congress, which is the Chamber that starts the drafting of the laws, with an *Exposición de Motivos* and all the antecedents to the proposed legislation, in order to facilitate the activities of Congress in elaborating the laws.

The Chambers of Parliament also have the power to initiate the law making procedure. The draft proposals—*proposiciones de ley*—must be endorsed by 15 *diputados* or a Parliamentary group, and any antecedents and aims of the legislation must be included. The Chamber then decides whether it wants to adopt the *proposición de ley* or not; if so, the law-making procedure starts. The approval by the Chambers of the proposal as a whole or in part is necessary because only the Chambers of Parliament have vested "legislative initiative" and not individual members or parliamentary groups. If the *proposición de ley* is presented in the Senate, once the Senate—as a Chamber—has decided to go ahead and endorsed the proposition,

---

[33] See Ch.2, pp.63–3.

[34] Art.1(2) CE. "*La soberanía nacional reside en el pueblo español.*"

[35] This legislative initiative is for a national law and different from the independent legislative power of the Autonomous Parliaments on matters within the power conferred on them by their respective *Estatuto de Autonomía*.

[36] There is a requirement of 5,00,000 signatures endorsing the proposal which can only affect matters which are not reserved to *ley orgánica*, international matters or the *prerogativa de gracia*.

the draft proposal will be passed to the Congress for discussion. The Executive then, has an opportunity to give its opinion and eventually oppose the progress of a particular law if it affects certain matters.[37]

As regards the "popular initiative" or "citizen's initiative", the exercise of this is regulated by the LO 3/1984, of January 26,[38] which is fairly restrictive. First, the Constitution restricts the areas on which legislation based on "popular initiative" is possible.[39] Secondly, any project presented by the "popular commission" in charge of the project needs to be analysed and accepted by one of the *Mesas del Congreso*. If it is accepted, a period of six months begins to run during which it is necessary to collect 50,000 signatures supporting the project presented by the *comisión promontora*. If, after this, the project goes ahead the State will reimburse the expenses of authentication of signatures and of the publicity for the campaign. If the project fails, it is an expensive process which makes it difficult for certain groups/sectors of society to have access to this possibility. Some writers criticise this constitutional regulation as unduly restrictive.

The assemblies of the Autonomous Communities may demand that the Government and/or the Chambers of Parliament exercise their power(s) of legislative initiative.[40]

As far as the ordinary legislative procedure is concerned the Constitution establishes the main lines, while the Chambers have the possibility of complementing and developing these guidelines in their own *Reglamento*. Draft legislation is examined first in the Congress and then in the Senate. The procedure starts with a discussion in Congress where there are clear, differentiated steps. The first stage is the *fase de enmiendas a la totalidad* (period of amendments) during which the project or proposition can be totally rejected and substituted by a different one, by returning the text to the Executive or the Senate. These amendments to the whole of the proposal can only be presented by a parliamentary group and need to be discussed and approved by the *Pleno* (Art.110(3), 126 and 127 RC). It is not possible to make a total amendment to a proposition coming from the Congress or from "popular initiative". The second stage is the discussion in the relevant commission, depending on the subject matter of the proposed text—*fase de comisión*. Here the amendments are studied

---

[37] The Executive can oppose legislative proposals which vary the national budget (Art.134 CE); or which contain measures contrary to a previous delegation of legislative power to the Executive (Art.84 CE).

[38] *Ley Orgánica Reguladora de la Iniciativa Popular* LO 3/1984 of March 26.

[39] Arts 87(3), 131 and 34 CE.

[40] See Art.87(2) CE.

and a report is prepared for a subsequent discussion in the plenary session. The last stage in the Congress is the plenary discussion and vote—*fase de pleno*—where it is decided which text is accepted, the original one, the amendment or an intermediate text.

After discussion in the Congress, the text goes to the Senate where, within a period of two months, the text must be approved, amended, or rejected. The procedure in the Senate is very similar to the discussion in the Congress: the text goes first to the commissions for discussion and is then referred to the plenary session for final approval. The Senate has the right of veto, i.e. the rejection of the text by absolute majority.

If the text is approved by the Senate, the new law is ready to be sanctioned by the King and published in the official journal and the legislative procedure ends. If the Senate, however, exercises its right of *veto* or introduces changes, the text must be returned to the Congress. It is in this situation that the superiority of the Congress is clearly apparent because even in the case of veto by the Senate, the Congress can approve the text by absolute majority. In the case of suggested amendments, these can be adopted or otherwise rejected by a simple majority, in which case the initial text can be approved after two months by a simple majority.

Before the draft discussed in the Chambers becomes a *ley*, there are some formalities it needs to comply with, namely to be signed by the King—*sanción* and *promulgación*—and its publication in the official journal. *El Boletin Oficial del Estado* (BOE).[41]

3. THE GOVERNMENT

THE GOVERNMENT

The executive power in modern monarchies is identified with the Government and thus differentiated from the King. However, as has been pointed out by some writers,[42] there is a lack of historical and modern literature explaining the nature and function of modern governments. One reason for this, can be that the liberal division of powers concentrated on rationalising the exercise of power and subjection to the Law, thus giving Parliament preferential attention and

---

[41] The official journal is published daily, except on Sundays.
[42] See Antonio Torres del Moral, *Principios de Derecho Constitucional Español*, (1992), Vol.2, pp.159–61.

leaving a block of differentiated and heterogeneous powers—which in absolute monarchies belonged to the King—grouped collectively as "executive power". This is why, in the early Constitutions, the Government as such did not exist.[43] It was only when the evolution towards a parliamentary monarchy started to take place that the Government, as a separate organ of the State, appeared.

In the British Constitution the separation of the Government as a separate organ started to emerge clearly with the electoral reform of 1832, when the enlargement of the electorate diminished the power of the Monarch in favour of Parliament, and therefore in favour of the Cabinet and the Prime Minister.[44] In the progressive consolidation of the parliamentary system the Cabinet exercises practically all of the powers of the Crown and the Monarch is an institution symbolising political unity, who can give advice and counsel, and should be kept informed, but does not designate the *Premier* or Prime Minister, as this is determined by the electorate. Because of the relationship between the electorate and the majority of the House of Commons, the British Cabinet effectively directs Parliament.

In Spain the Constitution clearly distinguishes the Government from the King. Article 98 states that the Government is composed of the President, Vice-Presidents, ministers and any other members determined by the law.[45] There are, according to the Constitution, certain essential members in the Government: the President and the Ministers. Together with these there is the possibility of having one or more Vice-Presidents and other members whose existence and functions will be determined by the law.[46] In 1983 the LOACE[47] established 15 ministerial offices and any variation of these must be passed by a law of Parliament. However, since 1985 the different *leyes de presupuestos* (general budget law) have altered this situation by conferring on the President the power to change the number, denomination and powers of the different ministers by *Real Decreto*, this is by a

---

[43] The 1812 Constitution did not mention the Government because the executive power was vested in the King.

[44] A. Torres del Moral, *op. cit.*, p.160.

[45] Art.98(1) CE: "*El Gobierno se compone del Presidente, de los Vicepresidentes en su caso, de los Ministros y de los demás miembros que establezca la ley*".

[46] Not necessarily by a formal *ley*, STC 60/86, *Caso RD ley de medidas urgentes de reforma administrativa; a reglamento* can, according to the main guidelines fixed by a formal *ley*, determine how many and which are the ministerial offices according to the needs and circumstances of each case.

[47] *Ley de organización de la administración central del Estado; Ley* 10/1983 of August 16. The LOACE has been substituted by the LOFAGE *Ley* 6/1997 of April 14. See below.

reglamentary disposition. This system has the advantage of having flexibility and speed, by which ministerial offices can be adapted to the changing circumstances of the nation.[48] Today there are 16 ministerial offices.[49]

In 1997 a specific law was approved to regulate the Government[50] and to complement the more general law on the organisation of the central administration of the state.[51] This law gives a definition of the Government[52] by referring to its functions.

There are three main characteristics that inform the Government according to the law 50/1997: the direction of the Government by the President, the joint responsibility of its collegiate members and the wide autonomy granted to each of the Ministers in their own area.[53]

The Government is one of the central organs of the State. It has executive power and controls the direction of the national politics. The Government is a collegiate entity and functions as a *collegium*. At the same time each of its members has its own functions. It is usual to identify the Government with the Council of Ministers—*Consejo de ministros*—and when the Constitution refers to the Government as a collegiate entity this expression is used.[54]

The President

The President of the Government is a post which has its own characteristics which clearly differentiate the incumbent from other members of the Government. He is not a Prime Minister, in the sense that his position is not that of a *primus inter partes*, but he enjoys a pre-eminence and a power to direct the Government as a whole. Historically, the President was the only member of the Government who had *investidura parlamentaria* which meant that he enjoyed the

---

[48] See Luis López Guerra, *op. cit.*, pp.140–3.

[49] See *www.moncloa.es*.

[50] *Ley* 50/1997 of November 27, *de Organización, Competencia y Funcionamiento del Gobierno*.

[51] The very important LOFAGE, *Ley* 6/1997 of April 14. See below, "The Public Administration".

[52] Art.1, *Ley* 50/1997 that repeats Arts 97 and 98 *CE*.

[53] See the *Exposición de Motivos* of the *Ley* 50/1997 and the Comment and Introduction from Luis Martin Rebollo, *Leyes Administrativas*, (8th edn, Aranzadi) pp.945–8.

[54] Arts 88, 112, 115, 116(2) and (3). Although in Art.116(2) uses both "Government and Council of Ministers" which has given rise to doctrinal discussion as to whether these two expressions should be identified or not. See Luis López Guerra. *op. cit.*, p.145.

initial confidence of Parliament. It is this parliamentary confidence on which the President bases his power. Other ministers are chosen by the President (Art.100 CE) although all Ministers and the President are formally nominated by the King.[55]

The main function of the President is the direction of the Government and the co-ordination of the activities of its members.[56] He also has other functions specifically designated in the Constitution, including the nomination and dismissal of Ministers, the petition of the King to preside over the Council of Ministers (Art.62(9) CE), initiation of the *cuestion de confianza* (Art.112 CE), the dissolution of Parliament "under his exclusive responsibility (Art.115(1) CE), and proposing the submission of a decision to popular referendum (Art.92(2) CE). In most cases the President will consult the Council of Ministers[57] but the above can be called "acts of the President" because in the last instance they are dependent on his exclusive decision.

The President has the support of specific agencies in order to prepare and perform his functions. These organs are not necessarily ministerial departments and they are integrated in the "Presidency of the Government". These two agencies are the "General Secretary of the President" and the "Cabinet of the President". Both agencies are regulated by reglamentary rules according to the general provisions of the LOFAGE.[58]

The Vice-President

Although the existence of one or more Vice-Presidents is optional according to Art.98 CE, a Vice-President of the Government has been a constant presence in Spanish post-constitutional politics. The *Ley del Gobierno*[59] provides for the possibility of having more than one Vice-President and also regulates the main characteristics of his office. The Vice-President supports the President and substitutes for him in cases of illness, death or absence from the country. In practice his main function is the co-ordination of governmental action and planning. He also presides at the meeting of the General Commission of Secretaries of State.

---

[55] The Ministers are appointed by the President and the President by Parliament (Art.99 CE).

[56] Art.2 *Ley* 50/1997.

[57] This is compulsory in the case of the *cuestión the confianza*.

[58] *Ley* 6/1999, see below p.213.

[59] Art.3, *Ley* 50/1997.

The Ministers

The Ministers are the heads or directors of a section of the administration—ministerial departments.[60] However, it is possible to have Ministers who are not the head of any department,[61] usually when it is necessary to resolve a specific task of a very specialised character and of such importance that it seems sensible to include it in the council of Ministers.

The position of Minister is both political and administrative since they are at the same time heads of a department of the Public Administration and members of Government. Ministers are chosen by the President and formally nominated by the King.[62] The President can decide on the termination of the office of Ministers. Their office will also end when the Government as a whole is dissolved, for instance in the case of new general elections or when Parliament withdraws its confidence from the Government.

Each Minister has a Cabinet as a support organ. The Cabinet is a political organ and its members are chosen by the Minister. Members of Government, like Members of Parliament, have a special status, rights and duties. The Constitution accepts the possibility of being Members of Parliament at the same time as Ministers,[63] but Members of Government are not able to have any other public office, nor practice a private profession or commercial activities. The *Ley de incompatibilidades de altos cargos* (*L*25/83 details the regime of incompatibility which extends even to the administration of their one estate if this conflicts with their ministerial duties. Members of Government enjoy criminal protection and the Criminal Code specifies certain crimes against the freedom to exercise their functions by the Members of Government (Arts 160, 161 and 163 CP). Members of Government also enjoy special jurisdiction since it is the Criminal Chamber of the Supreme Court which hears cases against the President and Members of the Government (Art.102 CE). Another procedural particularity, established by the LECrim, is that it is possible for them to give evidence from their office or residence or make any declarations to court in writing, instead of orally, in court.

An important duty of members of Government is the duty to keep secret any matter which could endanger the internal or external safety

---

[60] See Art.4 *Ley* 50/1996 and Arts 12 and 13 of the *Ley* 6/1997.
[61] "*Ministros sin cartera*" according to Art.4 of the *Ley de Régimen Jurídico de la Administración del Estado* of July 26, 1957 (LRJAE).
[62] This is one of the "acts of the President". See above.
[63] Art.98 CE.

of the nation, even in judicial proceedings. In the case of Members of Government this provision extends to the deliberations of the Council of Ministers.

The functions of the Government

The Government is today regulated by its own law, the *Ley* 50/1997. Traditionally the Government has been associated with the executive power and its main function would be the execution of the laws previously approved by Parliament. However, this understanding of the division of powers does not reflect the reality of modern democracies in which the Government clearly does more than execute laws approved by Parliament. The functions of the Government can be divided into functions of political direction and executive functions,[64] since Art.97 of the Constitution seems to differentiate between these.[65]

With regard to the political direction of the State, the powers and functions of the Government extend to the preparation of the political agenda which is explained by the President to the Congress when he demands a vote of confidence of Parliament (Art.99(2)), the drafting of the general budget of the State (later approved by Parliament) and the general planning of the economy. Also included in the political functions of the Government are the exercise of legislative initiatives, the power to dictate *decretos-leyes* in cases of urgency and extreme need (Arts 82–85 CE) and the defence of the State.[66] Finally, the Government directs the foreign relations of the State.

In the exercise of its executive function the Government can legislate by "delegated legislation"[67] and dictate rules of law, *reglamentos*, subject to the *ley*—regulatory power. It also directs the Public Administration and ensures the effective performance of public services.

---

[64] Antonio Torres del Moral, *op. cit.*, Vol.2, p.168.

[65] Art.97 CE "*El gobierno dirige la política interior y exterior, la Administración civil y militar y la defensa del Estado. Ejerce la función ejecutiva y la potestad reglamentaria de acuerdo con la Constitución y las leyes.*"

[66] Because even if the King is the nominal head of the armed forces (Art.62(h)) it is effectively the Government which directs and controls the Military.

[67] See Ch.2, p.40.

4. THE PUBLIC ADMINISTRATION[68]

While there is a clear separation between the King and the Government it is not so easy to differentiate the Government from the Public Administration. Theoretically the Government is the "directing mind" while the administration "the hand which executes".[69] The administration appears to be an entity subordinate to the Government, legally established and responsible for its activities. In practice there is continuity between the Government and the Administration because the Government "administers" and the Administration has a clear political dimension since all its senior positions are politically designated.

The State needs both personal and material means in order to perform the duties established by the Constitution. The instrument by which these functions are performed is the Public Administration. The Public Administration is a complex organisation whose function is to carry out the tasks of the State and whose activities are subject to particular rules, some of which are to be found in the Constitution and some in subsequent legislation.[70]

As a "social and democratic State" (Arts 1 and 9(3) CE) the functions of the State are very complex since the State is present in different areas of activity, many more than in the original liberal State of the last century, when the State's main function was to guarantee individual freedoms and to provide minimum services such as the defence of the realm and the administration of justice. Although the Public Administration is the main instrument of the State in performing the duties and services imposed by the fundamental laws, it is not the only one. Sometimes the State employs private individuals or corporations to perform certain public services and sometimes the Administration provides services as a private organisation without exercising any public authority.

So far "the Public Administration" or "the Administration" has been referred to as an abstract entity connected to the State which is also an abstract entity. The concept of administration is abstract, but in practice there are different public administrations. The existence of a decentralised State in the form of a "State of Autonomies" has the consequence that there two different levels of administration: the

---

[68] It is not the object of this work to provide a detailed exposition of the constitutional regulation of the Administration. The major authority on the subject of Administrative law which should be consulted by anybody intending to approach the subject seriously is E. Garcia de Enterria, *Curso de Derecho Administrativo* (6th edn, 1993). See also Ch.8.
[69] A. Torres del Moral, *op. cit.*, p.192.
[70] Including not only formal *ley* but also *reglamentos*.

central administration or the administration of the State as a whole, and the autonomous administrations for each of the Autonomous Territories. The central powers of the State have their own administration (*Administración del Estado*) through which they develop the functions reserved to them by the Constitution, and each of the Autonomous Communities has its own administrative organisation to perform its functions and powers (*Administraciones Autonómicas*). At a different level the Constitution recognises the autonomy of other territorial entities—*provincias* and *municipios*—for the carrying out of their functions and the protection of their interests (Art.137 CE). Each of these provincial and municipal entities has its own administrative organisation (*Administractiones locales*).

Together with this territorial distinction of public administration there are other organisations with non-territorial foundations. These are dependent on a territorial administration but they enjoy separate legal personality. Amongst these non-territorial administrative entities some of them are based on a personal element, i.e. belonging to a professional body (Art.36 CE), and are called *Corporaciones Públicas*; others are created in order to perform specific public services—*Instituciones Públicas*; good examples are provided by the different institutions in charge of the health administration such as the National Institute of Health (INSALUD) or the National Institute of Social Security (INSS).

A third category of public administration, is that of the administrative bodies of the constitutional organs. The different constitutional organs are independent and each of them needs independent administrative support. Therefore there is an independent administration for Parliament, the judiciary, the Constitutional Court; all of these being totally separated from the administration of the State. The final example of independent administration is the electoral administration, the purpose of which is to "guarantee the transparency and objectivity of the electoral proceedings".[71]

The main principles of the organisation of the Administration are stated in the Constitution (Arts 103–107 CE). They reflect the main ideas that inspire modern public administration as initially conceived during the French Revolution and subsequently modified by the requirements of the "Social State" in the second half of the twentieth century. The basic constitutional principle can be said to be that of Art.130 CE: ". . . the Administration is subject to the laws".[72]

---

[71] Art.8(1) LOREG "*garantizar . . . la transparencia y objectividad del proceso electoral*".

[72] Art.103(1) CE: "*La administración pública sirve con objectividad . . . con sometimiento pleno a la ley y al Derecho*".

Three points should be mentioned here: *a la ley y al Derecho* means that the actions of the Administration are subject to all the sources of law—the Constitution, statutes, by-laws and general principles of the law. The subjection is "total" and applies to all the areas of activity of the pubic administration. The action of the Administration is legitimate only when there is previous legal consent. As a consequence administrative activity is subject to the control of the courts both in the exercise of its "regulatory capacity" and in any other activity.[73]

Other principles governing the activities of the Public Administration are found in the Constitution. These are as follows: administrative activity must be objective[74] and neutral,[75] which means that even if the Administration follows the lines established by the Government its subjection to the law is a guarantee against arbitrariness; it must also be efficient, which is more a *desideratum* than a directly applicable principle; it must allow the participation of the citizens by guaranteeing access to registers and documents of direct interest to any persons involved in the matter. Citizens also have the right to express their views before the drafting of general rules might affect individuals.[76] The Administration is responsible for its activities; any damage caused as a consequence of any action of the Administration should be compensated for by the Administration[77] (independently of any liability under contract or tort).

The Administration has the dual function of applying and executing the laws on one hand, and of being instrument of the Government for the execution of governmental policies on the other. As a consequence a dual parameter must be applied to the control of administrative activity. Parliament, as the organ of control of the Government, controls administrative activity with respect to its political responsibility,[78] but control of the legality of administrative activity is left to other organs, some of which have a jurisdictional character—ordinary courts and the Constitutional Court—and others which have a dual or non-jurisdictional nature, such as the *Tribunal de Cuentas* and *Defensor del Pueblo*.

One of the main principles of the "*Estado de Derecho*" is the subjection of all the powers to the law. As such the Administration is

---

[73] Art.106 CE: *Los tribunals controlan la potestad reglamentaria y la legalidad de la accion administrative, asi como el sometimiento de esta a los fines que la justifican.*

[74] Art.103(1) CE: *"la administración sirve con objectividad . . .".*

[75] STC 77/1985, *Caso LODE.*

[76] Arts 105(a) CE and 105(b) CE.

[77] See below, *Responsabilidad del Estado*, pp.225–6.

[78] See above p.179.

subject to judicial review by the ordinary courts.[79] The Constitutional Court controls the subjection of the Administration to the Constitution in three main ways: first, by the *recurso de amparo*,[80] which is an extraordinary procedure for the protection of fundamental rights and civil liberties (s.1, Ch.II, Title I CE) used when public powers have infringed one of these by their activities; secondly, by resolving conflicts of power between the Central State and the Autonomous Communities, thereby ensuring that both the acts of the Central Administration and the Autonomous Administrations are within the powers conferred by the Constitution and *Estatutos de Autonomia*; and thirdly, through the control by the Constitutional Court, on the request of the Government, of the constitutionality of regulatory dispositions dictated by the Autonomous Communities (Art.161(2) CE).[81]

To this it is necessary to add the control of the respect for local autonomy by the new process created in Ch.V of the LOTC.[82]

5.   *EL TRIBUNAL CONSTITUCIONAL* (THE CONSTITUTIONAL COURT)[83]

COMPOSITION AND FUNCTIONS

The Constitutional Court is one of the organs of the State. It is not included in the judicial power and it is only subject to the Constitution and to its own *ley orgánica* (LO 2/1979 of October 12 (LOTC)). Some writers[84] suggest that the Constitutional Court is a real "jurisdiction" in the sense that its decisions are made according only to the Constitution. However, it is important to distinguish this organ from the judicial power.

The origins of constitutional justice can be traced back to the famous American case of *Marbury v Madison*,[85] in which Marshall J. constructed the theory of judicial review of the law. It seemed quite logical that a system which recognised the supremacy of judicial

---

[79] See below "Administrative Courts" and *Recurso contencioso-administrativo*.
[80] See below.
[81] As developed by Tit.V of the LOTC.
[82] Arts 59(2) LOTC. See below.
[83] Visit *www.eltribunalconstitucional.esl*, the official website of the constitutional court where all decisions of this court can be found as well as information on the structure and functions of the court.
[84] Pablo Perz Tremps, *op. cit.*, p.254.
[85] (1803).

decisions through a system of precedent, should adopt such an approach, in contrast to continental Europe where the supremacy of the law as "the expression of popular will", as formulated by Rousseau was nearly a dogma. In its original formulation by the United States' Supreme Court in 1803, the control of constitutionality of legislation[86] was not only a power, but a duty of the judge. The judge was obliged to declare the law, and if two different laws were in conflict and one of them was in the Constitution, the judge had to respect the latter because this was hierarchically superior. This model is known as "diffuse control of constitutionality", because all the judges are responsible for controlling the legislation by refusing to apply any which is contrary to the Constitution. However, the judge does not have the power to derogate or declare legislation void, because this function belongs exclusively to Parliament. The system works well because the principle or precedent creates a special relationship between Acts of Parliament and case law, by which a statute has no other meaning than that which is attributed to it by judicial decisions.

In continental Europe it was only after the First World War that the idea of the supremacy of Parliament began to weaken in favour of the supremacy of the Constitution. Some writers[87] have pointed out that only when universal suffrage was introduced, did the fear of a more "democratic" Parliament, in which the majority might take decisions which were contrary to the interest of the dominant class, stimulate consideration of the introduction of a mechanism for controlling Parliament. This mechanism was the Constitutional Court. The first constitutional courts in Europe can be found in the Czech and Austrian Constitutions of 1919 and 1920 which followed the ideas of K. Kelsen regarding constitutionality. According to Kelsen the Constitution provides only rules and mandates to Parliament and not directly applicable rules. The Constitution is applied through Acts of Parliament and these, in turn, are applied by judges in their decisions. It is then necessary to establish an organ outside the judiciary to control the adequate compliance of Acts of Parliament to the Constitution. This organ, the Constitutional Court, has a function of negative legislator because when it declares that a statute is unconstitutional it rejects it from the system. In this respect the Constitutional Court shares legislative power with Parliament. This model has been followed in Europe only as far as there is an organ responsible for the control of constitutionality of legislation but most of the European

---

[86] *Leyes* and dispositions on the same hierarchical level.
[87] Antonio Torres del Moral, *op. cit.*, pp.381–2.

Constitutional Courts—the Spanish, Italian, and German—have elements of both models.

In Spain the first Constitutional Court appeared in the Constitution of 1931, which created a *Tribunal de Garantias Constitucionales* (Court of Constitutional Guarantees). When the draftsmen of the 1978 Constitution met to draft Title IX, they all agreed on the need to establish an organ to control the legislative and also that this organ should be independent of all the other powers of the State, partly because this was the model followed by other countries with a similar legal culture,[88] and partly because there was a great reluctance to leave the control of constitutionality in the hands of a judicial class mainly drawn from the period of dictatorship.[89]

The Constitutional Court is a real jurisdiction neither dependent on, nor incorporated in the judicial power. Its main function is the interpretation of the Constitution (Art.1 LOTC) and in doing this it plays a key role in the distribution and organisation of the powers of the State. The Constitutional Court controls the exercise of the legislative power by Parliament, ensuring that any legislation approved by Parliament which is contrary to the Constitution is declared null and void. However, it is not only Parliament that is controlled by the Constitutional Court; the Executive and the Judiciary are also subject to the control of constitutionality over their activities, exercised through the procedure of the *recurso de amparo*.[90]

The Constitutional Court is composed of 12 Members, four of whom are chosen by Congress, four by Senate, two by the Executive and two by the *Consejo General del Poder Judicial*. Judges of the Constitutional Court are selected from lawyers, judges, civil servants and university professors with more than 15 years experience and "recognised professional standing". All the Members need to belong to the legal professions.[91] Their mandate is for nine years, which means that they do not necessarily coincide with the period of the legislature and so are not chosen by a given majority in Parliament at the time. For the election of the Members of the Constitutional Court a qualified majority of three-fifths is required in order to ensure a consensus of the main political forces. The Members of the Constitutional Court are subject to very similar

---

[88] It is important to remember the influence of the German Constitution of 1949 in Spanish public law.

[89] Pablo Perez Tremps, in Luis López Guerra, ed., *op. cit.*, p.254.

[90] See below.

[91] For a list of current members visit *www.tribunalconstitucional.es*.

principles as those of judges and magistrates; they are independent, cannot be removed (Art.159 CE) and their tenure of office is incompatible with the exercise of any other trade, profession or public office (Art.159(4) CE). The difference between judges and Members of the Constitutional Court is that judges cannot be members of any political party while Members of the Constitutional Court may be.[92] They also enjoy the benefit of "special jurisdiction" by which any criminal action against them will be heard by the Criminal Chamber of the Supreme Court.

The Members of the Constitutional Court elect their President—by majority—and their Vice-President. The work is organised by the President who also represents the institution.

The function of the Constitutional Court as the supreme interpreter of the Constitution can be summarised as follows: control of the constitutionality of the rules with *fuerza de ley*[93] (Arts 161(1)(a) 163 and 95 CE); protection of the fundamental rights and freedoms recognised in Arts 15–30 of the Constitution (Art.161(1)(b) CE); control of the constitutionality of the legislation of the autonomous Communities (Art.161(2) CE); guarantee of the territorial distribution of power between the State and the autonomous communities (Art.161(1)(c) CE); and control of the distribution of power among the different organs of the State (Art.59(3) LOTC) and control of the distribution of power between the central, autonomic and local administration (Art.61(1)(d) CE).[94]

In order to perform these functions most effectively the Constitutional Court organises itself in three different ways: in Sections (*Secciones*), in Chambers (*Sales*) or in full (*Pleno*). The Chambers, each of which has six Members and is presided over by the President or by the Vice-President, have jurisdiction to hear the *recurso de amparo*. The different sections decide on the admissibility of different cases and each of them is composed of three Members.

THE DIFFERENT PROCEDURES OF THE CONSTITUTIONAL COURT

El recurso de inconstitucionalidad[95]

This procedure is established in order to control the constitutionality of the rules with *fuerza de ley*. These are not only rules approved by Parliament (*leyes* in the formal sense) but also *Estatutos de*

---

[92] They cannot, however, have any executive position on the political organisation.
[93] See above, Ch.2, p.31.
[94] Introduced be the LO 7/1999 April 21 of protection of local autonomy.
[95] "Appeal of unconstitutionality" against rules with *fuerza de ley*.

Autonomía, decretos leyes, decretos legislativos, Reglamentos of the Chambers of Parliament and international treaties (Art.27(2) LOTC) and rules of the Autonomous Communities equivalent to those mentioned. The Constitutional Court has expressly ruled out any competence to control the derivative law of the European Community[96] even if this is directly applicable because the parameter for control is Community Law itself and not the Constitution and it is up to the European Court of Justice to effect any control. With respect to any legislation approved prior to the Constitution, the problem can be looked at from a double perspective; first, any subsequent legislation derogates previous legislation and in this case the judge has to apply the latter rule on the matter; secondly, an issue of the hierarchy of sources should be resolved by recognising the superiority of the Constitution. From this second perspective the Constitutional Court will have to decide whether or not there is a conflict. In one of the earliest decisions of the Constitutional Court,[97] it was decided that a mixed approach should be adopted to control the position of pre-constitutional legislation: the judges can automatically refuse to apply the rule that they understand has been abrogated by the Constitution or, if they have any doubt, they can demand a ruling from the Constitutional Court.

The *locus standi* for starting a *recurso de insconstitucionalidad* is restricted by Art.162(1) CE to 50 *Diputados*, 50 *Senadores*,[98] the President of the Government, the Ombudsman, the Government of the Autonomous Communities or the Legislative Assemblies of the Communities.[99] The *locus standi* of the *Defensor del Pueblo* seems to be associated with his role of protecting of fundamental rights,[1] although there is a wide spectrum of laws which can directly or indirectly affect these fundamental rights.[2]

An appeal of unconstitutionality must be initiated within three months following the publication of the legislation which is being contested in the BOE.[3]

---

[96] STC 64/1991, *Caso APESCO.* See Ch.2, pp.35–8.

[97] STC 2/81, *Caso Ley de Bases de Régimen Local.*

[98] In order to protect the rights of the minoritary groups in Parliament who can thereby contest actions of the majority.

[99] Against rules "affecting their autonomy" (Art.32(2) LOTC) not only in the sense of revindication of powers taken by the State through its legislation but also in cases in which the legislation of the State affects any of the interests of the Community, STC 56/1990, *Caso Ley Organica del Poder Judicial II.*

[1] P. Perez Tremps, in L. López Guerra y otros, *op. cit.*, p.269.

[2] STC 150/1990, *Caso Recargo del tres por ciento.*

[3] If it is an appeal against legislation of an autonomous community which is published both in the BOE and the Autonomous Community Journal the period starts to count from the date of the first publication. ATC 597/1990, *Caso Ley asturiana de caza.*

Procedure

An appeal is started by any of the persons/organs with *locus standi* by means of a written complaint specifying the law which is being challenged and the reasons for the complaint. If the Constitutional Court accepts the case—which is decided by one of its sections—it will pass a copy of the complaint to Congress, Senate and to the Government or to the organs of the Autonomous Communities, if the rule which is being challenged was passed by one of those Communities. If these organs consider it appropriate they can put forward any arguments which they believe to be pertinent.

The decision of the Constitutional Court will be effective from the day after its publication in the BOE (Art.164 CE) and the effect will be the nullity of any law declared to be "unconstitutional". Nullity, strictly speaking, means that the legal provision has never existed. However, Art.40 of the LOTC modifies the effects of this nullity, by providing that it will not affect those decisions which are *res iudicata*, except when the application of the law resulted in the imposition of criminal or administrative sanctions which would not have been imposed had the law not existed. Also, the Constitutional Court itself has some-times modified the effects of the declaration of "unconstitutionality" by limiting the period of applicability, if the circumstances of the case so demand.[4]

The decisions of the Constitutional Court are binding on all the powers of the State (Art.38 LOTC) and have full *erga omnes* effects. There are no appeals against these decisions and it is not possible to start new proceedings in the Constitutional Court based on the same legal provision once a decision has been given. This effect of decisions of the Constitutional Court has resulted in some writers including Constitutional Court decisions amongst the sources of law. Without entering into a doctrinal discussion about this, it is important to note that these decisions are not *case law* in the strict sense of the word, given the peculiar nature of the Constitutional Court.[5]

La cuestión de inconstitucionalidad[6]

According to this second procedure it is possible to control the constitutionality of a legal provision when a judge, in the course of judicial proceedings, believes that the rule he has to apply to decide

---

[4] STC 45/1989, *caso* I.R.P.F.
[5] See Ch.2, pp.47–8.
[6] Question of unconstitutionality.

a case may be unconstitutional (Art.35(1) LOTC). Doubt about the constitutionality of a rule can be brought either by the parties or by the judge himself, in any type of proceedings. If that doubt arises, the judge, will first, try to interpret the rule in a way which is compatible with the Constitution. If he cannot do so, he will request an interpretation from the Constitutional Court once he has heard the parties to the proceedings and the *Ministerio Fiscal*. The procedure in the Constitutional Court is very similar to the procedure for *recurso de inconstitucionalidad* and the decision will have the same effects.

Control of international treaties

This control has a different nature from the two previous procedures because it is consultative. The control occurs prior to the signature of the treaty and its purpose is to determine whether the terms of the international treaty will in any way be contrary to the Constitution. If this is so, the Constitution will need to be modified (Art.95 CE) before the treaty is signed and ratified, otherwise the treaty should not be entered into. Both Parliament and the Government have the right to initiate consultation (Art.78(1) LOTC). The only case to date in which this mechanism has been used has been in relation to the Treaty of the European Union.[7]

Once the Treaty has been ratified and has become a rule of the legal system it is possible to challenge the constitutionality of any of its provisions by way of either a *recurso* or *cuestión de inconstitucionalidad*.[8]

Recurso de amparo

This procedure, directed at the protection of rights and freedoms recognised by the Constitution, is the last of the internal appeals available to a citizen for the protection of such rights and freedoms.[9] Whilst, in principle, the protection of such rights come within the jurisdiction of the ordinary courts,[10] this procedure is extraordinary and is only used as a last resort. It is only justified when judicial intervention has proved inefficient, because the

---

[7] STC of 1 July, 1992, *caso Tratado de la Union Europea*.

[8] See Ch.2, pp.34–8.

[9] It is possible to appeal to the European Court of Human Rights if the person believes that any of these rights has been violated.

[10] The Constitutional Court has repeated its subsidiary character on the protection of fundamental rights several times

object of the *recurso de amparo* is protection against any act of public power[11] which violates any of the following rights: Art.14 CE (principle of non-discrimination), Arts 15–19 CE (fundamental rights and public freedoms) and Art.30(2) CE (right to military objection). As a consequence of the subsidiary character of this procedure, several requirements need to be met in order to be able to start such an appeal. The main requirement is that all ordinary procedures for the protection of the right invoked have been exhausted (Arts 43(1) and 44(1) LOTC). These procedures will vary depending on the origin of the violation, the organ which is responsible, the time and occasion of the violation. It is important to note that Art.53(2) CE provides a special and summary procedure for the protection of the same rights which can be pleaded in *amparo*[12] and it will always be necessary to have previously exhausted this procedure.

The right to commence proceedings rests with any natural or juridical person who was party to the proceedings (Art.46(1)(b)) and who claims a legitimate interest, the Ombudsman and the Attorney General.

The time limit to start the procedure of *amparo* varies. In the case of acts or omissions of the judicial power (Art.44 LOTC) the period is twenty days from the date of notification of the judicial decision; in the case of acts of the legislative organs of the State or of the Autonomous Communities[13] it is three months from the date when the act becomes definitive;[14] against an act of the Executive—State and Autonomous Communities—or the Public Administration, it is twenty days from the date of notification of the judicial decision concerning any previous judicial proceedings.

Procedure

The procedure consists of two stages; the first stage, admission, involves of an examination of all the legal requirements, limitation

---

[11] This has been interpreted quite flexibly allowing *amparo* against acts of entities such as *TVE* which has a mixed public and private nature; STC 35/1983, *Caso Hermanos Bengoechea v TVE*. The criteria to apply is whether there has been an exercise of *imperium*, that is public power, or not.

[12] *Procedimento Preferente y Sumario para la protección de derechos fundamentales*. See above.

[13] These acts do not include legislation approved by the Parliament of the Autonomous Assemblies.

[14] If there is an administrative procedure available, for instance in cases of internal administration, it is necessary to exhaust this and any available judicial proceedings first.

periods or the existence of a previous decision by the Constitutional Court on the same matter (Art.50 LOTC); the second stage is the actual procedure in which the public prosecutor and the parties are present and can formulate any statements they think are applicable. After this the *Sala* hearing the case will make a decision.

The decision can have several effects. If it admits the claims of the plaintiff, the most obvious consequence is the declaration of nullity of the act or resolution against which the appeal was initiated, and the recognition and reaffirmation of the right or freedom claimed by adopting whatever measures are necessary.

Conflictos de competencias[15]

In this type of procedure the Constitutional Court will rule on the distribution of powers, determined by the Constitution and the *Estatutos de Autonomia* between the State and the Communities, or between different Communities, when a disagreement regarding the exercise or the extent and method of the exercise of one of these powers arises.[16]

The only organs with capacity to initiate this procedure are the Government—of the State—and the executive of the different Autonomous Communities (Arts 62 and 63 LOTC). There is a difference in the position of the central Government and the autonomous governments. The former is in a position of superiority because it can either start the proceeding in the Constitutional Court when it is believed that an autonomous community is acting outside its powers, or demand the annulment of the disputed act or disposition of the autonomous community (Art.62 LOTC). If it is the autonomous community which considers that the central Government is acting outside its powers it is always necessary first to make a request to the State (Art.63 LOTC). The time limit to effect the request to the State or the Community, or to start the proceedings if it is the central Government which is initiating these, is two months from the date of publication of the act or law complained of. If there has been no response within one month or if this is negative, then, the procedure can be started in the Constitutional Court. The difference in position between the central Government and the autonomous community is reflected in the fact that there will be an automatic suspension of a legal provision of the community for a maximum period of five months

---

[15] Conflicts of power between the State and the Autonomous Communities or between the Autonomous Communities themselves (Art.161(1)(c) CE and Title IV LOTC).

[16] The conflict can be positive, when more than one Community or both the State and an Autonomous Community exercise a power; or negative, when none of them exercise the power.

(Art.161(2) CE), while any legal provision of the Central State can only be suspended by the Constitutional Court once it has considered the possible prejudicial effects of such an application, until a definitive ruling is made (Art.64(3) LOTC).

The procedure of the Constitutional Court consists of an analysis of the allegations of both parties and giving a decision determining to whom the power belongs according to the Constitution and the *Estatutos de Autonomia*. The Constitutional Court will also determine what action is necessary to restore the initial positions of the parties which have been altered as a consequence of the law dictated outside the competence of one of the executive powers.

The original period of three months to promote a *conflicto de competencias* was extended to six months for those cases in which a *Comision Bilateral de Colaboracion*[17] has been created and the ongoing discussion or agreements of the *Comision* have been notified to the Constitutional Court.[18] The aim is to avoid unnecessary constitutional litigation and to encourage communication and collaboration between the different administrations.

Conflictos de atribuciones[19]

This type of procedure was introduced by the LOTC, Ch.II, Title IV, Art.10(b) according to Art.161(1)(d) *CE*: "The Constitutional Court has jurisdiction . . . in any other matter according to the Constitution or the Organic Laws".[20] The object of this procedure is the resolution of any conflict between the organs of the State—the Executive, Parliament and the Judiciary—as to the powers that each of them enjoy and the exercise of those powers. It can only be commenced when one of these powers considers that one of the others has invaded its sphere of influence. The capacity to initiate the proceedings rests with on the Executive, the Congress, the Senate and the General Council of the Judiciary (Art.59(3) LOTC). The organ which believes another organ has invaded its powers must communicate this to the "intruder", demanding the withdrawal of such intrusion. If the organ which has been requested refuses on the grounds that it has

---

[17] Created according to the provisions of Art.5(2) of the *Ley 30/1992* of November 26 *de RJA-PAC*, with the aim of exchanging information and avoiding conflicts between the different administrations.

[18] Art.33 LOTC as amended.

[19] Conflicts between the Constitutional Organs of the State concerning the extent and exercise of their powers.

[20] "*El tribunal constitucional tiene jurisdicción . . . las demás materias que le atribuyan la Constitución ó las leyes orgánicas*".

acted within its powers, then it is possible to initiate the procedure in the Constitutional Court, which will hear both powers and make a decision confirming the attribution of the disputed power and any *ultra vires* activity null and void.

There is a special type of *conflicto de atribuciones* in respect of the powers of the *Tribunal de Cuentas* regulated in Art.8 LOTC which is identical to any other resolution of a conflict of powers.

Conflicto en defensa de la autonomia local

This new procedure was introduced in 1999[21] and allows local administrations to resort to this procedure to challenge invasions of their autonomy by the central State or the autonomous communities. The legitimate right to start this procedure lies with the provinces or municipalities that are representative enough according to the criteria fixed by the law.[22] The procedure must be brought within three months from the date of publication of the law or disposition that is being challenged.

6.   THE AUTONOMOUS COMMUNITIES AND THE TERRITORIAL MODEL OF THE STATE

Spain has opted for a territorial model of distribution of powers based in the principles of unity and autonomy. These two principles have, at times, been difficult to reconcile and the Constitutional Court has built a considerable archive of decisions interpreting the fine line that divides the power between the central state and the different autonomous communities.[23]

The autonomous communities have their origin in the Constitution itself, and more precisely in its Title VIII that allowed—although did not force—those territories and provinces that had enjoyed historical independence to organise themselves into self-governing entities called autonomous communities. In fact although Spain is one of the oldest European states in its actual formation it has also only been a centralised state since the absolutism of the 18th century and, later, during the regime of General Franco. The different regions and his-

---

[21] LO 7/1999 *de modificación de la Ley Orgánica del Tribunal Constitucional.*
[22] Art.75(3) LOTC, the provinces or municipalities must have a minimum number of inhabitants representative of all those affected by the law of the state or autonomous communities that is being challenged.
[23] See *www.eltribunalconstitucional.es.*

torical territories—many of them with their own language and distinctive culture—saw the arrival of democracy as the open door to their long awaited independence.

Today Spain is territorially divided into 17 autonomous communities, each of them with their own Parliament, Executive and Administration. Those autonomous communities have a core of powers or *competencias* that are exclusive and others that are shared between the community and the central State.[24] Not all autonomous communities have opted for the same level of powers. The legislation of the central state is subsidiary for all those areas that the autonomous communities have not legislated upon or for all those areas that belong in exclusive to the state.[25]

The main rule of the autonomous communities is their *Estatuto de Autonomía* that is equivalent to their "autonomous constitution". The *Estatuto de Autonomía*, however, needs to be approved by *Ley Orgánica* of the central State Parliament. The first *Estatuto de Autonomía* was the *Estatuto de Autonomía Del Pais Vasco*[26] followed by the *Estatuto de Cataluña*.[27] To this followed the *Estatuto de Galicia*,[28] *Andalucia*,[29] *Asturias*,[30] and *Cantabria*.[31] Two years later Murcia,[32] Valencia,[33] Aragón,[34] Castilla-La Mancha,[35] Canarias[36] and Navarra[37] obtained their *Estatuto*. Extremadura,[38] Baleares,[39] Madrid[40] and Castilla y Leon[41] became autonomous communities a year later. Finally, in 1995 Ceuta and Melilla had their autonomy regulated.[42]

---

[24] For example the State may provide the general legislative framework and the autonomous community is in charge of the "enforcement" of the power.
[25] See, above, Ch.2, "Autonomy and the system of sources: relationship between state law and the laws of the autonomous communities", pp.46–48.
[26] LO 3/1979 of December 18
[27] LO 4/1979 of December 18.
[28] LO 1/1981 of April 6.
[29] LO 6/1981 of December 30.
[30] LO 7/1981 of December 30.
[31] LO 8/1981 of December 30.
[32] LO 4/1982 of June 9.
[33] LO 5/1982 of July 1.
[34] LO 8/1982 of August 10.
[35] LO 9/1982 of August 10.
[36] LO 10/1982 of August 10.
[37] LO 13/1982 of August 10.
[38] LO 1/1983 of February 25.
[39] LO 2/1983 of February 25.
[40] LO 3/1983 of February 25.
[41] LO 4/1983 of February 25.
[42] LO 1/1995 of March 13 and LO 2/1995 of March 13 respectively.

The territorial model of the State is under review currently in Spain with all the autonomous communities immersed in the process of reviewing the *Estatuto de Autonomía* under the Government of Jose Luis Rodriguez Zapatero and some communities demanding a more radical change in the organisation of the State.[43]

Cataluña and the Basque Country have requested that their relationship with the State is not framed under the umbrella of autonomy but rather under the more ambitious of "free association".[44]

7.   THE PROTECTION OF FUNDAMENTAL RIGHTS AND FREEDOMS

The wide scope of activities of the public powers in general has the potential of affecting people's enjoyment of their fundamental rights. In some cases the common good requires that individual rights are restricted; in others the interference with the individual's enjoyment of his fundamental rights may not be legitimate. What characterises a democratic society is not necessarily the total and perfect lack of interference with the fundamental rights of individuals; that would be more a utopian aspiration than a realistic view of the function of modern societies. Democratic societies, though, have the mechanisms to evaluate acts which interfere with fundamental rights and the procedures for restoring individuals their freedom.

In Spain the protection of the fundamental rights recognised by the Constitution is a constitutional mandate in itself.[45] The rights recognised in Art.14 (principle of non-discrimination) and Arts 15–29, including the right of conscientious objection of Art.30, are considered to be fundamental rights and freedoms that warranted a special procedure for their protection and the possibility of exercising the *recurso de amparo* to the Constitutional Court if judicial procedures were exhausted.

The special procedure that the constitution referred to had to be based on the principles of preference and speed of actuation in order to avoid the pitfalls of the ordinary administrative proceedings that the

---

[43] See also *www.elpais.es/articulo/elpporesp/20040524* for an excellent article on the projected reforms by each autonomous community.

[44] Visit the website of the *Generalitat de Cataluña* for a copy of their new *Estatuto de Autonomia* approved by the Catalan Parliament and currently under debate in Congress.

[45] Art.53(2) CE.

citizens could always resort to. This special procedure had been called the *Procedimiento Preferente y Sumario de Protección Jurisdiccional de los Derechos Fundamentales de la Persona*[46] until 1998. This law preceded the Constitution by one day and had to be adapted in order to coincide exactly with the scope contemplated in Art.53(2).

Until 1998 it was possible for those whose fundamental rights had been infringed to choose between the ordinary administrative proceedings in the ordinary courts or the procedure of *Ley 62/1978*. The advantages of the latter were that it was not necessary to exhaust the administrative route before going to court and that the procedure was indeed much faster. It also usually suspended the act or resolution under dispute. The disadvantages lay in the limitations of the object of the proceedings, which did not extend to ordinary infractions of the legality, such as procedural infractions, or deviation of power that had to be resolved by the ordinary *contencioso-administrativo*.

Once the judicial avenue had been exhausted it was possible to appeal to the Constitutional Court through the procedure of the *recurso de amparo*.[47]

The new law of administrative procedure[48] seeks to eliminate the distinction between the protection of fundamental rights and ordinary jurisdiction by creating a special procedure for the protection for fundamental rights that encompasses the advantages of speed and simplicity of the old preferential and summary procedure but at the same time allows for all type of claims (Art.114(3)) including challenges to the activity or inactivity of the administration and challenges to general dispositions.

Under the new procedure nothing is said about the need to exhaust the administrative route before starting the judicial proceedings but this is understood by a reading of Art.115 when it states the period of time for bringing the proceedings.[49] The documents that need to be presented are extremely straight-forward—a simple writing by the parties stating the right affected by the disposition, actuation or inactivity of the administration. The same day or, at the latest, the following day, a copy of the claim is passed on to the corresponding body of the administration that must, during a maximum period of five days, reply to this claim and provide any information. The court will then dictate an *auto* accepting to proceed with the claim or rejecting it. If the claim is accepted the

---

[46] *Ley* 62/1978 of December 26.
[47] See above, p.199.
[48] *Ley* 29/1998 of July 13 *de la jurisdiction contencioso adminsitrativa*.
[49] Which the law 29/1998 calls "*recurso*".

parties are called for further allegations within eight days and the court having heard both sides will dictate a decision in five working days.[50]

It is possible to appeal against this decision and this appeal is necessary if the parties wish to proceed later to bring a *recurso de amparo*.

---

[50] Arts 116–121 LJCA, *Ley* 29/1999.

Chapter Eight
Administrative law
and procedure

1. THE PUBLIC ADMINISTRATION

The Public Administration is a complex organisation that provides the different powers of the State with the personal and material means to enable them to develop their constitutional functions.[1]

The Public Administration is endowed with special and extensive powers[2] in order to aid the performance and development of its function and mandate. These extensive powers are needed to perform those duties efficiently but are open to abuse by individual officials. In order to control this powerful entity with its exorbitant powers the Constitution[3] sets out the main lines and principles of a special regulation—the body of administrative law—that has been created and developed in order to control and assess the legality of administrative activity, and redress any damage or disturbance caused to citizens in the enjoyment of their legitimate rights if the Administration goes beyond the legal boundaries established.

The legal rules that provide the outline for administrative action regulate the powers of the Administration, establishing the controls available and the rights of individuals, constituting the main body of the discipline of administrative law. The Administration has reached gigantic dimensions at the current time, as has the body of administrative law. The list of its scope includes town planning, taxes, health and safety, licences, contracts for public services and local administration. Today many areas constitute sub-disciplines of administrative law such as town planning or taxes and are studied separately. We will in this Chapter only look at some aspects of the central administration concentrating on administrative procedure (both internal and in judicial review).

---

[1] P. Pérez Tremps, in López Guerra and others, *op. cit.* p.187. See also Ch.7, p.193.
[2] Among them perhaps the most distinctive is the power of *autotutela* or power to declare rights and enforce its own decisions. See below.
[3] Arts 103–107, Art.130(1).

TYPES OF PUBLIC ADMINISTRATION

The Spanish State is territorially divided in political entities that enjoy different degrees of autonomy and power. These territorial entities are the autonomous communities,[4] provinces and municipalities.[5] Each of these entities has got a different administration. We can then talk about an *Administración del Estado* (Administration of the Central State), *Administraciones Autonómicas* (administrations of the autonomous communities) and *Administraciones Locales* (local administration).

The territorial division of the state has effects beyond the existence of different public administrations, central, autonomic and local. The central administration of the state is organised for ease of operations around the territorial unit of the province. This organisational division of the central administration creates what is called the *Administración Periférica del Estado* (APE). The APE is co-ordinated by one *Delegado del Gobierno* for each autonomous community and one *Gobernador Civil* in each of the provinces.

Beyond the territorial criteria of division of power and organisation of the central administration there are what are called non-territorial administrations.[6] These are branches of the Public Administration created with an institutional base that aims at meeting a public goal for example the provision of public health services. They are called *Instituciones Publicas*. Finally, there are *Corporaciones Públicas* which are based in a personal element such as belonging to a professional body.[7] All constitutional organs have their own administrative support which forms part of the Public Administration.[8]

2.   SOURCES OF ADMINISTRATIVE LAW

The Constitution sets up the limits of subjection to the law of the Public Administration in Arts 103–107. The volume of activity of the Administration today and the territorial variations make administrative law one of the areas with the largest volume of legislation. The

---

[4] See Ch.7, pp.206–7 and Ch.2, pp.49–52.

[5] The autonomy of provinces and municipalities is recognised in Art.137 CE.

[6] For an informative account of sections, branches and dependencies visit the website of the M.A.P., *Ministerio de las Administraciones Publicas*, at *www.map.es* and follow the links to the different departments.

[7] For example a *Colegio de Abogados*, see Ch.4, "The Legal Professions" and Ch.7 where an introduction to the Public Administration is provided.

[8] Parliament, the Constitutional Court, the Government, see Ch.7, above.

main laws relating to administrative law are the *Ley de Régimen Jurídico de las Administraciones Públicas y del Procedimiento Administrativo Común* (LRJ-PAC), the *Ley* 6/1999 of April 14 de *Organización y Funcionamiento de la Administración Central del Estado*; the RD 429/1993 of March 26 *de procedimiento en caso de responsabilidad de las Administraciones Públicas*, the *Ley* 29/1998 of July 13 of the *Jurisdicción Contencioso-Administrativa*.

3. Administrative Acts (el acto administrativo)

The regulation of the procedure for these acts, their effects and the ways of challenging them in front of the administrative authorities are regulated by the *Ley* 30/1992 of November 26, LRJ-PAC. This law was passed by the central State and applies to all public administrations according to the exclusive powers granted by Art.149(1)(18) CE on the regulation of the Public Administration and the rulings of the Constitutional Court in the matter.[9]

Administrative acts are any acts of the Administration that can create rights, duties or have an influence in the enjoyment of rights by individuals. Administrative acts need to be approved by the department or section of the administration with power to do so[10] and must follow certain procedures for their elaboration and publication or notification to those affected. They also need to be "reasoned" or justified (*motivados*) and must include a reference to the facts to which they refer and the laws or other regulations in which they are based.[11] Administrative acts produce effects from the date they are approved unless something different is specified by law for that particular act or type of acts.[12] There are certain circumstances that require that administrative acts have retrospective effect, for example when an administrative act is dictated in replacement of another act that has been declared null and void.

The Administration is under the obligation to notify individuals of all acts that may potentially affect their rights and interests within 10 days from the date in which the act was dictated. Notifications to individuals must also conform to a certain procedure and formalities and must include the full text of the act or administrative resolution and an indication of whether it is possible to appeal it internally by the *recurso de alzada* or *reposición* or whether the act or resolution puts

---

[9] STC 76/1983 of August 5 and STC 32/1981 of July 28.
[10] Otherwise they will be null and void, see Art.53 LRJ-PAC.
[11] Arts 53(2), 54 and 55 LRJ-PAC.
[12] Arts 56, 57 LRJ-PAC.

and end to the administrative procedure and the parties interested need to challenge it in court (through the *procedimiento contencioso-administrativo*).[13]

4.   ADMINISTRATIVE PROCEEDINGS (INTERNAL)

There are a great variety of types of administrative procedures if we understand by these any procedures that the individuals or the Administration must follow in order to vary the rights of obligations of the citizens. Individuals may want to apply for a building licence to the Administration and this request must follow a certain procedure. The Administration on the other hand may start a sanctioning procedure against an individual that has built without a licence. Individuals may denounce de facto situations to the public administration and urge action to be taken. In all these cases certain formalities, periods of time and notifications must be made.

The proceedings are started by one or several individuals with the same or a very similar interest (for example all the neighbours affected by the noise produced by a disco-bar that the local administration has just licensed) by presenting a written claim (*solicitud*) in the registry of the Administration that approved the act or regulation that they wish to challenge. This written claim must contain the name and address of the claimant/s and or the legal representatives (if any)[14] and the place where all notifications by the Administration must be addressed. It must also contain the facts, reasons and explanations of the claim and a clear statement with the request or demand to the Administration (for example to demolish an illegal building) and the section of the Administration to which it is addressed.[15]

Once the procedure has been duly started it is possible to request that the Administration takes precautionary or provisional measures.[16] The Administration itself may decide to do so ex officio if it believes that there is a danger to people or property, as may be the case with a falling building, or noxious fumes from a factory.

The parties to the procedure can bring any evidence that they wish and can, in due course, challenge any irregularity from the part of the

---

[13]   Arts 58–61 LRJ-PAC.
[14]   At this point it is not necessary to be represented by an *abogado* or *procurador*. If the parties, once the internal administrative procedures for challenging decisions have been exhausted, proceed to the *contencioso* then they must employ the required legal representatives. See below.
[15]   Arts 68–71 LRJ-PAC.
[16]   Art.72 LRJ-PAC.

Administration in the instruction of the procedure. Before the Administration gives its final resolution the parties can formulate further allegations, and if the case affects the general public a period of public information can be established by publishing details of the act or resolution, the proceedings that are under way and the period in which the parties can formulate their allegations and express their views.[17] This is published in the *Boletin Oficial* of the state, of the autonomous community, or of the province, depending on the territorial scope of the resolution. It is not necessary to have formulated allegations in order to be able to appeal a resolution dictated later that affects an individual's rights. Once the period for further allegations has expired the Administration must dictate a resolution.

The Administration is under the obligation to resolve all administrative proceedings whether these have been started by individuals or by the Administration itself. The maximum period for a decision is expressly stated in the Regulations for that particular procedure. If nothing is stated the maximum period is of three months.[18] This three-month period can be extended to a maximum of six months if the nature of the case makes this extension necessary. Citizens have the right to be informed of the maximum period in which the Administration will resolve the procedure and of the effects of a lack of resolution. This lack of resolution is called *silencio administrativo* or "administrative silence" and it is of great importance because a large percentage of proceedings started in front of the Administration do actually end by administrative silence.

The *Ley de Régimen Jurídico de la Administración del Estado y del Procedimiento Administrativo Común* (LRJ-PAC)[19] contains the rules about the effects of a lack of resolution from the Administration. The area was modified in 1999 with the aim of providing a more coherent treatment of this important aspect of administrative action. The main novelty lies in stating the general rule that the administration is under the obligation to decide all administrative procedures[20] except in the limited cases listed in Art.42(1)(3) when the proceedings end by agreement between the citizen and the Administration or when the proceedings are about the exercise of a right in respect of which it is only necessary to notify the Administration.[21]

---

[17] Arts 78–86 LRJ-PAC.
[18] Art.42 LRJ-PAC, *Ley* 30/1992 of November 26.
[19] Ley 30/1992 of November 26. Modified in Arts 42, 43 and 44 in relation to the *"silencio administrativo"* by the *Ley* 4/1999 of January 13.
[20] Arts 42 and 89(4) LRJ-PAC.
[21] See the excellent commentary to this article by Martin Rebollo, *op. cit.* p.460.

In proceedings started by individuals if the maximum period that the administration has according to Art.42 for giving a decision has lapsed the person/s that started the proceedings can understand that his petition has been successful.[22] This has been traditionally known as *silencio positivo* or positive silence. This rule has got the following exceptions: when the individual has exercised the individual or collective right of petition,[23] when the decision estimating the request from the individual would amount in giving to the claimant rights over a public service or when the proceedings were started in order to challenge a general act or disposition. In these cases the silence will be negative, meaning that the petition or claim is rejected by the Administration.

In those cases in which the proceedings were started by the Administration, for example a sanctioning procedure for lack of requisite licences, the effects of silence by the Administration are different. If the Administration has not decided on a sanctioning procedure within the necessary time the administrative act lapses. In any other type of proceedings started by the Administration lack of a resolution within the specified time is understood as having rejected the claim if there was the possibility that the proceedings could end by conferring a right to the individual.

MEASURING TIME

Days in administrative procedure are understood to be working days and these are all days except Sundays or other official holidays. Months or years are counted starting with the day after the notification or the date when the proceedings could be understood to have ended by silence. Periods of time start running the day after the notification (or end of proceedings by silence). If the last day of the period is not a working day the period is extended until the next working day.[24]

Once the Administration has decided expressly or by way of silence the individuals can appeal first internally through a *recurso administrativo de alzada* or *reposición* and, after, externally to the courts through the *recurso contencioso-administrativo* or proper judicial proceedings.

All acts and resolutions of the Administration are enforceable from the date that they are approved. Usually the Administration will give

---

[22] Art.43 LRJ-PAC.
[23] Right of petition recognised by Art.29 CE, see STC 242 1993 of July 14 and LO 4/2001 of November 12, regulating the right of petition and modifying the LRJ-PAC by forcing the Administration to give a decision in all case in which this right is exercised.
[24] Arts 47–49 LRJ-PAC.

the individuals a period of time for complying with the resolution (for example two weeks to cut the branches of a tree in a garden that is a danger to those walking by, or the period of time allowed to voluntarily pay certain taxes). If the time passes and the individual does not comply with the resolution then the Administration can, depending on the circumstances of the case, proceed to enforce it (for example send a contractor to cut a tree and later invoice the individual or freeze the bank accounts of those who owe taxes to the State).

RECURSOS ADMINISTRATIVOS

Recurso de alzada[25]

This is an appeal against those administrative acts that do not put an end to the internal administrative procedure. The appeal is addressed to the hierarchical superior section or organ of the Administration. This appeal needs to be filed within a month from the date when the resolution or act that is being challenged was notified or within three months when the proceedings ended by silence.

The Administration has a maximum period of three months to resolve this *recurso*. If the three months have passed and no resolution is notified to the parties these must understand that their claim or appeal has been rejected unless the act that has been challenged was an Act also "presumed" by silence of the administration. In this case of two consecutive resolutions by silence, the individual can understand that his appeal has been successful.

Against the resolution (or lack of one) in a *recurso de alzada* it is only possible to appeal through the *recurso extraordinario de revisión*.

Recurso de reposición[26]

This is an appeal presented to the same body or department that gave the resolution against Acts that end the administrative procedure. It is not necessary to file this appeal before going to court and starting a *contencioso-administrativo*. The individuals can choose whether or not to file it, but if they start the *recurso de reposición* they need to wait until the end of the period granted to the Administration to resolve it.

---

[25] Arts 114–115 LRJ-PAC.
[26] Arts 116–117 LRJ-PAC.

Recurso extraordinario de revisión[27]

This is an extraordinary appeal that is only possible in those cases in which an obvious mistake had been made when dictating the act or resolution challenged and when new documents appear that can prove the error or mistake in the resolution or a criminal decision declaring fraud in the documents or declarations used to arrive to the resolution has been passed. It is also possible when the members of the Administration involved in the decision have been condemned by a final criminal court decision of fraud or abuse of position.

This extraordinary appeal can be made up to four years after the date of the resolution that is going to be challenged due to the length of time that it can take to obtain a decision of fraud in the criminal courts.

5.   CONTROL OF THE ADMINISTRATION

The administration is controlled in different ways. First, there is a political control by Parliament that is really a control of the Government as the head of the administration. Secondly the ordinary courts and tribunals have a general control over the activities of the administration. The courts control the regulatory power of the administration, the legality of all administrative activities and their subjection to the constitution and the law.[28] Thirdly there are specialised jurisdictional controls. Finally there is a control exercised by non-jurisdictional institutions such as the *Defensor del Pueblo* and the *Tribunal de Cuentas*.

ORDINARY JURISDICTIONAL CONTROL

All administrative activities are subject to the control of the ordinary courts or tribunal according to Art.106(1) of the CE, which excludes the possibility of any areas that escape jurisdictional control. However it is necessary to remember that the Government as the head of the administration has the political discretion to take certain decisions and those decisions do not fall under the control of the ordinary courts. These types of political acts include things such as the calling of a referendum, or the dissolution of the Chambers of

---

[27]   Arts 118–119 LRJ-PAC.
[28]   Art.106(1) CE.

Parliament.[29] The Constitutional Court has acknowledged this realm of political discretion[30] where the control belongs to Parliament.[31] The distinction between administrative and political acts is for the courts to make, and, in the last instance it would be necessary to resort to the Constitutional Court.

The control of administrative activities by the Court takes into account the margin of discretion the Administration has and needs in order to properly develop its functions. This discretion, understood as opportunity or convenience, is not revised by the Court. The jurisdictional control is limited to that of adequacy of administrative action to whatever procedures are in place for that particular actuation. For example control on whether the Administration requested all necessary information or reports, gave the prescribed time to individuals for questions or allegations, and respected the time limits when dictating a decision. The jurisdictional control of the administration allows the courts to establish whether the Administration has achieved the aims provided for by law. Otherwise it would be possible for the Administration to conform to procedural limits but use its power between the procedural limits to achieve aims that are outside the law. This is what is called *desviación de poder* (deviation of power).

All regulatory activity of the administration is subject to jurisdictional control by the *jurisdicción contencioso administrativa*.[32]

SPECIALISED JURISDICTIONAL CONTROL

This control is also done by ordinary courts but because of the nature of the activity or the right that is being affected by the administrative activity the control takes place by some special procedures. These are the procedure of habeas corpus[33]; the procedure for the protection of fundamental rights and freedoms of Art.114 of the *Ley* 29/1998 and the procedure to challenge electoral irregularities.

The Constitutional Court controls the Administration in different ways. First through the *recurso de amparo*[34] as the subsidiary and last guarantee of protection of fundamental rights and freedoms. Secondly through the *conflicto de competencias* between the State and

---

[29] Eduardo Espin, in *Luis Lopez Guerra y otros, op. cit.* p.207.
[30] STC 45/90 *caso Administraciones Justicia de Euskadi*; *caso STC 196/90 caso Denegacion de Informacion*, in *Lopez Guerra y otros, op. cit.* p.207.
[31] See Ch.7, p. 179 et seq.
[32] See below, p.22.
[33] LO 6/84, see Ch.6, p.156.
[34] See Ch.7, pp.202–3.

the autonomous communities.[35] Thirdly by the new constitutional procedure for the protection of local autonomy.[36] Finally by the control of the constitutionality of all rules passed by the autonomous communities according to the procedure of Art.1612 of the LOTC.[37]

NON-JURISDICTIONAL CONTROL OF THE ADMINISTRATION

El Defensor Del Pueblo

El Defensor del Pueblo[38] is an agency designated by Parliament and responsible to it. Its main function is to survey administrative activity and ensure that there are no violations of the fundamental rights recognised in Title I of the Constitution. The *Defensor del Pueblo* does not have executive judicial power and his activities are limited to persuasion and advice.

The involvement of the *Defensor del Pueblo* can be initiated by any individual without restrictions of age, gender, nationality or even capacity. It can also be initiated ex officio. A complaint must be addressed to the *Defensor del Pueblo* with statement of the facts in plain language. This complaint must be signed by the person making it but it does not require the intervention of *abogado* or *procurador*. The aim is to make this first complaint as informal as possible and open to all individuals.

The *Defensor del Pueblo* has got wide powers of investigation and all public authorities are under the obligation to assist and provide any information that is requested by his office. Only the Government by a decision approved by the Council of Ministers can decide not to facilitate certain information or documents if these are declared secret.

Once the investigation has finished the *Defensor del Pueblo* may decide to pass on any evidence obtained to the *Fiscal General* and the *Fiscal General* can start criminal proceedings if the facts alleged amount to a crime.[39] He can also write to the administrative department against which the complaint was made, giving its view as to whether there has been a violation of an individual's fundamental right and what steps should be taken in order to avoid it happening again. The administrative authority must reply to this information within a month

---

[35] See Ch.7, p.204.
[36] See Ch.7, p.205.
[37] See Ch.7.
[38] The ombudsman, contemplated by Art.54 CE and Regulated by the LO 3/1981, of April 6 (LOPD) as amended by the LO 2/1992 of March 5 and the LO/1995 of November 23.
[39] See Art.262 LECrim and 25 LODP.

acknowledging receipt of the suggestions made and specifying the measures that will be implemented to avoid further violations of rights.

The *Defensor del Pueblo* can also make recommendations to Parliament or other administrative authorities if the outcome of his investigation is that a certain piece of legislation has produced unfair results to individuals. He will always inform the person who made the complaint about the outcome of his involvement and will send an annual report to Parliament with conclusions and suggestions.

The different autonomous communities have similar institutions regulated by their respective autonomic laws that control the activities of their autonomous administrations. These are:

- the *Ararteko* in the Basque Country[40];
- the *Sindic de Greuges* in Calaluna[41] and Baleares[42];
- the *Valedor del Pueblo* in Galicia[43];
- the *Defensor del Pueblo Andaluz*[44];
- the *Síndico de Agravios* in the Comunidad Autónoma de Valencia[45];
- the *Justicia de Aragón* in Aragón[46];
- the *Defensor del Pueblo* in Castilla la Mancha[47];
- the *Diputado del Común* in Canarias[48];
- the *Defensor del Pueblo* de la Comunidad Foral de Navarra[49];
- the *Procurador del Común* in Castilla-Leon.[50]

There is also a European Ombudsman created by the Treaty of Maastricht.[51]

El Tribunal de Cuentas

The Tribunal de Cuentas controls the public finances and the accounts of the State. The name tribunal is deceptive because this

---

[40] *Ley del Parlamento Vasco* 3/1985 of February 25.
[41] *Ley del Parlamento de Cataluña* 14/1984 of March 20.
[42] *Ley del Parlamento de las Islas Baleares* 1/1993 of March 10.
[43] *Ley del Parlamento de Galicia* 6/1984 of June 5 as amended.
[44] *Ley del Parlamento de Andalucia* 9/1983 of June 1 as amended.
[45] *Ley de las Cortes Valencianas* 11/1988 of December 2.
[46] *Ley de las Cortes de Aragón* 4/1985 of June 27.
[47] *Ley* 16/2001 of December 20.
[48] *Ley* 7/2001 of July 31.
[49] *Ley foral* 4/2000 of July 3.
[50] *Ley* 2/1994 of March 9.
[51] Arts 21 and 195 of the TJCE and Decision 94/262 of the European Parliament of March 9, 1994.

special type of court is directly connected to Parliament and not to the judiciary.

The members of the *Tribunal de Cuentas* enjoy the same independence as judges.[52] The *Tribunal de Cuentas* is composed of 12 counsellors nominated by both Chambers of Parliament. These counsellors must be of recognised standing within the Legal profession. The *Tribunal de Cuentas* has competence or jurisdiction over any matter connected to the expenditure of public funds. Its jurisdiction ceases where the jurisdiction of the administrative or criminal courts starts.[53]

6. JURISDICTIONAL CONTROL OF THE ADMINISTRATION: THE "CONTENCIOSO-ADMINISTRATIVO"

The French revolution introduced the idea of control of the public powers by their subjection to the law. Any act which goes beyond their sphere or powers, is unjust or unjustified is an arbitrary act against which the individuals could legitimately resist enforcement and a criminal sanction could be imposed. The main problem at the time was that the doctrine of separation of powers made the control of the Administration by the judiciary difficult, and not least because the revolutionaries were duly reluctant to let a judicial class that came from the nobility and the old *Parliaments* dominate, curtail and control the much needed new and vigorous public administration that was in charge of building the new State.[54] The French system had to find a mechanism that could control the activity of the Administration and took into account the separation of powers (*juger l'Administration c'est encore administrer*). The *Conseil d'Etat*— an administrative consultive organ created by the Napoleon Constitution—will soon adopt a role in hearing patrimonial claims against the Administration. These claims extended with time to any complaints that citizens had against the Administration. In 1806 a special tribunal of a mixed administrative and judicial nature was created by Napoleon himself. This is the section of the *contencieuse-administratif* in the *Conseil d'Etat*.

In Spain the origin of the judicial control of the Administration is heavily influenced by the French model even though the drafters of the Constitution de Cádiz favoured the Anglo-Saxon model of separation and control of the Administration by a proper judicial

---

[52] See Ch.3, pp.59–60 and Ch.4, pp.86–9.
[53] LO 2/1998 of May 12, *Del Tribunal de Cuentas*.
[54] Garcia de Enterria, *Curso de Derecho Administrativo*, Madrid, Civitas (1993), p.548.

tribunal. In 1845 two laws declared that the *contencioso* was to be resolved by the *Consejos Provinciales* and the *Consejo Real* (later to become the *Consejo de Estado*). Their jurisdiction is based on a list of matters that can be checked and challenged. It is also a type of second instance once an internal or administrative procedure has been exhausted. During the 19th century the debate about the nature and scope of the control of the Administration followed the political polarity of the time with liberals favouring a system of total and external judicial control and moderate and conservative parties favouring the model of the *Consejo de Estado* of mixed nature and partial control. In 1888 the *Ley de Santamaria de Paredes* introduced a general clause of jurisdiction in respect of administrative matters, but the exceptions to this general clause were so numerous that all the matters related to the *exceso de poder* (the French *excès de pouvoir*) were excluded. The situation continued with small modifications until in 1956 a *Ley de la Jurisdicción Contencioso Administrativa* was finally passed. Despite being a law of the Francoist era this was a highly technical piece of legislation that was celebrated by experts of all political ideologies. It dealt with many of the shortcomings of the regulation before that date and tackled the main problems of administrative jurisdictional control by placing this firmly in the judiciary, maintaining a "general clause" system of jurisdiction but accepting all cases related to the *excès de pouvoir* and excluding from control only those acts that fall into the category of political acts or acts of government and made great advance in matters related to the enforcement of decisions. This law remained in force[55] after the approval of the Constitution and has only recently being derogated by the *Ley 29/1998* of July 13 *de la Jurisdicción Contencioso Administrativa*.[56]

The *jurisdiccion contencioso adminsitrativa* is a mechanism of control of the multiple and varied privileges enjoyed by the public administration. It is a requirement of the *Estado de Derecho*. Its main problem today is the overload of the courts in administrative matters. This overload makes it very difficult to comply with the constitutional mandate of effective judicial protection of citizens.[57] The courts

---

[55] Subject to changes and clarifications by the Constitutional Court.
[56] For the history and a general overview of the *jurisdicción contencioso-administrativa* see, Garcia de Enterria, op. cit., Ch.XXIV, pp.546–572 and Martin Rebollo, op. cit. pp. 1360–1380.
[57] Art.24 CE. Data about the overload of the courts dealing with administrative matters can be found in the yearly *Memories* published by the *Consejo General del Poder Judicial*, *www.cgpj.es*. Martin Rebollo, op. cit. pp.1371–1375 reproduced and comments upon some of this data. As an example in the year 2000, 24,434 cases were pending in the administrative Chamber of the Supreme Court while 12,146 had been resolved and 12,691 new cases were admitted.

will entertain claims against administrative acts, inactivity of the administration, factual activity outside procedure (*via de hecho*) and regulatory dispositions (either *reglamentos* or *decretos legislativos*[58].

The courts that integrate the *orden jurisdiccional contencioso* are:

- the *Juzgados de lo Contencioso* finally created and functioning from December 1998;
- the *Juzgados Centrales de lo Contencioso*;
- the *Salas de los contencioso-administrativo de los Tribunales Superiores de Justicia de las Comunidades Autonomas*;
- the *Sala de lo contencioso-administrativo de la Audiencia Nacional*;
- the *Sala de lo contencioso-administrativo* of the *Tribunal Supremo*.

The distribution of matters relates to the origin of the act, the subject matter of the act, the claim and the amount of money at stake (Arts 8–13 LJCA). The new *Ley 29/1998* states that the *jurisdiccion contencioso-adminsitrativa* will deal with four types of claim. An individual can request a declaration of nullity of an act (Art.31(1)), a declaration recognising an existing situation (Art.31(2)) a declaration that the administration must do something (Art.32(1)) or a declaration precluding the administration from doing something.

The proceedings start with a brief written claim in which the plaintiff states the resolution or administrative act that he wishes to challenge. This claim needs to be signed by an *abogado* and a *procurador*.[59]

The period to start judicial proceedings against the administration is restricted to two months if the act challenged was expressed. This is extended to six months if the claimant is challenging a presumed act or decision by silence.[60] In cases of an action against a factual activity of the administration (*via de hecho*) the period is of 30 days.

Once the written claim is accepted the court will request the file from the administration to which the claim refers and will notify and cite all interested parties.[61] The claim is given a number and when the time for this case arrives the court will notify the claimant so that he and his legal team can formalise the *demanda*. This *demanda* is passed on to the Administration, which has a period of time to reply.

---

[58] See Art.1(1) LJCA and Ch.2, "Sources of Law", for an explanation of *Reglamento* and *Decreto Legislativo*.
[59] Art.45 LJCA.
[60] Art.46 LJCA see above for decisions by silence and the effects of administrative silence.
[61] Arts 48 and 49 LJCA.

The court will present any evidence and this will open the period of conclusions or the oral hearing. After the hearing the court will dictate a decision (*sentencia*) which can either; refuse to admit the claim (*inadmitir*),[62] estimate the petition (*estimar*),[63] or reject the case on the merits (*desestimar*).[64]

It is possible to appeal against the decision of the court via the *recurso de apelación* or the *recurso de casación*.[65]

Together with the góeneral proceedings the LJCA establishes three special procedures: the procedure for the protection of fundamental rights and freedoms,[66] the procedure in cases of a *cuestion de ilegalidad* (Arts 123–126)[67] and the procedure in case de *suspension adminsitrativa de acuerdos* (Art.127).[68] In all special proceedings the periods are reduced and the need to exhaust all internal administrative channels is eliminated.

7.   EXTRA-CONTRACTUAL LIABILITY OF THE STATE

The regulation of the extra-contractual or civil responsibility of the State has its origins in the *Ley de Expropiación Forzosa* of 1954[69] and in Art.106(2) of the Constitution that establishes that any damage suffered by individuals as a consequence of the normal or abnormal functioning of public services will be compensated unless the damage was due to *fuerza mayor*. This general statement is complemented by Arts 139–146 of the *Ley de Régimen Juridico de las Administraciones Públicas y del Procedimiento Administrativo Común*[70] that regulates in detail the responsibility of the public administration, its civil servants and other personnel and the *Reglamento de procedimientos en materia de responsabilidad de las Administraciones Públicas*.[71]

---

[62] Art.69 LJCA.
[63] Art.71 LJCA.
[64] Art.70 LJCA.
[65] Arts 81–102 LJCA.
[66] As we saw in Ch.7, pp.208–10.
[67] This is a new procedure for challenging regulations passed by the Adminsitration.
[68] The *acuerdos* or agreements are those of local corporations whose autonomy has been reinforced by the *Ley 7/1985 De Bases de Régimen Local*. See Martin Rebollo, op. cit. p.1459.
[69] Law of Compulsory Purchase of Land, see Martin Rebollo, *Leyes Adminsitrativas*, (Aranzadi, 2002) p.514.
[70] *Ley* 30/1992.
[71] RD 429/1993 of March 26.

The main concept around which the system is organised is the concept of *"lesion"*. *Lesion* is damage suffered by an individual. This damage is illicit because the individual is under no obligation to tolerate the damage. Damage, as such, is not enough to create the responsibility. An individual may have indeed suffered damage by an action of the public administration but he may not have a cause of action to claim compensation because he was under the obligation to suffer it. The *lesión* must be real, individual and susceptible of evaluation.[72]

The damage must be due to the activity or inactivity of the Administration or the provision of public services. There must be a proven causal relation between this activity and the damage suffered although the courts have softened this requirement so that concurrent and indirect causality are acceptable.[73]

The regulation of responsibility of the State has several characteristics:[74]

- It is a unitary regulation that extends to all Public Administrations.
- It is general as it covers all administrative activity—or inactivity—in cases of responsibility for omission.
- The responsibility is direct even in cases in which the Administration pays damages for actions or omissions of its employees.
- It is a type of objective responsibility or responsibility for risk since it is not necessary any element of fault by the state. The only requirement is the actual damage suffered to trigger the mechanism of responsibility.
- It aims for the total reparation of the damage suffered.
- It needs to be claimed within a year of suffering the damage.[75]

The responsibility needs to be claimed by administrative proceedings first and later, if appropriate, by an action on the *jurisdiccion contencioso administrativa*.

---

[72] Art.139(2) LRJ-PAC.
[73] See, Martin Rebollo, *op.cit.* p.515.
[74] Martin Rebollo, *op. cit.* p.14.
[75] Art.142(5) LRJ-PAC, *Ley* 30/1992 of November 26.

Chapter Nine
The law of obligations

1. INTRODUCTION

The word *"obligación"* comes from the latin *obligare* which means, "to tie in, to subject physically", and by extension, morally. The word "obligation" *(obligación)* is constantly used in legal and non-legal language and does not always refer to what obligations are in strict legal terms. Obligations, technically speaking, are particular types of legal duties because the content of the obligation can be translated into a patrimonial value or, in Diaz Pairo's words:

> "obligations are legal relationships whereby a person—the debtor—must do or refrain from doing certain activity in order to satisfy a private interest of another party—the creditor. The creditor can, in case the debtor does not fulfil his duties, address the economic value of his interest against the property of the debtor."[1]

Puig Brutau defines obligations or rights of credit as,

> "The right of the creditor to request from a debtor that the debtor gives, does or doesn't do something. This right is guaranteed by all the property of the debtor."[2]

Sometimes what the law or the speaker are really referring to when they use the word "obligations" are what some authors call *"deberes jurídicos"* or "legal duties".[3] Legal duties involve a request for certain behaviour from an individual because of the position that he is in. For example Art.3 of the Spanish Constitution states that: "all Spanish

---

[1] Definition by Diaz Pairo in Castán Tobeñas, *Derecho Civil, Tomo 3*, p.45.
[2] Puig Brutau, *Concepto del Derecho de crédito*, in *Estudios de Derecho privado* Vol.1 (Barcelona), p.167.
[3] Carlos Lasarte, *Curso de Derecho Civil Patrimonial* (9th edn, Madrid, Tecnos, 2003), p.395.

citizens have the duty to know Castilian", this is really a legal duty and not an obligation.[4]

The Spanish Civil Code does not really define what a (civil) obligation is. Article 1088 says, "*toda obligación consiste en dar, hacer or no hacer alguna cosa*", which can be translated as, "The obligations consist of giving, doing or not doing something". This Article explains what the content of the obligation is but not what an obligation itself is,[5] because the services or the things that the debtor must give are the content of the obligation; they can disappear and the obligation itself can still exist.

The law of obligations (*el derecho de obligaciones*) is the branch of civil law that regulates the right that one person[6]—the creditor (*acreedor*)—has to request from another—the debtor (*deudor*)—that the latter gives, does or refrains from doing something.[7]

All obligations have the following elements: subjects, object, relationship between the subjects and a *causa*. The parties or subjects are the creditor and the debtor. They are referred to sometimes as active subject (creditor) and passive subject (debtor). The first has the right to demand and enforce performance of the obligation by the debtor. The positions of creditor or debtor may be taken by one or several people.[8] The object of the obligation is the performance that can be demanded by the creditor. This performance can consist of doing, not doing or giving something. The last element, the *causa* is the objective and immediate reason of the obligation, the "why", the reason of the power of the creditor to demand a performance by the debtor.[9]

THE LAW OF OBLIGATIONS IN THE SPANISH CIVIL CODE

The law of obligations is regulated in the *Libro IV* (Book IV) of the Civil Code, following in part the French model but improving it in several ways. The main difference between the Spanish Civil Code and the French Code or the Italian Civil Code of 1865 is that the Spanish Code introduces a separate book—the *Libro IV* just mentioned—to regulate obligations and contracts in a methodical and independent manner while the French and Italian Codes looked at obligations in the context of acquiring real rights.

---

[4] See Lasarte, *op. cit.* p.395.

[5] Martin Perez, in Castán, *op. cit.* p.46.

[6] Note that it is possible to find a plurality of people in the position of creditors or debtors. See below, *Obligaciones mancomunadas* and *Obligaciones solidarias*.

[7] Art.1088 CC, "*toda obligación consiste en dar, hacer o no hacer alguna cosa*".

[8] See infra, *obligaciomes solidarias y mancomunadas* where there are either several debtors, creditors or both.

[9] We shall return to the concept of *causa* when we study the law of contract below.

This Book IV of the Code has, however, a very wide content and includes matters that go well beyond what we could legitimately identify as the core of the law of obligations. There is, for example, a Chapter on matrimonial economic regimes[10] that will fit better into the area of family law; rules about evidence[11] and acquisition and extinction of rights by prescription[12] that affect all types of rights—real and personal—in general and not only obligations.

For a long time the academic debate revolved around whether, from a didactic point of view, the law of obligations should precede or follow the study of real rights.[13] Opinions are varied but most Spanish universities study the law of obligations first.

The original version of the Code containing a regulation of the law of obligations was drafted with a very different society and model of economic traffic in mind. The late 19th century agrarian and localised society demanded a very different system of regulation from the guarantees needed today when mass contracts, internet and multinationals throw a very different light on the original ideas of "freedom of contract" and "equality of parties". Today we also live in a society where the traffic of services is bigger than the traffic of goods. Like in so many other areas it is said that the Civil Code is obsolete in the treatment of obligations and most contracts are regulated by subsequent legislation.[14]

REAL RIGHTS AND PERSONAL RIGHTS

Obligations are also called rights of credit or personal rights, as opposed to real rights because they are subjective rights held by an individual[15] against another individual. It has been common to differentiate between real rights and personal rights or rights of credit.[16]

- Real rights[17] give the holder of the right a power over the thing itself independently of who is the owner or possessor. For

---

[10] *Capitulaciones matrimoniales*, Arts 1315–1444. See Ch.11.

[11] Arts 1214–1253 CC.

[12] Arts 1930–1975 CC.

[13] See Lacruz *Berdejo y otros, Derecho de Obligaciones*, Vol.2, p.14.

[14] See *Ley Contrato de Seguros, Ley de venta de bienes a plazo, Ley comercio electronico*.

[15] See note above about possible plurality of parties as creditors and debtors.

[16] We are using here the classification made by C. Lasarte, *op. cit*. p.396, but this shared by all authors. See for example Castán Tobeñas, op. cit. p.52, Diez Picazo, *Sistema de Derecho Civil* Vol.2, p.18.

[17] See Ch.10, p.260.

example the holder of a right of usufruct[18] has the right to enjoy the use and fruits of the property independently of whether the (bare) ownership of the property has been passed to another person.[19]

- Real rights are absolute rights and can be enforced *erga omnes* while rights or credit are "relative rights" that can only be enforced against the debtor. An example of the above can be seen with the most typical of both types of right: ownership as a real right which entitles the owner to exclude trespassers (everybody must refrain from trespassing) and the right of the seller (a right of credit) to request the price from the buyer (only) in a contract of sale.
- Real rights are concerned with attribution or distribution of property[20] and have a tendency to *permanence*; personal rights or rights of credit are structurally *transitory* rights that will be extinguished when the debtor fulfils his obligation.
- Real rights can be acquired by prescription (Art.1930 Civil Code)[21] while this possibility will be totally inappropriate for rights of credit.

SOURCES OF OBLIGATIONS

This expression is unanimously used for those acts that create obligations in the legal sense. Article 1089 of the Civil Code states that "obligations are created by law, by contracts and quasi-contracts and by those illegal acts and omissions in which there is fault or negligence". According to this Article there are two main sources of obligations: the law or the free will of the parties expressed in contracts. Obligations are divided into: *Obligaciones legales*, which are those obligations created by law and include all extra-contractual obligations[22]; and *obligaciones contractuales*, which are those obligations created by contract. To this a third category of quasi-contracts is sometimes added. This rather obsolete terminology includes, according to Art.1887 of the Civil Code the, *"gestion de negocios ajenos sin mandato"* and the, *"cobro de lo indebido"*. They are of marginal importance in Spanish legal literature and belong to the general category of the law of restitution in English Law.

---

[18] Usufrut is a real right, see Ch.10, pp.263–4, for explanation and characteristics.
[19] For an explanation of the right of usufruct see, Ch.10, pp.263–4.
[20] Castán Tobeñas cites Betti's classical formulation about the different function of real and personal rights. Real rights he says, resolve a question of *attribution* of property and rights, personal rights or obligations solve a problem of *co-operation*—as in the case of contracts—or *reparation*—as in the case of extra-contractual responsibility.
[21] See Ch.10, p.274.
[22] See below.

2.   TYPES OF OBLIGATIONS: CLASSIFICATION

Beyond the main division between contractual and extra-contractual obligations the doctrine has made different classifications of the different types of obligations. These are useful for pointing out different aspects of the nature and regulation of obligations in Spanish Law.

ACCORDING TO THE NUMBER OF SUBJECTS

According to the number of subjects (active or passive) obligations can be *unipersonales*, when there is only one subject in the active or passive role, or have a plurality of subjects. In the later case there are two possibilities: *obligaciones mancomunadas* and *obligaciones solidarias*.

Obligaciones mancomunadas are regulated in Arts 1137 and 1138 of the Civil Code and, despite what their name suggests, have very little of "obligations in common" since each party is liable to perform only their own part of the obligation. These obligations have also been called *obligaciones pro-rata*. This type of obligation is the general rule according the Civil Code[23] but of course, in order to have a pro-rata performance or right of credit the obligation itself must be of such a type as to be able to be divided. There are cases in which it is not possible to divide the obligation. An example given by Lacruz[24] is that of two buyers who buy a horse. One of them pays half the price but the other doesn't. The seller has the right to terminate the contract despite payment from one of the buyers (Art.1124 CC).

In those cases in which the credit or debt are divisible (*mancomunados*) the original obligation is in practice divided into different credits and debts with a different existence as to performance and extinction.[25]

Obligaciones solidarias are those in which there is also a plurality of debtors, creditors, or both but in contrast with the *obligaciones mancomunadas* all debtors are liable for the whole performance and all creditors have the right to demand performance of the whole

---

[23] Art.1137 CC states that, "the concurrence two or more debtors or two or more creditors does not imply that each of them has the duty to perform the obligation or the right to demand the whole performance". This is complemented by Art.1138 of the Civil Code, which adds, "unless the obligation establishes something different, in the previous instance—of several creditors or several debtors—the credit or the debt is presumed to be divided in as many equal parts as creditors or debtors and each credit or debt is independent from the others".

[24] Lacruz Berdejo, *op.cit.*, p.21.

[25] See below.

obligation. They have been graphically described as "obligations of all and each of them for the whole".

The "solidarity" can be active (of several creditors), passive (of several debtors), or mixed (of several creditors and debtors). In this type of obligation payment by one of the debtors extinguishes the obligation.[26] Internally, these type of obligations are like the *obligaciones mancomunadas*. This is, among the various debtors and creditors each of them is responsible for the performance—or has the right of credit—of his part of the obligation in equal or unequal parts according to what was established when the obligation was created. This means that if one of the debtors pays the whole debt to the creditor or creditors that request payment from him, he has the right to claim back from his co-debtors payment of their respective shares. These co-debtors are now not in a position of solidarity and therefore he must request from each of them payment of his part. This is known as *accion de regreso* (Art.1145(2) CC).

There are today several examples of "solidarity" imposed by law and geared towards the protection of consumers. Good examples are provided by the L.O.C.M., which establishes that in cases of vending machines the owners of the premises where the machine is installed respond jointly to the consumer. Another example is provided by the *Ley de Ordenacion de la Edificacion* de 1999,[27] which establishes the responsibility of all agents of the construction—architects, builders, surveyors and others—for any defects of construction if liability cannot be directed exclusively to one of these parties.

ACCORDING TO THE PERFORMANCE DUE BY THE DEBTOR

Obligaciones de dar

The performance of this type of obligation requires that the debtor "gives" something. This means a physical transfer of a corporeal thing to the creditor. If the object is a specific thing the creditor can compel the debtor to give it, for example a particular picture by Picasso. If it is a generic thing he can request performance at the expense of the debtor, for example if the debtor is obliged to deliver 500kg of top soil, this is a generic obligation. Should the debtor default or refuse to deliver the top soil by the time agreed, the creditor can buy it elsewhere and the debtor will now be responsible for the expenses incurred according to Art.1101 CC.

---

[26] Art.1145 CC. Other ways of extinguishing these obligations are by novation (Art.1143 CC), compensation or for supervening impossibility (Art.1147). See below.
[27] See Ch.10, "Property", p.280.

The debtor is obliged to keep the object of the obligation—the thing that he must give—in a good state, acting at all times with the "diligence of a good father", an expression equivalent to that of a "reasonable man".

Obligaciones de hacer

These can be of two main types: those that consist of the performance of a certain activity without expecting any precise result—*obligación de medios*; and those that require the obtainment of a specific result, for example we ask the decorator to paint the dining room—*obligación de resultado*.

Both of these type of obligations, *de medios* and the *resultado*, can be "personal" (*obligaciones personalisimas*) if the creditor entered into the relationship only because of the person that was to perform it. For example in the first case of *obligaciones de medios* we can employ a famous lawyer to defend us and a substitute is not acceptable, or, in the case of *obligaciones de resultado* we may book an appointment for a haircut with a particular stylist.

Obligaciones de no hacer

These consist of the imposition to the debtor of an obligation to refrain from certain behaviour. This may be just any material activity—not to take the dog onto school premises—or legal activity—not to sell an item for a determinate period. In the second case some of these restrictions are imposed by law as accessory obligations. An example is the obligation not to sell property acquired through the exercise of a right of preferential acquisition during a certain period of time.[28]

3.   CONTRACTUAL OBLIGATIONS

HISTORICAL EVOLUTION OF THE LAW OF CONTRACT

In Roman law only certain types of contracts created obligations between the parties.[29] In modern law, all agreements are, in principle, capable of creating a contractual relationship with the only

---

[28] See Art.51 LAU and Lasarte, *op. cit.* p.403.
[29] This was known as the system of *numerus clausus* for contracts whereby the parties' will had to be expressed in one of the pre-accepted models for one the contracts

limits imposed by the general principles of good faith,[30] morals,[31] law or public order. This evolution from a system of *numerus clausus* to an open system where all agreements are valid involved the influence of canon and mercantile law. Canon law, with its emphasis on the importance of good faith and the binding nature of promises, endowed engagements with an action in the ecclesiastic courts.[32] In principle dealings between secular subjects were subject to the jurisdiction of the King but the idea that promises and agreements should be enforceable penetrated the civil laws of different kingdoms.[33]

It was necessary, however, for the school of natural law to defeat the principle that simple agreements are not enforceable as a general principle of the law. It was in the 17th century that the idea that the source of obligations is the human will, expressed in such a way that can be recognised and enforced by the law, evolved until it was introduced in the Napoleon Civil Code with the now classical formulation of Art.1134 of the French Civil Code; "Agreements legally formed take the place of the law (*loi*) between the parties (those who have made them)".

Domat and Pothier were the two great authors of the period and their work is instrumental on the formulation of modern civil law.[34] The Spanish Civil Code follows the French Civil Code although develops some of the principles in what Lacruz describes as much more "expressive way". Article 1091 of the CC is a copy of Art.1134 FCC stating that, "obligations that arise from contracts take the place of law between the parties". This statement needs some explanation because there is always a difference between the law, understood as a general law with normative vocation, creator of objective rights and the agreement between the parties that can only create subjective rights and duties. The function of a contract is not really normative. The parties to it are not intending to create law when they enter into

---

recognised by the law. See Lacruz Berdejo. "*Derecho de Obligaciones. Vol 2: Teoria general del contrato*", p.10.

[30] Art.7 CC, in the exercise of any right and more specifically, Arts 1473 and 1688 CC being contrary to moral, law or public order.

[31] Art.1116 CC.

[32] *Condictio ex canone* and *denuntiatio evangelica*. See Lacruz, *op. cit.* p.13.

[33] In Spain in particular it is possible to find early references to this concept in the *Ordenamiento de Alcala*, el Fuero de Navarra and the *Observancias de Aragón*. For more detail on these texts and the areas they covered see Ch.1, pp. 9–12.

[34] Domat's main work was *Le droit public, suite des lois civiles dans leur ordre naturel* and Pothier's *Trait des obligations* (1761). For a discussion of the two authors' influence on the French law of contract see, Bell, *Principles of French Law*, p.306 and Lacruz, *op. cit.* p.14.

an agreement, but they are disposing of their own rights and creating duties with a patrimonial content.[35]

The contract is basically an agreement between the parties addressed to the production of legal effects. At the time of the drafting of the European Civil Codes, the philosophical and political ideas of the time influenced a view of contracts that rested upon the principles of equality and freedom of the parties that could decide to agree on rights and obligations according to their interest. Arts 1255 of the CC reflects this conception of the Liberal State authorising the parties to enter into any agreements, clauses or conditions that they wished.

It soon became clear that the evolution of the economic model and the expansion of the role of the State on the one hand, and the big economic groups and companies on the other, made this idea of equality of parties deciding what, how and whether to enter into a contract a complete fallacy. Even in its simpler form, contractual parties to a mere sale are rarely free to agree any terms. Nobody in Western Europe can walk into a shop pick up a litre of milk and try to negotiate the price with the person at the counter. Nor is the shopkeeper totally free to fix the prices since those will be dictated by the conditions of competition between similar or equal establishments if he wants to keep in business.

The situation is even clearer in major contracts with big economic forces like banks, insurance companies, transport or with contracts with the main utilities' providers. The parties who want or need to use these services need to agree to the contractual terms imposed by the companies.

This means the State needs to intervene and moderate the full impact of the principle of freedom of contract by imposing certain duties—mainly of publicity and a spectrum of minimum rights for the weaker party—on the party that was perceived to be in a stronger position.

Modern civil law has complemented this with specific legislation for the protection of consumers. In Spain there are two laws: the *Ley General de Consumidores y Usuarios* of 1984 and the *Ley de las Condiciones Generales de la Contratacion de 1998.*

ELEMENTS OF A VALID CONTRACT

In order to have a valid contract three elements are essential: consent of the parties, object of the contract and *causa* of the obligation.[36]

---

[35] Lacruz, *op. cit.* p.18.
[36] Art.1261 CC.

If one or more of these elements are missing, there is no contract according to Art.1261. In addition, the parties—according the principle of freedom of contract or *autonomia de la voluntad* that we saw in the previous section—can introduce other elements into the contract, namely, *condiciones ó termino* (conditions), which are referred to by the doctrine as accidental elements in the sense that they are not essential for the existence of the contract.[37] We will look at both essential and non-essential elements starting with the former.

Capacity of the parties

The parties to a contract must be able to understand, want and express to enter into that contract. In order to do so they must have both *capacidad natural* and *capacidad legal*.[38]

Minors are not able to enter into contracts according to Art.1263 CC. This rule is designed to protect minors from their own inexperience and lack of judgement in particular cases. However a strict application of this rule will suffocate and make the development of those who have not reached the necessary age and the economic agent impossible. Minors today enter into a variety of contracts everyday and in most cases they fully understand the implications of those simple sales. Think of teens buying clothes, records, food and other goods. The legal system today understands this and despite the persistence of this rule in the Civil Code, contracts entered into by a minor are not null and void but merely voidable at the request of the legal representative of the minor or the minor himself at the time of reaching the statutory age.[39] It is clear that this is designed for relatively large economic transactions and not the everyday sales that minors enter into as a matter of course.

Together with these general situations of lack of capacity there are situations referred to as "special incapacity" to contract. These are really prohibitions to enter into specific contracts between specific people or in respect of specific objects because of the situation in which one or both parties are. There are no true examples of lack of capacity[40] because the person who is restricted from entering into a

---

[37] Once these conditions are introduced they become essential to that particular contract. See more below.

[38] Art.1263 CC indicates in a negative way who cannot be a party to the contract because they cannot consent: *menores no emancipados, locos o dementes y sordomudos que no sepan escribir* (non-emancipated minors, those of unsound mind, and dumb and deaf individuals who cannot write).

[39] See Art.1.301 CC.

[40] See Art.1459 CC.

particular contract due to the position he finds himself in can enter into contract with different people or with different objects. The aim of these prohibitions or restrictions is to avoid a possible abuse of the position that some people have because of their profession or relationship with the other party or the unjust enrichment of one party to the other party's detriment. Examples of this prohibition are tutors in respect of the property of the tutees,[41] agents in respect of property of their principal that they are to sell or manage,[42] *albaceas*[43] or executors in respect of the estate, civil servants or other public sector employees in respect of that property of the State that they are in charge of, and judges and magistrates in respect of property involved in a case being heard in front of them.[44]

CONSENTIMIENTO

The agreement of the parties to the contract is the starting point of any contract. There is no contact without consent (*solus consensum obligat*). This consent or agreement can be expressed in many ways and with different degrees of formality. Spanish law gives priority to the agreement of the parties over the formalities of expressing the agreement and insists that contracts are valid and enforceable from the time at which the parties' consent coincides over the object and the cause of the obligation. It has also been said that the parties can express their consent in any way they wish, although there are some methods that will make it easier to prove the existence of the contract and its content if disagreements arise in the future.

The principle of freedom from formalities applies to all contracts, even those for the creation or transmission of real rights despite the confusing language of Art.1280 CC. Ownership and other real rights can be created and transferred by private agreement complemented by *traditio* and the exigence of public documents is only related to the fact that none of the rights created can be entered into the Land Registry if that type of document is not used, therefore depriving the parties of the protection granted by the registry.[45]

The agreement of the parties or consent in order to be valid depends on two different things: the capacity of the parties and the freedom from defects on the formation of consent—*vicios del consentimiento*.

---

[41] Drafted according to the LO 1/1996, of January 15, see also Art.221(3) CC.
[42] Art.1709 *et seq.* CC, Arts 96(4) and 267 of the C.Com.
[43] Art.901 CC.
[44] Art.1459 CC and the numerous restrictions introduced by the *Ley* 53/1984, of 26 December, *de incompatibiliades* and the *Ley* 30/1984, of 2 August *de reforma de la función publica*.
[45] See Ch.10, pp.282–5.

Vicios del consentimiento

The formation of a contract rests upon the premise that two (or more) free parties agree on obliging themselves to certain behaviour. The doctrine calls *vicios del consentimiento* to those situations in which the consent of one or more of the parties is vitiated either because of their own mistake or because of external interference. In those cases and depending on the seriousness of the interference or the mistake the law either declares the contract non-existent for lack of consent or allows the party that suffers the interference or mistake to annul the contract and recuperate any damages suffered.

The following examines these situations in order.

Error

The Civil Code does not give a definition of what constitutes an error but it establishes the characteristics that this error or mistake must have in order to be relevant. It is clear that if contracts could be annulled because one of the parties made "a mistake" this would create a situation of legal uncertainty that would make impossible the normal flow of economic activity. In consequence Art.1266 of the Civil Code declares that the mistake must be essential or substantial and in respect of the object of the contract. To these two requirements the *Tribunal Supremo* has added that the mistake must be excusable; this is that the person suffering the mistake must have exercised due diligence and cannot be blamed for the mistake itself.[46]

The mistake must also have been recognised by the other party to the contract or should have been recognised if that party had exercised due diligence. The legal system is not denying the party who does not suffer the mistake his legitimate expectations of legal consequences since that party knows or should have known of the mistake. Mistake is sometimes confused with *dolo* since it is possible to argue that somebody who knows that the other parry is entering into a contract suffering a serious mistake about the object and who does nothing to correct the mistaken understanding is not acting in good faith. The main difference between the two is that in cases of mistake the party who does not suffer it does nothing to induce the mistaken belief in the other party while *dolo* requires an active conduct as the definition of *dolo* indicates.

---

[46] See *Sentencia 21 de junio 1978* in which the requirement of "excusability" is based in the principle of responsibility for one's own acts and errors, protection of good faith and security of legal transactions. See Lacruz, *op. cit.* pp.72–73 for a good commentary on the *Tribunal Supremo* decisions on this point.

Dolo is defined by Art.1269 of the Code as occurring when one of the parties by words or "insidious machinations" induces the other party to celebrate a contract that he would have not celebrated in the absence of those words or conduct. In order to be sufficient to annul the contract the *dolo* must be serious (*grave*), performed with the malicious intention of confusing the other party and modifying their judgement and intention. *Dolus bonus* or publicity exaggerations about a product or a service are not considered to fall under the category of *dolo*. It is understood that everybody can exercise their own judgement as to whether or not to believe those often exaggerated claims.[47]

Violence or intimidation

Violence is the use of irresistible force in order to exact the consent of one of the parties.[48] This force has traditionally considered to be physical but Lasarte uses the example of an hypnotist who substitutes the consent of the party under hypnosis.[49]

Intimidation is defined as a threat that produces in one of the parties to the contract a rational fear of suffering a serious and imminent harm in his person, property of the person or property of his spouse, descendants or any other close member of the family.

Violence and intimidation act in different ways because in a contract conducted under actual physical violence there is no consent at all while in a contract celebrated under intimidation there is consent even if this is vitiated. The Civil Code[50] establishes the same consequences for both types of interference with the free formation of consent and gives the party who suffered the violence or intimidation the possibility of annulling the contract. This has been criticised by the doctrine because if there is no consent there can be no contract and therefore in cases of violence the contract should be null and void *ab initio*.[51]

In cases of intimidation, the consent is still present, because the person who suffers intimidation has a choice between entering into the contract or suffering the damage that constitutes the threat. There is ample case law in this matter determining that the fear must be evaluated taking into account the personal circumstances of the

---

[47] The limit to a good faith "exaggeration" and what the legislation on consumer protection calls *publicidad enganosa* needs to be determined by the courts. See *Ley General de Consumidores y Usuarios* of 1984.

[48] Art.1267(2) CC.

[49] Lasarte, *Elementos del Contrato, op. cit.* p.329.

[50] Art.1268 CC.

[51] See Lasartae, op. cit, p.331 and for a more detailed treatment of the question, Lacruz Berdejo y otros, *Derecho de Obligaciones, op. cit.* pp.387–389.

person suffering it. The damage threatened must be illegitimate[52] and the consequences acceptable.[53]

The so-called "*temor reverencial*", which could be translated as "reverential fear", or fear to disappoint those to whom respect is due, will not affect the contract.[54]

Formation of contract: offer and acceptance

A contract usually starts with the offer made by one party to the other and it is perfected when the other party accepts that offer.[55] The offer, in order to be binding, must be complete, precise and definitive and be addressed to either a proposed party or to the general public. Acceptance of the offer, in turn, must be directed to the offeror, and be definitive. It must also be made within the period during which the offer is valid. The acceptance must be over the same object and *causa* which constitute the contract and must be coincident in all material points with the offer; otherwise it would constitute a counter-offer.

Contracts between absent parties

There are four possible solutions in order to determine when a contract is made between absent parties. At the one end of the spectrum the contract may be made when the acceptance is declared. At the other end it may not be made until the acceptance is received or known by the offeror. In between those two it is possible to chose a point of completion for when the acceptance is sent; this is when the acceptor posts the acceptance. In Spanish law the Civil Code opts for the solution that the contract is made when the offeror knows of the acceptance or ought to have known of it in good faith. This solution has been criticised as extreme[56] by the doctrine and incongruous with other sectors of the law, like commercial law where the criteria of declaration of the acceptance has been chosen.[57] The

---

[52] It is not intimidation to announce, or threaten to exercise a legitimate right; for example to go to court to request payment of a pre-existing obligation. Ss July 4 and 28, 1947; December 15, 1966; and March 21, 1970.
[53] For example, S of March 8, 1958, establishing that intimidation affects the freewill of the person suffering it but there is still a will from the party to the contract; S February 15, 1943, and November 18, 1944, on the same line. S November 18, 1944, and April 22, 1944, on the type of threat that amounts to intimidation and the need to take into account the personal circumstances of the person suffering it, for example education, culture and isolation.
[54] Art.1267(4) CC.
[55] Arts 1261 and 1262 CC and ample case law.
[56] Lacruz, *op. cit.* p.92.
[57] See Art.54 C. Com.

contract is understood to have been concluded in the place where the offer was made. If the contract was made by phone it is understood to have been made between present parties since communication is immediate.[58]

For contracts made by automated electronic means the *Ley* 34/2002 of July 11[59]establishes that the contract is made at the time of manifesting the acceptance. For example if somebody buys goods or services by internet the acceptance of the terms and conditions will be determined by clicking the required button on the computer. The same is applicable to tickets bought from automatic machines.

Pre-contractual talks do not generally entail any responsibility or obligation to complete the contract in normal circumstances. Only if one of the parties has acted in bad faith can the other request compensation for damages suffered.[60]

Objeto del contrato

The object of the contract is one of its essential elements.[61] There has been a large doctrinal debate about what the Code means by "object of the contract".[62] A large of part of the classical civil law writers understand that the object is the *prestación*, the performance, the goods[63] or services[64] that are the subject matter of the contract.

The French *Civilistes* argued in respect of the similar wording of the Code Napoleon about the object of the contract that a contract itself has no object, only effects; those effects are the obligations that the contract creates and those obligations have got an object. The object of the obligations is provision of goods or services.[65] This view is supported by many of the Spanish writers among whom are Puig Brutau and Diez Picazo.[66]

---

[58] S *de 3 de enero de 1948* cited by Lacruz in *op. cit.* p.92.
[59] *Ley* 34/2002, July 11 de *servicios de la sociedad de la informacion y comercio electronico.*
[60] Arts 1258 and 1902 CC. The responsibility will be extra-contractual in this case since there is, and will not be, a contract.
[61] Art.1261 states that there is no contract unless this has a certain and legitimate object.
[62] See Lacruz Berdejo, op. cit. pp.437–440 and Lasarte, *op. cit.* p.332.
[63] The term here includes not only corporeal objects but also incorporeal things such as rights.
[64] Services in this context include any negative behaviour in the sense of "not doing" something, if this abstention has got a patrimonial value.
[65] Ripert, cited in Lacruz, *op. cit.* p.437.
[66] See Puig Brutau, *Derecho de Obligaciones, op. cit*, p.22 and Diez Picazo, *Sistema de Derecho Civil* Vol.II, pp.85–87.

They argue that the object of the contract is referred in Art.1261 of the Civil Code as the, "object that is the subject matter of the contract", indicating with these words an understanding of goods or services like the object of the contract. This understanding is furthered by the so-called requirements of the object of the contract of Arts 1271, 1272 and 1273 CC. The object must be "legitimate, possible and determinate".

Legítimo

The object must be legal, which in respect of goods means that these must be able to be transferred and therefore cannot include property that for reasons of public interest or the public good is outside trade, such as public property or traffic of human organs (the *res extra commercium* of Roman Law). Further, all goods and services that constitute the object of a contract must comply with the law and good morals (Art.1271(3) CC).

Posible

The Code states this requirement in a negative way: "the object of the contract cannot be impossible" (Art.1272). Possible means possible in the world of physical reality as opposed to legal impossibility. For example it would be physically possible to make a contract selling a human organ for money but it would not be legal according to the previous requirement. On the other hand it may be legal to have a contract for the sale of a litre of stardust but it will not be physically possible.

Determinado o determinable (ascertained or ascertainable)

This requirement applies both to things and services, for example to sell a particular model of car or to repair any window frames damaged by rot (Art.1273 in fine).

Causa

Causa in Spanish law has both an objective and a subjective meaning. In an objective sense *causa* is the socioeconomic function of the contract (Art.1274 CC). The subjective meaning of *causa* serves the purpose of controlling the conformity of the contract with the law and morals of the community at a particular time.[67] We will look at both these aspects in turn.

---

[67] See, among others Lasarte, *op. cit.* p.54.

Causa in an objective sense (Art.1274 CC)

The Spanish Civil Code understands that "the objective socio-economic function of the contract" constitutes the *causa* and distinguishes in Art.1274 between an onerous *causa* and a gratuitous *causa*. For gratuitous contracts the *causa* is the "liberality of the donor" (the reason why he is being liberal is irrelevant according to the doctrine) and in onerous contracts the *causa* is for each of the parties the performance or promise of a good or service by the other party.[68]

This understanding of what constitutes the *causa* as the socio-economic function of a contract allows a function for each main type of contract to be objectively identified. For example the contract of sale has the function of exchanging things for money.

The *causa* must not be confused with the parties' motives for entering into that particular contract. The *causa* is one of the essential elements of the contract and it is not dependent on subjective reasons. For example, I buy a bunch of flowers for a colleague who is in hospital. The contract of sale has got what the Code calls an "*onerous causa*": I give money and the flower seller gives me the bunch of flowers. My actual motives in buying the flowers are, at this point, irrelevant.[69] The law does not endow to particular and personal motives any relevance, even if those are known to both parties unless the motives or "internal subjective reasons" are included in the contract as a condition.[70] An example of this will be when a person buys land in order to build a house on it and this is known to the seller. If nothing is said in the contract the sale will be valid whether or not the buyer can actually obtain a licence to build on the land. If, on the other hand, the buyer specifies that he buys the land with the condition that the actual dimensions of the plot are sufficient for him to obtain a building licence and, later, it is found that the plot is actually not large enough, the contract will come to an end. The parties will have to return what they received until they are in the same position as they were before they entered into the contract.[71]

Causa in a subjective sense (Art.1275 CC)

If the *causa* is the objective socio-economic function of the contract how is it possible to have an illegal cause? If motives are not relevant all sales of goods, whatever the goods, must be legal if the

---

[68]   Art.1274 CC.
[69]   My motives can be varied: I may be expecting a promotion at work, I may just be a kind person or I may even fancy the shop assistant.
[70]   See below, *Condiciones*.
[71]   Arts 1.122 and 1.123 CC.

object is legal. If the actual motive is irrelevant all donations would
be valid whatever the motive or intention the donor had in mind when
donating the goods. If the *causa* of the contract had only an objective meaning no motive will ever play a role in the validity of the contract from the point of view of the *causa*. However Art.1275 destroys
the neat categorisation of *causa* of Art.1274 by stating that contracts
with no *causa* or illegal *causa* do not produce any effect. It is clear
from the wording of this Article that *causa* is something more for the
legislator than the objective function of the contract; expecting to
obtain goods or services for money cannot be illegal per se. The *causa*
must therefore be the specific *causa* for that particular contract and
in this sense it is very difficult to differentiate from the motives of the
parties. This has been the view that the courts have taken when trying
to curb the validity of otherwise valid contracts that pursued an
objective contrary to the law or the moral of a particular time.[72]

Diez Picazo and Sancho Rebullida argue that the reason for the
sanction and lack of effect of a contract that is objectively immoral
or illegal has nothing to do with the *causa* itself but with the limits to
the "autonomy of the parties" or freedom of contract. Saying that the
causa is illegal is, in the strict sense, incorrect, adds Cariota Ferrara,[73]
because although there are illegal motives (subjective) the *causa*
cannot operate in an individual case—the one that is illegal—in a
different way to the general and abstract sense that the law generally
understands.

The implications of a subjective type of *causa* are complex. On the
one hand it poses questions as to how important—to the parties—
and crucial to the particular contract the illegal motive should be in
order to affect the *causa* in the sense of Art.1275. On the other it is
necessary to establish whether both parties must know and co-
operate in the pursuance of this illegal motive in order to render the
causa illegal as per Art.1275 CC.

The answer to these questions is not straightforward. The doctrine
of the Supreme Court understands that *causa* is not only the objective and typical socio-economic purpose of the contract but also the
specific end sought in each particular case. In this sense there is
"*causalization*" or integration of the motive into the contract.[74]
Lacruz adopts a practical view by saying that in order to have an
illegal *causa* (*causa ilícita*) this must be the determinant or *decisive*
motive for *both* parties, or at least be known to both, and one party

---

[72] See Lasarte, op. cit. pp.334–7 or Lacruz Berdejo for a great and detailed exposition
of the different views on motives of different authors, *op. cit*. pp.180–189.
[73] Member of the "school of the objective *causa*", in Lacruz, *op. cit*. p.186.
[74] S of December 14, 1940; S of April 1, 1982.

must exploit in his own benefit the illegal motive of the other. An example of this is: A rents a flat to B at an exorbitant price because he knows he wants it to traffic illegal drugs; or A buys B's property at a much lower price that the open market because he knows that B wants to avoid his creditors.[75]

Absence of causa and falsa causa

The Civil Code also rejects the possibility of contracts with no *causa*, what are called "abstract contracts", in German Law by establishing in Art.1275 that "... contracts without a *causa* will not produce any effects". The *causa*, we have just said, is one of the essential elements of the contract according to Art.1261; therefore if there is no *causa* there is no contract. Article 1277 further adds that the *causa* is presumed to be existent and legal even if it is not stated in the contract unless the debtor proves otherwise.

The *falsa causa* of Art.1276 is somehow different to the previous situation of absence of causa, a *falsa causa* is really within the realms of the defects of consent. The *causa falsa* is a fundamental error on which consent was based and therefore on the contract. The error falls over the existence of one of the requirements that one or both parties consider fundamental for the existence of the contract. Most of the Spanish doctrine deals with the *falsa causa* as a type of "*simulación*". The parties agree to enter into a contract that none of them really wants in order to produce certain effects that are only superficial and not real. What the parties really want is to achieve other effects, those of the *contrato disimulado* or hidden contract. An example of this will be a "simulated" sale of a house from a father to his favourite child. The *causa* is *falsa* because there is an absence of price given for the house. None of the parties really wanted a sale; the sale was the vehicle by which the father tried to avoid the rules of legitimate shares[76] or perhaps certain taxation on inheritance. The real "*causa*" is found in the hidden, *real intention* behind a transaction, a gift or donation. The consequences of a simulated contract of sale in order to defeat compulsory shares in inheritance will be that the sale is null and void because there is no *causa*—for onerous contracts the *causa* is the *prestación* or promise of the other party and in this example there really was no price given, only a simulated declaration pretending that there was such delivery of the price (Art.1274 CC). In addition in this case the

---

[75] Lacruz, *op. cit.* p.187.
[76] For "compulsory" or "legitimate shares" in succession in favour of descendants see, Ch.12, p.318, "Succession".

simulated or hidden contract, the donation or gift will also be void because the *causa* here is illegal—to defraud the legitimate rights of the other future co-heirs.[77]

Accidental elements of the contract: conditions

Conditions are very common on contracts and perfectly valid according to the general principle of freedom of contract. The parties can agree whatever they wish in whatever terms they wish and therefore they can subject the contract, and its perfection, to whatever conditions they think fit (Art.1113 CC).

Contracts subject to a condition are perfect contracts but their effects depend on a "future and uncertain" event. It is clear that the contract already exists, otherwise it would not make sense to insert a condition; it would just be a case of pre-contractual talks.

The Civil Code requires that conditions meet certain characteristics in order to be valid: the fact or event that constitutes the condition must be possible (Art.1(116) CC), legal according to the law and good morals, and it must be independent of the parties (Arts 1(115) and 1(119) CC). For example, I might say to my neighbour, "I will sell you my surf board if I get bored with surfing". This is worded as a conditional sale, "if something future and uncertain happens", but it is not a real condition because it is up to me to understand whether or not I am bored with surfing. It will be against Art.1256 of the Civil Code to allow the validity and enforcement of a contract to be subject to the will of one of the parties.

There are two types of conditions in Spanish law; *suspensivas* and *resolutorias*. *Condiciones suspensivas* make the effects of the contract subject to a future event; the contract is left awaiting for its effects to take place. *Condiciones resolutorias*, on the other hand mean that when the future event eventually takes place, the contract ceases to produce effect.

4.   DISCHARGE OF THE CONTRACT

A contract is discharged by performance, frustration or breach.

---

[77] See *S.* of December 20, 1989, *S.* of December 21, 1981, *S.* of October 8, 1981, all of these cited in Lacruz Berdejo et al. *op. cit.* pp.176–179.

PERFORMANCE (PAGO O CUMPLIMIENTO)

The concept of *pago* involves the satisfaction of the performance due by the debtor of the obligation that therein extinguishes it.

The word *pago* encompasses all type of performances, not only of payment of money. The Code refers indistinctively to *pago* and *cumplimiento* to describe performance of the obligation. In common language some types of performance, or non-performance are referred to as *pago* while for others it is more common to use the word *cumplimiento*.

Performance of the obligation/s due is the normal, expected and lawful way of discharging a contract and extinguishing any obligations created by that contract.[78]

The debtor is the person obliged to perform the obligation but it is possible, in certain circumstances, that a third party effects the performance in place of the debtor discharging the obligation vis-à-vis the creditor that has his right satisfied by the third party's performance. The Civil Code makes a distinction between "personal obligations" (*obligaciones personalísimas*) and other types of obligations. *Obligaciones personalísimas* are those that were entered into because of the person and attributes of the debtor, for example employing a famous lawyer to defend us in court, and therefore do not admit performance by any other person.[79] For all other obligations the Code accepts the possibility of a third party to the original contract performing in lieu of the debtor.[80] The debtor may either approve or indeed he might have instigated this performance by another person, disapprove of or even ignore the performance effected by the third party. If the debtor knows and approves the performance of his contractual duties by a third party[81] a substitution (*subrogación*) takes place whereby the original creditor is substituted by the third party who performed the debtors duties. The terms of the original contact remain unchanged and any guarantees, conditions or clauses withstand unchanged. The debtor is now obliged to pay (in the sense of perform) to the new creditor.

If the debtor ignores that payment or performance of the obligation by a third party has taken place, or if knowing it opposed it, the original contractual relationship is extinguished and a new right of credit is created in favour of the third party who payed.[82] This right

---

[78] Arts 1156 and 1157 CC.
[79] Art.1161 CC.
[80] Art.1158 CC.
[81] Art.1158(1) CC. The Article applies equally to extra-contractual obligations.
[82] Art.1158(3) CC.

of credit is called *acción de reembolso o reintegro*. The claim by the new creditor is limited to the benefit derived by the debtor from the performance of the obligation by the third party.

The payment or performance of the contract discharges the debtor from his obligation if this payment is coincident with what it was agreed between the parties.[83] The creditor has a right to reject it if it is not exactly coincident.[84] The payment must also be made to the creditor himself or to a person who appears to be the creditor[85] in order to be valid for the discharge of the contract. Payment to a third party will only discharge the obligation if it reaches the creditor.[86] The time of performance will have been agreed by the parties in the contract. It is common to introduce conditions or terms in contracts and if this is the case the happening of the events that constitute the conditions or that determine the beginning or end of the *termino* will mean that the performance is due.[87] The place of performance is also that agreed in the contract or, in the case of a defective agreement and having considered the nature of the obligation in each case, the domicile of the debtor if the obligation does not point out to another obvious place of performance.[88]

Caso Fortuito and Fuerza Mayor

Nobody can be held responsible for those events that could not have been foreseen, or that if foreseen could not have been avoided.[89] The Civil Code reflects this by exonerating the debtor of any liability if the performance of the contract becomes impossible due to *caso fortuito* or *fuerza mayor*.[90]

The two terms are used as synonymous in some Articles of the code,[91] on other occasions the code refers to only one of them[92] and although the case law and the doctrine have elaborated a distinction between them,[93] their effects are coincident. They both refer to those

---

[83] Arts 1166 and 1157 CC.
[84] Art.1169 CC.
[85] Art.1164 CC, even if he is not the actual creditor.
[86] Art.1163(2) CC.
[87] See above, *Condicion* and *termino*.
[88] If the place is not clear the court will determine what is the appropriate place of performance. The subsidiary rule is that the creditor must seek the debtor.
[89] Art.1105 CC.
[90] In English law such events will fall under the category of frustration.
[91] Arts 1602 and 1625 CC.
[92] Arts 1136, 1183, 1744, 1745 refer to *caso fortuito*, while Arts 457, 1784 and 1905 refers to *fuerza mayor*. See Lasarte, *op. cit.* at p.429 for a discussion of these terms.
[93] See Lasarte, op. cit. pp.429–30 for a discussion, also Lacruz Berdejo, *op. cit.* pp.287–89.

events and circumstances external to the debtor and over which he had no power, that make it impossible for him to perform his obligations. The debtor must prove that he can no longer perform due to these circumstances.[94] In exceptional circumstances the debtor is still obliged to perform despite the impossibility created by those external factors.[95] These exceptional cases have their origin in the previous fault of the debtor who was already in breach before the unforeseeable events took place.

BREACH OF CONTRACT AND REMEDIES

Breach of contract takes place when the debtor does not perform his obligations under the contract. The breach may take place because the debtor does not perform on time, or the performance is not adequate, for example it is not complete, exact or according to the terms of the contract. If the debtor is late in performing he is said to be in *mora*, a legal situation that immediately creates an obligation to pay damages[96] (Art.1108).

In cases of breach the creditor has the right to request the *ejecucion forzosa* or "forceful execution" of the obligations. This can take different forms depending on the nature of the obligations. If it is still possible the court will order specific performance or performance *in natura* (Art.708 LEC), and in the case of generic obligations, generic performance (Arts 701 and 702 LEC). If specific performance is not possible the court will order the payment of damages (*daños y perjuicios*).[97] Damages can also be added to any order of specific or generic performance if appropriate.[98]

The measure of damages is calculated by taking into account two different concepts: the *daño emergente* and the *lucro cesante*.[99] The first of these concepts, *daño emergente*, is the damage or loss suffered by the creditor as a consequence of the debtor's breach. The *lucro cesante* is the loss of earnings or loss of profit due to the breach of contract. These are easier to theorise about than to ascertain in practice. The courts have been cautious to limit the *lucro cesante* to those loses that were either contemplated for in the contract or that are

---

[94] Arts 1124 and 1183 CC and Arts 281, ss. LEC.

[95] Arts 1744, 1745, 1182,1184, 1988 CC.

[96] Art.1088 CC. The effects of the *mora* are very serious. As it has been mentioned above it does not exonerate the debtor of his liability even if performance becomes later impossible due to *fuerza major*.

[97] Art.1101 CC.

[98] Arts 1096 and 1124 CC. See also Lasarte, *op. cit.* p.437.

[99] Art.1106 CC.

naturally and directly caused by the debtor's breach and could have been foreseen by a reasonable man.[1]

If the debtor has acted in bad faith he is responsible for all damages produced by his breach of contract[2] and not only those which could have been foreseeable. In both cases, both good and bad faith from the debtor, it is necessary to prove the damage suffered.[3]

5.　EXTRA-CONTRACTUAL LIABILITY OR EXTRA-CONTRACTUAL OBLIGATIONS

The name "extra-contractual" referring to obligations or "responsibility" as it is more commonly referred to in the Spanish legal literature (*responsabilidad extracontractual*) encompasses all those obligations created by the so-called "illicit acts" by Art.1089[4] when there is fault or negligence. This extra-contractual responsibility is also known as civil responsibility to contrast it with the criminal responsibility that arises from the commission of a crime. The regulation of extra-contractual responsibility can be found in Arts 1902–1910 of the Civil Code.[5] These Articles regulate what is described in the Code as responsibility for fault or negligence but they also include cases of strict liability.[6] Like in many other areas of civil law the regulation of the Code is rather obsolete and reflects an economic and social reality very different from today's. With the evolution from industrial to post-industrial society and the generalisation of situations of risk, most legal systems have recognised that an increased risk of damage to individuals and their property requires faster mechanisms devoid of the element of fault or negligence of the general provisions of extra-contractual responsibility. Responsibility for risk or objective responsibility has replaced in many cases the traditional type of subjective or fault responsibility at least in the number of cases of extra-contractual liability. A system based on fault will be

---

[1] See Lasarte, op. cit. p.438 and Lacruz Berdejo, *op. cit.* pp.208–216. The later has an excellent overview and analysis of case law in the area.
[2] Art.1107(1) and (2) CC.
[3] See Lacruz, op. cit. especially pp.212–213.
[4] Art.1089 CC, "*Las obligaciones nacen de la ley, de los contratos y cuasi contratos, y de los actos y omisiones ilicitos en los que intervenga cualquier genero de culpa o negligencia*".
[5] Perhaps it is important to clarify that sometimes civil responsibility is accessory to criminal responsibility as a crime can originate both. See Ch.6, p.142.
[6] For example liability for fallen trees (Art.1908 CC).

inappropriate for air accidents, terrorist attacks or industrial accidents that may cause damage to third parties.

Extra-contractual responsibility as it is generally referred to is often defined by default. It arises when there is no pre-existent legal obligation between the author of the illicit contract and the victim. The obligation to repair the damage suffered does not arise as a consequence of the breach to fulfil a previous contractual obligation: "*el que por acción u omisión causa daño a otro interviniendo culpa o negligencia esta obligado a reparar el daño causado*" (whoever causes damage to another with fault or negligence is obliged to repair the damage caused), Art.1902 CC.

ELEMENTS MENTIONED IN ART.1902

Act or omission

The first of the elements in the regulation of extra-contractual responsibility is an act (a voluntary action) or fact (involuntary) or omission that the person responsible commits (Arts 1093 and 1903 CC). This act or omission must be illegal even if Art.1902 does not mention this requirement, otherwise it will not create an obligation to repair. Lasarte[7] is of the opinion that there is no need to describe the act or omission as illegal because all acts (or omissions) that cause damage to another person are automatically presumed to be against the law unless there are special circumstances that justify the action (or omission).

Damage

In order to be able to demand the payment of damages it is necessary to prove that some damage has been suffered. If the damage is material or consists of damage to property it is relatively easy to calculate the amount of the reparation. In the case of moral damages or damage caused to incorporeal rights like honour, health or freedom it is not so easy to ascertain the amount that the damages should reach in terms of pain and suffering. It is left to the court to fix it for each particular case.[8] The damages are calculated on two different

---

[7] *Op. cit.* p.383.
[8] The first court decision recognising moral damages was the STS of December 6, 1912, in which a newspaper published the news that an unmarried woman had left the city with a priest with the immediate damage to the honour of the parties that the publication of the news produced.

grounds: *daño emergente*—the damage actually caused; and *lucro cesante*—the loss of income suffered as a consequence of the former. For example, if an injured victim of an accident could not go to work for a month, it would be the victim who demands the type of reparation that he or she feels will put him or her in the position they were in before the damage occurred. This may include replacement of an object, publication of the truth in a newspaper to correct previous inaccurate statements by a journalist, monetary compensation or a combination of several of them. The judge will look at the circumstances of the case and order those measures that he thinks will put the victim in the same or a more similar position to where he was before the act took place.

A limit to judicial discretion has been placed in the case of damages suffered as a consequence of the operation of motor vehicles. The disparities in the quantum of damages awarded by different courts for very similar injuries[9] was such that the *Ley 30/1995 de 8 de noviembre de ordenación y supervisión de los seguros privados* gave a new wording to Art.1(2) of *the Ley de responsabilidad civil y seguro en la circulación de vehiculos a motor*. This wording implies that all damages will be fixed according to the criteria of this law and with a maximum ceiling fixed in the same.

Causal link between the act and the damage

The proof of this causal link is sometimes difficult because there may be several acts that contribute to the final damage. There is only one Article—Art. 1902—of the Civil Code dealing with this aspect and it is left to the courts to evaluate all the different concurring causes and their effects in the causal relationship. This is, perhaps, one of the areas of civil law where judicial freedom and even creation of the law is at its greatest.[10]

Fault or negligence

"*Culpa o negligencia*" are the subjective requirements for the existence of extra-contractual responsibility. The type or degree of fault is of no importance in the case of extra-contractual liability, which is in contrast to what happens in the case of contractual responsibility; any type of fault or negligence is sufficient according to Art.1089 CC.

---

[9] It is important to point out that the quantum of damages is not subject to *recurso de casación* and therefore the *Tribunal Supremo* cannot fix a general or homogeneous limit.
[10] Despite what we said in Ch.2 about the sources of law.

This is not to say that when reaching a decision the courts will not look at all the circumstances of the case.

Only those who the law considers with certain mental maturity and capacity can be held responsible for damage caused to another by fault or negligence. A minor, for example cannot be said to have acted with "fault" or with "negligence" since he cannot discern these standards and yet he can cause damage by his actions to another person or his property. In these cases the law holds those who care for minors are responsible for any damage caused by the minor's actions. The Civil Code and complementary legislation establish that parents are responsible for the actions of their children,[11] tutors and wardens for the acts of the wards,[12] employers for the damages caused by their employees while performing their functions,[13] and schools are responsible for any damages caused by their pupils during any activities under their supervision and control.[14]

If more than one person is responsible the obligation to repair is a *obligación solidaria*.[15]

The period to demand extra-contractual responsibility is of one year from the date that the victim knew of the damage according to Art.1969(2) of the Civil Code. Special legislation establishes different periods for specific cases such as six months for air traffic accidents[16] or 10 or 20 years for damages derived from nuclear installations.[17]

RESPONSIBILTY FOR RISK

The system of objective responsibility is associated with the existence of compulsory insurance for all the agents that engage in what the legal system deems to be high risk activities. An example of this is the compulsory motor insurance that all drivers must take. Responsibility for risk is also called objective responsibility because it

---

[11] Art.1903(2) drafted according to the *Ley* 11/1981.

[12] Art.1903(3) CC.

[13] Art.1903(4). This is a slightly different case because employees are not mentally unaccountable like minors but the Code gives the employer the role to ensure that all conditions to avoid damage, mostly to the public, are present and to train employees accordingly.

[14] *Ley* 1/1991 of 7 January. Note that the actual teachers are only responsible if they are found to have acted with gross faulty or negligence (Art.1904(2) otherwise it is the school itself that carries the responsibiltity.

[15] See above, p.231 for the general characteristics of this type of obligations.

[16] Art.124 *Ley de Navegación Aerea*.

[17] Art.67 *Ley de Energía Nuclear*.

does not rest upon any fault of the person responsible. It arises as soon as the damage occurs even if the person held responsible exercised all due care. The main examples of objective responsibility in Spanish law are: air travel[18]; motor cars[19]; nuclear energy[20]; hunting[21]; terrorism[22] and consumers.[23]

---

[18] *Ley* July 21, 1960, note that there is not necessarily any fault or negligence from the travel operator.

[19] *Ley sobre responsabilidad civil y seguro en la circulación de vehiculos a motor* of 1964 with the modifications introduced by the *Ley 30/1995* of November 8, *del seguro privado*. The driver of the car is responsible in the case of an accident unless the accident was due to the exclusive fault of the victim or *fuerza mayor*.

[20] *Ley 29 de abril de 1964*.

[21] Ley *de caza de 4 abril 1970* and *Real Decreto 63/1994* of January 21 *Reglamento de Responsabilidad Civil del Cazador de subscripción obligatoria*.

[22] *Ley 32/1999, de 8 de octubre*.

[23] Art.25 of the *Ley 26/1984* de *Consumidores y usuarios* establishes a system of objective responsibility in favour of consumers for any damage suffered as a consequence of the use of goods or services unless the damage is exclusively his own fault or the result negligence.

Chapter Ten
Property law

1. INTRODUCTION

The Law of property was originally conceived for the regulation of tangible, physical property. The Spanish Civil Code of 1889 reflects this conception not only in the language used, "*Derecho de Cosas*" ("law of things"), to refer to property law but also in the whole articulation of a system of ownership and other real rights based, essentially, on the ownership of land.

Land in the 19th century constituted the main source of wealth and power and the basis of the economy. Spain remained an agrarian and comparatively underdeveloped country for much longer that its European neighbours. Capitalism with its emphasis on the law of contract and the plethora of rights over incorporeal property took a long time to take hold in Spain. When the Spanish economy finally evolved and new rights were created, ad hoc laws were necessary as the Civil Code referred—and still does—to livestock, boundaries, fallen trees and rights of way in its articles on property law.

Within the Civil Code the main regulation of property is found in Book II *(Libro II)*: *De los bienes, de la propiedad y de sus modificaciones*; complemented by *Libro III—de los differentes modos de adquirir la propiedad* (of the ways of acquiring property) and numerous provisions of *Libro IV* on obligations and contracts that regulate rights of guarantee such as *prenda* and *hipoteca*, and rights of exploitation like *arrendamientos* and *censos*.

The main special laws and legislation complementing the Civil Code are:

- *Ley Hipotecaria y Reglamento Hipotecario.*[1] These laws contain all regulation of the Land Registry and some important rules about the creation and transfer of real rights. We will refer to them throughout this chapter.

---

[1] *Ley Hipotecaria, Decreto* August 2, 1946, modified by the *Ley 7/1988 sobre condiciones generales de Contratación* and by the *Ley 1/2000 de Enjuiciamiento Civil.*

- *Ley sobre el Régimen del Suelo y Valoraciones.*[2] Note that this legislation is subsidiary to the legislation passed on the matter by the autonomous communities.[3] For example for the *Comunidad Valenciana de LRAU* of 1994[4] takes priority over the *Ley del Suelo.*
- *Ley de Reforma y Desarrollo Agrario* of January 12, 1973, regulating the exploitation of rural land.
- A collection of public law legislation such as the *Ley de Expropiación Forzosa,*[5] *Ley de Régimen Local,*[6] *Ley de Aguas,*[7] *Ley de Costas,*[8] *Ley del Patrimonio del Estado,*[9] *Ley de Minas,*[10] *Ley de Montes*[11] and *Ley sobre el Patrimonio Histórico y Artístico.*[12]

2.   THE CLASSIFICATION OF PROPERTY

GENERAL CONCEPTS

Cosas o bienes

The Spanish Law of Property refers to property as *cosas.*[13] *Cosas* can loosely be translated as chattels or things. The Civil Code also uses the word *bienes* (translated as "goods", more similar to the French *bien*). *Bienes* are any type of property that can be appropriated by man and has an economic value.[14]

As the Civil Code was based in a predominantly agrarian society with wealth resting upon land ownership and with a system of rights

---

[2] Ley 6/1998 of April 13, *sobre régimen del suelo y valoraciones,* referred to as *Ley del Suelo.*

[3] The Constitutional Court declared that two articles of the *Ley del Suelo* arts 16.1 and 38 and the *disposicion final* were unconstitutional because they invaded the powers that the autonomous communities had in these matters.

[4] *Ley Reguladora de la Actividad Urbanistica de la Comunidad Valenciana* of 1994, *Ley* 6/1994 of November 15.

[5] *Ley* of December 16, 1954 *de Expropiacion forzosa.*

[6] *Ley* 7/1985 of April 2, *Reguladora de las Bases del Régimen Local.*

[7] *Texto Rejundido de la Ley de Aguas* of July 20, 2001.

[8] *Ley 22/1988,* of July 28 *de Costas* and *Real Decreto* 1471/1989 of December 1.

[9] D. 1022/1964 of April 15.

[10] *Ley* 22/1973 of July 21.

[11] *Ley* of June 8, 1957 *de Montes.*

[12] *Ley* 16/1985 of June 25 *del Patrimonio Historico Espanol.*

[13] Hence the denomination *Derecho de Cosas,* that we referred to at the beginning of the Chapter.

[14] See Art.333 Civil Code.

based upon physical powers of enjoyment of property the Code does not make much provision for incorporeal property. This is regulated by modern laws like the Law of Intellectual Property[15] or the Law of Patents[16] and Trade Marks.[17] Nor did the Code have many provisions for the so-called "special properties", that is, natural resources such as water, electricity and gas that are, again, regulated by ad hoc legislation that has been modified depending upon the economic model of exploitation of these resources chosen by the government at any particular time.[18]

BIENES MUEBLES E INMUEBLES

Corporeal property is divided between *bienes muebles* (movables) and *bienes inmuebles* (immovables).[19] The distinction is similar to the classification of property as real or personal property in English law but it is not identical.

Bienes inmuebles are all land and buildings, or constructions attached to them, trees, plants and crops while they are attached to the land, machinery used for agricultural purposes, mines and water, any real right over immovable property and any work of art permanently attached to the land; for example a fresco or sculpture.

Bienes muebles, are defined by default[20] in Art.335; all property not listed as immovable is movable. *Bienes muebles* are any property that can be appropriated and moved from one place to another without detriment to the property itself. Movable property is subdivided in turn between *bienes fungibles* e *infungibles*. The first are those that are consumed by normal use, for example vegetable produce, the second are those that can be used according to their nature and not be consumed, for example a piece of furniture.[21]

The distinction between movables and immovables is important for a number of reasons:

- possession of movables can amount to a title whereas this is not the case with immovables, although immovables may be acquired

---

[15] *Ley de la Propiedad Intelectual, RDLeg 1/1996* of April 12.

[16] *Ley 11/1986,* of March 20, *de Patentes.*

[17] *Ley 17/2001,* of December 7, *de Marcas.*

[18] These laws have been listed under the first section, see *Ley de Aguas, Montes* etc. In the last few years we have seen a change in the regulation of natural resources that traditionally were supplied by state companies holding a monopoly and today are supplied by private companies that compete for a share of the market.

[19] Art.334 CC.

[20] This is due to the main aim of the Code drafted before the arrival of capitalism to Spain, that as we said above dealt with land as the main property and symbol of wealth.

[21] Art.337 CC.

by adverse, unchallenged possession over a period of time. This is called *usucapio* or *prescripcion adquisitiva*[22];

- it is important to establish whether an item of property belongs to one or the other category when establishing ownership at the dissolution of a matrimonial regime[23] or at the time of succession.[24]

PUBLIC AND PRIVATE PROPERTY

The law of property constitutes the basis of the economic design of a society. The informing principles of the law of property in Spain are found in the Constitution itself—Art.33—that establishes a political choice for a system of private ownership of land and public ownership of natural resources.

Although the Constitution recognises and endorses a system of private ownership, the State itself and other public law bodies, such as local administrations and autonomous communities, need property for performing their duties. Property owned by public law entities such as the State, autonomous communities,[25] provinces and local entities, is classified as either *bienes de uso o dominio público* or *bienes patrimoniales*. The heading of the Civil Code, "*De los bienes segun las personas a que pertenecen*" (which can be translated as "classification according to the owner of the property") is misleading because the State may own property but if the property is not subject to public use in the way defined in Art.339 it is private property for the purposes of this classification.

Bienes de dominio público are those put to public use or to the fulfillment of a public service.

There are two main types of "public property" or more accurately *bienes de dominio público* (Art.339): those destined for public use, such as rivers, roads, harbours, public built bridges, beaches[26]; and those that belong to the State but are not open to public use, such as mines, buildings for the defence of the territory or any other that is destined to a public service or to the promotion of public wealth. This rather archaic formulation is complemented for a more up-to-date collection of rules that regulate the use of public roads, telecommunications,

---

[22] Art.1915 CC. See below, *usucapio*, pp.273–4.
[23] See below, Ch.11, "Family Law", pp.298–301.
[24] See Ch.12 "Succession", pp.318–20.
[25] Autonomous communities are not mentioned in the Code because they obviously did not exist when the Chapter was drafted. The regulation of this property is found in the laws passed by the different autonomous Parliaments.
[26] *Ley de Costas* Art.31(1)(d), "all beaches belong to the public . . . and cannot be of private use".

mines, defence and national harbours in a manner more adequate to the traffic of the 21st century.[27]

The same differentiation is made in respect of property owned by other public law entities such as provinces and municipalities.[28]

Bienes de uso público are roads, squares, streets, fountains and public waters, promenades and public buildings of general use paid for with money from the municipality (or the province, or the autonomous community) as opposed to money from the state.

All other property is a *bien patrimonial*, also referred to as "private property of the state", in Art.340 CC and it is subject to the general provisions of the Civil Code on property.

3. OWNERSHIP AND RIGHTS OTHER THAN ABSOLUTE OR "FULL OWNERSHIP"

THE CONCEPT OF OWNERSHIP

In the Civil Law, ownership is said to be absolute. There are no "layers of ownership" as in English Law with its different estates and interests.

Merryman[29] uses the graphic metaphor of a box with the name ownership written on it to explain the concept of ownership in civil law countries:

". . .whoever has the box is the owner. In cases of complete and unencumbered ownership the box is full of rights including use, enjoyment, power of alienation, power of exclusion and others. The owner may transfer some of these rights but as far as he keeps the box, he is the owner".

Ownerships entails a right of enjoyment, a power of disposition and a power or right of exclusion of others. The owner has, according to Art.348 of the Civil Code, the right to enjoy and dispose of the

---

[27] *Ley 25/1988,* of July 29, *de Carreteras; Ley de bases del Patrimonio del Estado, D 1022/1964,* of April 15; *Ley 22/1973 de Minas* of July 21; *LO 6/1980* of July 1 *regulladora de los criterios basicos para la Defensa Nacional y organización Militar; Ley 27/1992,* of November 24, *de Puertos del estado y de la Marina Mercante; Ley 3/1995* of March 23 *de Vias pecuarias; Ley 11.1998* of April 24 *General de Telecomunicaciones.*

[28] Art.343 Civil Code; see *Texto refundidio de Régimen Local RDLeg. 781/1986* of April 18.

[29] Merryman, *Comparative Law: Cases and materials* (1978), p.915.

property without more limitations than those established by law. This emphasis on enjoyment by the Code has been criticised by some authors[30] who think that the most distinctive characteristic of the right of ownership is power of exclusion of others. Ownership means that something belongs to the owner exclusively (even if it is a so-called lesser right—see below, the lesser right also belongs exclusively) and the owner can therefore decide what to do with it and, more importantly keep others away from it.

The power of enjoyment (*goce*) varies enormously in how it can be exercised depending on the type of property and the right held by the owner. In this context if the object over which the ownership right falls is productive property (in the legal or physical sense), the produce (*frutos*) will belong to the owner. In the agrarian society for which this Article was conceived this was reflected by the owner of the land receiving any agricultural produce from the land.[31] Today the majority of owners receive what are called *frutos civiles*,[32] this is, interest from money, royalties from intellectual property rights or rents from real or contractual rights established over property. The right of enjoyment can also consist of peacefully occupying certain land,[33] enjoying the views or passing through my neighbour's land in order to access my own.[34]

The third main component of the right of ownership is the power of disposition. Property is characterised by the economic value of the object, land or rights over which it falls.[35] This patrimonial or economic value derives from the value of exchange of the thing or right and enables the owner to exchange his property in the open market for money, other property or rights.

Notwithstanding the absolute character of ownership in the Civil Law it is possible to create different rights over the same thing. These can be "real rights", such as easements; or land charges, such as mortgages; or contractual rights like tenancies. When any of these real rights are created by the owner or by law they constitute a limitation on the extensive powers that the owner had prior to the constitution of

---

[30] Among these, Lasarte, *op. cit.* p.182.

[31] Note that the Code differentiates two types of produce from the land, the so called *frutos naturales* or spontaneous products of the land or of animals (Art.355(1)) and *frutos industriales* that are those produced by the land due to man's intervention (Art.355(2)).

[32] Art.355(3) CC.

[33] This is one of the many and natural powers of the owner of land.

[34] The owner of a *predio dominante* enjoys a *servidumbre de paso* over the *predio sirviente*. See below, *servidumbres*.

[35] Art.334 CC. Remember the definition of *bien* which included the patrimonial value of the property. See above, p.256.

the real right. If an easement is created by law the owner cannot exclude the beneficiary of it from his land to the extent of the rights granted by the easement; therefore the owner's power of exclusion is reduced to that extent. The same can be said if an usufruct is created, the property subject to the usufruct is now enjoyed by the usufructuary who can, "use and enjoy as owner" during the period for which the usufruct is constituted[36] while the owner's rights and powers are substantially reduced to what the Code calls fittingly "bare ownership".

There are other types of limitation in the use of property by the owner that are imposed by administrative regulations directed at the protection of "the public good and general interest". A good example of these regulations is the planning restrictions that may limit the owner's ability to build on his land or the division of land in the different types of *suelo urbano, urbanizable* and *rústico* by the *Ley del Suelo*[37] that limit the use of the different types of land.

POSSESSION AND OWNERSHIP

Possession in itself is not a right but a fact. The importance that the legal system attaches to the protection of possession is a fundamental measure to keep order and peace. In effect the law will, in principle, protect the possessor over the owner until it is proved that the possessor has no right to enjoy the property. This is due to the fact that possession does not require legal determination in order to ascertain its existence and it is then possible to protect by means of a fast procedure[38] without the need to resort to the usual civil proceeding for the determination of rights. In order to protect the possessor, and because of the potentially disturbing effect that disputes about possession can create, a special summary and fast proceeding called *interdicto*[39] is available. In these proceedings what is at stake is the fact of possession and whether the person who was in possession was disturbed in it. The judge does not decide or even look at legal issues such as whether the possessor had a right of possession in the first place or whose right is better: the possessor's or the person who has disturbed his possession. If the person claiming to be the legitimate owner wants a court decision to establish that the person in actual possession has no right to the property he needs to

---

[36] Usually the usufructuary's lifetime. See below.

[37] See below for an explanation of these concepts.

[38] Possession was traditionally protected by means of a fast procedure called *interdicto*. See below.

[39] Note that although the LEC 2000 has abandoned this terminology the proceedings and effects are the same.

go to the general declarative proceedings and exercise an *accion reivindicatoria.*[40]

Possessors enjoy three very important presumptions in their favour. First, that the possessor has got good title, that is, a good right that allows him to possess[41]; second, that he is a possessor in good faith[42]; and third that he has been the continuous possessor of the property.[43] These are presumptions *iuris tantum*, and whoever wants to challenge the existence of a right to possess, the continuity of possession or the good faith in the current possessor must prove it.

The importance of the protection of those who peacefully possess one thing is obvious in cases of those who purchase movable property in good faith from shops or other establishments open to the public. In these cases the *Código de Comercio*[44] establishes an exception to the general principle of *nemo dat quo non habet*, in its Art.85 by allowing the buyer to become the owner. The buyer cannot be disturbed in the possession of the goods that he has acquired irrespective of whether or not the seller had the title or authorisation to sell the property. The original or "real owner" has got the right to pursue the matter against the unscrupulous seller in court by exercising the appropriate civil or criminal actions.

The convoluted version of Art.464 of the Spanish Civil Code seems to establish a different rule for civil sales. In fact, Art.464 seems to have two contradictory statements: in the first phrase it establishes that, "the possession in good faith of movables[45] amounts to title . . .", followed by, ". . . however, whoever lost or was deprived illegally of any movable property can request that this property is returned to him". The first part seems to imply that possession is equivalent to ownership for the good faith possessor, but is this "title" equivalent to ownership, or as it is called by the Spanish doctrine is this an acquisition a *non domino*? The Supreme Court has interpreted this Article in quite a wide manner allowing claims to be made that endanger, in the opinion of some authors,[46] the security of traffic in civil matters. The explanation for

---

[40] Art.250(1)(4) LEC 2000 and old Art.1651 LEC 1881.

[41] This is called "*justo título*", see Art.448 CC.

[42] This derived from the general principle and presumption of good faith and it is established by Art.434 CC.

[43] Arts 459 and 466. This may become relevant in cases of prescription and acquisition of ownership and other real rights. See below.

[44] *Código de Comercio* 1885.

[45] Note that what is being said here, and also the rule of Art.85 CCom, is applicable only to movable property. Immovables hare subject to different rules that we shall consider in due course.

[46] See Lasarte, *Curso, op. cit.* pp.216–217.

this Article, argue those authors, is that Art.464 CC was inspired by Art.2279 of the French Civil Code. The French version limits the cases of exclusion of acquisition of the thing *a non domino*[47] to those of theft. The Spanish Supreme Court has, however, widened the interpretation of what constitutes a *privacion ilegal* (illegal deprivation) beyond those cases of theft contemplated in the French version. In order to acquire *a non domino* the effective possession of the movable following an acquisition in good faith is necessary. The transaction, also, must be one that in normal circumstances is able to transfer the rights in question, for example a sale.

Possession, for the law, goes beyond the physical or external manifestation and it is acknowledged that sometimes the owner does not have the immediate possession of the property. The owner may, for example, allow somebody to use his property by contract. In this case, the immediate possessor (*el poseedor inmediato*) is not the owner although he has a contractual entitlement to the property[48] while the actual owner is what is called *poseedor mediato* and has a *ius possidendi* or delayed right of possession.

OTHER REAL RIGHTS

The Civil Code recognises other "real rights" other than full ownership. We will divide them into three main groups: rights of enjoyment, rights of guarantee and rights of preferential acquisition. This classification is widely used in most Spanish textbooks on property law.

Rights of Enjoyment

Usufruct (Arts 467 et seq. CC)
Usufruct is the right to use and enjoy the benefit of a thing which belongs to another person without altering its substance. The usufructuary enjoys the sole possession of the thing and has got the power to exclude the owner, fittingly called "bare owner".[49]

---

[47] "*A non domino*" is the name given to the assimilation between acquisition of movables in good faith and ownership of the first part of Art.464 CC.

[48] The immediate possessor has what is called the *ius possessionis*, Art.451, and the right to enjoy any benefits of the property.

[49] For a comprehensive and detailed explanation of the right of usufruct and of the different types see, Diez Picazo and A. Gullon, "*Sistema de Derecho Civil*" Vol.III, *Derecho de Cosas y Derecho Inmobiliario Registral*, pp.391–435 and Albadalejo y Doral, *Comentario a los artículos 467 a 529 del Código Civil*, en "*Comentarios al Código Civil*" dirigido por M. Albadalejo, Tomo VII, Vol.1 (Madrid, 1980).

Usufructs can fall over rights as well as over other types of property insofar as those are not rights of a personal nature.[50] A right of usufruct can be created over any type of property. It can be created by law[51] or by contract. Usufructs can be created for any length of time. Those created by law usually extend to the duration of the life of the beneficiary.[52]

The institution of the usufruct is useful because it provides a division between the management of ownership[53] and enjoyment of the property.[54] In Spanish law the usufruct is commonly used to achieve some of the effects that in England will be achieved by the creation of a trust. Their most common use is in succession matters where the parties can create an usufruct in favour of the surviving spouse, partner or co-owner that will allow them to ensure enjoyment and use of the property.[55]

Servidumbres (easements) (Arts 530–603)

Servidumbres are limitations on the use of land generally imposed by law. The main characteristic of all of the different types of *servidumbres* that can be encountered is that one property—*predio sirviente*—is subject to another—*predio dominante*—to the extent of the particular *"sevidumbre"*.[56] These limitations imposed on the absolute powers of the owner of certain land are usually imposed by law (*servidumbres legales*)[57] in order to facilitate the peaceful enjoyment of rights of owners of different land[58] but they can also be

---

[50] See Art.469 CC and Diez Picazo, *op. cit.* p.428 for a longer and authoritative exposition on the subject.

[51] For example the statutory usufruct of the surviving spouse of Art.944 CC. See Ch.12, "Succession", p.320.

[52] This is the case in succession law in respect of the usufruct of the surviving spouse.

[53] Bare ownership, equivalent to a certain degree to the legal ownership of trustees.

[54] Making it possible to compare the usufructuary's right to that of the beneficiaries under a trust.

[55] In Spanish, there is no right of survivorship for co-owners which means that when one of them dies, his share forms part of the estate and it is divided or allocated to the heirs as appropriate. This could be very disruptive for the surviving partner and in order to ensure the right of occupation a lifetime usufruct over the share that is not his or hers can be created.

[56] Art.530 CC. "A servidumbre is a charge imposed over one land for the benefit of another belonging to a different owner". See also *ley Hipotecaria* Arts 2(3) and 13, for Cataluña see *Ley* 22/2001, of December 31, *de regulacion de los derechos de superficie, de servidumbre y de acquisicion preferente*; in particular Arts 6 and 8(1). For Navarra see *Leyes* 365, 393 and 394 of the *Compilación de Navarra*.

[57] Art.536 CC and Arts 549–593 CC.

[58] A typical example is a right of way or *servidumbre de paso* in favour of the land locked in with no direct access to a public highway.

created by individuals voluntarily—*servidumbres voluntarias*.[59] These rights are said to be "attached to the land"[60] and will bind the new owner. Some of them are imposed by law in the public interest, for example for telecommunication networks, or the establishment of rights of way for the provision of electricity, water and sewage. These are public law *servidumbres*. Others, although also imposed by law, are created for the benefit of individuals, for example a right of way for the owner of land with no direct access to the highway,[61] *servidumbres* regulating party walls and other boundaries between properties[62] or *servidumbres de luces y vistas*.[63]

In the past *servidumbres* revolved around the agrarian economy that the Civil Code regulated. Today, these have diminished in importance in front of the so-called public utility *servidumbres* but private *servidumbres* are still relevant. Today the complex and detailed administrative rules of planning law fulfil a large part of the role performed by the *servidumbres* in the past.

Rights of guarantee

Rights of guarantee are a type of real right that guarantee the performance of a right of credit by charging the property of the debtor. The great advantage of rights of guarantee is that the owner of land or other property can obtain credit based on the value of the property and, at the same time carry on enjoying and using the property. From the point of view of those advancing credit the advantages lie in the reinforcement of what would be a mere contractual right of credit with a real guarantee, this is with the security that the property attached to the performance of the obligation provides. The most important rights of guarantee in Spanish law are the *hipoteca* and the *prenda*.

This *prenda* is reserved to movable property and it is a rather old fashioned right, somewhat inadequate to the economic needs of the 21st century.[64] The person requesting and obtaining the credit—the debtor—must transfer possession of the object to be charged to the creditor who must keep it safely until such a time when the debt is satisfied. The object is then returned to the debtor. If the debtor

---

[59] Art.536 CC and Arts 594–604 CC.
[60] Art.534 CC and Art.108 of the *Ley Hipotecaria*.
[61] Arts 564–570 CC.
[62] Arts 571–579 CC.
[63] Arts 580–585 CC.
[64] Today it has been largely substituted by the *Ley de la Hipoteca M'ovil y la Prenda sin desplazamiento Ley* December 16, 1954, modified by the RD 828/1995 of March 29.

defaults the creditor becomes entitled to sell or use the property given.[65]

Hipotecas (mortgages)

The Hipoteca differs from the *prenda* in that the *hipoteca* falls over immovable property[66] and it does not imply displacement of the property, allowing the owner to continue the enjoyment of the property. Mortgages or *hipotecas* need to be registered in order to be properly constituted in Spanish law.[67] Because the inscription in the Land Registry is constitutive, mortgages in Spain are always created by a public document,[68] a notarial public deed or judicial decision. This is logical because the lack of displacement of the property subject to the *hipoteca* needs of the publicity afforded by the Land Registry and only transactions recorded by public documents have access to the Registry. *Hipotecas* can be created over any type of real right that can be transferred (Art.107 LH), for example ownership, usufruct or a right of *hipoteca* itself. They cannot fall over *servidumbres* because those are entwined to the land in such a way that it would make it impossible to separate the right from the *predio dominante*[69] should the debtor default, and therefore the creditor would be unable to enforce its right.

Hipotecas are an accessory guarantee to the main obligation. *Hipotecas* are often constituted as guarantees for bank loans for the purchase of land. If the debtor fulfils his obligations of monthly (or other) agreed payments and pays the whole amount due for the satisfaction of the credit the *hipoteca* will be cancelled. In case of default by the debtor the *Ley Hipotecaria* guarantees enforcement by establishing the so called *accion hipotecaria*.[70] The *accion hipotecaria* that can be exercised by the summary proceedings of Arts 681 *et seq.* of the LEC,[71] the ordinary proceedings of the LEC[72] or by resorting to the extrajudicial sale of the property if this was agreed between the parties according to Art.129 LH as amended by the LEC.[73]

---

[65] Art.1864 CC.
[66] Although today it is possible to create *hipotecas* over movable property, see above.
[67] This is the only case in Spanish law in which the inscription in the Land registry is constitutive, this is, essential for the creation of the right. See Arts 1874 and 1875(1) CC and Arts 106, 145 LH and 595 *LECrim*. And below, "The Land Registry", p.282.
[68] Only public documents have access to the Registry. See below.
[69] See above.
[70] Art.1964 CC, this action prescribes in 20 years.
[71] In the past this was regulated in the *Ley Hipotecaria* itself Arts 131 *et seq.*
[72] See Ch.5, "Civil Procedure".
[73] This procedure was developed by the *Real Decreto* 290/1992 of March 20. See Lasarte, *op. cit.* p.264.

Usually the value of the property charged with an *hipoteca* is superior to the debt that it guarantees and in case of default by the debtor and enforcement by the mortgagor the bank must pay any surplus to the debtor. If this is not the case[74] and the amount of loan exceeds the value fetched by the property the debtor is personally liable for the remaining amount with all its present and future property.[75] In order to enforce this right of credit the mortgagor (the bank or building society) will have a personal action that will have to be enforced in ordinary proceedings.[76] It is possible to have an *hipoteca de responsabilidad limitada* (Art.140 LH) whereby the liability is limited to the value of the property subject to the *hipoteca* and not does not extent to the debtor's other property.

Rights of preferential acquisition

In certain circumstances the law recognises that certain people have a special relationship with a particular property even though the property belongs to another person and on these basis it grants those people what are known as rights of preferential acquisition. These rights are the rights of *tanteo* and *retracto* and the *opción de compra*.

These rights are granted in favour of co-owners (Art.1522), co-heirs (Art.1066) and those sharing boundaries of neighbouring agrarian properties (Art.1523). In the later case the *Ley de Arrendamientos Rusticos*[77] in order to encourage access to the land of those exploiting agricultural holdings has created several rights of *tanteo y retracto* and preferential acquisition in favour of tenants of agricultural land.[78]

Tenants of urban land also benefit from preferential acquisition. Under the "new"[79] *Ley de Arrendamientos Urbanos*,[80] tenants have

---

[74] For example because of fluctuations in the value of immovable property due to market forces.

[75] Art.1911 Civil Code, universal patrimonial liability.

[76] Art.1447(1) LEC.

[77] *Ley 83/1980* of December 31.

[78] The protection of agricultural tenants is carefully designed though, and has its own limits. The aim is to avoid the creation of large agricultural holdings (*latifundios*) while protecting small land holdings (*minifundios*). In this respect it establishes limits to the extension of the land previously owned by the person who wants to benefit from these rights of preferential acquisition. Art.97 of the law restricts access to those who own more that 20 hectares of irrigated land or 200 of dry land. It is also necessary to prove that the person benefiting is a "professional of agriculture" (Art.93(2)(2)) and not just a rich landowner!

[79] New, in respect of the old LAU of 1964 (D 4104/1964) that is still in force for contracts entered into before 1985 due to the very generous rights of subrogation in favour of relatives.

[80] LAU *Ley* 29/1994 of November 24.

certain rights of preferential acquisition. These rights are not mentioned by the Civil Code as real rights but the *Reglamento Hipotecario* makes reference to them and their inscription in its Art.14. Since only real rights have access to the Land Registry the doctrine has included this right within the group of real rights of acquisition. The importance of having access to the Land Registry lies in the possibility of enforcing this right on third parties. Given the nature of the right this is of essence.[81]

The function of the rights of *tanteo* and *retracto* is identical: to ensure that certain persons acquire a particular property with priority to others (the general open public). The only difference is the time at which they operate: *tanteo* before the transfer has taken place and *retracto* after it.[82]

The first of these rights, *tanteo*, gives the holder a right of first refusal or preferential acquisition of any other share of the property that is being offered for sale, by paying the same price (*tanto*) that the property is being marketed for.

The second right (*retracto*) operates after a sale has taken place and allows the holder (the co-owner or tenant) to subrogate and occupy the place of the buyer by his better, preferential right, by reimbursing to the buyer any price that he paid plus related expenses.[83]

Opción de compra

This contract makes it possible to synchronise buying and selling property in Spain since it allows the buyer to "hold" securely the property he wishes to purchase for a period of time during which he can finalise the sale of his own property.[84] The maximum time that a contract of *opción de compra* can be registered for is four years. In practice it would be difficult to find a seller willing to wait that time.

The main characteristics of the contract are that it gives one party—usually the buyer[85]—the option to decide unilaterally whether or not the sale contract should take place. If the party who hold the "option" decides that he wants to perfect the sale then the other party is obliged to do so and if he refuses the judge will order performance

---

[81] See below, "Land Registry and third parties", p.285.
[82] This right is not mentioned in the Civil Code but it is recognised in Art.14 of the *Reglamento Hipotecario* and the law regulating Landlord and Tenant: the *Ley de Arrendamientos Urbanos*, *Ley* 29/1994 of November 24, Arts 25 and 31.
[83] Art.1521 CC.
[84] For sale of land and conveyancing in Spain see below.
[85] It is possible to have a contract of "option to sell" in which the seller holds the option previous payment to a particular buyer of the premium agreed.

of the contract or damages if for whatever reason specific performance is not possible.

The property, the price and the way of payment are all agreed at the time of entering into this contract and cannot be changed later at the time of the contract of sale proper. The establishment of a period of time *el plazo* for the exercise of the option is essential to the contract.[86] The option must be exercised during the time agreed. This is a period of *caducidad*[87] and the buyer must prove that he offered the full price and required the seller to complete the sale. If the option is not exercised during the agreed time the right of the buyer is extinguished. If the seller refuses to complete the sale the buyer can go to court. The action is a personal action and can be exercised during a period of 15 years.[88]

This real right is not regulated in the Civil Code although it is frequently used by the parties and can be registered in the Land Registry (Art.14 of the *Reglamento Hipotecario*) if it is documented by public deed. This is highly advisable since it will provide a protection to the would-be purchaser against third parties.

CO-OWNERSHIP

If a property is acquired by more than one person it will become subject to a situation of co-ownership. This may be suitable in the case of a second or holiday home as the financial investment and enjoyment can be spread among the different parties. Co-ownership can also arise by law, for examples in cases where there is more than one heir[89].

Co-ownership is regulated in Arts 392–406 of the Civil Code. Co-ownership in Spanish law is organised around the concept of *cuotas* or shares. Each co-owner owns the property *pro indiviso* proportionally to his participation or share and can enjoy it accordingly. He must also contribute to its maintenance and satisfy expenses in a proportional way.

Each co-owner retains the right to transfer or dispose of his share at any time[90] subject to a right of preferential acquisition in favour of the other co-owners.[91] This right must be exercised within nine days

---

[86] STS October 24,1990; December 23, 1991, and October 29, 1993.

[87] This means that it cannot be extended or stopped by any actions of the buyer.

[88] There is lot of case law in this area among the most interesting are STS December 13, 1989; STS November 13, 1992; STS January 4, 1992, and November 2, 1995.

[89] See below, Ch.12, p.317, "Succession".

[90] Art.400 CC.

[91] Arts 1521–1525 CC, see above for rights of preferential acquisition.

from the date of inscription of the transfer in the property register or from the time in which the co-owner had knowledge of the sale.

The administration of the property is subject to the general rules of the Civil Code but the parties can agree something different. Each co-owner is granted a right of requesting the division of the property. This can be potentially very disturbing because if there is no agreement between the co-owners the property may be put to sale by public auction under a court order and invariably fetch a lower price than it would have done in the open market. This right can be counter-acted by the right of preferential acquisition of the other co-owners and by the possibility of agreeing not to divide the property for a period of time.

There is another type of co-ownership of "common parts of a building" mentioned in the Civil Code and regulated by the *Ley de la Propiedad Horizontal* of 1999. We will look at this type of co-ownership as it applies to a large numbers of Spanish properties.

Co-ownership under the Ley de la Propiedad Horizontal[92]

For those properties that consist of different flats or different parts of a same building, it is necessary to regulate the ownership, rights and obligations over the common parts of the building or the grounds if it includes more than one building. This is done in Spanish Law by the strangely called "Law of Horizontal Property", which articulates the regulation on the basis that each owner is the absolute owner (equivalent to holding a freehold) of his or her individual unit and all these individual owners are a particular and legally regulated type of co-owners of the common parts of the building. As co-owners they have the duty to contribute proportionally to the maintenance and upkeep of those common parts of the property. They also have powers of decision and vote also proportional to the share or size of their interest. This situation of co-ownership is called *comunidad de propietarios*.

The *comunidad* is governed by a *Junta*, or council of owners; a president and vice-presidents if necessary; a secretary and an administrator. The president is elected among the owners, usually through a rota by which all owners are to become presidents at one time or another. The mandate lasts a year. All owners have the obligation to become presidents and accept their turn except in exceptional circumstances in which they may be relieved from it. The president is the legal representative of the community in court and in all other legal matters. It

---

[92] *Ley de reforma de la LPH, Ley 8/1999* of April 6, *de reforma de la Ley 49/1960,* of July 21, *sobre Propiedad Horizontal* (BOE no.84, of August 4, 1999).

is optional to have different people performing the roles of secretary and administrator. These two can be taken by the president although it is common to have one president and one secretary for each calendar year. In many cases communities may decide to appoint somebody with the required professional capacity to perform the role of administrator, and this, although more expensive, may be particularly suitable for those properties in which a large number of owners are foreign or when the property is used as a second or holiday home and the owners cannot take responsibility for performing these roles.

Small communities of less than four owners are not subject to this law and can regulate themselves according to the general principles of the Civil Code on co-ownership of Arts 398 *et seq.*

The main obstacle to the smooth functioning of communities under the old law was the rule that required unanimity for taking decisions. Unanimity, as it is well known in other spheres of decision making, is more a utopian aspiration than a reality of communal living. This need for unanimity blocked many decisions that would have resulted in changes beneficial for the community or for the majority of its members. In fact the quest for unanimity created more friction and frustration than it sought to eliminate. The new law of 1999 reflects this reality and proceeds by giving a more flexible approach to the majorities required for the introduction of certain services like lifts, removal of barriers and installation of adequate services for those with disabilities, or the installation of solar panels for the production of energy.

The second major point in respect of the communities was to make sure that everybody paid its dues and contributed according to their quota to the expenses and upkeep of the community. A plurality of measures has been employed in order to achieve this. First the creation of a contingency fund to which all members must contribute regularly by law. Second, the introduction of a requirement to provide evidence of payment of all charges to the community at the time of transfer of the property. The community charges are considered a preferential credit (Art.1923(5) CC) and any debts to the community will pass with the property to the new owner (Art.5 LPH). Third, the agreements reached by the *Junta* of owners are directly enforceable and there is a fast and efficient procedure for collecting the monies due.[93]

The new law has also updated the more administrative aspects of the old law by reviewing the rules relating to the drafting of the agreements and decisions of the *Junta*, establishing the different functions

---

[93] El *procedimiento monitorio*, see Ch.5, "Civil Proceedings", p.120 and the new wording of Art.21 LH by the LEC 2000.

of the community organs and particularly of the administrator, the procedures for calling meetings, how to exercise of the right to vote or be deprived of it for non-payment of charges.

Perhaps the most successful measure of the new law has been the way in which any reforms and improvements are divided between necessary and unnecessary (Arts 7(1) and 7(2)). Improvements and building work to communal areas caused unnecessary standstill and frustrations under the old law which required unanimity and it is expected that many long-standing conflicts can finally be solved. A typical example of a situation that used to created friction and disagreement was the installation of lifts in older properties. In the past nothing could be done if there was no agreement on the matter. Today, Art.7(2) establishes that if the cost of installing a new facility is over three times the monthly contribution then those who opposed it are not obliged to pay. It is to be seen what will happen if those in the first floor who opposed the installation of the lift are seen using it or if visitors to their house, or those who may buy the property from them want to benefit from it. Article 7(2) established in its final paragraph that in those cases they must contribute a proportional share paying interest. This might become the new cause of friction.

It is advisable to contact the president of the *comunidad* or the administrator if there is one since either of them can provide useful information beyond the statutes of the *comunidad*, the parts that are private to our unit and the parts that are common and, the percentage that we must contribute towards the general expenses and up keeping of the community. It will also be relevant to check that no major works are planned, for instance the construction of a communal swimming pool, unless there are pre-existing funds for this or unless, of course, that we are happy to contribute and can budget for this major new expenditure.

Perhaps one the most welcomed reforms introduced by this law is that of Art.24 LPH which contains the regulation for *complejos inmobiliarios privados* sometimes called communities of detached villas[94] or *urbanizaciones*. The new Art.24 tries to adapt the traditional law of horizontal property to these urbanisations.[95]

---

[94] Although this translation chosen by Searl, *You and the Law in Spain* (15th edn), p.355 is only partially correct as the regulation include, semidetached and even terraced villas with common grounds.

[95] See, Searl, *op. cit.*, above at p.335 for some information about this type of communities.

4. THE ACQUISITION AND TRANSFER OF REAL RIGHTS

The different ways of acquiring and transferring ownership and other real rights is regulated in Book III of the Civil Code.

The doctrine has traditionally distinguished between original acquisition of ownership and derivative acquisition. Original acquisition is the acquisition of property by the first owner. This is possible by occupation, as listed in Art.609 and developed in the first title of the Book III, Arts 610–617 CC.

OCCUPATION

In order to acquire ownership by occupation the property needs to be susceptible to being acquired in this way. It is possible to acquire in this way animals (by fishing or hunting), hidden treasures, and movable objects that have been abandoned.[96]

Hunting and fishing are regulated by special legislation that takes into account the numerous international conventions signed by Spain in the matter and the special regulations of the different autonomous communities.[97]

Any money, jewellery or other precious objects whose existence was unknown and that appear to have no owner are called *tesoro oculto* or hidden treasure.[98] Those who discover a treasure in their own land become the owners subject to the provisions of the *Ley del Patrimonio Histórico Español*[99] that places restrictions on the ownership of certain objects that are listed as forming part of the historic heritage. If the treasure was found in land belonging to another person or to the state ownership of the treasure depends on whether the discovery was fortuitous or not.[1] Fortuitous discoveries are split between the owner of the land and the person who made the discovery. All others belong to the owner of the land who must pay a certain price to the person who actually found the treasure.

USUCAPIO

This way of acquiring ownership and real rights is based on possession of the property "as an owner", in public, peacefully and for

---

[96] Art.609 CC.
[97] *Ley 4/1989* of March 27, *de conservacion de los espacios naturales y de la flora y la fauna Silvestre*, modified by the *leyes 40 and 41/1997* of November 5.
[98] Art.352 CC. See also Lasarte, Curso, *op. cit.* p.227.
[99] *Ley 16/1985* of June 25.
[1] See Arts 614 and 351 CC.

an uninterrupted period of time.[2] The Civil Code refers to this way of acquiring ownership and other real rights as *prescripción adquisitiva* or *usucapión*. Prescription (*prescripcion extintiva*) means that rights can be lost if they are not exercised during a period of time.[3] In the same way the law recognises that rights may be acquired if a certain factual situation is maintained during a period of time. The law requires that the person who wants to acquire ownership in this manner publicly and to everybody's knowledge detents the possession of the property without any interference or challenge. There are two types of *usucapión* or *prescripción*, ordinary and extraordinary. In order to benefit from the shorter period required for the *usucapión ordinaria* the possessor must be so in good faith and needs to have a "fair title" to the property.[4] This title to the property must be proven and real. An example of this would be a purchase from somebody who appears to be the owner even if later it was discovered that he was not the real owner of the property. If the buyer acquired the property in good faith the sale itself will be considered fair title since that contract in objective and normal circumstances can transfer possession and ownership. In the circumstances of our example—sale by somebody who was not the actual owner as it is later discovered—ownership cannot be transferred, but it is sufficient to constitute the good title at the basis of the requirements for the *ucucapio ordinaria*. For movable property the period of possession in order to acquire full ownership is of three years,[5] for immovables it is 10 years, except on those cases where the owner lives abroad when the period is extended to 20 years.[6]

The code also refers to the *usucapio extraordinaria* that allows the possessor to become owner without title or good faith just by the mere fact of possessing the property over a longer period of time. In this case the periods are of six years for movables[7] and 30 for immovables[8] without distinction between present and absent owners.

DERIVATE ACQUISITION OF OWNERSHIP

Ownership and other real rights can be acquired and transferred by law, by donation, *mortis causa* by testate and intestate succession and

---

[2] Art.1941 CC.
[3] Prescription of rights. The period of time varies depending on the right. References are made throughout the text to the different period for exercising rights and actions.
[4] Arts 1953 and 1954 CC.
[5] Art.1955(1) CC.
[6] Arts 1957 and 1958 CC.
[7] Art.1955(2) CC.
[8] Art.1958 CC.

by certain contracts and *traditio*.[9] These quite diverse methods are called by the doctrine derivative methods of acquiring ownership because they require the existence of a previous owner. Several real rights have their origin in the law itself that determines their existence, *servidumbres*, usufructs, legal rights of acquisition. These have been explained above. Although intestate succession is a creation or transfer of rights by law, and as such could be included in creation or transfer by law, both testate and intestate succession are generally studied together and I will refer to the Chapter on succession for a more detailed study of this type of transfer.

In Spanish law in order to transfer ownership and other real rights by contract it is necessary to actually transfer the property in question. In respect of immovable property the *traditio* can be, and usually is, symbolic by giving the keys to the property,[10] or by putting the ownership documents at the disposal of the buyer.[11] For those real rights that do not entail possession of the property, such as mortgages, the transfer or *traditio* is fictitious, taking the form in this case of the public deed creating the mortgage and its registration.

Donation is a gratuitous contract but the Civil Code allows the transfer of ownership or other rights without the need to transfer the property (*traditio*) that is required for other contracts. Donations of movable property can be oral or in writing; if the intention is expressed orally the property will need to be transferred for the donation to be complete. If the intention is in writing the transfer is not necessary for the donee to acquire his rights. He only needs to accept the written donation.[12] For immovable property donations must be done by public deed.[13]

5.   THE SALE OF LAND—CONVEYANCING IN SPAIN

We are going to look at the sale of land in this Chapter as the conveyance of land is today the most common way of acquiring immovable property and this contract has some special characteristics that differentiate it from any other contract of sale. The general principles of the law of contract discussed in the Chapter on obligations remain applicable unless otherwise indicated.

---

[9]   Art.609 CC.
[10]   This should also be applicable to movables, for examples the keys to a motor boat or car.
[11]   Art.1464, for example by giving the deeds of ownership of an immovable.
[12]   Art.632 CC.
[13]   Art.633 CC.

GENERAL PROVISIONS

The contract for the sale of land follows the general regulation of the Civil Code for all contracts and just like any other contract needs to have all essential elements of capacity of the parties, identification of the object of the contract (the property), *causa* and agreement over the price.[14]

In addition Art.1280 of the Civil Code seems to establish the need for the contract to be done by public deed.[15] The need for complying with the formalities of a public deed need to be considered in the context of land registration: only public deeds have access to the property register and only then can all the guarantees of the register be effective. The contract of sale of land is, however, complete and enforceable between the parties without the need to comply with any specific formalities.[16]

This means that it is not compulsory to conduct a sale of land by public deed and indeed many transfers of land are conducted by private contract. This is fully effective between the parties but has no effect in respect of third parties.[17]

PRE-CONTRACTUAL NEGOTIATIONS

Arras

This contract is perhaps the most dangerous as it is often signed in a hurry when the parties want to make sure that they won't miss out on what they think is a good deal.

This contract has its base in Art.1454 of the Civil Code which describes what is known as *arras penitenciales*:

> "If the parties give an amount of money in the context of contract of sale, the contract can be repudiated. With the consequence that the buyer will lose his deposit or the seller will have to return the amount received in duplicate."

This seems very straightforward but consider that there are different types of *arras:*

---

[14] Arts 1278; 1279; 1280 and 1450 CC.

[15] "All acts relatives to the creation, transmission, or transformation of a real right over immovable property must be documented by public deed."

[16] Art.1278 CC general principle of freedom of formalities.

[17] Sometimes the parties will present a copy of the private sale contract to the tax office in order to pay the tax over land transfers which gives it a type of publicity. However this is not comparable to the publicity and protection of the Land Registry.

- *arras confirmatorias*: the deposit is part of the price and therefore the contract already exists and cannot be terminated by either party without legal consequences;
- *arras penales*: these are slightly different because the money of the deposit is a guarantee of performance of the contract or a guarantee of compensation for damages in the case of non performance.

The Supreme court has stressed on several occasions[18] that the parties are free according to Art.1255 Civil Code to enter into whatever type of contract they wish. If the parties' intention is not clear the court will resort to the principles of interpretation of the parties' will of Arts 1281–1289, but the parties should not assume the application of Art.1454 Civil Code as subsidiary.

Opción de compra

This contract is explained in a previous section.[19]

Promesa de compra o de venta

This is really a "pre-contract of sale" by which the parties agree on the object of the sale (the property) and the price to be paid and the fact that they can request the other party to perfect the contract but leave the completion of the contract pending on the fulfilling or happening of certain events.

It is common to use this type of contract when the property has yet to be built and has yet to obtain different permits and certificates, or when the buyer has to sell his own property or obtain finance.

Problems often arise (and there is extensive case law on the matter) when the parties do not use expert legal advice and draft a contract which does not clearly state their intentions or the conditions necessary for the right to request completion of the sale contract.

THE CONTRACT OF SALE

The contract of sale is regulated in Art.1445 of the Civil Code which establishes as essential requirements the agreement on the object of the sale (identification of the property, flat, land) and the agreement of a fixed price even if there is no instant delivery of the property or the price.

---

[18] STS July 31, 1992; April 31, 1988.
[19] See above p.268.

The price becomes due at the time agreed by the parties.[20] The delivery of the property can either be fictitious, by delivery of the title deeds, or actual, by taking possession of the property.

Spanish law requires that all contracts that create, transfer, modify or extinguish rights over immovable property should be done by public deeds Arts 1280(1), 609 and 1059 Civil Code. But these Articles need to be read together with Art.1278 of freedom of formalities of the parties to a contract.

The private contract of sale of immovable property is fully valid and effective and the parties can request each other to have it formalised by the notary on a public deed. If this is not done and the sale remains only private it cannot be entered into the registry and the parties (especially the new owner) miss all the protection that the register gives to property owners. It cannot be stressed enough that going to the notary and registering the sale at once are of crucial importance,[21] otherwise nothing prevents the unscrupulous seller from selling the same property to a second buyer who may enter his title of acquisition into the registry first and take priority over the first buyer. The first buyer would in this case be left with an action in contract for damages against the seller. Not a good prospect when the seller may be impossible to trace or resident in another country.

TAXES AND OTHER EXPENSES

The purchase of land in Spain attracts taxes and fees that as a gross figure amount to 10 per cent of the cost of the property. This figure is made up by adding the main taxes on transfer to the fees of the notary and the Land Registry.

Taxes

Impuesto sobre bienes inmuebles (IBI)
This is a direct tax, collected locally (similar to our council tax). It is important that the purchaser of a second hand property obtains proof from the vendor that he is up to date with his payments. Otherwise the new owner will be responsible for them. The amount of this tax depends on the *valor catastral of* the property and there are slight variations from each local authority.[22]

---

[20] Art.1500 CC.
[21] See below, the Land Registry.
[22] For a detailed list and explanation of this tax see; Marques Fdez, Flores, *op. cit.* pp.187–189.

Plusvalia

This is a tax over the increase in value of urban land is another local tax that needs to be paid when the land (or property in general) is sold or when new real rights are created or transmitted. The vendor should pay this tax. If the transfer is gratuitous then it will be charged to the beneficiary. This tax can be set off in the tax declaration. Sometimes the contract of sale will have a clause establishing the liability of the buyer for the payment of this tax. This is possible due to the principle of freedom of agreements between the parties.

Impuesto sobre transmisiones patrimoniales

This is a tax that establishes different charges for different types of contract: option to buy, contract of sale, usufruct. The tax is chargeable as a percentage of the value of the property. This value is the value declared by the parties at the time of the sale and it has been frequent to declare a value inferior to the "real or market value" in order to save on this tax. This is, however, a mistake that may cost dear to the unaware buyer because he may find himself having to pay extra taxes when he sells his property as capital gains tax. In many cases it may be difficult to resist pressure from the seller. The buyer is responsible for the payment of this tax and must be paid within 30 days of the date of the contract (public or private). This tax is applicable in all sales by a private seller and resale properties when the property has been previously occupied for a minimum period of two years.

The tax has different values depending on the type of contract. For the contract of sale it is 6 per cent of the value of the property (this value is the value declared by the parties but it must be close to the value recorded by the local authorities for payment of the IBI). For the contract of "option to buy", the charge is 6 per cent of the deposit given or 5 per cent of the total value of the property whatever the greater. Any property brought into a *"sociedad"* (*anónima o limitada*) only has to pay a tax of 1 per cent of the value of the property. The creation, transfer or modification of a right of usufruct will attract a tax of 6 per cent of the percentage indicated on the chart of the *Ley del Impuesto de Transmisiones patrimoniales*. This percentage is calculated in relation to the age of the usufructuary (starting at 19 years and ending at 89 years: 70 per cent of the value of the property at 6 per cent for a usufructuary aged 19 and 1 per cent less for each year).

Impuesto sobre actos juridicos documentados

This tax is payable for the use of public documents. The tax is quite low, 0.5 per cent of the value of the property, and it is only payable if the property is subject to VAT. Those public deeds that are subject to the ITP do not have to pay IAJD.

Impuesto sobre el valor anadido
Only transfers or sales of property from developers are subject to IVA (or VAT in English), all other sales pay ITP. The current charge is 7 per cent of the sale price. The tax is collected by the seller that must pay it into the State.

Guarantees and protection of purchasers

There are two types of guarantees for those buying property: remedies against the seller in contract; and guarantees as a consumer if the seller is a developer granted by the general laws of consumer protection and the more recent *Ley de Ordenación de la Edificación*.[23]

Protection for consumers

The *Ley de Ordenación de la Edificación* was passed in order to regulate the increasing number of developments that had been talking place in Spain in the last decade. This construction boom was regulated by obsolete legislation and reliance of general principles of consumer protection. The new law drafts a more comprehensive system of guarantees and establishes the responsibilities of all those involved in the building process. It is applicable to all building works started after May 6, 2000. For buildings started before that date the system of Arts 1(909) and 1591 of the Civil Code is applicable. The old system of the Civil Code establishes the responsibility of builders and architects for 10 years for what it calls *ruina* del edificio (and could be translated by structural defects). These defects needed to be substantial and make the building inhabitable.

The new law of 1999 develops this basic system by establishing the personal and individual civil liability of all those involved in the building process (*agentes de la construcción*). One of the main

---

[23] Protection by the *Ley* 26/1984 of June 19 *general para la defensa de consumidores y usuarios modificada* by *Ley* 23/2003, of July 10, *de garantías en la Venta de Bienes de Consumo*, BOE November 7, 2003; *Ley* 7/1998, of April 13, BOE April 4, 1998; *Ley* 22/1994, of July 6, BOE July 7, 1994 and the *Sentencia* 15/1989, of January 26 *del Tribunal Constitucional*, BOE February 2, 1990, that declares some of the Articles of the *Ley* 26/1984 as amended as non-applicable in those autonomous communities that chose to have powers for the protection of consumers. Extra protection is also granted by the *Ley* 38/1999 of November 5, *General de la edificación*. We will see some of the main points of this law in the main text.

problems of the old system was that it was not possible to ascertain who exactly made a mistake or where the responsibility lay among all those involved: architects, engineers, builders or technicians. In this case the law of 1998 establishes that if it is not possible to establish who is responsible the liability will be *solidaria*[24]; this is all agents will be joint and severally liable.

There are three main guarantee periods: a period of one year during which the main developer is liable for material damages suffered as a consequence of the poor workmanship; three years during which all those involved in the process (architects, builders, structural engineers) are responsible for all damages caused by defects that affect the habitability of the building; and a period of 10 years of liability or guarantee of the structural safety of the building.[25]

All these guarantees are underwritten by compulsory insurances.

The notary and the registrar will check that these guarantees has been duly put in place before they authorise the sale and the inscription respectively.[26]

Remedies against the seller in contract

Hidden defects
The seller is not liable for obvious defects or for defects that should have been noticed by the buyer because of his profession or training. He is liable for hidden defects if these made the property unusable for its purpose or if they greatly diminish its value to the extent that if the buyer had been aware he would not have bought the property. This is known as the guarantee against hidden defects.[27]

If the seller is found to be liable he must return the price received plus any other expenses incurred by the buyer. He will also be liable for damages if he is found to have acted in bad faith. The main drawback of this action is the brief period in which it needs to be exercised which is only six months.

Inaccurate description of the boundaries or the dimensions of the property
The description of the dimensions of the property may be crucial to the purchaser. Planning permission if often granted on the premise of a plot of certain size and usually the building authorised will be

---

[24] For *responsabilidad solidaria*, see Chapter 9, "Obligations", pp.231–2.
[25] Arts 19 and 20 of the *Ley* 38/1999.
[26] See *Instruccion de la Dirección General de los Registros y el Notariado* of September 11, 2000.
[27] Art.1484 CC.

limited in size proportionally to that of the plot. It is clear that a property bought on the basis of certain size, or having certain boundaries may be unsuitable if it is discovered, at a later date, that the size was not that indicated in the contract.

The Civil Code, Arts 1469–1472, give the buyer the option to demand a reduction of the price proportional to the smaller size of the plot or property or to repudiate the contract. The buyer must exercise any action based in those ground in the six months that follow the date of the transfer of the property.[28]

Eviction from the property

The buyer may be deprived or evicted from the property because somebody with a better right exercises it. These rights can be the rights of preferential acquisition of a co-owner,[29] or the right of the spouse who refused to give his or her consent for the sale of the family home.[30]

Article 1320 establishes a measure of damages that will always cover the price paid by the buyer and any associated costs of buying. These damages can be increased if it is found that the seller acted in bad faith.

6. THE LAND REGISTRY

The Land Registry is a register of ownership and other rights over immovable property. This registration ensures publicity of title and gives protection to those involved in real estate transactions.

Registration, in Spanish law, is voluntary. There is no obligation to register most transactions[31] since the creation, transfer and modification of real rights takes place according to the rules of the Civil Code. Registration is not constitutive but merely declarative. In practice, however, it may be difficult to sell unregistered property as purchasers will be wary (if duly advised) to acquire a plot without any protection against unforeseen surprises.[32]

---

[28] Art.1472 CC.

[29] Or any other right of preferential acquisition, see above, pp.267–9.

[30] Note that in order to dispose of a home that is the "habitual residence" of the family it is necessary to have the consent of both spouses, even if the property belongs exclusively to one of the spouses and therefore there is no evidence in the registry of the other spouse's interest. The spouse that was not consulted can have the transaction set aside. More disturbingly for the purchaser the action can be brought within the four years following the transaction according to Art.1320 CC.

[31] The exception is mortgages for which registration is compulsory Art.1875 CC.

[32] The dangers are serious: the seller might had charged the property in different ways, encumbrances may not be apparent, he may have granted other real rights or he may even have previously sold the land to somebody else.

The Spanish land register is organised according to an operative principle called the principle of *folio real*. This means that there is a separate page (*folio*) for each plot of land and each of these plots is allocated a serial number. The whole legal story of each plot is then entered onto each page: ownership, mortgages and any other legal charges.

The Land Register is divided territorially into different offices[33] and every Land Registry office is run by a *registrador de la propiedad*. This officer is a lawyer with a special training in property law and registry matters. He is a member of the Spanish civil service and his role is crucial as he will assess each document and transaction before he makes an entry on the registry.[34] The *registrador* has the power—and the duty—to refuse making an entry if he thinks that all the necessary requirements are not present. These requirements may be pre-payment of taxes and duties to the treasury, manifestation of consent of all parties involved or respect of certain mandatory or public policy rules in property or succession matters.[35] Once an entry has been made the content of the register is then presumed certain and true and the rights thereby declared will be enforced by the courts. Entries are made on application and it is possible to appeal against a refusal to make an entry by the registry officer.[36]

The system of land registration operates a principle of priority. This priority refers to priority of registration, not necessarily of creation of the real right. Whatever right is registered first, it will have priority against others registered after it on time.

The Land Register is public and everyone who has a legitimate interest can request a *nota simple* or any other information about a particular property. The registry officer will assess whether there is a legitimate interest in each case. Foreigners have the same rights of access to the Land Registry as Spanish nationals.

---

[33] For a list of all offices of the land registry in Spain and varied information about registration see: *www.registradores.org*.

[34] See for example *Resolución de la Dirección general de los registros y el notariado* of March 1, 2005, BOE no.95, April 21, 2005, 13667. In this resolution the Notary of Denia challenged the refusal by the registrar of the same locality to effect and entry of allocation of property according to the Spanish will of a British citizen on the grounds that there was no sufficient proof of the law applicable to the substance of the act—in this case English Law.

[35] For example if a will does not respect the *legítimas* of the compulsory heirs it would be impossible to register the property on the name of the will's beneficiary.

[36] See fn.12 above, appeal by the Notary, but the appeal can also be made by individuals to the *Dirección General de los Registros y el Notariado* (DGRN). Against the decision of the DGRN it is possible to appeal by *juicio verbal* in the first instance court of the place where the property is situated. See Ch.5, "Civil Proceedings", p.112 for details of this procedure.

There are two usual ways of obtaining information from the register: a *nota simple* (simple extract) and a *certificación* (certificate). The *nota simple*, contains a brief description of the land and identifies the owner and any charges or rights affecting the property. Its value is purely informative. The certificate contains basically the same information but is signed by the registry officer and is the only document that legally proves the content of the register.

The costs of making an entry vary according to several factors. The cost is approved by the Government by *Real Decreto* of the Council of Ministers and published in the BOE. Currently it is contained in the *Real Decreto* 1427/1989 of November 17. There is a copy available to all users in each of the registry offices. The charges are made according to two parameters; type of entry (*clase de asiento*); and value of the land or right that is to be registered.

As a general rule it is necessary to present the documents to be registered at the registry office of the place where the land is situated. Notaries and judges can use fax transmission. It is also possible to use mail or to go to the land registry office where the document relating to the real right was signed, if this is not the same place where the land is situated and request that they forward the entry. In order to effect an inscription all taxes and charges relating to the transaction must have been paid and certificates of payment provided.

THE FINCA

Finca is the name given to immovable property in land registry terminology. The first entry that is made for a *finca* is called *inmatriculación* and it opens a new page or folio in the Registry. For each *finca* the very first right to be registered is the right of ownership (Art.7(1) LH). The first registration on a *finca* can be obtained by three different procedures: by *expediente de dominio* (Art.201 L.H.); by *Título público de acquisicion* and *acta de notoriedad* (Arts 203, 204 and 205 L.H.), or, by a *certificación de dominio de Entidades Publicas* (Art.206 LH).

Once the first registration has taken place all other rights, charges and encumbrances affecting the property can be entered insofar as they comply with what is known as *principio de tracto sucesivo* which means that they must originate or be authorised from the person that is the registered owner (Art.20(1) LH). If the *tracto* (which can be translated as chain of title) is broken it is possible to resort one to two of the procedures mentioned above: *expediente de dominio* or *acta de notoriedad* (Art.200 LH) for the registration of the new owner's right without the need to re-recreate all intermediate transactions. The chain of title can be broken for several reasons. For example if one of the heirs does not register the property in his name in order to save the taxes that will charge his inheritance, this heir then leaves the property to his own children and these after their father dies sell the property to a third party who wishes to register his ownership right.

Protection of third parties—El Tercero Registral

Those who acquire a right relying on the content of the Register and in turn register their acquisition are protected by Art.34 of the LH and can claim title to the property even more convincingly than the transferor. In order to be in this privileged position the party must fulfil four requirements: the person acquiring the right or property must have acted in good faith; must have acquired the right from a person that appeared to be the owner according to the registry; must have given consideration (not received by gift); and must have registered the right or title himself.

Together with the Land Registry a *Catastro*[37] is maintained locally primarily for taxation purposes. This *cadaster* is an administrative register attached to the *Ministerio de Hacienda* (the Tax Office) and none of the legal effects of the Land Registry. It is, however, very useful in rural areas because in many cases it contains a more detailed physical description of the property than the Land Registry.

7. ADMINISTRATIVE RULES AND REGULATIONS: LEY DEL SUELO

Today the law of property cannot ignore the growing body of limitations and rules on land issued by the public administration. One of the most relevant laws is the *Ley del Suelo*. Most of the powers relating to town planning belong to the autonomous communities[38] and the *Ley* 6/1998 of April 13, *sobre el Régimen del Suelo y Valoraciones*, was passed by the central Government in order to fix a very minimum framework about the classification of the land and rights and duties of owners of different types of land. In any other matters it is necessary to refer to the law of each of the autonomous communities.[39]

---

[37] This *Catastro* is regulated by the RDLeg. 1/2004 of March 5 of the *Texto refundido de la ley del Catastro*.

[38] STC of March 20, 1997, where the Constitutional Court made a ruling on the distribution of powers.

[39] There are variations both in the letter of the different laws and on the way in which they are applied. A good example is provided by the famous (and rather infamous) *Ley*

The *Ley del Suelo* divides land into three different types: *suelo urbano*, *urbanizable* and *rústico*. *Suelo urbano* (urban land) is suitable for building, subject to the necessary permits and consents and to the regulations stating the different sub-categories. *Suelo urbanizable* is land "suitable to become to be urban". It is only possible to build on this land after the necessary specific plan has been approved and the area has been designated as an area to be "urbanised", which usually will involve considerable investment in infrastructure and services. *Suelo rustico*, or rural land, is agricultural, forest, or protected land-scape land. Building is severely restricted and very limited as to the dimensions, use and type of building.

The type of land will determine what can be done to it in terms of use and construction. This information can be easily obtained from the respective Local Council or the Provincial Commission of Urbanism. This information must be obtained for all projected purchases of land from the particular area where the property is situated. It is also important to check the local *"Plan General de Urbanismo"* that will zone the land as *urbano, urbanizable o rustico* and the plans that the local corporation has to develop the area. In general, prices for urban land are much higher than for other types of land in Spain and this is due to the fact that one of the characteristics of urban land is that all services and utilities are connected to it. In the case of *suelo urbanizable* the owners of this type of land may have to contribute towards the cost of bringing services or extending those exiting to a degree sufficient for the land to be "urbanised". This is the premise over which the "land grab law" was based, the re-zoning of land previously considered rural into *urbanizable* and the demand to the owners to contribute to the cost of development.[40]

It is important to bear in mind that in order to be able to build it is necessary to obtain a building permit or *permiso de obra* (planning permission) and make sure that the building complies with the local building regulations. For this it is necessary to go to the local *section de urbanism* of the Town Hall. Once the building is done it will need to be inspected in order to be issued the corresponding certificates, the *cedula de habitabilidad*. Obtaining these documents guarantees that the building regulations have been complied with[41] and that

---

de Reglamentacion de la Actividad Urbanistica de Valencia of 1994, or as it is usually referred to the "Land Grab law". For those interested in the topic and up-to-date information of the different actions started against this law visit: www.abusos-no.org.

[40] The contributions requested were usually extortionate and disproportionate to the value of the property since the problems arise when the development of the land has been granted by the local corporation to an unscrupulous private developer.

[41] For example minimum dimensions for the different rooms, size of windows providing natural light or fire escapes.

the building complies with safety and other regulations for human habitability.

In order to inscribe and register a newly built property the notary first and the registrar later will request presentation of all permits and certifications.[42] Buying a property which is not registered means that these certificates were not available and represents a risk, perhaps structural or a health and safety hazard or simply a risk that registration may be refused if this paperwork cannot be obtained.

---

[42] Arts 26, 33, 37, 242 and 243 of the *Ley del Suelo*.

Chapter Eleven
Family law

1. FAMILY LAW

Spain is the fourth country in the world[1] that has extended the institution of marriage to persons of the same sex.[2] It has also recently approved a new law on separation and divorce that enables the spouses to end their marriage easily and quickly. All that is needed is the willingness of one or both of the spouses to separate or divorce.[3] Personal freedom is at the centre of the radical family law reforms that the government of Jose Luis Rodriguez Zapatero has introduced. This focus on the individual and on the equality of all citizens irrespective of faith, age, gender, age or sexual orientation reflects a very different society and a different model of regulation of the institutions of family law. The Spanish State makes a clear distinction between those areas of family law that affect the public interest and require control, regulation and intervention from the public powers[4] and those other areas which are private and therefore are best left to the individuals involved to decide.[5] Gender is no longer a main factor for the enjoyment of rights and duties in family law, nor is sexual orientation. However, just over thirty years ago, Spain was a country where married women were under the control of their husbands and marriage was a sacred institution that lasted until death!

In Spain the lengthy right-wing dictatorship under General Franco meant that women's liberation and equality before the law took place much later than in other European countries. It also meant that a concept of a patriarchal, unitary family was maintained for much longer. With no divorce and a heavy religious influence in

---

[1] After Holland, Belgium and Canada.
[2] *Ley* 13/2005 of July 1.
[3] *Ley* 15/2005 of July 1, see below.
[4] For example all matters relating to minors including custody, maintenance and safety.
[5] For example, deciding whether to remain married or not, although the state regulates a minimum agreement that the spouses must reach in respect of patrimonial matters, especially if there are children involved.

society, only families that complied with the dictator's ideas notion of a "family" were recognised and supported.[6] Illegitimate children were discriminated against and stigmatised; women left the paternal house to enter under the (legal) dominion of their husband like a human being with diminished capabilities; adultery was severely punished, particularly women's adultery which was not tolerated in society; and family law followed society's rules by constraining women and children under the patriarchal dominium. The model of the Civil Code, reflecting a 19th century agrarian society model, was maintained and any innovation or adaptation, which had taken place during the brief progressive period of the Second Republic, was promptly amended.[7]

It was in May 1975, a few months before Franco's death that the first step towards reforming family law was taken. A law of May 2, 1975[8] that aimed at establishing the legal equality of spouses was passed. It was only partially successful. The main innovation introduced by this law was the elimination of the so-called *licencias matrimoniales* which were authorisations given by the husband to the wife that enabled her to enter into contracts and other legal relationships. After this law was passed it was clear that a more thorough reform was urgently needed as the legal equality introduced in the economic field sat uneasily with the widespread inequality in all other areas of family law.

Soon a new democratic regime under the Constitutional Monarchy of King Juan Carlos I emerged. The new Constitution of 1978 with its principles of equality, dignity and freedom made urgent reform of the family provisions of the Civil Code imperative. For example, Art.14 of the Constitution introduced a need to eliminate all forms of discrimination against children born outside marriage. It also sat uneasily with a system that afforded better rights over children to fathers than mothers.

As a consequence of these political and constitutional changes two new laws that were to dramatically change family law were passed in 1981. The *Ley* 11/1981 of May 13[9] modified the Civil Code in matters of filiation, custody of children and economic matrimonial regimes

---

[6] This support took the form of great financial incentives for larges families—*familias numerosas*. This was partly due to social and religious reasons but more due to the practical task of populating Spain after the great life loss of the Civil War.

[7] For example, the law on divorce.

[8] *Ley* 14/1975 of May 2 *Reforma del Código Civil y del Código de Comercio sobre situacion juridical de la mujer casada y derechos y deberes de los conyuges* (BOE no.107 of May 5).

[9] *Ley* 11/1981 of May 13 *de modificación del Código Civil en materia de filiación, patria potestad y regimen económico matrimonial* (BOE no.119, May 19).

and the *Ley* 30/1981 of July 7[10] modified marriage in general and established the possibility to end a marriage by divorce. These two laws were the cornerstone of the modernisation of family law in Spain.

2. MARRIAGE

Until the *Ley* of July 7, 1981 the only marriage recognised in Spain was the religious marriage regulated under canon law. The law of 1981 changed this scenario and made clear that marriage was an institution of civil law. It did, however, still recognise and give civil effect to the regulation of marriage by the Catholic Church and other religious denominations.

The current Spanish system of marriage follows the so-called Anglo-Saxon model in which there is only one type of marriage—civil marriage—recognised by the State. That marriage can be conducted in different forms, including a religious form.[11] This is logical if we consider that the Constitution establishes the secular nature of the State in Art.16 and the principle of freedom of religious beliefs together with the principle of equality of Art.14. These constitutional principles and the change that society had experienced in the last years of General Franco's regime resulted in the need to revise the agreements that were in force within the Catholic Church on the regulation of marriage. These agreements had been formalised in the *Concordato con la Santa Sede* of August 27, 1953 whereby the State gave full effect to the marriage celebrated according to canon law and made it very difficult to celebrate the subsidiary civil marriage.[12] The new agreements with the Catholic Church did not have the form of a *Concordat* (convention) they were called just *Acuerdos* (agreements) and were signed in January 1979 and ratified by Spain in December 1979. The most relevant of these *Acuerdos* is the one dealing with legal matters and in particular with marriage. In this agreement it is said that "the state recognises the civil effect of marriage conducted according to canon law".[13] This paragraph seems to recognise two

---

[10] Ley 30/1981 of July 7 *de modificación en la regulación del matrimonio y del procedimiento a seguir en los casos de nulidad, separación o divorcio.* (BOE no.172, July 20).
[11] The other system is the Latin system which recognises various *types* of marriage; civil and religious regulated by different legal systems and gives the parties the option to chose one or another. See Diez-Picazo, *Sistema de Derecho Civil*, Vol. IV, Madrid, ,Tecnos (1992) p.74.
[12] See, Diez Picazo, *op. cit.* p.79.
[13] Apto. 1, Art.VI of the *Acuerdo con La Santa Sede* of August 27, 1979.

types of marriage. Those "celebrated according to Canon Law" could mean those conducted according to the substantive requirements of Canon Law and in the form prescribed by Canon Law. However, if we look at the articles of the Civil Code introduced by the *Ley* of July 7, 1981 we will see that this is not the case. In effect, Arts 49, 59 and 60 of the Civil Code make clear that there is only one valid marriage (civil) which can be conducted in a religious form (including a form according to canon law).[14]

The Civil Code, following the *Acuerdos*, gives full civil effect to the marriage conducted according to Canon Law but for these effects to take place it is necessary that the marriage be registered in the Civil Registry.[15] Some commentators argue that Art.63 of the Civil Code seems to go a bit further than originally envisaged in the agreements with the Catholic Church since it authorises the registrar to check that the marriage fulfils the requirements of the Civil Code before authorising registration.[16]

Marriage, until July 2, 2005,[17] was the permanent union of two people of different sex[18] through certain rituals. This union was given special legal effect. Article 32 of the 1978 Constitution ensured the right of both men and women to enter into a marriage with full legal equality. The characterisation of marriage as an heterosexual union, has, however, changed with the approval of the *Ley* 13/2005 of modification on the Civil Code on marriage. This law was passed by the central state in the exercise of its exclusive power on civil legislation

---

[14] Article 60 of the Civil Code treats the marriage celebrated according to Canon Law as marriages conducted according to the formalities of other religions. Note also that Art.60 is under the rubric of the Civil Code " of the forms of celebrating marriage".

[15] "The marriage is valid since the date of conduction but will not have civil effects until its registration"—Art.61 of the Civil Code.

[16] See in this matter Diez-Picazo, *op. cit.* pp.69–74.; Diez-Picazo: *El sistema matrimonial y los acuerdos entre la Santa Sede y el Estado espanol, en "Curso de Derecho matrimonial y procesal canonica" IV, Salamanca 1980;* Jornado Barea: *El nuevo sistema matrimonial espanol* Madrid A.D.C. 1983; Lopez Alarcon, *El nuevo sistema matrimonila espanol* Madrid, 1983. Also, below.

[17] July 2 is the day of the entry in force of the *Ley* 13/2005 of July 1, *por la que se modifica el Código Civil en materia de derecho a contraer matrimonio*; (BOE no.157, July 2) *www.boe.es/boe/dias/2005-07-02/pdfs/A23632-23634.pdf.*

[18] Marriage, until July 2005, was limited to heterosexual unions. The Supreme Court had in the past established that transsexuals could not marry in the S. of March 3, 1989. Homosexual couples were afforded certain rights as a type of civil partnership but there was a considerable social opposition towards the use of the word "marriage" to define or regulate these unions. The opposition of a certain sector of the population persists today and the *Ley* 13/2005 has been challenged as unconstitutional in the Constitutional Court. See *www.unav.es/civil/pagina_6.html* for a list of articles and resources on the topic.

recognised by Art.149(1)(8) of the Constitution.[19] It was approved by a vote of 183 in favour, 136 votes against and 6 abstentions. The *ley* contains a single article whereby all references to marriage in the Civil Code and complementary legislation are to be understood as including homosexual as well as heterosexual marriages.[20] The law also modifies some Civil Registry rules in order to eliminate references to the gender of the spouses or parents that could discriminate against homosexual spouses.[21] The opponents of this law, which is currently being challenged in the Constitutional Court[22], base their arguments on the moral, religious or philosophical about the nature of marriage[23] as well as Art.32 of the Constitution itself that refers to the equal rights of "man" and "woman" to engage in marriage. They argue that including gay unions into the institution of marriage is therefore unconstitutional and that the otherwise legitimate claims of legal equality can be achieved by passing a comprehensive law about rights and duties of stable unions.[24]

Proponents of the new law point out that in order to understand this constitutional provision it is necessary to go back to the pre-constitutional period in which, as it has been said above, man and woman were not equals before the law and married women had a status of diminished capacity. This, they point out, made necessary the mention of "man" and "woman" in the constitutional text in order to stress the equality of women. It would be necessary to wait until the *Tribunal Constitucional* decides whether the new law is unconstitutional or not. In the meantime several same sex couples have celebrated their marriages and there is a long waiting list for more to take place.

---

[19] See *Disposicion final primera* of the *Ley* 13/2005 and Art.149(1)(8) of the Constitution. This is without prejudice to the rights of the autonomous communities to the conservation, modification and development of the special or *foral* civil laws in the areas where those exist. See Ch.2, distribution of powers between the State and the autonomous communities. pp.49–52.

[20] This single article modified the wording of Arts 44, 66, 67, 154, 160, 164(2), 175, 178.2, 637, 1323, 1344, 1348, 1351, 1361, 1365, 1404, and 1458 of the Civil Code.

[21] *Disposicion adicional segunda* of the *Ley* 13/2005, that modifies Arts 46, 48 and 53 of the *Ley de 8 de junio de 1957, sobre el Registro Civil* (BOE no.151 of June 10).

[22] Three judgments, of Denia, Canarias and Burgos respectively, have raised a *cuestion de inconstitucionalidad* to the *Tribunal Constitucional* when requested to celebrate an homosexual marriage in the territory or their demarcation.

[23] See L. Martínez-Calcerrada, *La Homosexualidad y el matrimonio* (2005, Ediciones Academicas), for a good overview and analysis of the different views on the legality of homosexual marriages.

[24] There are, in fact, several of these laws in force in Spain, *Ley* 6/1999 of March 26, of stable unmarried couples in Aragón; *Ley* 18/2001 of December 19, of stable couples of Baleares; *Ley* 10/1998 of July 15 of stable unions of Cataluña; *Ley* 11/2001 of December 19, of de facto unions of Madrid; *Ley Foral* 6/2000 of July 3, of legal equality of stable couples; and *Ley* 1/2001 of April 6, that regulates de facto unions in Valencia.

THE REQUIREMENTS FOR A VALID MARRIAGE

According to the Spanish Civil Code, in order to enter into a valid marriage the spouses must enjoy full legal capacity to marry and must express their free consent following certain formalities.[25]

Capacity

The Civil Code does not define marital capacity but instead lists the cases in which this capacity is non-existent. It does so in Arts 46 and 47. In order to be able to enter into a valid marriage a person must be of legal age or emancipated and not be married to anybody else.[26] The future spouse must not be a close family relative or have been convicted of the death of a previous spouse.[27]

The only real impediment to the capacity of marriage is already being married to somebody else. With the exception of this impediment, the Ministry of Justice or the first instance judge[28] can dispense with the other restrictions on capacity.

Consent

Consent is crucial to the institution of marriage. The spouse must consent specifically to marriage and must accept the effects and duties of Arts 67 and 68 of the Civil Code.[29] Consent must also be expressed in a form recognised by the Code as valid.[30] The marital consent must be unconditional. Any condition attached will be treated as non-existent by Art.45.

This solution is comparable to the option taken when regulating illegal conditions in succession law.[31] In succession matters it is deemed that consent cannot be given twice by the deceased. In marriage it would have been possible to treat the unlawful condition as indicating a lack of consent to marry.[32] However, Diez-Picazo explains that this second option wasn't chosen because it would give the parties the means to claim the nullity of the marriage. Today, with the progressive privatisation of the institution of marriage and

---

[25] Art.45 CC.
[26] Art.46 read *a contrario*.
[27] Known as "criminal impediment" by the doctrine, Art.47(3) CC.
[28] Art.48 CC.
[29] The effects or duties of Arts 67 and 68 Civil Code.
[30] This will be in one of the forms of Ch.III of Title IV, Book I Arts 49–60 CC.
[31] See below. Art.792 CC.
[32] As is Art.1116 CC in respect of obligations.

the possibility of dissolution of marriage by mutual consent in the new law of separation and divorce, this option would appear more logical[33].

There are two cases of consent being deemed absent: first, mistake in the identity of the other spouse[34] and secondly, coercion or fear.[35] In these two cases the marriage is void *ab initio* since it lacks one of its essential elements.

Formalities

The marital consent must be given in a predetermined form established by the Civil Code or by the rules of a religious faith.[36]

Civil form

Civil marriage is conducted in front of the judge in charge of the Civil Registry in the area in which the parties are domiciled. Since 1994 the town mayor is also authorised to conduct the marriage.[37] This change in law was introduced for two reasons: first, to make it possible for a democratic representative of the people to conduct an act of important social consequences such as marriage; and secondly, the increase in the number of civil marriages and the simultaneous pressure on the judge in charge of the Civil Registry, together with mounting criticism due to the anonymity and depersonalisation of the ceremony made a practical change necessary. For Spanish citizens abroad the diplomatic or consular authority in charge of the Civil Registry has the authority to conduct marriages.[38] Non-nationals can marry in Spain according to the formalities established by Spanish law or to those established by their own national law.[39]

---

[33] See Diez Picazo *op. cit.* pp.81–82 and, for the dissolution or termination of marriage, see below, pp.301–9.

[34] Art.73(4) CC.

[35] Art.73(5) CC.

[36] As authorised by the Code in Art.42.

[37] *Ley* 35/1994, of December 25. This Law modifies Art.51 of the Civil Code which only authorised mayors or delegated authorities to conduct marriages in the absence of the judge. However, the increase in civil marriages to the detriment of religious marriages had put a heavy burden on the judge in charge of the Civil Registry and it was thought that it was appropriate to introduce the option of the mayor conducting marriages.

[38] But note that Spanish nationals can also marry abroad according to the formalities of the place of conduct Art.49 CC and Art.51 CC.

[39] Note this is a private international law rule. See below, Ch.13.

Civil ceremony

In order to be able to celebrate a marriage the parties must establish that they fulfil the requirements established by the Code. This is done by filling out a form—*expediente*—according to the regulations of the Civil Registry.[40] The *expediente* is processed by the judge or the civil servant in charge of the Civil Registry. Marriages conducted according to a religious form do not need to fill in the form previously mentioned. This is the reason why those marriages must be examined before their listing in the registry in order to check that the parties fulfilled the criteria (of capacity) necessary for entering into a valid marriage.

Once it is established that the parties have the necessary capacity to marry, the marriage ceremony takes place in front of the required authority[41] and two witnesses.[42] The civil authority will read Arts 66, 67 and 68 of the Code to the parties to be married and will ask them whether they consent to take the other party as their spouse. If they reply "yes" they are declared husband and wife.

Marriage "in religious form"

Marital consent can be given in any of the forms prescribed by a religious faith registered in the Religious Entities Registry.[43] Marriage according to the rules of canon law is treated in the same manner as any marriage conducted according to the formalities of any of the recognised and registered religions.[44] These marriages celebrated in any "religious form" will have civil effect[45] from the time of celebration. However, the marriage will need to be entered into the Civil Registry for these effects to be recognised fully. The registrar will, when there is a petition to register a marriage conducted in a religious form, check that all requirements of the Civil Code for a valid marriage are present[46] before he registers the marriage. This is necessary because if the marriage is celebrated in a religious form there is no need to fill in the previous expedient of Art.56 which had the aim of checking that the Code's requirements for a valid marriage were

---

[40] Art.56 CC. See also Art.250 of the *Reglamento del Registro Civil* (RD of August 29, 1986).

[41] See above.

[42] Art.57 CC.

[43] See Art.59 CC. *The Registro de Entidades Religiosas* is kept in the *Minister de Justicia* according to the RD of January 9, 1981.

[44] Art.60 CC.

[45] This means the rights and duties of marriage start from the date of celebration if this date were to be different from the date of registration.

[46] Consent, capacity. See Arts 45, 46 and 47 CC.

present. It is therefore logical and coherent that, at some point, the registrar checks that those requirements are present.[47]

EFFECTS OF MARRIAGE

Traditionally a distinction has been made between "personal effects" of marriage and "patrimonial effects". Personal effects will be the focus of this paragraph and patrimonial effects will be discussed in the section on matrimonial property regimes below.

Article 66 of the Civil Code opens the chapter relating to the "Rights and duties" of the spouses with the statement that both spouses have equal rights and duties. This is a consequence of the Constitutional Arts 14 and 32. It means that marriage alone does not change or affect the nationality of either spouse[48] and that neither of the spouses can assume the legal representation of the other unless this has been voluntarily and expressly given to the spouse.[49] Legal equality is also applicable to parental responsibility.[50]

Some of the duties of this chapter are ethical duties rather than legal duties. This means that there are no legal remedies to enforce them. For example, Art.67 states that spouses must help and respect each other. This is a mixture of an ethical obligation and a legal one in the sense that there is a duty of support or economic help between spouses.[51] They are also obliged to act in the "interest of the family". Again, it is difficult to ascertain which actions are "in the interest of the family" and which actions are not. There is no clear answer to this and each case needs to be considered on its own merits. It is easier to establish the scope of the duty of faithfulness in Art.68 and the duty to live together. Although adultery is no longer a crime punished by criminal law[52] it was until recently a civil wrong and one of the reasons for initiating separation and divorce proceedings. The same is true of living separately. The Criminal Code of 1995 reduces punishable conduct to that of abandonment of minors[53] but, again,

---

[47] Which is exactly what Art.65 of the Civil Code states: "In all cases in which a marriage is celebrated without the previous *expediente* the registrar will check that all the legal requirements for the celebration of marriage are present before entering the marriage into the Registry."

[48] See *Ley* of July 13, 1982 of Nationality.

[49] Art.71 CC.

[50] Note the previous situation prior to the law of 1975 when only fathers had parental responsibility, as discussed above.

[51] Breach of such a duty of support can constitute a crime, see Art.226 CP 1995.

[52] *Ley* 22/1978 of May 26, on de-criminalisation of adultery and non-marital cohabitation.

[53] See Arts 226–233 CP 1995 and compare with the regulation of the CP 1974, Arts 487–489 *bis* that contemplated a much more ample spectrum of this type.

can be cited as one of the reasons to initiate separation or divorce proceedings.[54]

PATRIMONIAL EFFECTS AND MATRIMONIAL PROPERTY

Marriage has several economic implications for the property of the spouses. In Spain those consequences are regulated by law and institutionalised to a large extent by subjecting all marriages to what is called an "economic matrimonial regime". This concept may be alien to the English reader since in English law marriage alone does not change the property status of the spouses.[55] In Spain the economic matrimonial regime, on the contrary, will regulate the ownership and use of all property acquired during the lifetime of the marriage.[56] This economic regime is either a regime imposed by law in the absence of an explicit declaration by the parties[57] or that chosen by the parties before, or at any time during, the existence of the marriage.[58] In order to select a matrimonial regime, and because of the important consequences for the spouses and for third parties, a notarial contract called *capitulaciones matrimoniales* needs to be entered into. In these *capitulaciones*—sometimes called pre-nuptial contracts—the parties specify what is to happen to the property that they currently own and to the property that each of them shall acquire during their marriage. These dispositions—whether the contract was agreed by the parties or the subsidiary regime of the Code in the absence of *capitulaciones*—can be changed at any time by agreement duly documented by the parties.[59] The only limit that the Civil Code establishes for changes to the matrimonial regime is in respect of the rights acquired by third parties. For those cases in which the parties have not entered into an ante-nuptial contract for the regulation of the patrimonial effects of the marriage, or where that contract does not cover all areas that need to be regulated[60], the law establishes a subsidiary, general and common regime which for the territories of common civil law is that of the *sociedad de gananciales*.[61] This is generally referred to in the comparative literature as "community of

---

[54] See below for a study of these.
[55] Although of course spouses have a duty of mutual support.
[56] Property that was owned by the spouses prior to marriage, in general, will remain their own property. See below.
[57] Art.1316 CC.
[58] Art.1315 CC.
[59] Art.1317 CC.
[60] See below.
[61] Art.1316 CC.

goods," although, as we shall see in brief it is rather a "community of acquisitions".[62] The Code also has some general dispositions[63] applicable to the three regimes that it regulates: *gananciales*; *participación* and *separación de bienes*. The general dispositions establish the principles of freedom of the spouses to chose whatever system they wish[64], the freedom to change their regime throughout the life of the marriage[65]; the equality of the spouses, their equal duties to contribute towards the family expenses[66] and the limitation on the power of disposition of the family home, furniture and effects used in the family home even if these or the home itself belongs exclusively to one of the parties.[67] There are also some dispositions referring to the termination of the economic regime—by death, divorce, separation or nullity.

It is important to note that the rules of succession only start being applicable once the matrimonial property regime has been terminated and, in the case of the society of *gananciales* or the regime of participation, the relationship needs to be ended and all property accounted for and allocated to each of the spouses. To this effect in this chapter of the Code regulating matrimonial property regimes we find some rules that to the common lawyer may appear to belong to the law on succession. One of these rules is Art.1321, which establishes that the surviving spouse shall receive all personal belongings.[68]

Sociedad de gananciales

The main characteristic of the regime of the "community of acquisitions" is that there are three separate funds to which property is allocated. There is a private or personal fund for each spouse that includes all property that they owned before the marriage or any property acquired by *donatio mortis causa* or *inter vivos donatio* expressly addressed to one of the spouses only. Together with those two separate funds there is a third fund—the community proper—where all earnings of the spouses and all acquisitions made during the existence of the regime fall irrespective of whether it was actually acquired by one or the

---

[62] Arts 1344–1410 CC.
[63] Arts 1315–1324 CC.
[64] Art.1315 CC.
[65] Art.1317 CC, the only limitation to this is that the change cannot affect rights of third parties.
[66] Arts 1318 and 1319 CC.
[67] Art.1320 CC.
[68] This means before his or her share is calculated under the law of succession.

other of the spouses. In this sense the community of earnings is very similar to a partnership or *sociedad*[69] and in some articles of the Code there is reference to the "*sociedad de gananciales*". Since the reform of 1981[70] the Code stresses that what is created by the regime of *gananciales* is a "community".[71] This community is very different from the community regulated in the Civil Code for situations of co-ownership[72] since in the community of *gananciales* there are no quotas for each spouse but both own the whole of the assets of the community *pro-indiviso* until such time in which the community is liquidated because it is extinguished as a legal entity.[73]

It is important to understand that even in this, the most communal of the regimes regulated, not all property of the spouses belong to the community, each spouse is entitled to what is known as *bienes privativos* which is all property that belongs exclusively to one or other of the spouses.[74] The rationale behind this regulation is that in order to belong to the society or community of *gananciales* both spouses have to "contribute" in one way or the other to the acquisition. This idea is perhaps better understood by looking at which property belongs to the community. The Code classifies as *gananciales* those goods acquired by the work or industry of one of the spouses. Even if one of the spouses was more directly involved in obtaining the property it was also the work and co-operation of the other by not spending the earnings or saving them which makes it count as an asset for the community.[75] During the life of the marriage the community exists for the purpose of covering the family expenses in the widest sense of the

---

[69] See Arts 1655 *et seq*. Civil Code, in particular Art.1675 Civil Code, *sociedad universal de ganancias*. For a good discussion on the topic see Diez-Picazo, op. cit pp.172–174; in more detail, Blanquer Uberos: *La idea de comunidad en la sociedad de gananciales. Alcance, modalidades y excepciones* RDN, 1982, p.7.

[70] By the *Ley* 13/1981. See above.

[71] See Art.1344 "*se hacen comunes . . .*".

[72] Arts 392 *et seq*. Civil Code.

[73] For example, because the marriage ends by separation, nullity, divorce or death or because spouses enter into a different ante-nuptial contract ending the *sociedad de gananciales* and starting a new regime.

[74] Article 1346 lists these: the property which belonged to each spouse before the marriage; property acquired in substitution of the former; property acquired gratuitously—by gift or inheritance—by one of the spouses; rights of the personality and/or compensation for rights of personality for example honour, image, clothes and personal belonging of normal value, tools and instruments necessary for the exercise of one's trade or profession.

[75] Other property belonging to the community of *gananciales* is, according to Art.1347: the interests of capital whether this is private or common; property acquired with common goods; property acquired as a consequence of the exercise of a common right of preferential acquisition.

term,[76] but it is at the time of ending the marriage, or the community, if this happens earlier[77] that an inventory and computation of the assets is made and the "earnings" are ascertained and fixed in order later to be divided between the spouses. During the existence of the community both spouses have equal powers in order to manage and administer the common goods and have a duty to inform and be transparent towards each other. If one of the spouses breaches these duties or acts against the interests of the community the other spouse can request the court to bring the community to an end, even against the will of the defaulting spouse.[78]

Participation

The other two matrimonial property regimes are less used in Spain in the territories of common civil law.[79] The system of participation[80] is a system of deferred participation in earnings. This system is significantly different from the *comunidad de ganaciales* because there are two separate and distinct funds or *patrimonios* during the life of the marriage: the wife's fund and the husband's fund. These will remain separate throughout the duration of the marriage but, at the time of dissolution there will be a participation in the earnings of the other spouse. There are never common goods or common property but only a personal right of credit to the earnings of the other spouse. This is the main difference with the regime of *gananciales*. This system has the aim of combining the benefits of the regime of community with the system of separation of wealth. In practice, however, it is used rarely and it is very difficult to determine the parties' participation. This is very similar system to this regime of *Zugewinngemeinschaft* used in Germany.[81]

---

[76] Art.1362 CC. See also Art.142 CC.

[77] Art.1382 lists the cases of dissolution of the *sociedad de ganaciales* if the marriage ends or a new regime is chosen. Note that the *sociedad* can also be dissolved by judicial decision in the cases numbered in Art.1393: incapacity of one of the spouses, declaration of absence of one of the spouses, bankruptcy, desertion, repeated fraudulent actions or breach of the duty of information between spouses.

[78] See Art.1393 referred to in the footnote above.

[79] In Cataluña, for example, the regime of separation of wealth is the legal subsidiary regime in absence of choice by the parties. See *Código de la Familia, Ley* 9/1998 of July 15.

[80] Arts 1415–1434 CC. *Régimen de participacion*

[81] For a description of the German regime, in English see Foster, *German Legal System and Laws*, (2nd edn, 1996), p.308.

Separacion de bienes

The last of the systems is that of total separation of wealth.[82] This is perhaps the simplest of the regimes since each spouse remains the sole owner of all his property pre-and post-nuptial although both spouses share the duty to contribute to the expenses of the family.[83]

The choice between one or the other of the aforementioned regimes will depend largely on the socio-economic circumstances of the spouses. Separation of wealth and participation in earnings are better suited to couples in which each spouse works and has different property, and less well suited to the now increasingly old family model in which one spouse, usually the wife, stayed at home looking after the children. Perhaps with the recent social changes and the incorporation of women into the labour market those regimes will be chosen more often.

The area of marriage and, in particular, matrimonial property is one of those in which variations exists in the different areas of *derecho foral*[84] although it goes well beyond the purpose of this book to cover these variations.[85] It is also important to consider the new laws regarding non-married couples that exist in some of the territories of different civil law.[86]

3. MARRIAGE BREAKDOWN

SEPARATION AND DIVORCE

Separation

A married couple can decide at any point during their marriage that they want to live at separate addresses for a limited period or

---

[82] Arts 1435–1444 CC.

[83] Art.1438.

[84] See Ch.1, pp.21–2.

[85] *Código de Familia, Ley* 9/1998 of June 15, of Cataluña (Art.10(1)); Compilación de Aragón (Art.23); Compilación de Navarra (*Ley* 80); Compilación de Baleares (Arts 3 and 66); *Ley* 4/1995 of May 24 de Derecho Civil de Galicia (Art.112); *Ley* 3/1992 of July 1 de Derecho Civil Foral del Pais Vasco (Art 93).

[86] *Ley* 10/1998 of July 15 of stable unions in Cataluña, Arts 4, 5, 23 and 24; *Ley* 6/1999 of March 26 of stable non married couples, Aragón (Art.5(4)); *Ley Foral* 6/2000 of July 3, of Navarra of Legal Equality of non-married couples (Art.7); *Ley* 18/2001 of December 19 of non-married couples of the Islas Baleares (Art.5). See below for a general exposition of the law regarding stable unions.

indefinitely. In some cases one of the spouses needs time, and space, to think about whether they wish to remain married.

It is quite common for couples to begin an informal (without legal intervention) separation, then proceed to a legal separation and, ultimately, to a divorce.[87] The old law on separation and divorce of 1981 favoured this process instead of opting for a divorce directly (although it was possible to get divorced without having been legally separated). Today, separation and divorce have been radically changed in Spain with the approval of the *Ley* 15/2005 *de modificación del Código Civil en materia de separación y divorcio*.

Legal separation (or separation from now on) can be consensual or contentious. It is much cheaper[88] and less straining emotionally to try to agree on the terms of the separation than to get involved in a legal battle, especially if there are children involved. Unfortunately this is not always possible. Some autonomous communities have passed laws encouraging or forcing couples to seek the services of a mediator either before they are allowed to separate[89] or while they are in the process of separating in order to agree the terms of the separation. If this agreement is not possible it will be necessary to go to court and seek a judicial settlement.

In the past, couples needed to have been married for at least a year before they could separate. The explanation for this compulsory waiting time was that the law tried to avoid hasty separations during the first few months of what is often the difficult process of getting used to living with somebody else.[90] The new law on separation and divorce reduces this time to three months or one month if there are reasons to suggest that the safety of one of the spouses or children under their custody is in question.[91] While the reduction of the waiting period has indeed been welcomed by the majority, some

---

[87] If divorce is permitted by the religious beliefs of the spouses. Legal separation is all that is admitted by the Catholic Church besides cases of "nullity" or marriages being declared void.

[88] It is estimated that consensual separation can cost the parties about €1,100 while a contentious one will cost in excess of €2,000. See, Maria de Rosario Villas de Antonio and Pilar Luisa Sanchez Garcia, "*La separación matrimonial*" BOE, Madrid (2003), p.9.

[89] *Ley* 1/2001 of March 15 of Cataluña; *Ley* 4/2001 of May 31 of Galicia and *Ley* 7/2001 of November 26 of the Comunidad Valenciana.

[90] Art.81 CC today modified by the *Ley* 15/2005. This requirement is also present in English Law, s.3(1) of the Matrimonial Causes Act 1973. But see Hayes and Williams, *Family Law*, Butterworths (2004), at pp.510–511 comments as to whether it is at all better to try to force newlyweds to remain together or allow them to separate shortly after they realise the error they have made and before any offspring is born.

[91] Art.81 of the Civil Code according to the new wording to be given by the *Ley de modificación del Código Civil en material de separación y divorcio*. The *ley* is at the stage

have criticised the arbitrary nature of the period of three months.[92] Critics point out that if the main aim of the modification of the Civil Code was to give the maximum support to the individual freedom of the spouses to decide, at any time, that their marriage has run its course, imposing an arbitrary three months' wait is absurd. There is no need for any other reason to be present or made public in order to allow couples to separate. Separation is not based on fault, it is enough that one or both spouses think that they are better off following different paths and that they communicate this decision to the judge. In a consensual separation this really is a communication from the parties to the judge of the end of marital life, and a public endorsement by the judge which will, in turn, produce certain legal consequences.[93]

Whether consensual or contentious it is necessary to employ the services of an *abogado* and a *procurador* in all separation proceedings. If the separation is consensual it is possible, and advisable, to use the same *abogado* and *procurador* in order to save time and money. The intervention of a lawyer (or two) will ensure that the parties are aware of all legal consequences if they proceed with the separation. For example it may have financial implications in terms of succession rights or pensions, taxes or other entitlements that the parties did not expect. Or, if the separation is consensual and not necessarily with a view to an imminent divorce the parties may re-consider their decision. The *abogado* is under the general professional duty of giving the best legal advice and representation to his or her client but he is no under the duty to act as a mediator or counsellor. A good family lawyer will advise the client both in a consensual or contentious separation as to what is a reasonable agreement and a reasonable state of affairs to be expected as well as being able to suggest an early settlement instead of a long legal battle.

The petition presented to the court must be accompanied by an agreement called *convenio regulador*.[94] This agreement states who will have custody of the children,[95] the time, frequency and length of visits

---

of proposal at the time of writing (April 2005) but it is thought that it will be approved without any modifications by Congress and Senate in the next few months.

[92] Agustin Cañete Quesada, "*El Anteprojecto de ley por el que se modifica el Código Civil en material de separación y divorcio*" in *www.porticolegal.com/articulos/pa_183.php*.

[93] Art.83 CC, Arts 68 and 69 "common life of the marriage", Arts 102(2) and 1319 "*potestad domestica*", Arts 90–98 general effects, and Arts 834, 835 and 945 succession. See also *Ley del Registro Civil* Art.76 and *Reglamento del Registro Civil* Arts 263 and 264.

[94] Art.90 CC.

[95] One of the novelties of the *Ley* 15/2005 is the possibility of shared custody.

to the children by the other parent and grandparents,[96] the use and enjoyment of the family home, the agreement about mortgage payments (if any) in respect of the same family home, the dissolution of the economic matrimonial regime of *gananciales*, the request for a "compensatory pension" or *pension compensatoria*,[97] if appropriate, and the frequency and amount of child maintenance.

In fact, the *convenio* can include any provision that the parties or their legal advisors deem necessary for the regulation of future relations and the dissolution of existing ones. This *convenio* is particularly important in the case of couples with descendants since a certain degree of continuity and certain ongoing communication will be necessary, until the children reach 18 and can decide who they want to live with. It is advisable to be as precise as possible in the *convenio regulador* since it is not infrequent for couples who initiate separation proceedings in reasonably amicable terms to distance themselves even more after separation, resulting in conflict years later when one or both of the former spouses start a new relationship or wish for the agreed status quo to change in any manner.

Once the *convenio* has been agreed a *demanda* (petition) is presented to the Court of First Instance where the parties are domiciled. The judge will call the parties to a hearing within three days[98] and ask each of them separately if they agree and approve the *convenio*. If they do and the judge thinks that it is a fair agreement and not detrimental to either spouse or the children it will be approved. If the judge thinks that the agreement or *convenio* has any terms that are unfair or particularly onerous for one of the spouses, he will say so and suggest that each party employs separate legal representation. It is also common for the parties to disagree at the last minute and many separations that start as consensual turn contentious at the time of the hearing.

The *Ministerio Fiscal*[99] will be consulted about any term of the agreement if there are minors involved or affected by it.

The court decision will be entered into the Civil Registry and the Land Registry.

---

[96] Note that grandparents have got visiting rights according to the *Ley* 42/2003, of November 21, *de modificación del Código Civil y de la Ley de Enjuiciamiento Civil en material de relaciones familiars de los nietos con los abuelos*.

[97] New rules have also been established in respect of the *pensión compensatoria*. See below.

[98] This is likely to be a longer period due to the overload of most courts.

[99] As to the role of the Ministerio Fiscal in general see Ch.4, p.89.

Contentious separation

This was very common under the old law and occurred when one of the spouses did not want to end the marriage. It was possible to request a separation (and later a divorce) if any of the following causes were present[1]: desertion (*abandono del hogar*)[2]; infidelity; repeated violation of marital duties[3]; injurious or violent conduct of one spouse towards the other spouse or the children (physical or mental); any serious or continuous violation of parental duties towards the children of both or of one of the spouses living under the same roof; alcoholism; drug addiction or mental illness; a jail sentence of six years or more or effective end of marital cohabitation.

Due to the nature of these causes of separation it is easy to see why the parties could not be able to proceed to an amicable or consensual separation. It is possible that where the relationship has reached breaking point one of the parties may need to request provisional measures from the court that will regulate the couple's relations in matters such as use of the matrimonial home and contribution to expenditure for access to the children while the definite agreement of *convenio* is reached or imposed by the court. These provisional measures can be particularly important in cases in which there may have been physical violence towards one of the spouses or the children and a request has been made to exclude the violent spouse from the marital home.

The provisional measures will remain valid until definite measures are imposed by the court. The court decision always means that the *comunidad de gananciales* must be ended if the parties have not done so before.[4]

The new law of separation and divorce totally dispenses with the so called "causes of divorce" on the grounds that it is, as pointed out, the parties' free will to remain married or to initiate a separation or divorce. The State should therefore abandon the protective role towards the institution of marriage that it still has by eliminating all causes or reasons that allow the parties to initiate a separation or divorce. The only relevance given to the behaviour of the parties is in the new wording of Art.81 that reduces the period of time that the

---

[1] Arts 81(2) and 82 Civil Code.
[2] Note that desertion may constitute a crime under Arts 226–233 of the *Código Penal*, if the spouse abandons minors or a family member that needs assistance.
[3] See Arts 68–71, on marital duties. See above, "Effects of marriage", p.296.
[4] For a detailed explanation of the process of liquidating the *sociedad de gananciales* see J.J. Reyes Gallur "*Aspectos procesales de la sociedad de gananciales*" in *www.cgae.es/articles*.

spouses need to have been married from three to one month in cases of physical or mental abuse towards a spouse or the children of the marriage.

It is perhaps important to make a reference in this section to the ownership and use of the family home following separation proceedings. The family home is not only the greatest economic asset that most families own but is also the home of the children. Even if the home belongs, in strict legal terms, to one of the spouses the judge can, and usually will, allocate the use of the home to the spouse that has the everyday custody of the children irrespective of whether the spouse owns part or all of the home, or has no claim over the ownership of the home. Ownership and use are clearly differentiated and this right of use, which will almost always be exclusive, is protected by making an entry into the Land Registry and requiring the consent of the spouse in occupation before any sale of the property can take place. This use, if the occupying spouse is not the owner, will usually finish once the children are old enough to leave the parental home.[5] If there are no children the house will usually be allocated to the legal owner or sold and each spouse will obtain their part of the proceeds.

Separation does not terminate the marriage or extinguish the marital link. Marriage can only be dissolved by death or divorce.[6] Separation suspends the common life of the spouses[7] and as such there are certain legal consequences that stem from a judicial separation beyond those measures agreed in the *convenio*. The main consequences will be felt in the area of succession rights. The surviving spouse is a "compulsory heir"[8] with a right of usufruct over one third of the estate. But, is the separated spouse a "surviving spouse"? According to Art.834 of the Civil Code in order to be treated as a surviving spouse the spouses must have been married and not separated at the time of death.[9] Different territories of *foral* law have different

---

[5] This, of course, is a subjective time-limit because it is common for adult children in Spain to live with their parents until they marry or obtain a job in a different locality. This is due partly to the high unemployment and the cost of accessing the property market but also to tradition. The court will fix a time limit if there is disagreement.

[6] Art.85 CC. We have not included nullity here because it technically does not dissolve a marriage since the marriage was understood to have never taken place. See below.

[7] Art.83 CC.

[8] Arts 834 and 835 CC. Different amounts will correspond to the surviving spouse depending on whether there are older generations or descendants. For a detailed explanation see Ch.12, "Succession".

[9] The old Art.834 made a difference between spouses separated consensually or without fault and those separated because of the deceased's fault. By "fault", in this context, it is understood that the Code makes reference to the causes of separation of Art.82 that can be attributed to one of the spouses. For example, domestic violence

provisions as to the consequences of legal separation upon the succession rights of the surviving spouse.[10]

The consequences of separation are the same in cases of intestacy.[11] In effect Art.945 precludes the surviving spouse that is separated by the final court decision or by mutual agreement from inheriting any property from the deceased. "Separated by mutual agreement" is making reference to those cases in which the parties have been de facto separated for a long enough period of time but there is no court decision making the separation official. It will need to be proven that the spouses were in fact separated by those wishing to benefit from the terms of the will. This will presumably be those relatives called to inherit in the absence of a surviving spouse.

It is to be celebrated that the new law has eliminated the differential treatment of separated spouses' succession rights in cases of intestacy or in cases in which there is a valid will. The elimination of the second paragraph of Art.837 and of all differences of treatment based on "fault" by one of the spouses is coherent with the view that separation and divorce is a choice made by the spouses.

It is also important to note that under the new regulation the different shares to be allocated to the surviving spouses according to whether or not there were common descendants or only descendants of the deceased has been eliminated.[12]

DIVORCE

Divorce is, together with death of one of the spouses, the only grounds to dissolve a valid marriage.[13] The regulation of divorce

---

towards the spouse or children, alcoholism, infidelity, abandonment of the marital home, mental illness and drugs addictions. Article 82 is today without content after the *Ley* 15/2005.

[10] *Compilación de Navarra, "usufructo legal de fidelidad"*, *Compilación de Aragón*, Arts 72 *et seq., "viudedad foral aragonesa"; Compilación de Baleares*, Arts. 45 and 53, *usufructo viudal; Código de sucesiones por causa de muerte en el Derecho Civil de Cataluña, Ley* 40/2991, December 30, de Cataluña, Art 331; *Ley* 3/1992, July 1, *De Derecho Civil Foral del Pais Vasco*; Arts 59, 159 and 160; *Ley* 4/1995, of May 24, *de Derecho Civil de Galicia*, Art.146(2); *Ley* 10/1998 of July 15, *de uniones estables de pareja, de Cataluña*, Arts 34(a) and 35; *Ley* 18/2001, of 18 December, *de parejas de hecho, de las Islas Baleares*, Art.13.

[11] See Arts 944 and 945 CC.

[12] Some of the doctrine doubted whether this different treatment was in fact constitutional at all. For a good discussion see: A. Cañete Quesada, *"El anteproyecto de ley por el que se modifica el Código Civil en material de separación y divorcio" www.porticolegal.com/articulos/pa_183.php.*

[13] Art.85 CC.

in Spain is similar to that of separation, except that divorce is a definite dissolution of the marriage, irreversible once the court has made its decision.[14] In many cases divorce is the next step after separation and if this is the case the procedure is substantially simplified since the agreements reached previously can continue in place or be modified to suit the parties with minimum expense. The proceedings are virtually identical[15] and once the decision is final it will be entered into the Civil Registry and have legal effects in respect of third parties.

Nullity

Nullity is different from the separation or divorce because if any of the essential requirements for a valid marriage—consent, capacity and the observance of certain formalities[16]—were not present, the marriage could never have taken place in the first place and therefore does not need to be dissolved. In fact, what a decree of nullity does is to provide a court declaration that the marriage in fact never existed for lacking an essential element.

The law ensures that any innocent spouse, and particularly children who may have been born to the marriage, do not suffer after this declaration.[17] This was particularly important before the 1978 Constitution when legitimate and illegitimate children were treated very differently in law.[18]

A marriage is null and void whatever its form of conduct[19] if, and only if:

- there was no consent from one or both spouses;
- there existed a lack of capacity of either spouse[20];
- it was conducted without[21] witnesses or the necessary public representative (judge, town mayor or other public servant);

---

[14] See Arts 87 and 88 CC. Nothing stops divorced ex-spouses from marrying again.
[15] See Arts 770 and following of the LEC.
[16] See Art.45 CC.
[17] See Art.79 CC, LRC, Art.76 and RRC Arts 263 and 264.
[18] Today, happily, the law prohibits any discrimination between children born in or out of wedlock; the main reform was introduced by the *Ley* 11/1981 of May 13.
[19] This makes reference to religious marriages and seeks to clarify that whatever form the marriage is conducted there is only one type of marriage and one set of requirements the marriage must comply with.
[20] The lack of capacity can be absolute, for example the spouse is already married or is a minor (Art.46 CC) or is a close family relation (Art.47 CC).
[21] See above, p.294.

- there was an error in the identity or essential personal attributes of one of the spouses; or
- consent was vitiated by coercion or serious fear.

Either spouse, the *Ministerio Fiscal* or a party who has a legitimate interest (for example the previous spouse in cases of bigamy) can start nullity proceedings.[22] Depending on the cause that the party is relying upon there is a period of time before proceedings can be initiated. If the parties have lived together for a year after coercion or fear has developed nullity ceases to be possible. The law is obviously eager that there be a great degree of certainty in all cases affecting the civil status of individuals.

The consequences are very similar to those in cases of divorce and separation.[23] The main underlying policy is that the spouse who was "innocent" or entered into the marriage in good faith, unaware that the marriage was void, should not be unduly damaged by the declaration of nullity. In effect Art.98 establishes that a compensatory pension will be given to the spouse acting in good faith. The same preoccupation exists in respect of children or third parties who relied on the existence of the marriage.

4. UNMARRIED COUPLES AND FAMILY RELATIONS OUTSIDE MARRIAGE

The so-called "crisis" of marriage as an institution has meant that many individuals choose a model of family life that is not institutionalised within the framework of marriage.

This choice makes particular sense if we consider the only recently changed[24]culpability model of divorce and separation regulated by the Code and the long periods of time required in order to be able to legally end a marriage.

However, families outside the legally recognised marriage were in a situation where upon death of one of the partners they were left with no rights over their estate unless a will was made, and, even where a will was made their rights were limited and they would be treated

---

[22] Art.74 CC, also see Arts 748(3), 753, 769 *et seq.*, LEC, and Cir 1/2001, of April 5, *de la Fiscalia general del Estado*, on the intervention of the *Ministerio Fiscal* in civil proceedings.
[23] See Ch.9 of the CC, the Code regulates all the consequences together even though it establishes special provisions to take into account the different circumstances.
[24] See above, *Ley* 15/2005 of July 5 for the modification of the Civil Code on separation and divorce.

as "strangers" with a heavy tax liability and no benefit from the many tax allowances available to close family members.[25] Many Autonomous Communities have recognised this social inequality and provided adequate legislation to address the needs and rights of those individuals.[26]

There was, however, no general law applicable in the whole territory of Spain and only those under the *foral* vicinity of one of the territories with a law regarding unmarried couples could benefit from the legislation. It is not that the central state ignored the reality of an increase in the number of cohabiting partnerships or families as this was recognised in the laws of landlord and tenant[27] and in the criminal code.[28] However, nothing had been done to address this area in one single legal instrument.

Many sectors of society had repeatedly raised objections about this and suggested that the various forms of direct or indirect discrimination that the current status quo imposes on unmarried family members was unconstitutional, or at least, against the spirit of the constitution read as society stands today. The effects of this discrimination were felt, particularly by same sex unions, since they were precluded from marrying[29] and therefore could not opt for the various legal and financial advantages in place for married couples.

In April 2004 the Grupo Parlamentario Mixto put forward a *proposición de Ley* to the Congress called *Igualdad jurídica para las uniones de hecho* or "legal equality for de facto unions". This *proposición de ley* relies on several articles of the Constitution to justify the need for a new regulation in this area. Art.39 of the Constitution— social, economic and legal protection of the family, the equality of all children irrespective whether they are born into a marriage or out of wedlock, the general principle of equality of all citizens of Art.14 and, the now driving principle in family law of personal freedom.[30] The explanatory notes to the draft bill explain the purpose of the law as enabling those with a different sexual orientation (same sex unions) or those who did not want to formalise their union by marriage to still benefit from some of the aspects of marriage that have a public

---

[25] See Ch.12, "Succession".

[26] See fn. 24, p.292.

[27] Art.16 *Ley de Arrendamientos Urbanos* (LAU) 1994 acknowledges the right of those living "*more uxorio*" to subrogate on their partner's tenancy contract.

[28] Art.23 CP, circumstances mitigating, aggravating or excluding criminal liability. This article treats married and unmarried partners alike.

[29] This has now changed with the *Ley* 13/2005 of July 5.

[30] See comments on this acknowledgement of the right to personal freedom of Art.10 CE and its impact in the proposed new regulation of separation of divorce, see above pp.302–308.

dimension: paternity, maternity, protection of children and rights over them, succession rights and tax benefits, and social protection in the form of obtaining work permits and benefits.

The law suggests a wide definition of what a "union" is, which includes any two individuals of any sex that are not married to somebody else or included within the forbidden degrees of consanguinity that live together in a free, stable and public relationship. A union is presumed to be stable after one year, unless there is common descendents in which case the simple fact that they are living together makes the relationship or union "stable".

To prove the existence of the stable union the partners must register the union in the special registries available in most town halls, or by a public (notarial) document, or by any other means of evidence accepted by law.[31] At the end of the relationship either of the partners must request an amendment to the registry indicating the termination of the relationship.

The partners of the union can regulate the personal, and, especially patrimonial consequences of their union freely by private or public document[32], if they do not do this the law provides a basic framework of rights, duties and compensation, if relevant, at the time of breakdown.

Should this *proposición de ley* be finally approved by the Congress and the Senate, it would mean that several articles of the Civil Code will have to be modified,[33] together with other legislation. For example, the *Ley* 21/1987 of November 11 on adoption; the *Estatuto de los Trabajadores*; several laws of social security,[34] regulation of civil service[35] and taxes.[36]

---

[31] See Ch.5, p.117, "Civil Procedure", means of evidence.
[32] The advantages of using a public notary's document are many. The notary will advise on the content of the regulation and suggest changes if any of their requirements are against the law. A notarial document also has the influence of veracity and authenticity that make it much easier to enforce than a private document that has to be proved, if contested just like any other private document.
[33] See *Capitulo II, Proposicion de Ley de Igualdad Jurídica de las uniones de hecho.* BOCG. *Congreso de los Diputados, serie B, no. 55–1, de 23/04/2004*
[34] *Ley General de Seguridad Social, RD Legislativo 1/1994,* of June 20; *Decreto 2065/1974* of May 30.
[35] *Ley 30/1984,* of August 2.
[36] *Ley 40/1998, of December 9, sobre el Impuesto sobre la Renta de las Personals Fisicas and Ley 29/1987, of December 28, del Impuesto de Sucesiones y Donaciones.*

Chapter Twelve
Succession

1. THE MAIN PRINCIPLES OF SPANISH SUCCESSION LAW

The Law of succession is not uniform across the territory of the Spanish peninsula. In Spain the common or general civil law co-exists with different territorial regional systems of civil law called *derechos forales*. These are not complete systems regulating all and every matter of civil law but most of them have special provisions for family and succesion matters.[1] This text will only deal with the general civil law since it will be impossible in this space to cover all the other systems.[2]

The regulation of the law of succession can be achieved by two main principles: the principle of freedom of testation or the principle of restricted testamentary freedom. In legal history intestacy and the devolution of the estate according to fixed rules preceded freedom of testament. The rights of the family were considered to be much more important than the wishes or whims of individual testators and several public policy reasons supported the view that succession should take place according to the law.[3]

Roman law progressively allowed testators the freedom to make wills, bordered by various formalities.[4] The system was soon faced with the problem of testators excluding their own relatives and leaving them without the minimum subsistence (*officium pietatis*). These cases were originally resolved by challenging the validity of the will on

---

[1] See, Ch.1, pp.21–2.

[2] The main *derecho foral* of succession can be found in: *Ley* 3/1992 of July 1, *del Derecho Foral del Pais Vasco*, Arts 27–92 and 153–188. *Compilación de Baleares. Texto refundido* approved by *Decreto Legislativo* 79/1990 of September 6, Arts 6–53, 65 and 69–84. *Ley* 1/1999, of February 24, *de sucesiones por causa de muerte*, of Aragón. *Compilación de Navarra, reformada por la Ley Foral del Parlamento de Navarra 5/1987* of April 1; *Leyes* 172 and 345; *Código de Sucesiones por causa de muerte en el derecho civil de Cataluña*, approved by the *Ley* 40/1991 of December 30 *de Cataluña. Ley* 4/1995 of May 24 *de Derecho Civil de Galicia*, Arts 117–170.

[3] For an accessible discussion in English of testamentary freedom and the evolution and arguments behind this concept see Borkowski, *Textbook on Succession* (Blackstone), 1997 pp.237–243.

[4] See, among others, Borkowski, *op. cit.* p.238.

the grounds of lack of capacity of the testator; it was presumed that the testator was of unsound mind if he had excluded all his relatives. This avenue proved burdensome and time consuming. When the Roman Empire received the Germanic tribes with laws providing for the devolution of the estate according to legal principles and little or non-existent freedom of testament, these laws mixed with the Roman laws of freedom of testament. As a consequence,[5] the Spanish system today is a mixture of these two systems. There is some freedom of testament but there is a portion of the estate which by law should go to the relatives of the deceased (the *legítima portio*[6]) already known to Roman law and today called *legítima* in Spanish law.[7] This fixed share is automatic in Spanish law[8] leaving the testator with only a portion of his estate that he can dispose of freely by will. The system is quite different from English law where family provision is discretionary and has no fixed entitlement[9] and where the main informing principle still is that of testamentary freedom.

2. WILLS: TYPES OF WILLS AND FORMALITIES

Wills in Spain are called *testamentos*. Testaments are personal,[10] free unilateral declarations of will[11] made by a person with full mental capacity[12] that are to take effect after the death of the person making the declaration.[13] In his act the testator will dispose of part or all of his property. It is not necessary, however, to limit the content of testaments to patrimonial dispositions; testaments can also contain other declarations such as recognition of extramarital children, provisions for the care and custody of the testator's descendants or instructions about the funeral or ceremony to be held after the death.

Testaments are divided between common or ordinary and extraordinary. Ordinary testaments are the *testamento olografo* (holograph

---

[5] See Ch.1, "Legal History".

[6] Which can be translated as the "rightful share".

[7] See below.

[8] As it is in France and Scotland, see Borkowski, *op. cit.*, p.241.

[9] See, Borkowski, *op. cit.* p. 242.

[10] Art.670 CC, 2 "*es un acto personalisimo*" and Art.669 CC which forbids common testaments and mutual wills.

[11] Testaments given under the influence of violence or intimidation are null and void Art.673 CC.

[12] Art.663 CC, on capacity to give a will.

[13] Art.667 CC, see also *Código de Sucesiones por Causa de Muerte en el Derecho Civil de Cataluña*, Art.104.

testament); *testamento abierto* (open) and *testamento cerrado* (closed).[14]

Extraordinary testaments are those given when the testator is considered to be in out of the ordinary circumstances. In these cases the law dispenses with the observance of the normal formalities. There are three types of special or extraordinary testaments: military,[15] maritime,[16] and testament made in a foreign country.[17] In the case of military or maritime wills, the underlying idea is that in the absence of a notary it is possible to make a will in front of another authority. For those cases involving a Spanish national abroad Art.732 CC contains a rule of private international law that must be read in conjunction with Arts 11, 12 and 677 of the Civil Code. It authorises and recognises testaments made according to the formalities of the foreign country.[18]

The most common type of testament in Spain is the *testamento abierto* or open testament authorised by a notary public. This testament presents great advantages since it involves a legal professional, the notary, from an early stage. The testator will go to the notary and explain to whom he wishes to bequeath his property after his death. The notary will discuss and explain to the testator whether it is possible to carry out his wishes or not and will draft a will making sure the testator's wishes are taken into account as far as the mandatory succession laws allow, particularly the *legítimas*. The notary will swear to the identity of the testator, his mental capacity and his ability to understand the dispositions contained in the will. Once the testament is signed the notary will give a copy to the testator for safekeeping and will keep the original copy in the notarial protocol.[19] A copy is also sent to the *Registro de Actos de Ultima Voluntad* (which we shall translate as Central Wills Registry). This is a registry dependent on the Ministry of Justice and where a record of all wills authorised by all notaries in Spain and by the Consular or diplomatic authorities abroad is kept.[20] This Registry has a very important function because after the death and before the distribution of the estate can take place it is necessary for those interested to request a certification from the

---

[14] Art 676 CC.

[15] Arts 716–721 CC.

[16] Arts 722–731 CC.

[17] Arts 732–736 CC.

[18] This is also the rule of the Hague Convention of October 5, 1961 on choice of law rules applicable to the formalities of wills, ratified by Spain by Instrument of March 16, 1988.

[19] Note that documents are kept for a minimum of 100 years in each *Notaría*.

[20] See *www.mju.es* and follow links in "*Canal Ciudadano*" to "*Registro de Actos de Ultima Voluntad*".

Registro de Actos de Ultima Voluntad.[21] The certification issued by this *Registro* will state either that there is no will by the deceased or that indeed there is a will. If the former, intestacy rules will apply to the devolution of the estate. In the latter case, it will indicate the name of the *notaría* where the original last will and testament can be found.

This formality of obtaining a certificate from the Central Registry indicating where the last will is held is a pre-requisite of any distribution of the estate. This is the case even if the relatives of the deceased know that there is a will and that the will was authorised by the local notary. The reason is the right that the testator has to revoke his will at any time. It is possible for the testator to make a later, different will that the relatives did not know about.[22]

Once the certificate of the Central Wills Registry has been obtained the parties interested can go to the *notaría* and make an appointment with the notary. The notary will read the will, make an inventory of the deceased's property, pay the funeral expenses and any outstanding debts, liquidate and pay the *impuesto de sucesiones y donaciones*,[23] distribute the *legítimas* and any legacies bequested in the will, and allocate the remainder of the estate between the heirs. The notary will also send all necessary documentation to the Land Registry, where details of any change of ownership of immovable property will be noted. Note that the notary is not an executor of the will and that he performs all the tasks mentioned above as an agent for the heirs. Property is vested with the heirs from the time of death[24] including all debts and liabilities making the existence of executors unnecessary from the point of view of formal ownership of the estate. It is possible to name an *albacea*[25] whose role is similar to that of the English executor as he will distribute legacies, pay debts, collate an inventory and perform all legal formalities. The main difference is that ownership of the deceased's property is vested in the heirs even in cases of using an *albacea*. This is rarely done except for large estates. In these cases the *albacea* tends to be a lawyer.

The testator can also make a closed testament or *testamento cerrado*, which is a document drafted and dated by the testator that he takes to the notary's office explaining that this is his last will and testament. The role of the notary in this case is reduced to that of

---

[21] This can be done personally, by post or by a personal request in any of the provincial delegations of the *Ministerio de Justicia* by those interested by providing a copy of the death certificate.
[22] All testamentary dispositions are revocable, Art.737 CC.
[23] See below, "Taxes on inheritance".
[24] See below, "The heirs".
[25] Arts 892–911 CC.

swearing to the identity of the testator and the fact that he appears to be of sound mind and that he is receiving a document that the testator says is his last will or testament. This closed document is also sent to the Central Wills Registry and once the testator dies the procedure is exactly the same as before when those interested request a certification from the Wills Registry. The notary will open the testament for the first time after the testator's death. This document, the closed will, is not a document drafted by the notary and the testator has not in principle benefited from any legal advice.[26] The dangers of this are clear: the testator may have ignored some mandatory rules about the *legítimas* or compulsory heirs or expressed his intention in a contradictory or unclear manner. In the past this type of will was used when the testator wanted to keep something secret, for example, a declaration recognising an extramarital child. The testament, however, is a personal act and the notary has a duty of confidentiality like any other legal professional.

Holograph testaments only require to be handwritten by the testator and signed by him indicating the date and place in which the testament was drafted. They allow for the maximum confidentiality on the destination of the property after death. However, they present serious dangers. The first danger is that the testament may be lost or destroyed; perhaps by somebody who will benefit under the rules of intestacy if no will is found. The second danger comes from the possibility that even if the testament is found it will need to be formalised and recognised as the last and free will of the testator[27] and this process is expensive and not always straightforward. The third is that the testator may have made some dispositions that are not allowed by the mandatory rules of succession.[28] To have a holograph will recognised and executed is more expensive and time consuming than making an open testament in front of a notary.[29]

If there is no testament, the rules of intestacy apply. In this case it is necessary to resort to a different procedure called *declaración de herederos*. This can take place either in the notary's office, if the deceased and the heirs were domiciled in the same place or it may be necessary to resort to the judge of first instance of where the deceased was domiciled. The procedure is more time consuming and expensive

---

[26] Of course, the testator may have had independent legal advice by a lawyer and decided to proceed with a closed testament instead of an open testament in front of the notary.

[27] This is done by taking the holograph will to the first instance judge of the last domicile of the testator. See Arts 689–693 CC.

[28] See below, compulsory shares and *legítimas*.

[29] Prices for making a will vary from €30–60 for basic wills for Spanish citizens.

and it is regulated by the Titulo IX of Libro II of the old LEC until the new law on *jurisidicción voluntaria* is approved.[30]

3.   THE HEIRS

In English law, after a person's death the property is vested in his personal representatives (executors or administrators) who will distribute the estate according to the terms of the will or to the rules of intestacy if there is no will.[31]

In Spanish Law the estate of the deceased passes directly to the heirs as a whole, including debts and liabilities.[32] This transmission is *ex lege* and automatic and takes place as soon as the heirs accept the inheritance. When this acceptance takes place the vesting of the estate is retrospective to the time of death,[33] otherwise there would be a time when the estate had no owner which is not possible in law. Acceptance by the heirs can be tacit or express.[34]

The heirs (*herederos*) are the persons so named in the will.[35] If there is no will, or the will fails to make a valid nomination, the law determines the persons who are to become "statutory heirs".[36] Since the heirs have "taken the place" of the deceased and now own all his rights and duties (except those of a personal nature) they are in principle personally liable to the creditors of the deceased and will have to satisfy the estate's debts out of their own property if after the liquidation of the estate the debts prove to exceed the assets. This unlimited liability is tempered by the right of disclaimer[37] and the possibility of acceptance subject to the benefit of an inventory given to the heirs.[38]

The heirs can repudiate the inheritance. This is called disclaimer. They can also ask for the "benefit of an inventory". This is a type of partial acceptance whereby a person accepts becoming an heir after looking at the inventory and estimating whether the debts surpass the value of the property in the estate. In this case the heir keeps his own

---

[30] See *Disposicion Derogatoria* 1.2 of the *Ley* 1/2000 of January 7.

[31] Note that the will may fail partially or may not dispose of all the property. In these cases testate succession and intestate succession rules co-exist.

[32] Arts 657 and 661 CC.

[33] Art.989 CC.

[34] Arts 998 to 1002 CC.

[35] Arts 750 and 772 CC.

[36] Art.913 CC.

[37] Art.989 CC right of disclaimer (*repudiación de la herencia*).

[38] Art.998 CC, *Aceptación a beneficio de inventario.*

property separate and his liability is limited to those debts which can be satisfied out of the deceased's estate.

The problem of debts exceeding the value of the property left by the deceased and therefore becoming a burden for the heirs does not exist in English Law since the distribution of the estate by the personal representatives or administrators will only take place after all debts have been paid.

COMPULSORY HEIRS: THE LEGITIMA

The reserved fixed share of the estate that must by law go to certain people constitutes the *legitima*.[39] This share of the estate varies according to whether the deceased had descendants or other close relatives.

In those cases in which the deceased leaves descendants, the estate is divided into three equal parts: the first part is called *legítima* and by law must go to the compulsory heirs in equal shares; the second part is called *tercio de mejora*, this third must also go to the compulsory heirs but can be distributed unequally among them; the last part is the *tercio de libre disposicion* with which the testator can do as s/he wishes. For situations in which there are no descendants the parents and ascendants will get one third of the estate and the surviving spouse will get a usufruct of half the estate.[40]

Parents and older generations are entitled to half the estate if there are no descendants or surviving spouse. If there are no descendants nor older generation the surviving spouse is entitled to a usufruct of two thirds of the estate as his or her *legítima*.

Any disposition that ignores the *legítimas* of the *herederos legitimos* will be reduced insofar as it is necessary to satisfy the legitimate share that corresponds according to law.[41]

4.   INTESTATE SUCCESSION

Intestacy arises in the absence of a will or in the case of the defective naming of an heir. Rules relating to intestacy may therefore apply even if there is a will.[42]

---

[39] Art.806 CC.
[40] For an explanation on the right of usufruct see Ch.10, "The Law of Property", pp.263–4.
[41] The process of reducing this is called r*educcion de disposiciones inoficiosas*, Art.817 CC.
[42] Arts 658 and 912 CC.

In common with other civil law systems, Spanish succession law on intestacy is based on family relationships by blood or adoption.[43] It is a system of succession *gradum et ordinum* in which individuals are categorised according to the degree of closeness to the deceased so that in general the next of kin excludes the more distant relatives.[44]

The general rule is that of equality among relatives of the same degree. Among each group (*gradum*) the right of survivorship applies as they are placed in a special situation of co-ownership,[45] subject to the right of representation which allows certain relatives (i.e. grandchildren) to inherit if the relative of immediate degree (children) has predeceased. This succession is per stirpes.[46]

THE PRIORITY ORDER

There are three types of successors: relatives, the surviving spouse and the State.[47] The surviving spouse is entitled to a usufruct at the same time as other relatives.

The succession rights of the surviving spouse were improved after 1981[48] and he or she is now preferred to collateral relatives of the deceased in the order of succession.

Among relatives, succession takes place in lines, one excluding the other.[49] The first in the order of succession are descendants, followed by older generations. In the absence of these the surviving spouse will inherit and, in defect of a surviving spouse, collaterals (brothers or sisters of the deceased) are called to inherit. Within each grade the estate is divided per head in equal parts. In cases in which there is concurrency of different grades because of the right of representation the division takes place per stirpes. This is also the case if only grandchildren survive the testator.[50] When brothers of full blood concur with brothers of single blood the first will inherit twice the amount of the second.[51] The State will inherit when there are no relatives.[52]

---

[43] There is no difference between adoptive or biological filiation in the Code since the *Ley* of May 13, 1981, which incorporated the principles of equality of Arts 14 and 39 of the Spanish Constitution.

[44] With the exception of the widow/er who shares with descendants and ascendants. See below.

[45] See co-ownership, Ch.10, pp.269–270.

[46] Art.924 CC, *Derecho de representación*.

[47] Art.913 CC.

[48] *Ley de 13 de Mayo de 1981* which modifies Art.944 CC.

[49] Art.921 CC. The existence of relatives in one grade excludes the other grades except for the right of representation.

[50] Art.933 CC.

[51] Arts 949–951 CC.

[52] Arts 957 and 1023 CC.

The Spanish law of succession seems to prefer blood relatives to the surviving spouse. This is due to historical factors such as the agrarian traditional society where the Civil Code originated. In the 19th century it was thought that property should remain within the family and all blood relatives were preferred to the surviving spouse. This was partially changed after 1981 acknowledging the radical change in family relations in the last century. The new model of nuclear family demanded that the surviving spouse should inherit before collaterals, even if the law still favours descendants and older generations with whom the surviving spouse concurs with an usufruct over their inheritance.[53] The position of the surviving spouse in the law of succession, and, in particular on intestacy, needs to be seen in context with the rules of matrimonial property.[54]

In order to be entitled under the rules of intestacy the surviving spouse needs to have been married to the deceased at the time of his death. This means that he or she should have been legally married to the deceased at the time of death. The new drafting of Art.945 CC[55] eliminates the concept of "fault" that was present in the old law, which made a distinction between "guilty" and "non-guilty" parties in the context of separation and divorce. This has been superseded today; if the parties are legally or factually separated the surviving spouse is not entitled to succeed under the rules of intestacy, irrespective of whose "fault" it was that they separated. The same applies for those cases in which the parties are divorced.

5. TAXES ON INHERITANCE

The ISD, or *Impuesto sobre sucesiones y donaciones*[56] taxes inheritance, *inter vivos* donations and monies received as a beneficiary of a contract of life insurance.[57] It is a tax which is managed by the autonomous communities and therefore there are variations depending on where the property is situated and where the deceased (or donor) had its habitual residence.[58] In Spanish law there is not a

---

[53] Arts 944 and 945 CC.

[54] Matrimonial property regime. See Ch.11, "Family law", pp.297–300.

[55] According to the *Ley 15/2005 de modificación del Código Civil en materia de separación y divorcio*. See Ch.11, "Family Law", p 306–7.

[56] *Ley 29/1987* of December 18; and *Real Decreto 1629/1991* of November 8.

[57] Except if the beneficiary and the person who took out the policy are the same, as happens in certain cases.

[58] *Ley Orgánica 8/1980*, of September 22, *de Financiación de las CC.AA (Última modificación: Ley Orgánica 7/2001*, of December 27), *Ley 21/2001*, of December 27,

general and large tax free allowance per estate but rather different and smaller tax free allowances for the heirs. It is therefore very important to plan carefully who the beneficiaries of the property will be in order to maximise the allowances and benefits of the tax system. The tax free allowance applies to close relatives and these also benefit from a more generous system of taxation that those who are unrelated to the testator.[59] This tax applies to "inheritance"; this means the property that is gratuitously passed to the heir. The calculation is very complex as there are not only different tax free allowances for different people but different bands of taxation and percentages that apply depending on the relationship between the heir and the deceased, the amount of the gift and the pre-existing wealth of the beneficiary. For example, for gifts to parents, children, spouses and brothers and sisters there is a tax free allowance of €15,911 per person. Children under 21 further benefit from an allowance of €3,973 for each year if they are over 13 but under 21; uncles, cousins and nephews enjoy a tax free allowance of €7,995 each; all other relatives or beneficiaries do not benefit from any tax free allowance. In addition, it is possible to enjoy a further tax free allowance on the transfer of the family home to the spouse or children. For each group there are different tax bands and rates.

Professional advice is indispensable in order to plan the most tax efficient way of distributing the estate. This is particularly true for foreigners with property in Spain who may not be bound by the rules of Spanish succession law but they may fall foul of the taxation system by choosing to leave their property to somebody unrelated or by creating an institution unknown to Spanish law such as a trust which may potentially attract a very high tax liability. The notary will give an indication to the testator at the time of drafting the will as to the general tax liabilities that his dispositions may entail. He will, for example point out that leaving property to distant relatives or unrelated people may attract a tax as high as 70 per cent in some cases; but efficient tax planning requires the intervention of a specialised professional like a tax advisor.

---

por la que se regulan las medidas fiscales y administrativas del nuevo sistema de financiación de las Comunidades Autónomas de régimen común y Ciudades con Estatuto de Autonomía. Leyes 17/2002 a 31/2002 de 1 de Julio, específicas de Cesión de Tributos Estatales a cada CC.AA.
[59] For a general statement of the law, in English and Spanish see *www.aeat.es*, the Official Spanish Tax Office website, which has clear information and access to all legislation necessary to calculate tax.

6. PRIVATE INTERNATIONAL LAW RULES IN SUCCESSION MATTERS

All private matters that involve a foreign element are subject to the rules of Private International law or, as they are also known, the rules of the conflict of laws. These rules will determine which of the legal systems involved or connected to a particular legal situation is to regulate it. They do so by selecting what is called a "connecting factor". This connecting factor can vary from a personal connecting factor, i.e. nationality or domicile, to a real or geographical factor, like the place where real property is situated, the place where a contract was signed or the place where the goods were at the time of the accident. Once a connecting factor has been selected as the most suitable for the regulation of a particular legal situation private international law prescribes a "choice of law" rule for each type of legal matter. There are different choice of law rules for contract, tort, validity of marriages, divorce, filiation, wills, real estate or personal property matters.

The choice of law rule is a peculiar type of legal rule because it does not give a legal answer to a legal problem or scenario but points to the legal system whose substantive law rules will apply to the resolution of the matter.

In succession matters there are different possibilities of establishing choice of law rules. Some legal systems classify succession matters according to the nature of the property to be distributed and therefore divide succession between succession relating to immovable property or real estate and succession relating to movables or personal property. The former is usually subject to the *lex rei sitiae* (or law of the place where the property is situated); the latter can be subject to a different law, for example the law of the last domicile of the testator (the last personal law of the testator). This was the solution chosen by the Spanish doctrine and case law of the 19th century—pre-Civil Code—until the significant case of *Vazquez v Didier*,[60] which included for the first time succession of real property into the personal law of the deceased.[61]

When the Civil Code was drafted and approved in 1889 the solution chosen was that of a universal personal law to regulate all succession matters: the old Art.10 read:

---

[60] *Sentencia del TS* of November 6, 1867. In J. Gonzalez Campos y otros, *Derecho International Privado: Parte Especial*, p.540.
[61] Other cases in the same line: *Marti v Mart*, STS November 27, 1868, referring to a case of interregional law; *Martinez v De la Serna*, STS January 29, 1875, or *Choussant v Arjona* STS June 6, 1873. All in Gonzalez Campos y otros, *op. cit.* p.540.

> "Both legitimate and testamentary succession are regulated by the national law of the deceased whatever the nature of the property or the place whether it is situated. This national law will determine the validity of testamentary dispositions and the rules of intestacy."

It was thought that a territorial conception of succession will only promote unnecessary litigation and confusion between the parties in a country with a variety of *foral* laws.

In succession law the choice of law rules in Spain and England are, again, different and a legal phenomena called *renvoi* takes place. This is because English law establishes that succession of immovable property should take place according to the law of the place where the property is situated (in the case of an Englishman with property in Spain, Spanish law) while Spanish law adheres to the rule that all succession matters should be regulated according to the personal law of the deceased (in our previous example: English law). The content of Spanish and English succession law is very different as to restrictions on testamentary freedom and distribution of the estate in the case of intestacy which make the choice between one or the other legal system crucial.

From the point of view of Spanish law, this has been resolved by understanding that succession must be regulated just by one system of law and therefore rejecting the *renvoi* made by the English conflict of law rule. Those foreigners with real estate in Spain, can, in principle, dispose of it according to the rules of succession valid in the country of their nationality. However, we pointed out that the inheritance tax system works closely related to the succession rules and it may well be that it is clearly inefficient from the point of view of the tax to be paid to make use of the freedom of testament available to foreigners when disposing of their property. Foreigners who own property in Spain may also need to consider ease of enforcement of their will when drafting one and choosing the provisions of this. The faster and cheaper option is indeed to make a will in Spain, in front a Spanish notary, dealing only with the Spanish property.[62] The will can then be registered in the Central Wills Registry and the process of succession and devolution of the estate will take place in the same manner as that described for Spanish nationals. As to the content of the will, I said that it was possible for foreigners to dispose of their property according to their own national succession law. While this is

---

[62] Making sure that this will does not revoke any previous English wills, nor that any subsequent English will or changes to a previous English will revoke the Spanish will.

undoubtedly the case, it needs to be remembered that foreign law may need to be proved if any of the officials involved—either the notary, or the registrar when registration of new ownership is sought in the property register—does not know it.[63] The process of proving foreign law can be again, expensive and burdensome and it may just be more convenient to dispose of the Spanish property complying with the Spanish rules of succession as well as the formalities for the making of wills.

Registration and enforcement of foreign wills in Spain is possible. It is, again, a time-consuming and expensive procedure as all documentation, the will, the grant of probate and a certificate of law stating that the dispositions of the will are allowed by English law will need to be officially translated and certified with the *Apostilla de la Haya*.[64] It is also almost impossible to provide all documentation duly certified within the six months from the time of death that the Spanish tax authorities require for the liquidation of inheritance taxes.

---

[63] See the recent *Resolución* of the *Dirección General de los Registros y el Notariado* of March 1, 2005, whereby the Registrar in Denia refused to enter a change in ownership of a property by succession *mortis causa* of a British citizen until it was proved that the dispositions of the will were according to law. The will in this case had been authorised by the Notary of Denia who was party to the procedure requesting registration and challenging the registrar's refusal. The will did not make provision for the descendants of the testator and therefore differed substantially from Spanish succession law. The DGRN upheld the registrar's refusal to register until proof of foreign law and of the inexistence of a posterior English will was provided.

[64] Hague Convention of October 5, 1961, abolishing the requirement of authentication for foreign public documents.

Chapter Thirteen
Private international law

1. INTRODUCTION

The rules of private international law can be found in the Preliminary Title of the Civil Code, Arts 8–12. The area is of considerable interest as it determines which system of law will be applicable to any legal relationship or dispute of private law involving a foreign element. All those with property or commercial interests in Spain, with family relations across more than one country or just on holiday, will, at some point find it necessary to determine which system of law, among those connected to a particular legal relationship, is applicable.

Private international law as a discipline deals with three basic legal questions. First, it determines the court that has jurisdiction in the event of a dispute in a private matter involving a foreign element. Secondly, if the Spanish Court is competent to hear and decide the case it establishes which system of law will be applied by the court to the resolution of the dispute. The fact that the Spanish court is competent to decide upon a dispute for breach of contract does not imply that the Spanish law of contract is the law applicable to the resolution of the substantive issues of the dispute. Third and last, it establishes the rules for the recognition and enforcement of decisions of a foreign court or other official documents.

These questions are universal and each legal system deals with them with their own internal rules of private international law. Much harmonisation has taken place in the context of unifying jurisdictional rules with the signature of the Brussels and Lugano Conventions first and the European Council Regulation 44/2001[1] in the context of co-operation in civil matters. Progress has also been made in the harmonisation of choice of law rules with the signature of the Rome Convention.[2] The Hague Conference on Private International Law

---

[1] Council Regulation 44/2001 of December 22, 2000.
[2] Rome Convention on the choice of law on contractual obligations June 19, 1980, ratified by Spain by instrument of September 4, 1987.

has also contributed to this area with a number of important conventions signed under its auspices.[3]

The international jurisdiction of the Spanish courts and the recognition and enforcement of foreign decisions are dealt with in Ch.5.[4] We will, in this Chapter, concentrate on choice of law rules.

2.   GENERAL RULES OF PRIVATE INTERNATIONAL LAW

These are the general problems or questions of private international law and the responses provided by the Spanish legal system are similar to those of other countries with parallel legal traditions.

CLASSIFICATION OR CHARACTERISATION

The special nature of the choice of law rule requires that all matters get "classified" into a category in order to select a choice of law rule for that type of problem. There are choice of law rules for marriage, succession, contractual obligations, and extra-contractual obligations and so on. This could work relatively well if only one legal system was involved but problems arise because different legal systems have different types of rules and institutions to deal with their legal matters. Some countries, for example, do not have matrimonial property regimes and issues related to them will fall either under property, succession, or even personal effects of marriage. Another typical scenario is that of the formalities required for a valid marriage like the intervention of a certain official for persons belonging a religious faith, that may be classified as issues of substance or capacity under different legal systems.[5] Spanish law opts for the rule that classification of legal questions takes place always according to the lex fori, this is Spanish Law.[6]

---

[3] Visit the official site for list of all international conventions and work under way: *http://hcch.e-vision.nl/*.

[4] See Ch.5, pp.103–6.

[5] The typical example that most textbooks on the English conflict of law cite is *Ogden v Ogden* [1905], which concerned a French domiciliary who married in England without obtaining his parent's consent. The question was "was the consent of the parents" a formality—in which case the rule could be ignored because the marriage in England only needed to comply with the English formalities—or was the parents' consent a rule affecting the capacity to marry in which case it applied and made the marriage voidable. For a discussion of this case see any conflict of law textbook, for instance, Clarkson and Hill, *op. cit.* discuss it on pp.484–489.

[6] Art.12(1) CC, this is the solution chosen by most legal systems.

RENVOI

Renvoi presents various problems in private international law. In principle it is an exception to the general rule that a reference by the choice of law rule to a foreign system of law means a reference to the substantive law of that country on the matter because what renvoi does is to look at the foreign legal system as a whole, including the foreign choice of law rules. The problem with this approach arises due to the very different ways of "classifying" legal situations that different legal systems have. To this it is necessary to add the possibility that the foreign choice of law rule will point to yet another country making it necessary to decide when to stop looking at the new country's law as a whole. The answer to these issues is complex. Most legal systems opt for a total rejection of renvoi. Civil law systems accept in certain situations what is called single renvoi or *reenvío de retorno*, which occurs when the foreign choice of law points to the original country as the system that will govern the substance of the matter. Even those countries that accept renvoi limit it to accepting the choice of law of the country first selected by the original choice of law, even if this means looking at the substantive law of a third country.

Spanish law accepts single renvoi or *reenvío de retorno* in Art.12(2) of the Civil Code. Remission to a foreign law is understood as made to the rules of substantive law not the foreign conflict of laws. The only exception is when the *renvoi* is to Spanish law. An example of a case when the operation of this rule can operate is succession of a UK national with real property in Spain, who dies intestate in Spain. The Spanish conflict of law rule for succession (Art.9(8)) indicates that the personal law of the deceased regulates all aspects of succession whatever the nature of the property and the country where the property is situated. This means that according to the Spanish conflict of law rule the personal law is English law. The application of Art.12(2) of the Civil Code points to the substantive rules of intestacy of English law for the distribution of the estate. However the English conflict of law rule establishes that succession of immovable property should be done according to the law of the country where the property is situated,[7] in this case Spain. The English choice of law rule "returns" the case to the dominion of Spanish law. This is a typical case of renvoi and a case that is acceptable according to the Civil Code. Spanish succession rules are substantially and materially very different from the English rules.[8] We

---

[7] See Clarkson & Hill, *op.cit.* pp.477–79.

have dealt with this matter in the Chapter on Succession where I indicated that despite the acceptability of renvoi in this scenario, the Spanish *Dirección General de los Registros y el Notariado* has established a preference for the application of the principle of "unity of succession" of Art.9(8), allowing foreign testators to dispose of immovable property situated in Spain according to the substantive rules of their national law.[9]

PUBLIC POLICY: ORDEN PÚBLICO

All countries have a general exception of public policy that allows them not to apply a foreign law if this is contrary to the public policy of the forum. The difficulties arise in determining what exactly constitutes the *orden público* at any particular time as the concept of *orden público* is an indeterminate legal concept that changes with time and adapts to social beliefs.

The rule that contains the exception of public policy is found in two different Articles of the Civil Code: Arts 8(2) and 12(3). The first of these Articles states that Spanish public laws apply to all those in Spanish territory. By public laws the doctrine and the Supreme Court understand criminal laws, constitutional laws, administrative law—including the laws of the local and autonomic administration—and labour and social security law dispositions.[10] Procedural law is also the law of the forum.[11] The second Article (12(3) CC) excludes the application of foreign law if this is contrary to the "*orden público*". The determination of what is the *orden público* is left open in order to be able to incorporate the different changes in perception between the imperativity of certain rules. Some authors have made a difference between what they called the *orden público interno* and the *orden público internacional*.[12] The first will be integrated by all those mandatory rules that Spanish citizens cannot derogate by private agreement. It will include matters such as when majority of age is reached. This cannot be changed privately by a Spanish national but a foreigner can have a different legal age and this will be recognised in Spain. The *orden público internacional* will be much more restricted than the internal one and will

---

[8] See Ch.12, "Succession", pp.322–4.
[9] For a general commentary on this see, Ch.12, "Succession", above and *www.notariosyregistradores/leyesextranjeras/sucesiones*.
[10] See Castán Tobeñas, *Derecho Civil Español, Comun y Foral*, Tomo I, Vol.I, p.673.
[11] Art.8(2) CC derogated by Art.3 LEC.
[12] Castán Tobeñas, *Derecho Espanol Comun y Foral, Tomo I, Introduccion y Parte General*, p.672.

only include those matters that really affect the nature of the fundamental institutions of the Spanish system, for example a contract of domestic services for life is unacceptable as it is too close to slavery. It is left to the discretion of the judge to resolve for each case whether a particular provision of foreign law is acceptable or must be rejected because of this exception.

FRAUD OF LAW

It will be fraudulent to use a conflict of law rule with the purpose of evading the application of an imperative rule of Spanish law. This explicit reference to fraud was included when the *Titulo Preliminar* of the Civil Code was changed in 1974. It could be argued that the general rule of Art.4 of the code, *fraude a la ley*, could have been applied but most authors celebrate the introduction of a reference within the private international law rules section due to the special nature of the problem and the facilities that the choice of law rules offer to defraud the application of mandatory rules. The sanction for those who resort to fraud to avoid application of the imperative rules is the application of those rules that the parties were trying to elude. Nothing is said about the validity (or not) of the fraudulent act and it is understood that they stand in so far as they are not contradictory with the mandatory rules of imperative application.

APPLICABLE LAW

The rules of applicable law or the "choice of law" rule is a peculiar type of legal rule as it does not provide a substantive regulation to a legal problem. The "choice of law" rule operates by identifying and classifying a legal situation or dispute in the different categories available in the legal system of the court hearing a case and then choosing a connecting factor that will point out to the system of law whose substantive law rules will provide the regulation for the private legal situation that is being considered. Choice of law rules are not neutral, and are formulated to suit the particular circumstances of a country and that country's legal culture. For example countries integrated by various legal systems such as the United States or Spain with its different systems of civil and *foral* law will opt for a different choice of law rules from countries with unitary systems of law such as France. Other circumstances also play a role in this area. Spain, for example, has traditionally been a country of emigration and it was thought that giving those emigrants a personal law based on nationality (rather than domicile) would protect them and create a permanent link with Spain. Nationality is more difficult to change or obtain that domicile.[13] However the integration of Spain in the European Community first, and then the larger European Union, and the changes of the last part of the 19th century towards a more mobile and cosmopolitan society with increased personal and commercial links across countries, has reduced the scope of the personal law in the successive revisions of the Preliminary Title of the Civil Code to include more mobile and realistic connectors such as "habitual residence" or "choice by the parties".[14]

The personal law of individuals is the law of their nationality and it applies to the determination of their legal capacity, to any issues of civil status, to the rights and obligations within the family and to succession.[15]

MARRIAGE

Marriage is governed by the common personal law of the spouses at the time of celebration. In the absence of a common personal law of either this should be chosen by the parties by public document before the celebration of the marriage, or if the parties have not made such election by the law of the common habitual residence, it must be made immediately after the celebration of marriage. If there is not a place of common habitual residence the law of the place of celebration will apply.

Separation and divorce are regulated by the common national law of the spouses at the time of the presentation of the action; if there is no common nationality by the law of the common habitual residence or if the spouses had different habitual residences by Spanish law, the Spanish Courts have jurisdiction to hear and decide the case.[16]

This means that two Spanish nationals habitually resident in a foreign country who married in that country could resort to Spanish law,[17] which may be relevant particularly now that the law of divorce in Spain has been modified.[18] The second part of the rule applies

---

[13] Think for instance of the concept of domicile in the English private international law which is linked both to factual and intentional factors rather than to administrative requirements like nationality. This may have created uncertainty as to which law was applicable.

[14] This is particularly true following the modification of Family Law of 1981 and the introduction of separation and divorce in Spain, see below.

[15] Art.9(1) CC.

[16] Art.107 CC.

[17] Obviously, if they first secure the jurisdiction of the Spanish Court, which they could do by submission, Art.22(2) LOPJ. See Ch.5, pp.103–6.

[18] In effect with the introduction of the *Ley* 15/2005 the parties need only to have been married three months in order to request a divorce and this divorce is devoid of any cause or reason. See Ch.11, p.303.

when the spouses, one of them a Spanish national, the other not, move after their marriage to a country with very restrictive or non-existent divorce laws, where they fix their habitual residence. Since one of them is not a Spanish national, they cannot resort to the first rule of common nationality, nor can they resort to the last rule because it only applies to those cases in which each spouse has his or her habitual residence in different countries.

It appears that these rules do not give a choice to the parties as to which law they can resort to but constitutes a taxonomic system for each of the possible scenarios.[19]

The economic effects of marriage get a separate treatment which gives the option of any agreement relating to the constitution, modification or substitution of the regime of economic effects of marriage to be valid if they are in conformity with the law that governs the personal effects of marriage (to be determined by the second part, as above) or with the law of the nationality or the habitual residence of any of the spouses at the time of the agreement.[20]

ADOPTION AND GUARDIANSHIP

The new Law on Adoption LO 1/1996 of January 15, changed the content of paras 4 and 5 of Art.8. The aim of the change was to give priority to the law of the child or the person to be adopted. In matters related to adoption, Spanish law will be applicable if the adoption is made in by a Spanish Judge. The national law of the person to be adopted is taken into account on matters referred to his consent and capacity.

Guardianship is also regulated by the national law of the ward but Spanish law will be applicable in respect of all urgent and protective measures to be taken in respect of minors or incapacitated persons abandoned in Spanish territory irrespective of their nationalities.[21]

SUCCESSION

Succession will be regulated by the national law of the deceased at the time of death whatever the nature of the property—real or personal—or the country where the property is situated. If the national law changes from the time of making a will to the time of death all dispositions made under the previous national law will remain valid but the will shall be adapted in order to take into account modification in

---

[19] Gonzalez Campos et al. *op. cit*. pp.402–50.
[20] Art.9(3) CC.
[21] Art.8(6) CC.

respect of any compulsory shares (*legítimas*) that may become applicable according to the last national law.[22]

The rights of the surviving spouse will be regulated by the law which regulates the personal effects of marriage (Art.9(2)) always taking into account the compulsory shares of descendants (*legítimas*) which will be calculated according to the last national law.

CONTRACT

The regulation of international contracts is marked in most legal systems by the principle of parties' autonomy that gives the parties to a contract a considerable degree of freedom to enter into whatever contractual relationships they wish and to subject those relationships to whatever law or laws they think most suitable for their commercial or private interests. In today's largely liberalised market economy this principle is justified by the trend towards minimum intervention from the State in private commercial matters.[23] It is also more efficient to leave the parties to choose the law that they want to regulate their contractual relationship since in this way they can adapt it to their needs or chose a system with provisions appropriate to these and reduce the likelihood of going to court over a dispute concerning this legal relationship.[24] This freedom of choice of law must be mitigated, however, with the also increasing awareness of the legal and real inequality of the parties and the need for state intervention in certain areas such as consumer protection or employment contracts. The control of the parties' free choice can done in two ways: by subjecting these specific types of contracts to a different rule of conflict[25] or by maintaining the parties' total freedom but adding the special state regulation as a rule of police or a mandatory rule applicable in addition to the provisions of the law chosen by the parties.

The second solution is the solution chosen by the Rome Convention which in Art.3 states the principle of freedom of choice

---

[22] Art.9(8) CC, see also Ch.12, "Succession", pp.322–4, which has a section on private international law.

[23] Unless the protection of consumers is necessary. See Ch.9, "Contract", above, p.233.

[24] This was first argued by Professor Kahn Freund and referred to as the, "prophylactic value of allowing and encouraging parties' autonomy". Cited by Virgos Soprano in Gonzalez Campos y otras, *op. cit.*, p.204.

[25] See below, Arts 5 and 6 Rome Convention and the different forums afforded in jurisdictional matters by the EC Council Regulation 44/2001 Art.5.

[26] This choice must be expressed or implied with reasonable certainty and is subject to the provisions of Arts 5, "certain consumer contracts" and 6, "individual contracts of employment".

of applicable law by the parties[26] limited by the mandatory provisions of an otherwise wholly connected country,[27] the mandatory rules relating to consumer protection of Art.5 and to individual contracts of employment in Art.6.

The Spanish Art.10(5) sets a limit on the freedom of choice by the parties: the chosen law needs to have some type of connection with the contract. If there is no choice or if this choice is not valid—for example because they choose the law of a country with no connection—there is a system of alternative possible connections, namely, the national common law of the parties if any, or the common habitual residence, or if none of these are present the law of the place of completion of the contract. Much criticism can be made of this type of connection which reflects the commercial realities of an era now bygone by effects of the rapid changes imposed by electronic commerce and distance contracting. These rules, it must be remembered, are of very limited application since they will only apply to contracts entered into before 1993.

The Rome Convention chooses a different route from the old Art.10(5) of the Civil Code, if there is no choice or if the choice is, for whatever reason, not valid, the contract shall be regulated by the law of the country with which the contract has the most real and substantial connection.

NON-CONTRACTUAL OBLIGATIONS

The drafting of an instrument parallel to the Rome Convention's for the regulation of the law applicable to non-contractual obligations has been the subject matter of a long and fruitless debate. To date no such instrument has been agreed and it looks unlikely that it will in the near future. Spanish private international law chooses the law of the place where the event took place as the applicable law to extra-contractual obligations in Art.9(1). This choice is not uncommon in comparative law and the issue is often one of determining where such a place is: where the facts took place or where the effects are suffered. In jurisdictional matters the debate is resolved by giving the victim a choice between the two.[28] The place of the tort or the place where the tort took place has progressively lost favour though in some countries in favour of looking at what are called the "cumulative interests

---

[27] This is what is known as a "relatively international contract" this is, a contract in which all elements are connected with one country but it has a foreign choice of jurisdiction and or a foreign choice of law clause. See Gonzalez Campos y otros, *op. cit.* p.209.

[28] See Art.5(3) of the Brussels Regulation and ECJ.

of the parties", famously upheld in *Babcock v Jackson*,[29] on the basis that in some occasions the place where a tort takes place is purely fortuitous.

In fact it is so difficult to give an ideal and unitary choice of law for each and every possible case that countries where judicial freedom is limited have opted for passing ad hoc rules for different situations. The most relevant are road traffic accidents, product liability and patrimonial responsibility of the public administration.

Road traffic accidents

This is an important matter for everybody who drives or travels as a passenger in a motor vehicle in Spain. Spain ratified the Hague Convention on the Applicable Law to Road Traffic Accidents of May 4, 1971, in 1987, whose main objective is to determine the civil responsibility of those involved in a road traffic accident. The applicable law will regulate the requirements for liability and the measure of damages, mitigating circumstances, limitations, exoneration of liability and transferability of compensation (for example to the family if the victim is dead). The importance of this is clear: damages and compensation for physical injury vary widely from one country to another. In countries like Spain where tourism amounts to millions of visitors per year it is unavoidable that some of these tourists will find themselves involved in a road traffic accident. This accident may involve another tourist, perhaps even someone from his own country, or it may involve a Spanish national. It is obviously purely fortuitous whether the accident happens between people of the same or different nationalities.

The Convention chooses the *lex loci delicti commissi* (the law of the place of the accident) as the applicable law. To this general rule there are certain exceptions allowing the application of the law of the country of registration of the vehicle in certain cases, namely when there is a special and strong connection between this later state, the victim and the parties involved in the accident. If only one vehicle is involved it is possible to apply the law of the country of registration of the vehicle in respect of the driver, the owner and the passengers if these are not resident in the country where the accident took place (Art.4 Convention). If there is a plurality of victims, the applicable law will be determined separately in respect of each of them. If more than one vehicle is involved in the accident and these are registered in different states, the law of the place where the accident took place will be applicable to all of them.

---

[29] 12 NY 2d 473 (1963). The decision was reported in England: [1963] 2 Lloyd's Rep 286.

It must be noted that if the author and/or victim are habitually resident in a country but the accident takes place in another and the car is a hired car registered in the country where the accident took place then the law of this country will be applicable law despite the common habitual residence of both driver and victim.

Product liability

The Hague Convention of 1973[30] regulates product liability for both natural and industrial products when there is no direct relationship between the manufacturer and the consumer that could command any contractual liability.

The criteria chosen by the convention departs from the *lex loci delicti commissi*, since rules of health and safety in the manufacturing and distribution of products of both manufacturer's country and the final user or consumer may have certain relevance, making the actual place where the harm occurred perhaps merely fortuitous. The rules of choice of law on product liability must be read together with the jurisdiction forums granted by the Brussels and Lugano Conventions and the EC Council Regulation.[31] Arts 4, 5, 6 and 7 of the Convention on product liability provide a system of alternative laws. First, the law of the country where the harm took place will be applicable if this is also the country where either the victim has his habitual residence or the main responsible person has its principal establishment or where the product was acquired by the victim. If none of the above is applicable the victim has the choice between the law of the state where the manufacturer has its principal place of business or the law of the state where the harmful event took place.

The application of the law of the country of habitual residence of the victim or the law of the country where the harm was suffered is restricted by Art.7 by what is known as a "reasonable expectation clause". This clause means that the manufacturer can prove that he could not reasonably expect that his product/s would have been sold in the country where the victim is habitually resident or where the harmful event took place. This, of course, is more complex today due to the increase in e-commerce. Can somebody say that they could not reasonable expect to have their products sold wherever in the world if these are available on the internet? On the other hand, is it reasonable to expect a manufacturer to be responsible according to each and every national law?

---

[30] Ratified by Spain in 1998, BOE January 26, 1989.
[31] Art.5(3) BC, LC and BR.

Patrimonial responsibility of the Public Administration

Damage to property or rights of individuals generates a duty of compensation by the Public Administration according to Art.106(2) CE. If the damage takes place in Spanish territory and is caused by Spanish public services the Spanish courts will be competent and Spanish law will be applicable to determine the measure of damages as the lex loci delicti commissi. However, it is possible that the damage may take place abroad. In the later case, because of the principle of immunity of public international law, actions of diplomatic and consular missions will be judged not in the state where the harm took place but in the state that they represent and the applicable law will not be the lex loci delicti but the lex fori.

FORMALITIES

Article 11 of the Civil Code contains a general rule on formalities establishing that the formalities of contracts, testaments and other legal acts are those of the place where they take place. However in order to preserve the validity of these acts even if they don't meet the formalities of the place where they took place Art.11 provides a series of alternative laws whose formalities can be met by a contract, testament or other legal act and still be valid. These other laws are the law applicable to the substantive issues or the personal law of both or any of the parties.

In fact the principle of *favor negottii* obscures the fact that it is the law that regulates the substance that of major importance because as Art.11(2) reiterates,

"if the law regulating the substance of a contract requires any special formalities for its validity these will always be enforced even though the contract is celebrated in a foreign country".

In reality we are looking here at constitutive formalities, for example those required for the creation of certain real rights.[32]

---

[32] In Spanish law only mortgages need to be documented by public deed in order to be constituted. See Chapter 10, "Property", p.266.

3. APPLICATION OF THE DIFFERENT CIVIL LAW REGIMES IN THE SPANISH TERRITORY

INTERNAL CONFLICT OF LAWS

Spain is one of those states in which more than one system of civil law co-exist. These civil law systems are the systems of *Derecho foral* of the different territories and the civil laws developed by the Parliaments of those autonomous communities with power to do so.[33]

The application of common civil law (the general civil law found in the Civil Code) or a special *foral* law is determined by the criteria of "*vecindad civil*". *Vecindad civil* can be translated as civil vicinity and amounts to being resident or domiciled in one of the territories where *foral* law applies. All Spanish citizens have either *vecindad civil comun*, and are subject to the rules of the Civil code, or *vecindad civil foral*.

The *vecindad civil* can be acquired at birth or later in life by a change from the original *vecindad*:

- At birth; the child has the *vecindad* of the parents. In cases of adoption the person adopted acquires the *vecindad* of the adopter. If the parents or adopters have different *vecindad* (each in different territories of *foral* law, or one common and the other *foral*) the child acquires the *vecindad* of the parent who determines the affiliation, or the *vecindad* of the place of birth or, the *vecindad* of common civil law.
- By choice; children can choose once they reach 14 years and up to a year from the date of emancipation, the *vecindad* of either of their parents or the *vecindad* of the place of birth. The spouses can at any time chose the *vecindad* of the other spouse although marriage itself does not alter the *vecindad* of either of the spouses.
- Change of vicinity; it is possible to acquire a different *vecindad* by continuous residence of two years in the territory subject to any particular *vecindad* (*foral* or common) by making a declaration opting for that vicinity at the Civil Registry. Continuous residence of 10 years changes the *vecindad civil*

---

[33] See Ch.1, p.22, *Derecho Foral*, and Ch.2, p.49, "Autonomous communities", and *Compilación de Cataluña, Compilación de Baleares, Compilación de Aragón, Compilación de Navarra, Ley de Derecho Foral del Pais Vasco* and *Ley de Derecho Civil de Galicia*. For a complete list of the legislation in civil matters of each of these territories see Fernandez Urzinagui, *Código Civil Espanol, (edición anotada* 2002, Ed Aranzadi) p.55.

unless the individual expresses his desire to keep his original *vecindad civil*. This declaration also must be made in the Civil Registry.

- Foreigners that acquire Spanish nationality must opt between the *vecindad* of the place of residence, of the place of birth, of their spouse or of their parents if the later two are applicable.[34]

If it is impossible to determine the *vecindad* civil of a person it will be assumed that he has the *vecindad* of the place of birth.[35]

The systems of *derecho foral* in Spain do not cover all aspects of civil law, nor are all of them developed to the same degree. But for those areas that are regulated by special or *foral* law it is necessary to apply a rule of choice of law similar to those seen when deciding between the different systems of foreign law potentially applicable to any situation.

The rule of conflict contained in Art.16 of the Civil Code determines that the personal law is determined by the *vecindad foral*—which in this context operates as parallel to the criteria of nationality chosen for foreign or international conflicts of law. Conflicts of law are resolved by the rules of choice of law of Arts 9, 10, 11 and 12 with some exceptions.

Renvoi, classification and public order are inapplicable. Certain peculiarities are recognised for the rights of the surviving spouse according to the *foral* law of Aragón.[36] The effects of marriage between Spanish citizens will be regulated by the law indicated by the application of Art.9; if the laws of one or the other spouse indicated that a matrimonial regime of separation is applicable, the rules of the Civil Code in respect of separation of wealth are applicable.[37]

---

[34] Art.15 CC.
[35] Art.14 was drafted according to the *Ley* 11/1990 of *reforma del Código Civil*.
[36] See Art.16(2) CC.
[37] See Ch.11, p.301.

Glossary

abandono del hogar	desertion
abogado	a practising lawyer in charge of providing advice for, and the defence of, clients
abogado de oficio	a duty solicitor
abogados del estado	body of lawyers advising, defending and representing the State and the Public Administration
abogados en ejercicio	practising lawyers
acción de reembolso o reintegro	right of reimbursement
acción de regreso	right of repayment of part of a debt between co-debtors
acción reivindicatoria	claim for the declaration of title to land
accreedor	creditor
acta de notoriedad	notarial act that declares certain widely known facts as representing the truth
acto administrativo	administrative act
actor/demandante	plaintiff
Acuerdos	agreements
acusador particular	a private prosecutor
acusador popular	a "popular" prosecutor
Administración del Estado	Central State Administration
Administraciones Autónomicas	Autonomous Communities' Public Administrations
Administraciones locales	local public administrations
agentes de la construcción	all those involved in the building process
albacea	executor of a will
allanamineto	the acceptance of plaintiff's claim by the defendant
anotación preventiva de la demanda	precautionary inscription of a claim in public registries
antecentes de hecho	summary of facts
Apostilla de la Haya	*Hague Apostille* or certification for foreign documents

arancel	the fixed fee charged by *procuradores*
arras confirmatorias	deposit paid to confirm intention to enter into a contract
arras penales	deposit or earnest money that will be lost if the contract is not entered into by a certain date
aseguramiento de bienes litigiosos	attachment of the property in litigation
atestados policiales	Police reports about crimes
Audiencia Nacional	Court with jurisdiction over the national territory in certain criminal, administrative and employment matters
audiencia previa al juicio	pre-trial hearing
Audiencia Provincial	a Higher Court with seat on the capital of the province
auto	a decision of the judge ending the proceedings without deciding about the subject matter
autonomía de la voluntad	freedom of contract
beneficio de justicia gratuita	legal aid
bienes	property that can be appropriated and has an economic value
bienes de dominio publico	public property of the state put to public use
bienes de uso publico	public property of the state open to general public use
bienes fungibles	consumable moveable property
bienes immuebles	immoveable property
bienes infungibles	non-consumable moveable property
bienes muebles	moveable property
bienes patrimoniales	private property of the State
bufetes, despachos	law firms
calificaciones	submissions
calificaciones definitivas	definitive submissions
careo	confrontation, means of evidence in criminal proceedings
carga de la prueba	burden of proof
Cartas pueblas	the laws granted by the King to Christian settlers on territories bordering with the Muslims
catastro	Administrative Register of immovable property for tax purposes
Catedrático	university professor
capacidad legal	legal capacity
capacidad natural	natural capacity of individuals
capitulaciones matrimoniales	notarial contracts for the regulation of the economic affairs of a marriage

casación	annulment, cassation
caso fortuito	unforeseen events
caución sustitutoria	deposit of monetary amount to cover an eventual court decision
causa	consideration, function of the contract
cédula de habitabilidad	building inspection certificate
certificación	certificate
citación cautelar	cautionary summons
clase de asiento	type of entry in the Land Registry
Código de Comercio	Commercial Code
Código Penal	Criminal Code
Colegio de Abogados	Bar Association
Colegio de Notarios	Professional Association of Notaries
Colegios profesionales	professional associations
Comisión de Codificación	a special commission created for the drafting of the different codes
Comisiones	the commissions (in Congress)
competencia funcional	the jurisdiction to hear appeals and enforce judgments of a given court
complejos inmobiliarios privados	communities of detached villas
comunidad de propietarios	community of owners in cases of *Propiedad Horizontal*
Comunidades Autonomas	Autonomous Communities
Concordat	Convention between the State and the Vatican
condiciones	conditions
condiciones resolutorias	future uncertain events upon which a contract ceases to have effect
condiciones suspensiva	future uncertain events upon which a contract starts having effect
conflicto de atribuciones	conflict or dispute between constitutional organs of the State as to the extent of their powers
conflicto de competencia	conflict of powers between the State and the Autonomous Communities
conflicto en defensa de la autonomía local	procedure in the Constitutional Court for the protection of local autonomy from interference by the State or Autonomous Community
congruencia	when the judgment must meet the petitions of the parties
Consejeros	advisers
Consejo de Ministros	the Council of Ministers
Consejo General de la Abogacia	the General Council of Lawyers
Consejo General del Poder Judicial	the General Council of the Judiciary; the government body of the judiciary

consentimiento	consent
constitución	a special type of law passed by the king (historic law)
contencioso-administrativo	judicial procedure against the public administration
contestación a la demanda	answer (to a complaint)
convenio regulador	separation or divorce agreement
Corporaciones públicas	public corporations
Cort General	Parliament in Catalonia consisting of nobles, churchmen and the representatives of the cities
cosas	chattels or things
costas	costs originated by the proceedings
costumbre	custom
cuantía del litigio	the amount of the claim in civil proceedings
cuerpo del delito	the object of the crime
cuotas	shares in property
cuestión de inconstitucionalidad	procedure in constitutional court challenging the compliance of legislation with the Constitution
culpa o negligencia	fault or negligence
daño emergente	consequential damage or loss
daños y perjuicios	damages
deberes jurídicos	legal duties
decisión	a judicial decision (see *sentencia*)
declaración de herederos	declaration of heirs
declinatoria	a dilatory exception in civil proceedings for denouncing lack of territorial or international jurisdiction
decretos	by-laws
decretos legislativos	a statute made by the executive by delegation from Parliament
decretos-leys	a type of statute made by the executive in special circumstances
Defensor del pueblo	the Ombudsman
delitos	crimes
delitos graves	serious crimes
delitos menos graves	less serious offences
demanda	a complaint; document opening civil proceedings
demanda de reconvención	counterclaim
denuncia	information or complaint
denuncia falsa	false information or complaint
Derecho	law
derecho	right
Derecho administrativo	administrative law
Derecho civil	civil law (private law)

Derecho común o general	common law (as opposed to regional—*foral* law)
derecho constitucional	Constitutional law
derecho de cosas	law of things or law of property
derecho de obligaciones	Law of Obligations
derecho del trabajo	Labour law
derecho financiero y tributario	Tax law
derecho internacional privado	Private International Law
derecho internacional público	Public International Law
Derecho penal	criminal law
Derecho procesal civil	civil procedure law
derechos forales	regional customary laws
derogación expresa	the express derogation of laws
derogación implícita	the implied derogation of laws
desamortización	the compulsory sale of Church-owned property in Spain in the 18th century
desestimar	rejection of a claim by the court
despacho colectivo	partnerships of a maximum of 20 lawyers
desviación de poder	deviation of power
detención	arrest
deudor	debtor
días multa	new type of calculating monetary punishment introduced by the Criminal Code of 1995 that allows for personal circumstances to be taken into account
dispensa legal de nacionalidad	legal dispensation of nationality
Dictamen	the draft legislation presented by the commissions
Diputación	the organ of government of the provinces
Diputados	Deputies; members of the lower chamber of Parliament
disposiciones transitorias	transitional law
doctrina legal	doctrinal writings
Documento Nacional de Identidad	identity card
Dret Comú	the *ius commune* in Catalan
ejecucion forzosa	enforcement of court decisions
ejecutivalo	enforceable
El Congreso de los Diputados	Congress (Lower Chamber of Parliament)
El Pleno	the plenary session (in Congress)
El Senado	Senate (Upper Chamber of Parliament)
embargo preventivo	attachment
emplazamiento	a summons to appear at the proceedings on a certain date

encabezamiento	heading on a document
equidad	equity
escrito de calificación provisional	the submission of a report to the judge by the prosecution, requesting the presentation of evidence and provisional conclusions
escritura pública	public deed
Escuela Diplomática	the Diplomatic School
establecimientos de cumplimiento de penas	ordinary prisons
establecimientos especiales	special prisons
establecimientos preventivos	remand prisons
estado de sitio, alarma o excepción	state of siege, alarm or exception
Estatuto de Áutonomía	the supreme law of the Autonomous Communities
Estatuto de los Parlamentarios	the status of Members of Parliament
estimar	estimate the petition on the merits
excepciones dilatorias	dilatory exceptions
expediente	dossier, file, report
expediente de domini	special procedure for the determination of ownership of unregistered land
falsa causa	fundamental error on which consent based
falta de jurisdicción	the lack of jurisdiction of a court
falta de personalidad del demando	the defendant's lack of capacity to stand in court
falta de personalidad del demandante	the lack of capacity of the plaintiff to stand in court
faltas	minor offences
fase de alegaciones	allegations
fase de enmiendas	the period of amendments (for legislation)
fase de instrucción	the first stage of criminal proceedings in which the judge directs investigations
fase de plenario	an oral trial in criminal proceedings
fase de prueba	the evidentiary stage
fianza	bail
finca	plot of land in the Land Registry
Fiscal General del Estado	the Attorney-General
Fiscales	public prosecutors
Fiscalía ante el Tribunal Constitucional	the public prosecution office at the Constitutional Court
folio real	principle of land registration that involves the registration of each plot on a different page or file
foral	regional

formalización de objeto litigioso	statement of the grounds for litigation
fraude a la ley	fraud of law
frutos civiles	interest, royalties or rent
Fueros Municipales	the municipal laws of medieval Spain
Fuerza de ley	the position of certain laws in the hierarchy of sources
fuerza mayor	force majeure
fundamentos de derecho	legal principles applicable to the facts specified in the *demanda*
Furs	the *fuero* in Catalan
goce	power of enjoyment
hechos	facts
hechos extintivos	mitigating circumstances
hechos impedivitos	mitigating circumstances
herederos	heirs
herederos legítimos	compulsory heirs
Hermandades	associations of neighbours in the cities of the Basque country with certain legislative capacity
hipotecas	mortgages
homologado	approved, endorsed, recognised
impuesto	tax
impuesto sobre actos juridicos documentados	tax payable for use of public documents
impuesto sobre bienes inmuebles	Real Estate Tax
impuesto sobre el valor añadido	value added tax
impuesto sobre sucesiones y donaciones	inheritance tax
impuesto sobre transmisiones patrimoniales	tax on inter-vivos patrimonial transfers
Inciativa Popular	popular initiative (for the elaboration of laws)
infracción de ley	a mistake in law (one of the grounds for *casación*)
inmatriculacion	first entry of a *finca* in the Land registry
inspección ocular	visual investigation by the judge
Instituciones Públicas	public institutions
instrucción	investigations by judge
interdicto de adquirir	an injunction granting possession
interdicto de obra nueva	an injunction against new buildings
interdicto de obra ruinosa	an order for the demolition of an old, dangerous building
interdicto de retener o recobrar	an injunction restoring possession
interdictos	injunctions
interpretación auténtica	the interpretation of a law by Parliament
interpretación usual	the interpretation of a law by the judge

investidura parlamentaria	the declaration by which Parliament invests its confidence in the President
jueces	judges
jueces temporales	temporary judges
Juez	judge
Juez de gardia	duty judge
Juez de lo Penal	a judge in the Criminal Court
Juez de Paz	Justice of the Peace
Juez de Vigilancia Penitenciaria	prison judge
Juez Instructor	investigating judge in criminal proceedings
juicio cambiario	summary proceedings for the enforcement of bills of exchange
juicio de cognición	the procedure (civil) for small claims
juicio de faltas	proceedings for less serious crimes
juicio de mayor cuantía	the procedure (civil) for large claims
juicio de menor cuantía	the procedure (civil) for lessor claims
juicio ejecutivo	a special summary procedure for the enforcement of monetary liquidated claims
juicio oral	oral civil proceedings
juicio ordinario	ordinary civil proceedings
juicio verbal	the oral procedure for minor claims
Junta de Portavoces	the Assembly of Representatives (in Congress)
Juntas	see *hermandades*
Jurados	jurors
jurídico	legal
jurisidicción	jurisdiction
jurisidicción por razón del objeto	jurisdiction of the court based on the subject-matter of the dispute
jurisprudencia	case law of the Supreme Court
Jurisprudencia constitucional	constitutional case-law
Jurista	jurist, lawyer
Justicia	justice
Justicia Mayor	a special institution of Aragón with some resemblances to the Ombudsman
justo	just, fair
juzgado	a unipersonal court
juzgado central de lo penal	Central Criminal Court
juzgados centrales de instrucción	the courts in charge of the investigation of certain crimes
juzgados contencioso-administrativos	the courts for administrative matters
juzgados de familia	courts of first instance in charge of family matters (civil)
juzgados de lo mercantil	commercial courts

juzgados de lo penal	criminal courts
juzgados de lo social	courts for employment matters
juzgados de menores	juvenile courts
juzgados de primera instancia	First Instance Courts
juzgados de primera instancia e instrucción	Courts of First Instance in civil and criminal cases
La Jurisprudencia	case law of the Supreme Court
Las Cortes Generales	Parliament
laudos arbitrales	arbitral awards
legítima	part of the estate that by law must go to the compulsory heirs
lesión	damage suffered
Letrados del Estado	lawyers who represent the State and the Public Administration
ley	law, statute
Ley Cambiaria y del Cheque	Bills of Exchange and Cheque Act
Ley de Bases	law drawing the main guidelines to which subsequent legislation should adhere to
Ley de Enjuiciamiento Civil	Civil Procedure Act
Ley del Mercado de Valores	Stock Market Act
Ley de Matrimonio Civil	Civil Marriage Act
Ley de Sociedades Anónimas	Companies Act
Ley ordinaria	an ordinary law or statute approved by Parliament
Leyes	laws, statutes
leyes de presupuestos	general budgetary laws of the State
Leyes Orgánicas	"Organic" laws—a special type of legislation
Leyes temporales	provisional laws
libertad provisional	freedom on bail
licenciado en derecho	Bachelor of Law
licencias matrimoniales	authorisations from husband to wife to enter into contracts (before 1975)
lucro cesante	loss of earnings
Magistrado Ponente	the judge who drafts the main judgment
magistrados	a higher category of judges
Magistrados suplentes	temporary judges (see *magistrado*)
materias troncales	core subjects
medidas cautelares	provisional remedies or precautionary measures
medidas cautelares innominadas	non-specific precautionary measures
Mesa	the Board (in Congress)
Ministerio de Hacienda	Tax Office
Ministerio Fiscal	the Public Prosecution Service
ministro	minister

Mora	default or delay in performing an obligation
motivado	reasoned or justified
municipios	municipalities
negligencia	negligence
nota simple	simple extract from the Land Registry
Notarios	notaries
objeto del contrato	object of the contract
obligación	obligation
obligaciones de dar	obligations that involve giving something to the creditor
obligaciones de hacer	obligations that require the debtor to do something
obligaciones legales	obligations created by law
obligaciones mancomunadas	obligations with a plurality of debtors or creditors
obligaciones personalísimas	obligations that can only be performed by the debtor
obligaciones solidarias	obligations with several debtors of creditors in which each of them can request full enforcement or be obliged to full performance
oficiales	the officials at the service of the courts
oficina judicial	the judicial office run by the Court Clerk
opción de compra	contract of option to buy
ordenanzas	rules dictated by the *Hermandades* or *Juntas*
orden público	public policy
ordenes	by-laws
ordenes jurisdiccionales	jurisidictional orders
pacto de quota litis	contingent fee agreement
pacto palmario	a variant of the contingent fee agreement with a premium in case of victory
Pactos de hospitalidad o clientela	the agreements between Iberians extending the application of personal laws
pago o cumplimiento	performance of the obligation
participación (regimen de)	matrimonial regimen of deferred participation in earnings
partidos judiciales	judicial districts
pasante	unofficial category of lawyers similar to trainee solicitors
Pase foral	the non-application of the laws dictated by the King of Castile by the different territories and kingdoms in medieval Spain

pensión compensatoria	compensatory pension
permiso de obra	planning permission
Pleno	full constitutional court
plusvalía	tax on increase of value of urban land
poder suficiente	power of attorney
policía judicial	the judicial police
poseedor immediato	person that is currently enjoying the property
poseedor mediato	actual owner of the property with no current direct right of use or enjoyment
pragmágticas	the laws dictated by the King of Castile without consultation with Parliament
predio dominante	land with a right of servitude over another
predio sirviente	land subject to a servitude
prenda	right of guarantee that involves displacement of the object
prescripción adquisitiva	acquisition of ownership by possession
prescripcion extintiva	prescription
principio de oficialidad	principle of officiality (procedure)
principio de tracto sucesivo	requirement of uninterrupted registration of the chain of title on property transactions
principio dispositivo	dispositive principle (procedure)
principios generales del derecho	general principles of law
prisión provisonal	pre-trial custody
privación ilegal	illegal deprivation (on the enjoyment of a right)
Procedimiento Abreviado	the abbreviated procedure (criminal)
procedimiento abreviado para delitos menos graves	the abbreviated procedure for less serious crimes
procedimiento por delitos graves	the procedure for serious crimes
procedimiento del jurado	trial by jury
procedimiento monitorio	summary proceedings for the enforcement of monetary obligations
procedimiento ordinario	ordinary procedure
procesamiento	indictment
proceso de iniciativa autonómica	procedure by which provinces express their will to become an autonomous community
Procurador	lawyer whose function it is to liaise between the court and the parties
Profesor Titular de Universidad	university lecturer
promesa de compra o de venta	pre-contract of sale
proposición de ley	a proposal for legislation presented by the Chambers of Parliament

Protocolo notarial	notaries' registry of acts and transactions
provincias	provinces
Proyecto de ley	the project for legislation presented by the Executive
prueba tasada	legally-weighted evidence
quebrantamiento de forma	a breach of formalities during the proceedings (ground for *casación*)
querella	a special type of information or complaint by the victim of a crime
recurso contencioso-administrativo	the judicial appeal against administrative dispositions
recurso de alzada	internal administrative appeal against administrative acts
recurso de amparo	procedure of appeal to the Constitutional Court for the protection of fundamental rights
recurso de apelación	ordinary appeal
recurso de casación	an appeal to quash a decision of inferior courts
recurso de inconstitucionalidad	appeal challenging the constitutionality of a law
recurso de injusticia notoria	appeal "for notorious unfairness"
recurso de nulidad	nullity appeal
recurso de queja	petition in error
recurso de reposición	motion to set aside
recurso de revision	extraordinary administrative appeal possible when new documents or facts appear after a decision has been made by the Administration
recurso de súplica	petition for reconsideration
recurso en interes de la ley	appeal against decisions of Superior Court
recurso extraordinario de revisión	extraordinary appeal for review
recurso extraordinario por infracción procesal	appeal against decisions of *Audiencia Provincial*
recusación de magistrados	the removal of judges from particular cases
renvio de retorno	single renvoi
registrador de la propiedad	officer of the Land Registry
Reglamento del Congreso	a statute governing the functioning of Congress
Reglamento del Senado	a statute governing the functioning of the Senate
reglamentos	regulations
reglamentos administrativos	the regulations about the organisation of the Administration

Reglamentos de las Cámaras	a law for the regulation of the functioning of each Chamber of Parliament
reglamentos jurídicos	the regulations affecting the rights and duties of citizens
réplica	reply
responsabilidad extracontractual	extra-contractual liability
retracto	right of preferential acquisition
Salas	Chambers or divisions of the higher courts
sanción y promulgación	the formal procedure for the passing of legislation consisting of the King's signature and "approval"
Secretario judicial	court clerk
Senadores	Senators; Members of the Upper Chamber of Parliament
sentencia	a judicial decision ending the proceedings and resolving the subject matter of the dispute
separación de bienes	matrimonial regime of separation of wealth
servidumbres	servitudes, easements
silencio positivo	rule that establishes that a claim is understood to have been successful if the Administration does not reply by a certain time
sociedad de gananciale	matrimonial regime of community of acquisitions
suelo rústico	rural land
suelo urbanizable	land classified as suitable for development into urban land
suelo urbano	urban land
sumario	see *fase de instrucción*
tanteo	right of preferential acquisition
tasas judiciales	the fee payable to the court
temor reverencial	reverential fear
Tercero registral	protected party that acquires property relying on the Land Registry
tercio de libre disposición	part of the estate that can de disposed of freely by the testator
tercio de mejora	part of the estate that by law must go to one or more of the compulsory heirs
tesoro oculto	hidden treasure
testamento	will
testamento abierto	open will
testamento cerrado	closed will
testamento olografo	holograph will

titulos ejecutivos	documents upon which it is possible to start enforcement of a debt without previous declarative proceedings
Tribunal	a court with more than one judge
Tribunal Central de Trabajo	Central Labour Court (seat in Madrid)
Tribunal Constitucional	Constitutional Court
Tribunal de Cuentas	special office that controls finances and accounts of the State
Tribunal del Jurado	jury
Tribunal Militar Central	the Central Military Court
Tribunal Superior de Justicia	the Superior Court of Justice with a seat in each Autonomous Community
Tribunal Supremo	the Supreme Court of Spain
turno de oficio	the duty to give free legal advice to those entitled to legal aid
urbanismo	town planning
usucapio	acquisition of ownership by possession
vacatio legis	period between the publication of a statute in the B.O.E. and its application
valor catastral	value of property in the Land *Cadaster*
vecindad civil	civil domicile; connecting factor for the application of *foral* or regional laws
via normal	the normal route for achieving autonomy
via rápida	the quick route for achieving autonomy
vicios del consentimiento	defects of consent by mistake or other interference
Villas	the cities in medieval Northern Spain
vista pública	public hearings

Bibliography

M. Albadalejo García, *Curso de Derecho Civil* (Edisofer, 2004), 4 Vols.

J. Almagro Nosete and others, *Derecho Procesal Civil* (Tirant Lo Blanch, 2002).

F.J. Álvarez García, *Código Penal y Ley Penal del Menor* (11th ed., Tirant Lo Blanch, 2005).

R. Capilla, L. Roca and M.R. Valpuesta, *Derecho de Sucesiones* (Tirant Lo Blanch, 1992).

J. Castán Tobeñas, *Derecho Civil Español, Común y Foral* (Reus, 1988), Vol.4.

C. Conde-Pumpido Ferreiro, *El Ministerio Fiscal* (Aranzadi, 1999).

F. Cordón Moreno, *Las Garantías Constitucionales y el Proceso Penal* (2nd ed., Aranzadi, 2002).

R. Cotijoch Pratdesaba, *La Compraventa ed Inmuebles* (Editorial Planeta, 2001).

J. Damián Moreno, *Introducción al Sistema Judicial Español* (Aranzadi, 2002).

L. Díez Picazo and A. Gullón, *Sistemas de Derecho Civil* (Tecnos, 1998), Vol.IV.

D. Espín Cánovas, *Manual de Derecho Civil Español* (RDP, 1978).

E. Gacto Fenández and others, *El derecho Histórico de los Pueblos de España* (UCM, 1992).

E. García de Enterría, *Curso de Derecho Administrativo* (Civitas, 2002) Vols I and II.

V. Gimeno Sendra, *Introducción al Derecho Procesal* (Colex, 2005).

J.L. Gómez Colomer, *El Proceso Penal Español para no Juristas* (Tirant Lo Blanch, 1993).

E. González Pillado and L.D. Espino Hernández, *El Coste del Proceso y el Derecho de Asistencia Jurídica Gratuita* (BOE, 2004).

E. González Pillado and M.D. Fernández Fuster, *La Reclamación de las Deudas Dinerarias Civiles* (BOE 2004).

E. González Pillado and X. Teixeira Rodriguez, *La Detención* (BOE, 2004).

J.L. Lacruz Berdejo, *Derecho de Sucesiones. Parte General* (Bosch, 1990).

J.L. Lacruz Berdejo and F. de A. Sancho Rebullida, *Elementos de Derecho Civil* (Bosch, 1994), Vol.III.

C. Lasarte Álvarez, *Curso de Derecho Civil Patrimonial* (9th ed., Tecnos, 2003).

C. Lasarte Álvarez, *Principios de Derecho Civil: Derecho de Obligaciones* (9th ed., Marcial Pons, 2004), Vol.II.

C. Lasarte Álvarez, *Principios de Derecho Civil: Contratos* (8th ed., Marcial Pons, 2004), Vol.III.

C. Lasarte Álvarez, *Principios de Derecho Civil* (5th ed., Marcial Pons, 2005), Vol.IV.

L. López Guerra and others, *Derecho Constitucional* (Tirant Lo Blanch, 2003) Vols 1 and 2.

J. Marquez Fernandez-Flores, *Compra de Viviendas* (Piramide, 1999).

I. Otto Pardo, de, *Derecho Constitucional: Sistema de Fuentes* (2nd ed., Ariel,1997).

P. Perez Tremps, *El Recurso de Amparo* (Tirant Lo Blanch, 2004).

J. Puig Brutau, *Compendio de Derecho Civil* (Bosch, 1990).

F.J. Sánchez Calero, *Curso de Derecho Civil (IV): Derechos de Familia y Sucesiones* (4th ed., Tirant Lo Blanch, 2005).

P.L. Sánchez García. *La Comunidad de Propietarios* (2nd ed., BOE, 2004).

J. Sole Tura, *Los Comunistas y la Constitución* (Planeta, 1978).

F. Tomás y Valiente, *Manual de Historia del Derecho Español* (Civitas, 1992).

M. del R. Villas de Antonio and P.L. Sánchez García, *La Separacion Matrimonial* (BOE, 2003).

Index

(all references are to page number)

395